THE SOUTHERN OLIGARCHY

THE
SOUTHERN OLIGARCHY

*An Appeal in Behalf of the Silent Masses of Our
Country Against the Despotic Rule of the Few.*

BY

WILLIAM H. SKAGGS
OF ALABAMA

NEGRO UNIVERSITIES PRESS
NEW YORK

Originally published in 1924
by The Devin-Adair Co., New York

Reprinted 1969 by
Negro Universities Press
A Division of Greenwood Publishing Corp.
New York

SBN 8371-1739-9

To My Wife
JULIA OLLIS SKAGGS

"So then am I become your enemy, by telling you the truth?"

PREFACE

The object of this book is clearly stated in the first paragraph of the ensuing narrative. It is an authoritative and candid survey of the corrupt practices and criminal lawlessness of a provincial Oligarchy; it is also an appeal to the patriotism and sober judgment of the American people in behalf of the great mass of white and colored citizens of the Southern States, who are held in political subjection and economic serfdom. For the information of my readers, especially in view of the serious import of the public questions discussed in this book, it may be well to state a few personal facts which have a direct bearing on the value of this survey.

In the first place, it should be borne in mind that I am a native of the South. My parents were born in the South and are buried in the town where I was born and brought up. It would be impossible for me to have any prejudice against the people of my native section, and I desire that my readers should know, before beginning an examination of my work, that I am a Southerner and my sympathies are with the people of the South. It may be well also to state that this survey was undertaken, not only with the approval, but also at the earnest request of prominent and patriotic citizens of the Southern States, some of whom have made great sacrifices for the cause of humanity and liberty; and who have an abiding faith in the effective truth of that aphorism of modern history and civic philosophy uttered by Abraham Lincoln when he said: "Let the people know the truth and the country is safe."

My fight against corrupt practices and lawlessness in the South began when I cast my first vote. Contemporary newspapers and other published documents supply ample evidence in support of this claim. For many years my work has been for the industrial progress, civic and educational advancement of the people of my native section.

Much of the material included in this volume was gathered several years ago, while I was a citizen of my native State, Alabama. Some of the authorities upon which this survey is based are seldom found outside large public libraries. In view of this fact, I have thought it pertinent to insert in the ensuing narrative numerous and lengthy excerpts from official reports, standard reference books and contemporary documents. I am not unmindful of the objections which the reader may find to my method of discussing a subject of this character, but this method has at least one great advantage. It places my authorities before the reader in the words of the most credible witnesses and authentic documents that are available.

The outstanding facts narrated in this book are based upon official documents, including judicial and legislative records, current news items published in Democratic newspapers in the South, and the testimony of reputable white citizens of the Southern States, a large majority of whom were, and many still are, affiliated with the Democratic party. This indictment of the Southern Oligarchy is complete in detail, and it is severe. If it were not severe, it would be neither complete nor authoritative. A partial or superficial discussion of these portentous questions would do no good. Palliatives and nostrums have failed to remove the disorder and this method of treatment continues to aggravate the malady. We are living in troublous times. A crisis has come in the history of this country and the people demand the whole truth. I believe the publication of an authoritative survey of actual conditions in the Southern States will be welcomed by a large majority of the citizens of the whole country; it will correct erroneous impressions and remove misapprehensions among a large number of patriotic Americans who feel a deep interest in all questions which directly affect the welfare of the whole country.

With a firm belief in the doctrine that "the people have a right to rule." it is clear that my indictment is against the un-American policies, the corrupt and lawless practices of the Southern Oligarchy. With "the feeling that an end must be put to the lawless oppression of a privileged class," I have carefully avoided controversial questions and theories respecting racial and religious dogmas. I am not attacking good citizens;

I am exposing corrupt and lawless practices, and the national menace of evils which have arisen under the rule of a provincial Oligarchy. I believe this survey will direct public attention to certain disorders in the South and prevent a dangerous civic disease from getting a firmer foothold. In order to expose the root of the disease, I have pointed out the cause and continued menace of certain disorders which have afflicted this country for many years. I have not followed the old-fashioned practice of treating symptoms, which has brought untold suffering to both races in the South and trouble to the whole country.

During many years the attention of the country has been riveted on the Southern States. With a white population composed of the purest British and French stock in America, the economic backwardness, civic and social delinquencies of these States have aroused a widespread interest; not only because these conditions are a menace to the whole country, but also because it is so difficult to arrive at a satisfactory conclusion touching the cause of this lapse in the evolution of civilization among an English speaking people of British and French lineage. In no other part of the civilized world can there be found such striking evidences of backwardness and decline among a people of British and French extraction as is found in the Southern States.

It is evident that there is a fundamental cause for this hiatus in the history of a people whose forebears were among the heroic patriots and distinguished statesmen in the early history of America. The cause is found in one of many tragic epochs in the history of civilization, where untoward events have reduced a proud and liberty-loving people to a state of economic serfdom and political subjection under the rule of a privileged class of political exploiters. Concerning the actual situation in the Southern States before the Civil War, Abraham Lincoln gave utterance to the whole truth when (August 24, 1855), in a patriotic and statesmanlike letter to his most intimate friend, Joshua F. Speed, he said:

"The slave-breeders and slave-traders are a small, odious, and detested class among you; and yet in politics they dictate the course of all of you, and are as completely your masters as you are the masters of your own negroes."

Lincoln was fully informed about conditions in the South. He perceived the pernicious influence of the exploiters and the corrupt and reactionary politicians. In all of his public utterances and official acts he steadfastly adhered to the opinion that the great mass of the people in the South had no voice in the affairs of their government and that they were being exploited by the "slave-breeders and slave-traders." The present Oligarchy that rules the South is almost a complete replica of the radical and reactionary leaders of the Slave Oligarchy before the Civil War. The leaders of the present Oligarchy habitually affect a supercilious air of provincial and abnormal sensitiveness which has been easily and conveniently used in support of the spoils system and in perpetuating their rule over the great mass of white and colored people in the South. These leaders do not like to have their methods inquired into nor their corrupt and provincial practices censured. They object to any investigation of their record in public affairs. They demand to be let alone, even when their policies and practices menace the life of the Nation. They are united and solid for the protection of their "peculiar institution" and the enforcement of their sectional, strictly partisan and un-American policies.

The difficulty in discussing any question relating to the South—local, national or international, civic, social, political, economic, religious or hygienic—is the absence of free speech and the presence of a proscriptive intolerance that predominates in the Southern States. The safeguards of democracy—law and public opinion—have been set at defiance, and there is an absence of "that atmosphere which we call Tone and on whose purity the honor and worth of public life depend."

The leaders of the Southern Oligarchy have been so insidious with their propagandism of racial and partisan proscription that the pernicious influence of their practices has permeated the political, social, educational and commercial life of the whole country. For many years the provincialism and sectional prejudices of the ruling class in the South have been the cause of turmoil and strife in the United States. This condition is an anachronism. It has no place in modern civilization; certainly not in a country that boasts of its democracy and guarantees in its organic law a republican form of government. The amount of discontent among a people living under such depressing conditions has found ominous expression in various manifestations of unrest and civic disorder. Herein lies a menace to the Nation. It is clear that the present task of America is to maintain order at home and preserve the semblance of democracy.

WILLIAM H. SKAGGS.

New York City,
June, 1924.

CONTENTS

THE SOUTHERN OLIGARCHY

CHAPTER I

AMERICA UNDER RULE OF THE OLIGARCHY

The purpose of this book is the presentation of facts relating
to the policies and practices of an Oligarchy by which the
Southern States of America have been ruled for more than forty
years; and also a survey of the resultant evils of such policies
and practices. In the words of Viscount Bryce,—

what I desire is, not to impress upon my readers views of my own, but to
supply them with facts, and (so far as I can) with explanations of facts on
which they can reflect and from which they can draw their own conclusions.

According to popular belief, the United States is a federal
government composed of democratic States, and the Constitution guarantees to every State a republican form of government. As defined by the *Century Dictionary*, a democracy is
"government by the people; a system of government in which
the sovereign power of the state is vested in the people as a
whole, and is exercised directly by them or their elected agents."
An oligarchy is "a form of government in which the supreme
power is vested in the hands of a small exclusive class; also,
collectively, those who form such a class or body." The difference between a democratic and an oligarchical government is
fundamental. As stated by Lord Bryce in his work on *Modern
Democracies:*

The word Democracy has been used ever since the time of Herodotus
to denote that form of government in which the ruling power of a state
is legally vested, not in any particular class or classes, but in the members
of the community as a whole. This means, in communities which act

by voting, that rule belongs to the majority, as no other method has been found for determining peaceably and legally what is to be deemed the will of a community which is not unanimous. Usage has made this the accepted sense of the term, and usage is the safest guide in the employment of words. . . .

No one has propounded a formula which will cover every case, because there are governments which are "on the line," too popular to be called oligarchies, and scarcely popular enough to be called democracies. But though we cannot define either Oligarchy or Democracy, we can usually know either the one or the other when we see it.

In his *Lectures to American Audiences*, Edward A. Freeman, noted English historian, indicates the difference between a democracy and an oligarchy in these words:

In the Greek Commonwealths the best definition of democracy and oligarchy would be that in the democracy political rights are enjoyed by all who enjoy civil rights, while in the oligarchy political rights are confined to a part only of those who enjoy civil rights.

This definition clearly portrays the actual situation in the eleven States which constitute the Solid South, where the people have surrendered the functions of government to a "small exclusive class"; and this provincial, oligarchic class is a very small "part only of those who enjoy civil rights."

A survey of civic and political conditions, the educational and industrial situation, and a summary of corrupt practices and criminal lawlessness, under the rule of a provincial Oligarchy in the Southern States, will show the deplorable decline of the purest English stock in America. It will also show that this British-American stock which, in the formative period of our history, contributed so much in valor, patriotism and statesmanship to the creation and early advancement of American institutions, has declined in civic virtue, intellectual force and political liberty, until it has become the most portentous fact before the American people.

When America was ruled by the Southern Oligarchy, in actual administration of the Federal Government, the United States was not a republic of federated, democratic States. It was in fact an oligarchic government. As stated by Lord Bryce, "no one has propounded a formula which will cover every case," but during the Wilson Administration it was clear that the supreme power of the Government was "vested in the hands of a small exclusive class." When the American people at last awoke to a realization of the actual situation, the policies and practices of the Southern Oligarchy were repudiated and condemned.

It should be borne in mind, however, that the overwhelming victory of the Republican ticket in the Presidential election of 1920 was not a party victory; it was a great popular protest against the spoils system, and also, more emphatically, a protest against provincialism; a popular demand for the reëstablishment of democratic institutions under a republican form of government. But the victory of the people in the election of 1920 did not destroy the Oligarchy. The national menace of this provincial class remains, and the lurking danger will continue as long as this Oligarchy retains absolute domination in eleven States, over nearly one-fourth of the total population and with the power of nearly one-fourth the total electoral vote of the United States. It is a national evil which cannot be confined within the geographical boundaries of any group of States.

An authoritative narrative of actual conditions, while America was under rule of the Southern Oligarchy, necessitates brief reference to certain outstanding facts in the legislative record of this Oligarchy. From March 4, 1913, to March 4, 1921, the Democratic party was in control of the administrative department of the Federal Government, and for six years of this period the legislative branch of the Government was under the rule of a sectional faction of this party.

In the 64th Congress there were 59 committees of the House of Representatives, and the chairman of each of 31 of these committees was a Representative from one of the eleven Southern States; 11 were from the Democratic Border States, Maryland, Missouri and Oklahoma, and the remaining 17 were from the Northern and Western States. In this Congress, the Southern States controlled every one of the ten leading committees of the Senate; and the chairman of every one of the fifteen leading committees of the House, except the committee on Appropriations, of which Representative John J. Fitzgerald (Democrat) of New York was chairman, was from the South. The following is a list of the chairmen of these committees:

Chairmen of the leading committees, 64th Congress.
Committees of the Senate:

Appropriations,	Thomas S. Martin, of Virginia.
Banking and Currency,	Robert L. Owen, of Oklahoma.
Education and Labor,	Hoke Smith, of Georgia.
Finance,	F. M. Simmons, of North Carolina.
Foreign Relations,	William J. Stone, of Missouri.
Judiciary,	Charles A. Culberson, of Texas.
Naval Affairs,	Benj. R. Tillman, of South Carolina.
Post Offices and Post Roads,	John H. Bankhead, of Alabama.
Public Buildings and Grounds,	Claude A. Swanson, of Virginia.
Rules,	Lee S. Overman, of North Carolina.

Committees of the House:

Appropriations	John J. Fitzgerald, of New York.
Banking and Currency	Carter Glass, of Virginia.
Education	Dudley M. Hughes, of Georgia.
Foreign Affairs	Henry D. Flood, of Virginia.
Immigration and Naturalization	John L. Burnett, of Alabama.
Insular Affairs	William A. Jones, of Virginia.
Interstate and Foreign Commerce	William C. Adamson, of Georgia.
Judiciary	Edwin Y. Webb, of North Carolina.
Military Affairs	James Hay, of Virginia.
Naval Affairs	Lemuel P. Padgett, of Tennessee.
Post Office and Post Roads	John A. Moon, of Tennessee.
Public Buildings and Grounds	Frank Clark, of Florida.
Rivers and Harbors	Stephen M. Sparkman, of Florida.
Rules	Edward W. Pou, of North Carolina.
Ways and Means	Claude Kitchin, of North Carolina.

In the 65th Congress the committees of the Senate were the same as in the 64th Congress. In the House of Representatives there were only four changes in the chairmanship of the leading committees, and each of the four chairmen was from the South. During an important period in our domestic affairs and a serious crisis in our foreign relations, our laws were made by provincial politicians who represented neither the wealth, intelligence, civic virtue, nor virile patriotism of America.

With a total population a little less than one-fourth the total population of the United States, in the Presidential election of 1920, the eleven Southern States cast less than ten per cent. of the total vote in the United States. In order to illustrate the situation more clearly, a comparison may be made with eleven States selected from the New England, Middle and Western States which, in the aggregate, have a population approximately the same as the total population of the eleven Southern States which compose the Solid South. The figures in the tabulation which follows are from the census of 1910; statistics from the census of 1920 will be cited in later paragraphs.

11 Southern States, Solid South.	Total Population, 1910.	11 Northern and Western States.	Total Population, 1910.
Alabama	2,138,093	Indiana	2,700,876
Arkansas	1,574,449	Iowa	2,224,771
Florida	752,619	Maine	742,371
Georgia	2,609,121	Michigan	2,810,173
Louisiana	1,656,388	Minnesota	2,075,708
Mississippi	1,797,114	Nebraska	1,192,214
North Carolina	2,206,287	New Hampshire	430,572
South Carolina	1,515,400	New Jersey	2,537,167
Tennessee	2,184,789	Ohio	4,767,121
Texas	3,896,542	Rhode Island	542,610
Virginia	2,061,612	Wisconsin	2,333,860
	22,392,414		22,357,443

The total male population (21 years and over) of voting age (1910), and the total votes cast in the Presidential election of 1912, in the eleven Southern States, are shown in the following table:

Total white male population of voting age		3,650,298
Total Negro male population of voting age		1,856,057
Total male population of voting age,		5,506,355
Total vote, Presidential election, 1912		1,540,514
White males, voting age, who did not vote	2,109,784	
Negro males, voting age, not allowed to vote	1,856,057	
Total males, voting age, who did not vote	3,965,841	3,965,841
		5,506,355

Less than 28 per cent. of the total male population of voting age (1910), and only 42.25 per cent. of the white male population of voting age, voted in the Southern States, in the Presidential election of 1912; while in the same election, the eleven Northern States, with a total population approximately 150,000 less than that of the Southern States, polled a total of 4,438,415 votes. The Southern States polled less than 28 per cent. of their total voting strength and less than 43 per cent. of their total white male population of voting age. In the same election the eleven Northern States polled 64.96 per cent. of their total male population of voting age and more than 66 per cent. of their total white votes. These eleven Southern States had 126 votes in the Electoral College and 104 members of Congress, while the eleven Northern States had 129 electoral votes and 107 members of Congress.

In the eleven Southern States the total popular vote in the Presidential election of 1892 was 2,135,962, while in the eleven Northern States used for comparison, the aggregate population of which in 1892 was a little less than that of the eleven Southern States, the total popular vote was 3,746,198. In the Presidential election of 1900 the popular vote in the·eleven Southern States was 1,881,218, which was 254,744 less than the total vote in 1892, while the popular vote in the eleven Northern States had increased to 4,430,370. In 1916 the eleven Southern States polled 11,009 votes less than they cast in the election of 1900, and 265,753 less than the total vote in these States in 1892. During this period of sixteen years there was a marked increase in the population of the Southern States, but a very decided decrease in the number of votes cast.

The total popular vote for Presidential Electors in 1916 in the Southern States was 1,870,209. In the eleven Northern States the total popular vote was 4,980,736. The total population of the eleven Southern States, estimated as of July 1, 1916, was 465,042 more than the estimated population of the eleven Northern States as of the same date, and yet the popular vote of the eleven Northern States in the Presidential election of 1916 was 3,110,527 more than the total number of votes cast by the eleven Southern States at the same election.

The total popular vote in the United States in 1916 was 18,528,743, of which that of the eleven Southern States that dictated the policies and the legislation of the country during the Wilson Administration was only a little more (17,335) than ten per cent. The popular vote in the State of Georgia, for example, in 1916, was only 158,690, while the popular vote in the State of Indiana at the same election was 718,848, although the population of Georgia in 1916 was in round figures 40,000 more than the population of Indiana. In the same election, the popular vote of North Carolina was 289,912, while the popular vote of Iowa was 516,495, though the population of North Carolina in 1916 was 178,000 more than the population of Iowa.

With a little more than half as many votes as Michigan, the State of Texas has one-third more representation in Congress and counts for one-third more in the election of a President of the United States. In the Congressional election of 1918 Georgia elected twelve Congressmen with a total vote of 59,196; Louisiana elected 8 Congressmen on a total vote of 44,794, while in the State of Maine there were 120,836 votes cast to elect 4 Congressmen, and Iowa elected 11 Congressmen with 340,311 votes.

The apportionment by population for the election of Representatives in Congress in 1916 was 211,877, and in States in which woman suffrage did not prevail, and in which normal honest elections were held, the total average vote for Congressmen was between 35,000 and 40,000. Delaware, with only one Congressman, cast 51,810 votes, and that was at the rate of one vote for each four persons in its population. In the national election of 1916, the total popular vote in the eleven Southern States was less than one person in 13 of the total population of these States. In Texas less than one person in 11 voted; in Virginia, less than one in 14; in Mississippi, less than one in 22; and in South Carolina the vote was at the rate of one vote for each twenty-five persons in the total population.

Mr. Wilson owed his election in 1916 to the Solid South. His plurality over Mr. Hughes in the total vote cast was 591,385, his plurality in the eleven states of the Solid South was 866,904. Outside of the pocket boroughs, where the result of the voting is determined in advance, Mr. Wilson ran behind Mr. Hughes nearly 300,000 votes. The eleven States of the Solid South cast a total vote of 1,870,209, which was less than 8 per cent. of their total population in 1916. The States outside the Solid South cast a vote of 16,658,534, which was about 22 per cent. of their population. In the Solid South an Elector was chosen by every 14,000 voters; it required 40,000 voters to choose an Elector in the other States, taken together.

In *The North American Review,* September, 1920, Dr. David Jayne Hill describes the actual situation as follows:

The decline in the number of voters in the Southern States is appalling. In Alabama, for example, the total vote for President in 1912 was more than 30,000 less than it was in 1880, forty years ago. And yet Alabama is a great sea-port and industrial State, vitally interested in every national question. In 1912 the total vote in Georgia, Louisiana, Mississippi, North Carolina, South Carolina, Texas, and Virginia was less than it was in 1888. In Virginia and Louisiana the number of votes cast in 1912 was about half those cast in 1888. In those two States, twenty-two Presidential electors were chosen by a little over 200,000 voters, a proportion that would have given the voters of New York State about 160 electoral Votes in that Presidential election, instead of the forty-five actually cast. In 1916, these conditions were practically unchanged, the eight States just named casting over 200,000 votes less than in 1888.

In the Presidential election of 1920 the total popular vote in the eleven Southern States was 2,605,850; in the same election the eleven Northern States which we have named for comparison cast a total vote of 8,473,044. The census of 1920 gives these eleven Northern States a total population of 26,049,175; the eleven Southern States a total of 25,106,954.

The total popular vote of the Southern States in 1920 was the largest cast by these States during the past thirty years. This increase was made up largely of the votes cast in North Carolina, Tennessee, and Virginia, where there was some organized opposition to the Democratic ticket in 1920. In spite of equal suffrage, as provided for under the 19th Amendment to the Constitution of the United States, there was only a slight increase in the total vote of Texas in 1920 compared with the vote of 1916; the total vote was 38,965 more in 1920 than in 1916. The popular vote in this State in 1920 was less than it was in 1892, 1896, or 1900. In South Carolina the popular vote in 1920 was less than it was in 1892 or 1896. Mississippi cast fewer votes in the Presidential election of 1920 than in that of 1916. The total vote of Mississippi for eight Representatives and two Senators was 82,492, in the Presidential election of 1920; in the same election, South Carolina, with two Senators and seven Representatives, cast a total vote of 66,442, and Georgia with twelve Representatives and, as matter of course, two Senators, returned a total popular vote of 154,049, which was 4,641 less than the total vote of this State in 1916, and 67,567 less than its vote in 1892.

The State of Maine has four Representatives, just half the number of Representatives from the State of Mississippi. In the Presidential election of 1920, it cast 197,530 votes, which was 32,546 more than double the vote of Mississippi. Nebraska has six Congressmen, one less than South Carolina. In the Presidential election of 1920, Nebraska cast 382,653 votes; more than five times, and lacking only 15,999 votes of being six times, the total vote of South Carolina. New Hampshire has only two Congressmen, less than any Southern State, yet the total vote in New Hampshire (159,092) was greater than the total vote, respectively, in Florida, Georgia, Louisiana, Mississippi, or South Carolina. Florida has four Representatives, Georgia has 12, Louisiana and Mississippi 8 each and South Carolina 7. New Jersey has 12 Representatives, the same number as Georgia. The popular vote of New Jersey in 1920 was 908,638, nearly six times the total vote of Georgia. Wisconsin, with 11 Representatives, one less than Georgia, cast 705,686 votes in 1920, being 89,490 more than four times the vote of Georgia.

Outside of these States that compose the Solid South, national issues are presented to the voters, discussed, and finally judged by public opinion; but not in the South. Nobody seems to know, and no one has tried to explain, why a vote in one of the Southern States should be worth more, and count for more in the general result, than a vote in one of the Northern States. *The Chicago Tribune* summed up the situation in the following statement:

Thus we have in the South not only a voter whose judgment is foreclosed, but also a voter who carries something like three times as much weight in the Electoral College as a voter in the North whose judgment is not predetermined.

This preposterous wrong against government by free opinion ought not to be tolerated. We are not arguing the justice or expediency of giving the colored man the vote, or the wisdom of permitting a provision of the national Constitution to be neither repealed nor respected. But we do contend that if the negro vote is not cast at the polls it should not be cast by the southern whites in the Electoral College.

As stated by *The Des Moines Capital:*

> No law prevents a white from voting the Republican ticket in the South, but public opinion restrains him. . . . Under present conditions, there is no more freedom of ballot in the South than there was in Poland. You can make a campaign in Dakota or Nebraska or in Montana or Kansas, but you cannot make a campaign in the old South, in the Confederate States as they were.
>
> The entire civilized world knows of these conditions and knows that the American people have not had the courage to straighten the matter out by doing justice.

The political power of the South in national politics is a matter of vital importance to the whole country, because the fixed policies of the political leaders who rule the South are essentially provincial and reactionary. They are not able to grasp important questions in national affairs, and their loyalty to the Nation is seriously impaired by their intense sectionalism and partisan selfishness. Alison, the historian, has furnished a story of the first National Assembly of France which clearly describes the Southern Oligarchy:

> Two circumstances, however, were remarkable in the composition of the Constituent Assembly, and contributed in a great degree to influence its future proceedings.
>
> The first was the almost total exclusion of literary and philosophical talent, and the extraordinary preponderance of the legal profession. . . . No less than two hundred and seventy-nine of the *Tiers État* were advocates, chiefly from the provincial courts of France. . . . This class did not correspond to the barristers of England, who, although not in general men of property, were at least usually possessed of talent and information. . . .
>
> The second circumstance was the great proportion of the *Tiers État* who were men of no property or consideration in the country—mere needy adventurers, who pushed themselves into the Estates in order to make their fortunes amidst the public convulsions which were anticipated. . . . France, on this occasion, paid the penalty of her unjust and invidious feudal distinctions.

Of the 565 members of the *Tiers État,* 279 were lawyers. Slightly less than 50 per cent. of the total membership were advocates, and yet this high percentage of lawyers in the Constituent Assembly has been a subject of frequent comment by historians. The proportion of lawyers among Senators and

Representatives from the Southern States has been for many years, and still is, a matter of comment. The percentage of lawyers in the *Tiers État* was slightly less than 50 per cent. but in the 65th Congress the percentage of lawyers among the total number of Senators and Representatives from the South was nearly 90 per cent.

In *Democracy In Europe*, by Sir Thomas Erskine May, we find reference to the influence of lawyers, preceding the French Revolution, which, in several respects, correctly portrays the situation in the South under rule of the Oligarchy:

Lawyers swarmed throughout the country; and they exercised a prodigious influence over the people. Like the *curés*, they were of humble birth; and were generally repelled from the society of their privileged neighbors. But in education they were superior to all but the highest class, and men of letters. They knew all the abuses of the law, and of official administration; and they were familiar with the new philosophy. . . . Active and ambitious; with large opportunities for association, among themselves, and with other classes,—they prepared the way for a revolution, in which they were hereafter to play a conspicuous part.

In his essay on Mirabeau, Macaulay, commenting on the pettifoggers and provincial agitators, at the time of the Revolution, describes the situation in France in these words:

Practical questions of vast moment were left to be solved by men to whom politics had been only a matter of theory—that a legislature was composed of persons who were scarcely fit to compose a debating society— that the whole nation was ready to lend an ear to any flatterer who appealed to its cupidity, to its fears.

Observing the baneful influence of the lawyer-politicians in England, Oliver Goldsmith commented on those whom he regarded as dangerous to society in the following language:

The pawnbroker, the attorney, and other pests of society might, by proper management, be turned into serviceable members; and, were their trades abolished, it is possible the same avarice that conducts the one, or the same chicanery that characterizes the other, might by proper regulation be converted into frugality and commendable prudence.

Lord Northcliffe, noted editor and publisher of England, came to this country as British High Commissioner shortly after

America entered the World War, and while the 65th Congress, under control of the Southern Oligarchy, ran riot in sectional politics and corrupt practices, with provincial politicians in control of the affairs of the Government. In an interesting article, published in *The Metropolitan,* May, 1917, the British High Commissioner said:

You do not make effective political use of your aristocracy of birth. You do not make effective political use of your aristocracy of business. You do not make effective political use of your aristocracy of labor. You are governed to a degree, I never cease marveling at it, by just one class— the lawyer-politician.

In the 65th Congress there were 22 Democrats in the Senate from the Solid South. Every Senator from the South was a Democrat; 19 were lawyers and three planters or farmers. In the House of Representatives of the 65th Congress, there were 101 Democrats and 3 Republicans, a total of 104 members from the eleven Southern States, of whom 92 were lawyers, 6 business men, 2 farmers, one school teacher, one physician, one newspaper editor and publisher, and one of unknown vocation. From the eleven Northern States there were 6 Democrats and 16 Republicans in the Senate. Of the 22 Senators from the Northern States, 17 were lawyers, two business men, one physician, one newspaper writer, and one not stated. In the House there were 37 Democrats and 67 Republicans from eleven Northern States, and out of a total of 107 members of the House from these States there were 76 lawyers.

Of the total membership of the 65th Congress, there were 72 lawyers, 9 planters or farmers, 4 bankers or brokers, 4 business men, 3 physicians, 2 editors and newspaper publishers, and 2 contractors, in the Senate; in the House of Representatives there were 292 lawyers, 38 business men, 15 bankers or brokers, 23 writers and newspaper publishers, 18 manufacturers, 10 planters or farmers, 8 working men, 7 merchants, 2 physicians, 4 school teachers, 3 contractors, one preacher, and 12 whose vocations were unknown or not stated.

While America was under rule of the Southern Oligarchy, the predominance of the lawyer-politician was notorious. Our Ambassador to Great Britain was sorely vexed by the quibbling in the State Department at Washington. In a letter to Colonel House on this subject, as related in *The Life and Letters of Walter H. Page,* he said:

The lawyer-way in which the Department goes on in its dealings with Great Britain is losing us the only great international friendship that we have any chance of keeping or that is worth having. . . .

I sometimes wish there were not a lawyer in the world. I heard the President say once that it took him twenty years to recover from his legal habit of mind. Well, his administration is suffering from it to a degree that is pathetic and that will leave bad results for 100 years. . . .

We are—under lawyers' quibbling—drifting apart very rapidly, to our complete isolation from the sympathy of the whole world.

When, in July, 1916, Ambassador Page "received a cable-gram summoning him to Washington," he found on his arrival that the State Department was still engaged in petty legal quibbling. All the "talk was about cases," and the Department was apparently incapable of dealing with the mighty questions in which America was vitally concerned. The trouble was that the lawyer-politicians, who dominated in every department of government during the Wilson Administration, were without experience in the larger affairs of state, and their provincialism and extreme partisanship unfitted them for development in the broader field of statesmanship. *Harvey's Weekly* clearly stated the situation when it said:

The Southern Democrats now in control of all branches of the Government have had no experience in large affairs or in organizations, except political, of any considerable size and could not be expected to develop overnight a capacity for management of the greatest business enterprise the world has ever known.

Charles Sumner perhaps had in mind the domination of the Southern Oligarchy, with its preponderance of lawyers, when he said:

All ages have abounded in lawyers and judges; there is no churchyard that does not contain their forgotten dust. But the jurist is rare.

The political leaders of the South who dominate the Democratic party are essentially provincial. They seem to have neither the capacity nor the inclination to rise above their local environments and provincial prejudices; partisan and sectional issues guide them in all matters relating to national or international affairs. The Hon. David Jayne Hill, from whose writings I have quoted in a preceding paragraph, stated the situation in the Southern States very forcibly when he said:

> The greatest single misfortune to the further development of free and virile democracy was the loss in what is known as the "Solid South" of the power of political initiative and independent action. Adherence to a single political party had induced a condition of political apathy and stagnation. It is not extravagant to say that entire States were menaced with the complete extinction of civic virtue. The South had become wholly sectional and indifferent 'to the great national issues which there had no hearing, received no free discussion, and awakened no interest.

This summing up of the case clearly states the real gravamen of the imputations against the South, all of which plainly shows the penalty of provincialism, malfeasance and maladministration under the despotic rule of a privileged class. It is a serious thing to charge that eleven States of this Union, with nearly one-fourth the total population, "had become wholly sectional"; it is a still more serious matter to charge that in these eleven States "great national issues had no hearing, received no free discussion." But the most appalling phase of the situation is found in the further and graver charge that "entire States were menaced with the complete extinction of civic virtue."

It would be hard to frame more serious charges against a civilized people than are the specific imputations contained in the words quoted from Dr. Hill. If these things be true, eleven States of the American Union are dangerously near a great social and political catastrophe. If there be no foundation for these charges, if the late civic and political history of these States does not disclose facts which justify such imputations, then they are false and outrageous. Had these accusations been made by a partisan leader unfriendly to the South, they would call for less attention, but coming from so high an authority, they demand the most serious consideration.

An investigation of the actual situation, a non-sectional and non-partisan survey of present conditions, will show that the conclusions of Dr. Hill are fully justified. Not only the public records, but the warning admonitions of some of the ablest and most patriotic publicists and writers of the South, supply ample warrant for the serious charges made by Dr. Hill. A survey of corrupt practices, the educational situation, the appalling criminal record, the backwardness, financial dependence, delinquencies and defaults of the South, will furnish cumulative evidence to support these grave charges respecting conditions in the Southern States. In summing up the evidence relating to this distressing situation it will be plainly shown that the great mass of the citizens of the South, white and colored, are not responsible for the deplorable conditions under which they have existed for so many years. Before the Civil War in the South, as stated in *Southern Sidelights*, by Edward Ingle:

Protests were now and then entered against the professional politicians, as when it was announced that there was no room in Texas for them; and the lawyer, because of his connection with politics, came in for his share of condemnation. A critic of the convention that extended the suffrage in Virginia objected to the large proportion of lawyers in that body. Conceding that from the honorable membership of the bar had come some of the best men and the wisest statesmen of the country, he nevertheless asserted that whenever affairs of state were committed to them in large numbers they had rarely failed to make mischief; and he laid down as axiomatic the statement that a country governed by its lawers was a victim of misrule. "In fact," he added, "we have been cursed in Virginia with an abundance of small lawyers and still smaller politicians. These two characters are often combined together in the same individual, and form a class of political pettifoggers, the like of which cannot be found in any class of plagues or monsters that ever existed.

Under the institution of slavery, a large number of public men were lawyers, but they had attained eminence in the practice of their profession; great jurists and brilliant advocates; and there were men of ability in other professions, and planters who were prominent in public life in the South. The decline of the South is the result of the false economic and civic theories, and the provincial policies introduced into American institutions, and enforced upon a brave and liberty-loving people, for the sole purpose of extending and perpetuating the institution of slavery in the interest of a small minority of slave-holders.

The great mass of Southern people had no interest in slavery and they were bitterly opposed to it. Less than ten per cent. of the people owned slaves; but, against their will and better judgment, they were misled into taking up arms in defence of an institution which the great leaders of their fathers, almost without exception, openly and strenuously opposed, and against the Union which had been created largely through the foresight, statesmanship and patriotism of their fathers. Less than twenty per cent. of the soldiers in the Confederate Army were slaveholders, and yet they fought with heroic valor and suffered with undaunted fortitude for the preservation of an institution and an economic system which was rapidly reducing them to a state of industrial serfdom, and for the success of a privileged class which held them in political subjection. Referring to the public men of the South before the Civil War, in his *History of the United States*, James Ford Rhodes says:

The South did, indeed, produce good lawyers and able politicians. Their training was excellent. The sons of the wealthy almost always went to college, and there they began to acquire the knack at public speaking which seemed natural to the Southerner. The political life of their State was early opened to them, and by the time the promising young men were sent to Congress they had learned experience and adroitness in public affairs. If they made their mark in the national House or the Senate, they were kept there, and each year added to their usefulness and influence. The aspirants for political honors being almost wholly from the small privileged class, it was not difficult to provide places for those eminently fitted.

The Slave Oligarchy was a landed aristocracy. This aristocracy not only directed all governmental policies, but it also ruled with an iron hand in the commercial and financial affairs of the Southern States. It was not only imperious in fixing the social status in the South, but its power was absolute in a country where the whole civic and economic system was built on the institution of slavery. This imperialism was not only undemocratic in theory and practice but it was not even republican in form.

The great social and economic revolution following the war brought about not only a great increase in the number of tenants engaged in cultivation of cotton, but also a radical change in the relation of landlord and tenant. So long as the laborers engaged in production of cotton were a part of the chattel estate of the planter, it was not necessary for the landlord to exploit his labor. After the bondsman was given not only his freedom, but, practically at the same time, also vested with all the civic and political rights of a citizen, equal under the letter of the law to his former master, the landlord no longer had a sentimental or pecuniary interest in the laborer who worked his fields.

When the landlord no longer owned the laborer on his farm it became necessary for him to divide authority in order to control the newly emancipated labor. This division was one of the great economic changes that has so seriously affected the social and political status of the South. The landed aristocracy ceased to exist as an absolute political and economic power, and in its place there has grown up a triumvirate made up of the landlord, the money lender and the lawyer.

After emancipation, the resources of the landlord were so greatly reduced, and there followed so many changes in ownership, that it became necessary to call in the assistance of the money lender, and, as a matter of course, the landlord and the money lender needed the services of the lawyer; not only in making laws in the interest of the landlord, but also in taking care that the laws were so enforced as to control the labor and perpetuate the economic and political power of the new dynasty.

Four years of heroic struggle did not atone—so far as the results have determined—for the sins of omission which, justly or unjustly, were inherited by the people of the South. Reconstruction brought greater hardships and humiliation than Appomattox, and at the end of that dismal period the great mass of the people found little relief. The dark days of Reconstruction not only added to the sufferings and burdens of an oppressed people but afforded an opportunity for the rise of a less worthy, oligarchical class of oppressors.

The great curse of the South, which grew out of the institution of slavery and which has been accentuated and vulgarized under rule of the present Oligarchy, is the suppression of free speech. The fostering of sectionalism, and a propaganda of extreme partisanship and racial animosities, have been the agencies through which the South has been held in more complete subjection since the Reconstruction period than it was ever held by the Slave Oligarchy. The record of this Oligarchy is the darkest page of American history.

In narrating the plain facts relating to the policies and practices of the Oligarchy by which the Southern States have been ruled for forty years or more, my hope and fervent prayer is that a clear and authoritative survey of these portentous events will rivet public attention on the deplorable and menacing conditions in the South, and that the mass of the patriotic citizens of these States will be aroused to a full realization of the great peril of their unfortunate condition. It is for the sake of and in the interest of the majority of the people of the South that this narrative is written, with the firm belief that the truth will make them free and forever destroy the menace of a corrupt and provincial Oligarchy under the rule of which they have been so long oppressed.

CHAPTER II

BRITISH TORYISM DOMINATES THE SOLID SOUTH

In the history of the decline and fall of the Tory party in the United Kingdom we find an interesting parallel to the record of the Southern Oligarchy. In a brief reference to some outstanding events immediately preceding the fall of the Tory party my readers will easily perceive the points of similarity to which I refer.

Although there had been a steady though slow growth of parliamentary government in England, it was not until after enactment of the great Reform Bill (1830-32) that the absolutism of a landed aristocracy, working through the Tory oligarchy, was finally destroyed, or at least its political power weakened so that it no longer retarded the progress of democratic institutions and representative form of government.

Less than one hundred years ago, England was governed by a privileged class. It was, in fact, an aristocratic or oligarchic type of government. With a total population of about 20,000,-000, the ruling class during the Wellington Ministry did not exceed 100,000; and this was the period of which Professor Charles D. Hazen *(Europe Since 1815)* wrote:

Great Britain appeared in 1815, to the superficial observer, in a brilliant light. She had persisted, when others had faltered, in her bitter hostility to Napoleon. She had been the soul of the coalitions, and the crowning victory of Waterloo seemed to place her at the very head of the nations of Europe. Her energy and her wealth seemed to be unbounded. Her population had been only 14,000,000 at the beginning of the great war; at the end it was 19,000,000.

The proud position that England held was ascribed, in the general opinion of Europe, to the excellence of her government. This government enjoyed a great reputation on the Continent.

The renown of the British Parliament "had filled the world." It was supposed that Parliament in fact ruled in England, through the Ministry; that the Ministry was the real executive power, and that it was subject to the will of Parliament. In Europe, England was regarded as a land of freedom and representative government. Yet, in fact, it was a country under the rule of an oligarchy. Professor Hazen continues:

England remained a land of the old régime until 1832, forty years after, the great transformation in France. Power rested with the aristocracy, composed of the nobility and gentry. . . . The House of Lords was composed almost exclusively of large landed proprietors. This was the inexpugnable bulwark of the prevailing social class. But the House of Commons was also another stronghold hardly less secure. This body, supposed as its name shows, to be representative of the Commoners of England, conspicuously belied its name.

Men who were making their fortunes in industry sought to enter the class of landed proprietors by purchasing large estates. Thus the established order gained additional support in the ambition of the newly arising moneyed class. Well might the younger Pitt exclaim: ''This House is not the representation of the people of Great Britain; it is the representation of nominal boroughs, of ruined and exterminated towns, of noble families, of wealthy individuals, of foreign potentates.'' The government of England was not representative, but was oligarchical.

Thus it will be seen that we have in the United States, under rule of the Southern Oligarchy, a privileged class, a government that may be likened to the old Tory government in England, before the great Reform of 1832. As stated by the historian (Hazen), the ''government of England was not representative but was oligarchical.'' It was not wholly aristocratic except in a political sense, because the aristocracy of the governing class was made up largely of men who had acquired their positions, social and political, by purchase. Here again the situation in the Southern States may be likened to that in England less than one hundred years ago. While the government in each of the Southern States is oligarchical and aristocratic in a political sense, it is not aristocratic from a social point of view, because it does not represent the cultural intelligence, the refinement, nor the ideals and patriotism of the best elements in the South.

The old Tory party in England numbered among its leaders men of learning and great ability, but in its decline it was narrow and reactionary in political policies and civic administration. Even under leadership of the Duke of Wellington, this party was not able to comprehend the vital issues of that period and to deal with them in a broad and statesmanlike manner. Commenting on the situation under the Wellington ministry, and the electoral reform measures of 1830-32, Professor Charles Seignobos, in *A Political History of Europe Since 1814* (translation edited by Professor S. M. Macvane), says:

Wellington, the head of the ministry, did not appreciate the change in public opinion. Earl Grey, the leader of the Whigs in the House of Lords, made a speech in favour of Parliamentary reform. Wellington, in the course of his reply, said: ''I have never read or heard of any measure up to the present moment which could in any degree satisfy my mind that the state of the representation could be improved, or be rendered more satisfactory to the country at large than at the present moment. . . . I will go still further, and say that if at the present moment I had imposed on me the duty of forming a legislature for any country, and particularly for a country like this, in possession of great property of various descriptions, I do not mean to assert that I would form such a legislature as we possess now—for the nature of man is incapable of reaching it at once—but my great endeavour would be to form some description of legislature which would produce the same results.''

As stated by Hazen:

The result of this speech, which was entirely sincere but seemed the very abdication of the intellect, was to arouse such widespread indignation that the Wellington ministry was shortly swept from office, and the Whigs came in. Thus was broken the control the Tory party had exercised with one slight interruption for forty-six years.

Commenting on the speech of the Duke of Wellington, Alison —*History of Europe*—says:

Such was the Duke of Wellington's famous declaration against reform, which immediately blew up the smoldering elements of innovation in the nation into a flame. No words from any statesman in English history produced such an impression. . . . Thus fell the Wellington Administration, the most important event in the domestic history of England since the Revolution, in the general annals of Europe since the battle of Waterloo. . . . It induced a transference not merely of the reins of government from one party to another, but a political power from one class in society to another.

During a discussion of the Reform Bill of 1830-32, Macaulay delivered a speech that ''made his reputation as one of the foremost orators of the House." Replying to Sir Robert Inglis, he said:

> My honorable friend. . . . challenges us to show that the constitution was ever better than it is. Sir, we are legislators, not antiquaries. The question for us is, not whether the constitution was better formerly, but whether we can make it better now. . . . We must judge of the form of government by its general tendency, not by happy accidents.

The fundamental purpose of the Whig leaders who carried through the reform measures of 1830-32 was to make the House of Commons a more truly representative body of legislators. Among other demands of the reformers, was the claim that "the power possessed by the landowning class and by the rich in general belonged of right to the bulk of the nation." The steady growth of democratic institutions in the United Kingdom, since the beginning of the reform measures in 1832, was summarized by Lord Bryce in these words:

> The United Kingdom, though in form a monarchy, has a government in some respects more democratic than is that of France, and the process by which it passed from an oligarchy to a democracy through four constitutional changes in 1832, 1868, 1885, and 1918, is full of instruction for the historian.

During ninety years last past, the United Kingdom has passed through four periods of changes which may be classed as revolutionary in effect, and each of these periods has been an epoch to which we may refer as the beginning of a new era in the progress of democratic institutions and representative government. The beginning of each era of "constitutional changes" through which the United Kingdom "passed from an oligarchy to a democracy" was marked by great agitation and public excitement. The Reform Act of 1832 was the beginning of these "four constitutional changes," and as it was more radical and revolutionary than any subsequent changes, it aroused more excitement, created more agitation, and caused more serious apprehension, than any later measures of reform. The contest of 1830-32 was "almost bloodless. There were riots, but no civil war."

For more than forty years, the power of the Oligarchy in the

Southern States has been, and it is at the present time, more absolute and oppressive than was the power of the Tory oligarchy in the United Kingdom before the Reform Act of 1832. While England was passing "through four constitutional changes," the South has passed through no constitutional change except the change from slavery to emancipation, which was not voluntary and which has not been wholly effective. Slavery no longer has a legal standing, nor is it in common practice in the Southern States, but in all other respects the power of the present Oligarchy in the South is as absolute as was that of the Slave Oligarchy in 1860, or at any other time in the history of this country. And the great mass of the people in the South, white and colored, are more oppressed and dependent at the present time than they were before the Civil War. The situation was forcibly described by *The Chicago Tribune* as follows:

The fixed southern control of the Democratic party is individualistic in its thinking, sectional in its sympathies, and inherits a tradition against common labor as servile. The social organization is still semi-patriarchal in the rural communities, and the southern environment presents the maximum of natural and cultural resistance to necessary social and industrial standardization.

As pointed out in the preceding chapter, the power of the Southern Oligarchy was vastly increased and extended when, in 1913, it came into control of the administrative and legislative branches of the National Government. During the Wilson Administration, this provincial Oligarchy was a greater menace to democratic institutions than the Slave Oligarchy was under the Buchanan Administration. When it gained control of the Federal Government, the Southern Oligarchy introduced into the management of national affairs the same narrow provincial policies and corrupt practices that it had used in the States where it had been in absolute control for nearly forty years. Shortly after the election of Mr. Wilson, in 1916, *The New York Tribune* summed up the situation in these words:

The single question that now remains to be considered is whether the division of the nation hereafter is to be sectional or to be a cleavage based on principle.

The success of the Democratic party in national affairs, under leadership of the Southern Oligarchy, involves and necessitates the imposition of Southern thought upon Northern action. Political thought in the South has no conception of nationalism; it is essentially provincial and partisan. Partisan leaders of the South who dominate the national Democratic party are open champions of the spoils system and extreme partisanship. Quoting further from *The Chicago Tribune*, it is plain that the Democratic party—

thinks in terms of the parish and State. It does not grasp the fact that our economic organization is national or that to try to direct it by piecemeal local regulation is worse than futile. It has not learned of the industrial revolution and is only dimly conscious of the existence of the social and industrial problems a changed and changing order of society has created.

In May's *Democracy In Europe*, we find a description of the French *bourgeoisie* that fits the privileged and ruling class in the Southern States:

If we search for the middle class in French society, we must look to the *bourgeoisie*. But who were they? There was a time when they had a recognized place in the State. They exercised their municipal franchises; and they were represented as part of the *Tiers État*, in the Estates. But they had lost all these privileges; they performed no services to their country, or their order; but had become a race of greedy place-hunters. Vast numbers of small offices were created and sold for their gratification. . . . The petty placeman, who served the king, was set above his fellows. He gave himself the airs of a great man. . . . In every town, the government had created a privileged aristocracy, alienated from the people, useless to the State, and a just cause of popular discontent.

Writing from Wytheville, Virginia, October 16, 1916, to *The New York Tribune*, an "Old Confederate Soldier" frankly and forcibly expressed the attitude of the South. This letter is so clear and candid in its admissions respecting the menace of the situation in the Southern States, under the rule of a provincial Oligarchy, that it is well worth the careful study of my readers. I quote from this letter at some length as follows:

There is no sense in trying to evade the fact that the South is the brains and backbone of the Democratic party. The South is perfectly willing to assume all responsibility of running the government, but it is not laboring under any delusion as to its tenure of power. Be assured that every question of national importance which comes up will be settled in conformity with the welfare and happiness of the South, so long as the South is in the saddle. The South, of course, wants the North to pay the taxes and the taxes to be spent for the benefit of the South. The South has been taught that the North, when in power, taxed the South and spent the money for the North.

But aside from the question of who shall pay the taxes, and where shall the taxes be spent, there is staring the country in the face the fact that the Solid South is a real menace to the happiness and welfare of the country. The South can never vote any other way than Democratic. Let the Northern people face that fact. . . .

The South has stood for Sam Randall of Pennsylvania, a Democrat in favor of high protection. Then it went wild over Watterson and a "tariff for revenue only." It stood for Cleveland and the gold standard and then for Bryan and free silver.

The South is perfectly willing to form a coalition with any dissatisfied element in the North, provided that element is strong enough to assure victory and will for the time being allow itself to be called Democratic. Every question is of secondary importance to the South in comparison with the one which appeals to us every day, namely.—How does the solution of this question or that question affect our relations to the Negro?

The menace of the South is real. We are a menace to ourselves as well as you. Thousands of us vote the Democratic ticket, but in our hearts hope the good sense of the North will save us from a calamity of our own making.

It is a lamentable, historical truth, not only that the South has been "perfectly willing to form a coalition with any dissatisfied element in the North," but also that the Southern Oligarchy has succeeded, with remarkable shrewdness and intrigue, at the time of the most serious crises in the history of the United States, in forming a coalition with the "dissatisfied element in the North." And it is also an historical truth that the coalitions which the political leaders of the South have made with the North have been not only with the "dissatisfied element," but more especially with the un-American, the irresponsible and disloyal elements of the North; and herein lies a continued menace to American institutions. It was the power of this coalition that supported President Wilson when the country was not only menaced by the corrupt practices and evil policies of the Southern Oligarchy but also was exposed to the immediate peril of autocracy. This menace was very clearly portrayed in a series of articles by Dr. David Jayne Hill, and published in *The North American Review,* from which I quote the following paragraphs:

By all the early traditions of the South, and by all the present material interests of its people, we are warranted in believing that personal government is particularly odious to the citizens of that portion of our country. It is there, if anywhere, that pure Jeffersonian political philosophy might be expected to prevail; and yet, it is an undeniable fact that its adhesion to one party has led the South into a position of obsequiousness to executive dictation which generations ago would have seemed intolerable.

Under such a régime every important decision is made by the head of the party; and when the word is spoken, irrespective of its meaning, it becomes the shibboleth of the entire electorate. Dissent becomes a political death warrant; even the oligarchy that locally rules, is cowed; and from the ruins of democracy, when its prerogatives of free and deliberate debate are thus denied, arise the insolent pretentions of an undisguised autocracy. Herein is the explanation of the astounding fact that Democratic Senators, with a few courageous exceptions, have been voted *en bloc* by the mere word of command of a party chief, who by the very nature of the case they have made an absolute master in his party's house.

The power of the Slave Oligarchy which, like the old Tory party in England, was essentially a landed aristocracy, was destroyed by emancipation, but from the ashes of that Oligarchy there arose an inferior, less cultured and more sordid power which came as the aftermath of Reconstruction. The history of the origin and growth of this post-bellum Oligarchy is found in the tragic and pathetic story of the Solid South. The late Henry Watterson perceived the menace of the Southern Oligarchy, in the reorganization of the Democratic party, after the beginning of Reconstruction in the South, when, in 1873, he said: "The Democratic party, crucified in 1860, received no decent burial, and has been rotting away ever since in the open air." He amplified his opinion of the Democratic party when he added this condemnatory judgment:

The reorganization of the Democratic party after the war was a capital mistake, and the participation in that act by the South was a first-class blunder. In the past it was the party of slavery; in the present it is the party of obstruction.

The leaders of the Southern Oligarchy habitually affect a

supercilious air of provincial and abnormal sensitiveness which has been easily and conveniently used in support of the spoils system and in perpetuating their rule over the great mass of white and colored people in the South. The leaders do not like to have their methods inquired into nor their corrupt and provincial practices censured. They object to any investigation of their record in public affairs. They demand to be let alone, even when their policies and practices menace the life of the Nation. They are united and solid for the protection of their "peculiar institution" and the enforcement of their sectional, strictly partisan and un-American policies. These are the policies and practices which prevailed in this country for eight years immediately preceding the outbreak of the Civil War.

The fact that the Democratic party in the South is, and has been for seventy-five years, "willing to form a coalition with any dissatisfied element in the North, provided that element is strong enough to assure victory," is a portentous historical fact. On several occasions, leaders of the Southern Oligarchy have made substantially the same acknowledgment that we find in the letter quoted from an "Old Confederate Soldier." Their excuse, when they were disposed to offer an excuse, for the unfortunate situation has been found in the claim that their policies and methods were necessary in order to protect the South from the menace of Negro domination.

Our survey of actual conditions, together with a summary of the official record, will show the absurdity and inconsistency of this specious and hackneyed plea respecting the alleged danger of Negro domination in the South.

Leaders of the Southern Oligarchy have asserted, by way of palliation for their evil practices, that the political methods which they have adopted are no worse than the partisan practices which have prevailed in the North. And it may be well to note that the Democratic politician of the South never wearies of telling the people that slavery was introduced into the South by New England tradesmen engaged in the slave traffic, though he does not tell them that slavery would have been abolished in the early history of this country had it not been for the opposition of the leaders of the Slave Oligarchy in Georgia and South Carolina. Moreover, when these political leaders of the South assert that corrupt practices, the spoils system and political chicanery originated in the New England States, they fail to add that these pernicious practices were introduced into American politics by Northern Democrats who were subservient allies of the Slave Oligarchy and who, almost without exception, were lacking in virile American patriotism and were frequently disloyal, and during the Civil War were properly classed as "Copperheads."

So far as one phase of corrupt practices is concerned, which has been used to a large extent to perpetuate the power of the Southern Oligarchy since the Reconstruction period, it is true that it came from New England. It originated in the partisan brain of a Northern Democrat. It is the system of gerrymandering the Congressional districts in the Southern States, by which one Black Belt county is included in every district, without regard to geographic contiguity, so that frauds in that county, where there are five or ten times as many Negroes as there are whites, could be easily covered up and used to overcome possible majorities for the opposition in the white counties.

Elbridge Gerry was a native of Massachusetts. He was several times defeated for Governor of his native State, but was finally successful in 1810 and was reëlected in 1811. His administration was severely criticised for its extreme partisanship, and how well founded were the charges against him is suggested by the fact that the legislature enacted a law while he was Governor, which he supported and signed, for re-districting the State in such manner as to eliminate the Federalists majorities in several counties, and by such unfair means procure a majority for the Democrats.

According to *The International Encyclopaedia,*—

Gerrymander is a word belonging to the political vocabulary of the United States and used to denote an unfair division of electoral districts in a state, made in the interest of one of the political parties. . . .

The form of one of the districts into which Essex County was divided was somewhat like that of a monstrous animal, and when some one suggested that it looked like a salamander, the name of gerrymander was given to it instead.

The first organized effort to form a coalition for the purpose of maintaining sectional policies as the distinguishing tenet of a national political party assumed definite form during the administration of Jackson, when Calhoun came forward, as the recognized leader of the reactionary element of the Slave Oligarchy, and announced a provincial policy which placed the institution of slavery above the Constitution and any law and all laws made by Congress. Now President Jackson was a very pronounced partisan, and it was during his administration that the spoils system was first introduced into American politics. But in spite of his extreme partisanship, Jackson was first an American, as Calhoun learned to his sorrow and deep chagrin. Andrew Jackson never forgave an enemy, and he used his official position to punish his enemies and reward his friends, but his loyalty to the federal government and his national patriotism were never questioned.

President Jackson did not hesitate to use his power to prevent a coalition of the Slave Oligarchy with the Northern Democrats, which was attempted when Calhoun brought forward his seditious doctrine of "a peculiar institution" which he placed above the Constitution, and which was accepted as the leading tenet of the Slave Oligarchy. The attempt to form a coalition of the leaders of that Oligarchy with the radical and reactionary Democrats in the Northern States was not successful during Jackson's Administration.

The Slave Oligarchy again undertook to form a coalition with leading Democrats of the North during Van Buren's Administration, for the purpose of placing the country absolutely under the domination of a sectional party. While Van Buren did not possess the manly qualities and virile patriotism of Jackson, he could not be led, nor driven, into full endorsement of the proposed coalition. He gave to the Slave Oligarchy his hearty support with all the influence of his administration in extending and making more permanent the spoils system, which was introduced into American politics by Aaron Burr, and greatly extended by Van Buren during Jackson's Administration; but Van Buren refused to support the proposed plans for a coalition to extend slavery and increase the power of the Slave Oligarchy. He was punished for his opposition to the plans of the Slave Oligarchy, but it was not until 1844 that that Oligarchy finally succeeded in forming a coalition which continued down to the election of Lincoln and the beginning of the Civil War.

When, in 1844, Van Buren refused to support every sectional demand of the ruling Oligarchy in the South, he was defeated for renomination and Polk was nominated as the Democratic candidate for President. The election of Polk made secure the absolute domination of the Slave Oligarchy in the national government. Then followed the annexation of Texas as a Slave State and the defeat of the Wilmot Proviso. Van Buren finally came out in the open with the Free Soil Democrats of the North and he was their candidate for President in 1848. Referring to the defeat of Van Buren before the Democratic Convention of 1844, Rhodes *(History of the United States)* says:

A majority of the convention was in favor of the nomination of Van Buren, and his choice would have given satisfaction to Northern Democrats, but his opposition to immediate annexation caused his defeat. The old rule requiring two-thirds of the convention to nominate was adopted, and this resulted in the choice, on the ninth ballot, of James K. Polk. Had ability constituted the test, Polk would not have been selected, neither had a long service in the House of Representatives given him a claim to distinction; but he had written, ''I am in favor of the immediate re-annexation of Texas to the territory and government of the United States.''

The coalition of the Slave Oligarchy with the subservient Northern Democrats brought about the election of Pierce in 1852 by a large majority. He received 254 electoral votes and Scott, the Whig candidate, only 42. The popular majority of Pierce over Scott was more than 200,000, a larger majority than had been received by any candidate for President prior to that election. Rhodes explains the success of the Democratic ticket and the election of Pierce as follows:

The reason of Democratic success was because that party unreservedly endorsed the compromise, and in its approval neither platform nor candidate halted. . . . The country was tired of slavery agitation. The people were convinced that the status of every foot of territory in the United States, with regard to slavery, was fixed; that it had ceased to be a political question.

Everybody who voted for Pierce and, as stated by Rhodes, the majority of voters for Scott, thought that the slavery question was forever settled:

> The business interests of the country were on the side of the Democrats. . . . Trade was good, the country was very prosperous. . . . The Democratic party gained the confidence of the people because it professed to be the party essentially opposed to the agitation of slavery; because it was the party of pacification.

When, in 1853, President Fillmore retired from office, and was succeeded by Pierce, "the country abounded with prosperity." Fillmore was a staunch American, a man of high personal integrity and intense patriotism. He initiated and led the movement in New York which abolished imprisonment for debt, New York being the first State to start this great reform. Fillmore also led in the movement for abolition of religious test oaths, and at the same time he was a forceful and aggressive advocate of non-sectarian public education.

Although Fillmore had given the country a wise and safe administration, during which there had been great prosperity, the popular feeling was that the agitation of the slavery question would cease with the election of a Northern Democrat whose policies would meet all the demands of the slaveholders and cotton producers, and thereby avoid further discussion of a question which had so long harrassed the people and about which they very much desired rest and avoidance of further discussion.

Within less than a year after the inauguration of Pierce, the Kansas-Nebraska bill was the burning issue of the hour, and those in the North who supposed they had seen an end of the slavery agitation quickly realized that this vital question had not been settled by surrender to the Slave Oligarchy and the election of a Northern Democrat. The great question of the hour had in fact assumed a more portentous aspect. As evidence of the absolute subserviency of the Pierce Administration to the Slave Oligarchy, when the Kansas-Nebraska bill was before the House of Representatives, it was announced that the patronage of the administration would be used in the interest of those Representatives who voted for the bill.

The final test of the supremacy of the Slave Oligarchy came in the vote on the Kansas-Nebraska bill, and the vote on that measure established beyond question the existence of an un-American coalition absolutely under control of that Oligarchy. Commenting on the Kansas-Nebraska bill, Rhodes says:

It is safe to say that, in the scope and consequences of the Kansas-Nebraska act, it was the most momentous measure that passed Congress from the day that the Senators and Representatives first met to the outbreak of the Civil War. It sealed the doom of the Whig party; it caused the formation of the Republican party on the principle of no extension of slavery; it roused Lincoln and gave bent to his great political ambition. It made the Fugitive Slave law a dead letter at the North.

Six years after its passage, Alexander H. Stephens wrote this frank acknowledgment:

Never was an act of Congress so generally and unanimously hailed with delight at the South as was the Kansas-Nebraska act.

When the Slave Oligarchy dictated the nomination of Buchanan, the power of the coalition was again demonstrated, and the subserviency of the Northern Democracy was complete. Regarding the surrender of Buchanan to the demands of the Slave Oligarchy, Rhodes says:

Pierce had served the South well, but it could now be truthfully said that Buchanan was serving her still better. When the web of subterfuge was brushed away, the position of the President amounted to this: It is determined by the slavery propaganda that Kansas shall be a slave State. There is now one more free than slave State in the Union, and Kansas is needed to restore the equilibrium. To make it a slave State by fair means is impossible. We have now a chance to make it one under the color of law, and this opportunity we are going to use to the best of our ability.

One outstanding evidence of the conspiracy of the pro-slavery element in Kansas was the usual corrupt practices of Southern politicians in perpetrating election frauds. Concerning this phase of the trouble in Kansas, Rhodes says:

From Oxford there was a forged return of 1,628 votes; the town had but fifty voters. In McGee county, where there were certainly not twenty voters, 1,266 pro-slavery ballots were alleged to have been cast. If the Oxford and McGee returns were allowed, the legislature would be pro-slavery; if they were thrown out, it would be a free State.

Election frauds have long been one of the distinguishing practices of the Democratic party, especially when that party was dominated by the Southern Oligarchy. While summarizing some of the outstanding facts in the history of the Democratic party under the leadership of the Southern Oligarchy, it may be well to call attention to another phase of political chicanery which has frequently brought success to the coalition and disaster to the country. In the campaign which resulted in the election of Pierce as President of the United States, the business interests of the country were on the side of the Democrats.

It frequently happens that the ultra-conservative business interests of the country are allied with the non-resistants, that is, those who are unable or unwilling to meet the vital issues before the people. And it has often happened that great disasters have come which could have been avoided had the selfish business interests been able to comprehend the actual situation and look beyond immediate financial gain. The materialists and pacifists frequently fall a prey to the artful subterfuges of the designing and unscrupulous politicians. Daniel Webster foresaw the menace of a coalition between the Slave Oligarchy and the designing political leaders of the Democratic party in the North when he said:

There is no chapter in our history, respecting public measures and public men, more full of what would create surprise, and more full of what does create, in my mind, extreme mortification, than that of the conduct of the Northern Democracy on this subject.

Mr. Webster referred to the conduct of the Northern Democrats who voted for the acquisition of more slave territory and then took the lead in the Free Soil party. ''And there they stand, sir,'' said Webster:

They leave us here, bound in honor and conscience by the resolutions of annexation; they leave us here, to take the odium of fulfilling the obligation in favor of slavery which they voted us into, or else the great odium of violating these obligations, while they are at home making capital and rousing speeches for free soil and no slavery.

In the Presidential campaign of 1916 there was a coalition of the Southern Oligarchy with the un-American Democracy in the North; not only the "dissatisfied element" but also a very large satisfied element, largely composed of profiteers who were making vast fortunes out of the suffering of Europe, as well as the Pacifists and pro-Germans. It was a repetition of the political chicanery of the campaign in 1852 when Pierce was elected. False and misleading promises of peace and continued prosperity, a sordid appeal to the selfish and material interests above honor and patriotism; and the campaign slogan of the Democratic party in the Presidential campaign of 1916 was that "he kept us out of war." The late Joseph Choate, some time Ambassador to Great Britain, had in mind the menace of this coalition of the Southern Oligarchy with the Northern Democrats, and the men whom this coalition elected to office, when, shortly before his death, in a public speech, he said:

In 1856 we were fighting against James Buchanan, whose administration proved so disastrous to the honor of the American people. It seems to me that our present President more closely resembles Buchanan than any other of our Presidents since the birth of the Republic. In both there was the same vacillation, the same lack of courage and manhood under the cover of what both called "watchful waiting."

Mr. Choate went on to say that President Wilson, like Buchanan, did all he could at first to prevent preparedness, that "both catered to the South." Nor was former President Theodore Roosevelt unmindful of the pernicious practices of the Southern Oligarchy under the coalition through which it had been able to gain control of the National Government. In commenting on the situation he referred to President Wilson in these words:

In the great world crisis he has played a more evil part than Buchanan and Pierce ever played in the years that led up to and saw the opening of the Civil War. The times have needed a Washington or a Lincoln. Unfortunately we have been granted only another Buchanan.

The historical facts relating to the provincialism of the political leaders of the South, in connection with important events of national character, should be taken together and studied in their relation to one another. The blight of slavery and the great social and economic revolution which followed the Civil War and Emancipation, made possible the rise of an Oligarchy which has been able to perpetuate its power by misleading the people and appealing to sectional prejudice and racial animosities. A short summary of some salient events of that chaotic period after the Civil War and before the beginning of Reconstruction will bring us face to face with the anomalous situation that made possible the rise of the Southern Oligarchy.

CHAPTER III

In his plan for reconstruction of the Southern States, President Lincoln displayed that remarkable foresight and statesmanship, seasoned with a keen sense of justice and broad American patriotism, which distinguished his whole public career. Before and during the war, he had shown that he possessed a vast amount of authoritative information concerning actual conditions in the South which enabled him to take a broad, sympathetic and statesmanlike view of the whole situation. On more than one occasion, he had emphasized the fact that the Southern States were ruled by the Slave Oligarchy, and he knew that this Oligarchy was wholly responsible for the war. He had clearly perceived that the great mass of the people had no voice in the affairs of government in the South; and he knew they had been coerced and misled into an attempt to divide the Union and perpetuate the institution of slavery.

Lincoln's sympathies were always with the mass of non-slaveholding whites of the South. He had faith in their loyalty and he was willing to trust them, but he never wavered in his determination to put down the rebellion and destroy the institution of slavery. He had no confidence in the reactionary leaders of the rebellion and he was never willing to make any terms with them that contemplated compromise on the two vital issues of the war. For instance, in his last message to Congress, he repeated the determination to which he had strictly adhered from the beginning:

The public purpose to reëstablish and maintain the national authority is unchanged, and, as we believe, unchangeable. . . . On careful consideration of all the evidence accessible, it seems to me that no attempt at negotiation with the insurgent leader could result in any good. He would accept nothing short of severance of the Union—precisely what we will not and cannot give. . . .

Between him and us the issue is distinct, simple, and inflexible. It is an issue which can only be tried by war. . . . What is true, however, of him who heads the insurgent cause, is not necessarily true of those who follow. Although he cannot re-accept the Union, they can. Some of them, we know, already desire peace and reunion. The number of such may increase.

Thus it is seen that Lincoln had confidence in the mass of the people in the Southern States, and his plan of reconstruction contemplated government in the South by the loyal people of those States. His plan was very simple because it was based on the assumption that the act of rebellion in each of the seceding States was the illegal act of disloyal persons who had unlawfully subverted the loyal State governments of the eleven States which passed the so-called acts of secession. It was assumed that the Southern States continued as members of the Union, and that Lincoln's plan of reconstruction could be carried out by placing the loyal people in these States in control of the State governments. In answer to complaints from Louisiana about "the course of General Phelps of Butler's army," President Lincoln wrote a letter, on July 26, 1862, to Reverdy Johnson, who had been sent to Louisiana on government business, in which he "touched upon the subject (reconstruction) quite incidentally in connection with Louisiana matters." From this letter I quote the following:

The people of Louisiana—all intelligent people everywhere—know full well that I never had a wish to touch the foundations of their society, or any right of theirs. With perfect knowledge of this, they forced a necessity upon me to send armies among them, and it is their own fault, not mine, that they are annoyed by the presence of General Phelps.

As related by Nicolay and Hay *(Abraham Lincoln)*, "two days later the President developed his idea more fully in a letter to Cuthbert Bullitt:"

The people of Louisiana who wish protection to person and property, have but to reach forth their hands and take it. Let them in good faith reinaugurate the national authority and set up a State government conforming thereto under the Constitution. They know how to do it, and can have the protection of the army while doing it. The army will be withdrawn so soon as such State government can dispense with its presence, and the people of the State can then, upon the old constitutional terms, govern themselves to their own liking.

On December 8, 1863, President Lincoln issued his famous "Proclamation of Amnesty and Reconstruction," from which I take the following:

. . . Whenever, in any of the States of Arkansas, Texas, Louisiana, Mississippi, Tennessee, Alabama, Georgia, Florida, South Carolina, and North Carolina, a number of persons, not less than one tenth in number of the votes cast in such State at the presidential election of the year of our Lord one thousand eight hundred and sixty, each having taken the oath aforesaid and not having since violated it, and being a qualified voter by the election law of the State existing immediately before the so-called act of secession, and excluding all others, shall reëstablish a State government which shall be republican, and in no wise contravening said oath, such shall be recognized as the true government of the State, and the State shall receive thereunder the benefits of the constitutional provision which declares that ''the United States shall guaranty to every State in this Union a republican form of government, and shall protect each of them against invasion; and, on application of the legislature, or the executive (when the legislature cannot be convened), against domestic violence.

In his third annual message to Congress (December 8, 1863) President Lincoln said:

. Looking now to the present and future, and with reference to a resumption of the national authority within the States wherein that authority has been suspended, I have thought fit to issue a proclamation, a copy of which is herewith transmitted. . . .
By the proclamation a plan is presented which may be accepted by them as a rallying-point, and which they are assured in advance will not be rejected here. This may bring them to act sooner than they otherwise would.

The question of Reconstruction was before the 38th Congress for more than five months, in 1864, and it was debated at great length in the House. The ''famous bill'' which embodied a compromise of the Congressional plan for Reconstruction was finally passed by the Senate, July 2, 1864, two days before the adjournment of Congress. This bill did not meet the demands of the Radicals, because it did not give the ballot to the Negro, but it asserted the jurisdiction of Congress and provided expressly that the President should recognize by proclamation the State governments established under it, only "after obtaining the consent of Congress." The President did not approve this bill but defeated it by a "pocket veto."

The President issued a public statement in which he referred to a bill passed by Congress to " 'guarantee to certain States, whose governments have been usurped or overthrown, a republican form of government,' a copy of which is hereunto annexed." The bill, he said, was received by him "less than one hour before the *sine die* adjournment of said session." Among other things, he thought the "system for restoration" provided for in the bill was "one very proper plan for the loyal people of any State choosing to adopt it," but he was opposed to forcing it on any State by law. He would at all times—

be prepared to give the Executive aid and assistance to such people, so soon as the military resistance to the United States shall have been suppressed in any such State, and the people thereof shall have sufficiently returned to their obedience to the Constitution and laws of the United States.

Senator Benjamin F. Wade and Representative Henry Winter Davis replied in an angry protest, in which they stated that they had read the President's statement "without surprise, but not without indignation," and they charged that the President's claim of want of time for examination of the bill was a false pretense. "Ignorance of its contents is out of the question," they asserted. The protest alleged that—

the President, by preventing this bill from becoming a law, holds the electoral votes of the rebel States at the dictation of his personal ambition. . . . A more studied outrage on the legislative authority of the people has never been perpetrated.

The joint protest of Senator Wade and Representative Davis, chief authors of the bill for reconstruction of the Southern States, which the President failed to approve, was printed in *The New York Tribune,* of August 5, and, as related by Professor Charles H. McCarthy (*Lincoln's Plan of Reconstruction*),

. . . two of the boldest leaders, disregarding every consideration of prudence, arraigned the President in language which for severity was never surpassed by the invectives of his ablest political opponents. . . . Their fierce manifesto, addressed "To the supporters of the Government," was perhaps, the most bitter attack made upon Mr. Lincoln during his Presidential career.

The "fierce manifesto" made no perceptible impression on Mr. Lincoln, nor did it make any great impression on the American voters. The President did not change his plan of Reconstruction. Long after it had been published to the world the Republican party, in convention assembled, approved his "practical wisdom, unselfish patriotism and unswerving fidelity to the Constitution"; and in the Presidential election of 1864, Mr. Lincoln received 212 electoral votes to 21 for George B. McClellan. He received the electoral votes of twenty-two of the twenty-five States participating in the election. A few weeks after the people had expressed their approval of his policies, in his fourth and last annual message, President Lincoln reverted to his plan for Reconstruction in these words:

They can at any moment have peace simply by laying down their arms and submitting to the national authority under the Constitution. After so much the government could not, if it would, maintain war against them. The loyal people would not sustain or allow it. . . .

In stating a single condition of peace, I mean simply to say, that the war will cease on the part of the government whenever it shall have ceased on the part of those who began it.

Respecting the question of giving the ballot to the Negro, President Lincoln displayed that broad and far-seeing statesmanship which characterized all his public utterances and official acts, especially in matters relating to the Southern States, which always received his most thoughtful and sympathetic consideration. For example, in a letter to Governor Hahn of Louisiana, the President wrote as follows:

I congratulate you on having fixed your name in history as the first free-State governor of Louisiana. Now you are about to have a convention, which, among other things, will probably define the elective franchise. I barely suggest for your private consideration, whether some of the colored people may not be let in—as, for instance, the very intelligent, and especially those who have fought gallantly in our ranks. They would probably help, in some trying time to come, to keep the jewel of liberty within the family of freedom. But this is only a suggestion, not to the public, but to you alone.

In his last public address, April 11, 1865, alluding to the new constitution of the reconstructed government in Louisiana, President Lincoln said:

It is also unsatisfactory to some that the elective franchise is not given to the colored man. I would myself prefer that it were now conferred on the very intelligent, and on those who serve our cause as soldiers.

When Andrew Johnson became President, there was a great change, due not so much to the fact that President Johnson was not willing to carry out the Lincoln policies but rather to the unfortunate fact that Johnson was very headstrong, self-willed and aggressive. He had been a Democrat but a strong Union man. He was Senator from Tennessee when that State seceded, but he ignored the act of secession and treated it with contempt, by retaining his seat in the Senate and taking the position that the State he represented had no right to secede and could not withdraw from the Union. Johnson sympathized with the South, but he had no patience with secession, and he was bitter against the leaders of the slave-holding Oligarchy who had forced the South into secession. His manner was not conciliatory but very offensive, not only to Republican leaders in Congress but also to Democratic leaders in the Southern States.

Apart from the fact that Andrew Johnson was elected Vice-President on the Republican ticket with Lincoln, but as a Union Democrat, he had been a Democrat all his life, and the narrow, partisan prejudices and provincialism so characteristic of Southern Democrats were not lacking in his public policies. In a frank discussion of this question, the South cannot escape responsibility for the sins of omission for which a Southern Democrat was responsible while acting as President during a very grave crisis in our country's history. Referring to the inauguration of Andrew Johnson as Vice-President, Ben Perley Poore (*Perley's Reminiscences*) says:

To the surprise of everybody, the Vice-President, when called on to take the oath of office, made a maudlin, drunken speech. He addressed the Diplomatic Corps and the heads of departments in the most incoherent, and in some instances offensive manner. The Republican Senators were horror-stricken, and Col. Forney vainly endeavored to make him conclude his harangue; but he would not be stopped; the brandy had made him crazily drunk, and the mortifying scene was prolonged until he was told that it was necessary to go with the President to the eastern front of the Captial.

President Johnson's policy of Reconstruction, as outlined in a proclamation of Amnesty made May 29, 1865, suggested substantially Lincoln's policy. Provisional Governors were appointed and State Governments reinstated. In elections only those could vote who had exercised that privilege prior to 1860. The final qualifications for suffrage were to be decided by the State legislatures or constitutional conventions. Johnson's plan, like the plan that had been outlined by Lincoln, limited the voters to white men, but favored a qualified suffrage for Negroes, leaving the question of franchise for the Negroes as a matter to be finally determined by the States. Congress opposed Johnson's plan for the same alleged reasons that it opposed Lincoln's plan, and for other reasons, and refused recognition to the State Governments established under it, assuming that Reconstruction was a matter for the legislative instead of the executive branch of the Government to handle.

Shortly after the appointment of a provisional governor for each of the Southern States, and in connection with other measures undertaken to carry out his plan of Reconstruction, President Johnson sent General Grant and Major-General Carl Schurz as special commissioners on tours of inspection and investigation in the Southern States, for the purpose of gathering authentic information concerning actual conditions and the feeling of the people. The two reports were quite contradictory; for example, the report of General Grant contained the following frank statement:

I am satisfied that the mass of thinking men of the South accept the present situation of affairs in good faith. The questions which have heretofore divided the sentiment of the people of the two sections—slavery and State rights, or the right of the State to secede from the Union—they regard as having been settled forever by the highest tribunal—arms—that man can resort to. I was pleased to learn from the leading men whom I met that they not only accepted the decision arrived at as final, but, now that the smoke of battle has cleared away and time has been given for reflection, that this decision has been a fortunate one for the whole country, they receiving like benefits from it with those who opposed them in the field and in council.

General Grant also stated that there was "universal acquiescence in the authority of the general government throughout the portions of the country visited" by him and "that the mere presence of a military force, without regard to numbers, is sufficient to maintain order." And his "observations" led him to the "conclusion that the citizens of the Southern States are anxious to return to self-government, within the Union, as soon as possible."

The whole spirit of the report made by General Schurz was vindictive and indicated a prejudice which, as a matter of course, so brave an American patriot and so chivalrous a soldier as General Grant could not feel toward a foe whom he had met in open battle and to whom he had granted such liberal terms of surrender. The antithesis of the conclusions reached by General Grant about the Southern people is expressed in the following excerpt from the report of General Schurz:

> Treason does, under existing circumstances, not appear odious in the South. The people are not impressed with any sense of its criminality. And, secondly, there is, as yet, among the Southern people an utter absence of national feeling.

Carl Schurz apparently had no faith in the people, and it seems that he had no plan for dealing with a defeated foe except the brutal German military plan of physical force and oppression. His report had "considerable influence" with the Radical faction in Congress, and it was made the basis of the Reconstruction measures of that faction under the leadership of Thaddeus Stevens. Those policies prolonged sectional prejudice, accentuated racial animosities, brought needless suffering to the poor Negroes, and made possible the domination of a corrupt and sectional Oligarchy in the Southern States.

It seems unbelievable that Congress rejected the judgment and counsel of the commander-in-chief of the Union Army, the greatest hero of the Civil War, second only to Lincoln in the esteem of the people, and instead accepted and approved the recommendations of a German-American citizen who could not see the situation from an American point of view. In one of the most troublous periods of this country's history, and at the time of a most serious crisis in the Southern States, a German-American citizen was the instigator of a policy that brought great trouble to the whole country and to the South in particular.

Carl Schurz should have known that the policy he recommended would keep alive indefinitely sectional prejudices and race hatred in America. In his later career we find the same subtle German influences at work through his agency to the detriment of the United States. In an "Epilogue" to an interesting book under the title of *Why Europe is at War*, General Francis V. Greene refers to the attitude of Carl Schurz during the war between France and Germany, in 1870-71, as follows:

It is a well settled principle of international law that any change by a neutral nation, after the outbreak of hostilities, in its neutrality laws, is in itself a breach of neutrality. It is an interesting fact that in the war of 1870, Carl Schurz, then United States Senator from Missouri, protested in the Senate against the sale of arms to France; and his action had important political consequences in this country. It is one of the factors that led to the formation of the Liberal party in 1872, the nomination by that party of Horace Greeley for President, the endorsement of the nomination by the Democratic party, the overwhelming defeat of Greeley, and the death of Greeley soon after the election.

I had the story at considerable length from his standpoint, and a very interesting story it was, from General Grant at St. Petersburg in August, 1878, at the time that he was making his tour around the world. The enmity of Carl Schurz toward President Grant and his Administration dated from this controversy, and because the Administration did not accede to Schurz's view, Schurz set out to split the Republican party and to defeat General Grant for the nomination; or if he received the nomination, then to organize from a minority of the Republicans and from the Democrats a party which should defeat him at the election. The plans of Schurz and Sumner and Greeley, as is well known, came to an ignominious failure.

After the Southern States, except Tennessee, had rejected the proposed Fourteenth Amendment, the Congressional plan of Reconstruction was finally adopted, in February, 1867, under an "Act to provide for the more efficient government of the seceded States." The bill was vetoed by President Johnson and on the same day was passed over his veto. Under this act all the States that had seceded, except Tennessee, were divided into five military districts. Provision was made for calling a convention in each of these ten States to frame a constitution. All male citizens, twenty-one years old and upward, of whatever race, color or previous condition, resident in the State one year previous to election, except such as were disfranchised for participation in the rebellion, or for crimes of which they had been convicted, had the right to vote for delegates to these conventions. It was further stipulated that the State constitutions to be made must provide for Negro suffrage, and such constitutions must be ratified by popular vote and approved by Congress.

The situation in the South after the assassination of Lincoln was a crisis that called for a man of broad views and careful training in the affairs of statecraft, and President Johnson did not possess these essential qualities of statesmanship. In antagonizing Congress, Johnson brought on his own downfall and precipitated a crisis which resulted in placing the Radical faction of the Republican party in the ascendancy. The domination of the Radical faction of the Republican party destroyed the influence of the wiser and loyal leaders of the South and afforded an opportunity for the successful propaganda of sectional prejudices and race hatred. It was the failure of President Johnson to grasp the opportunities for the exercise of broad, patriotic statesmanship that made possible the rise and long rule of a corrupt and provincial Oligarchy in the South.

As stated in the report of General Grant, ''the mass of thinking men of the South accept the present situation of affairs in good faith.'' It was true that the mass of the people had accepted the surrender of Lee and Johnston as the end of their struggle; they accepted it in good faith and they were loyal to the Government against which they had been making war for four years. It was a lost cause for which they had battled heroically, albeit in many cases against their better judgment and best interests, but they had made the sacrifice and accepted the result with heroic moral courage no less commendable than the physical courage they had shown on the battlefield.

Nowhere in the history of civilization can there be found a record of more liberal and generous terms of surrender granted to a defeated foe than were the terms granted by General Grant and General Sherman. The men who actually fought the battles of the Confederacy intended to abide faithfully and honorably by the terms of their surrender. If they ever departed from those terms it was when they were misled by designing and unscrupulous politicians.

In the writings of General John B. Gordon we find unstinted praise of General Grant and expressions of the most sincere appreciation of the liberal terms of surrender at Appomattox. General Gordon commented on the attitude of General Grant in the following language:

General Grant's bearing at Appomattox, his acts and his words, did much to alleviate the anguish inseparable from such an ordeal. The tenor of his formal notes, the terms granted at the appointed meeting, the prompt and cordial manner in which he acquiesced in each and every suggestion made by the Southern Commander, left upon the minds of the Confederates an ineffaceable impression. . . .

There was no trace of exultation at his triumph. He was in word and act the embodiment of manly modesty and soldierly magnanimity, and from first to last he was evidently intent upon mitigating the bitterness of defeat and soothing to the utmost of his ability the lacerated sensibilities of his great antagonist. General Grant's own declaration, made many years after the war, that he felt ''sad and depressed'' as he rode to meet General Lee in the little village of Appomattox, is entirely consistent with every account given of his bearing at the surrender. . . .

The repeated manifestations of General Grant's truly great qualities— his innate modesty, his freedom from every trace of vainglory or ostentation, his magnanimity in victory, his genuine sympathy for his brave and sensitive foeman, and his inflexible resolve to protect paroled Confederates against any assault, and vindicate, at whatever cost, the sanctity of his pledge to the vanquished—will give him a place in history no less renowned and more to be envied than that secured by his triumphs as a soldier or his honors as a civilian.

Referring to the surrender of General Joseph E. Johnston, General Gordon said:

The generous terms of surrender given to Lee by Grant were exceeded in liberality by those which W. T. Sherman offered to Joseph E. Johnston in North Carolina.

The memorandum of agreement between Generals Sherman and Johnston (April 18, 1865) contained the following stipulations:

The Confederate armies now in existence to be disbanded and conducted to their State capitals, there to deposit their arms and public property in the State arsenals. The President of the United States was to recognize the several State governments on their officers and legislatures taking the oaths prescribed by the constitution of the United States. The Federal courts were to be reëstablished in the Southern States, the people of the South were to be guaranteed their political rights, and rights of person and property, with a general amnesty.

The terms which General Sherman made with General Johnston for the surrender of the army under his command did not meet with the approval of Secretary Stanton, who manifested his displeasure by trying to arrange the review of the Grand Army in Washington so that General Sherman would not appear in it in command of the Division of the Mississippi. According to the story as narrated in *Perley's Reminiscences,* General Sherman had been informed about the very discourteous action of Secretary Stanton, and when he ascended the reviewing stand where President Johnson, General Grant and Secretary Stanton were seated,—

he shook hands cordially with President Johnson and General Grant, but when Secretary Stanton advanced with outstretched hand, he remarked, ''I do not care to shake hands with clerks,'' and turned away.

General Grant was very positive in demanding that all officers of the Confederate army should enjoy their liberty. Among those who had been imprisoned by order of the Secretary of War was General Clement C. Clay, an ex-United States Senator from Alabama. According to the story as narrated by Ben Perley Poore, General Clay was taken ill in prison with asthma, and his wife came to Washington to solicit his release. She went to President Johnson, and he gave her the necessary order, which she took to Secretary Stanton, who read the order, and, looking her in the face, tore it up without a word and pitched it into his waste-basket. The lady arose and retired without speaking; nor did Stanton speak to her. Soon afterward she was advised to call on General Grant, who ascertained by consulting his roster of the Confederate army that her husband was a Brigadier-General, and then wrote an order directing his release, under the Appomattox parole, on giving the required bond, and added: ''I shall see that this order is carried out.'' Having signed the order, he gave it to Mrs. Clay, who the next day presented it to the Secretary of War. It may be well to recall that Edwin M. Stanton was originally a Democrat and served as Attorney-General in Buchanan's cabinet, although he was a strong Union man and very much opposed to secession.

The South has produced few greater men than James Longstreet, who was distinguished not only for his prowess and gallantry as a great military commander, but also for his far-sighted grasp of great affairs of state. He was born and brought up in South Carolina, but after the war he resided in New Orleans and later in the little town of Gainesville, Georgia, where he died in 1904. General Longstreet was with Grant at West Point, where he was graduated in 1842, and a few years later served with distinction in the Mexican War. He entered the Confederate service with the rank of Brigadier-General in 1861, was promoted a Major-General in the same year and commanded a corps at the second battle of Bull Run. Longstreet commanded the right wing of Lee's Army at Antietam and commanded a corps with the rank of Lieutenant-General at Gettysburg. At Chickamauga he commanded the left wing of the Confederate Army, and served with distinction in the Wilderness in 1864 and before Richmond. It has been said that he "shared the most intimate councils and executed the most difficult orders of Lee," and no Confederate commander was more dreaded by the North and more beloved by the Southern soldiers than was Longstreet. He followed with unfaltering bravery and devotion the fortunes of the Confederacy until the end; he was a member of the last council of war held on the night of April 8, 1865, and was the senior commissioner, on the part of the Confederate forces, appointed by General Lee, to arrange the details and terms of the surrender.

In his book, *From Manassas to Appomattox*, General Longstreet relates that, about the first of November, 1865, business of a personal nature called him to Washington. On his arrival in Washington he stopped at the Metropolitan Hotel. General W. A. Nichols of the United States Army, noticing the arrival of the distinguished ex-Confederate General, called and insisted that General Longstreet should visit him and his family. At first General Longstreet declined the invitation, remarking that the war feeling was too warm for an officer of the army to entertain a prominent Confederate, but General Nichols insisted, stating that his wife would not be satisfied unless General Longstreet accepted their hospitality, whereupon General Longstreet became his guest. Being the guest of an officer of the army, the usages of military life required that General Longstreet should call upon the commanding General. Here follows General Longstreet's own story of his visit to General Grant:

On the next morning I walked with General Nichols to make an official call on General Grant. He recognized us as we entered his office, rose and walked to meet us. After the usual brief call we rose to take leave, when he asked to have us call on his family during the evening. Most of those whom we met during the evening were old time personal friends, especially the father-in-law, Mr. Dent. When leaving, after a pleasant evening, General Grant walked with us to the gate and asked if I cared to have my pardon. I pleaded not guilty of an offence that required pardon. He said that he meant amnesty—that he wished to know if I cared to have it. I told him that I intended to live in the country, and would prefer to have the privileges of citizenship. He told me to call at his office at noon next day; that in the meantime he would see the Secretary of War and the President in regard to the matter.

When General Longstreet called on General Grant the following day, General Grant stated that he had seen the President and the Secretary of War, and he thought the matter had been arranged, and he gave General Longstreet a letter addressed to the President in which he wrote:

In the late rebellion, I think, not one single charge was ever brought against General Longstreet for persecution of prisoners of war or of persons for their political opinions. If such charges were ever made, I never heard of them. I have no hesitation, therefore, in recommending General Longstreet to Your Excellency for pardon. I will further state that my opinion of him is such that I shall feel it as a personal favor to myself if this pardon is granted.

General Longstreet states that on the following day he called on the Secretary of War who referred him to the President. He then called on President Johnson, who, after a lengthy interview, asked to have the matter put off until the next day. The following day when General Longstreet called, the President was still unprepared to make a decision, but, as stated by General Longstreet, after a long, pleasant talk he said: ''There are three persons of the South who can never receive amnesty: Mr. Davis, General Lee and yourself. You have given the Union cause too much trouble." "During a subsequent session of Congress," writes General Longstreet,

General Pope sent in a list of names from Georgia, for whom he asked relief from their political disabilities. General Grant after approving it made request of one of his friends in Congress to have my name put on the list, and I was extended relief soon after it was given to General R. E. Lee.

The Commander in Chief of the Union forces who received the surrender of Lee requested a Southern Democrat to pardon General Longstreet, and when the Southern Democrat declined, a Republican Congress passed an act which granted amnesty to General Longstreet and other Confederate commanders.

There is perhaps nothing in the record of partisan provincialism in the history of the Southern Oligarchy more unjust than the treatment which General Longstreet received from the people whom he had served so faithfully. In January, 1866, he engaged in business in New Orleans with two old soldiers of the Washington Artillery. General Longstreet states in his autobiography that his "affairs were more than prosperous until I was asked an opinion upon the political crises of 1867." One of the New Orleans newspapers requested several former generals of the Confederate army to present their views as to the course the Southern States should follow. In a letter dated June 3, 1867, General Longstreet very clearly expressed his opinion as to the situation and what the South should do with reference to the new amendments to the Constitution resulting from the Civil War. In that letter he said:

The serious difficulty arises from want of that wisdom so important for the great work in hand. Still, I will be happy to work in any harness that promises relief to our discomfited people and harmony to the Nation, whether bearing the mantle of Mr. Davis or Mr. Sumner.

It is fair to assume that the strongest laws are those established by the sword. The ideas that divided political parties before the war—upon the rights of the states—were thoroughly discussed by our wisest statesmen, and eventually appealed to the arbitrament of the sword. The decision was in favor of the North, so that her construction becomes the law, and should be so accepted.

Illustrative of the littleness and meanness of the partisan press of the South, I quote the language of General Longstreet:

The afternoon of the day upon which my letter was published the paper that had called for advice published a column of editorial calling me "traitor," deserter of my friends, and accusing me of "joining the enemy," but did not publish a line of the letter upon which it based these charges. Other papers of the Democracy took up the garbled representation of this journal and spread it broadcast, not even giving the letter upon which they based their evil attacks upon me. . . .

The day after the announcement old comrades passed me on the streets without speaking. Business began to grow dull. General Hood (the only one of my old comrades who occasionally visited me) thought that he could save the insurance business, and in a few weeks I found myself at leisure.

Two years after that period, on March 4, 1869, General Grant was inaugurated President of the United States, and in the bigness of his generous heart called me to Washington. Before I found opportunity to see him he sent my name to the Senate for confirmation as surveyor of customs at New Orleans.

In doing what he regarded as a patriotic duty General Longstreet was as fearless in peace as he had been in war. He sacrificed income and position for what he considered the wise and honorable course for the States which he had served so faithfully. He took the position which he believed to be right and which subsequent events proved to be right. The ostracism and persecution of General Longstreet began immediately after he wrote the letter in which he conscientiously advised the Southern people to accept the situation as it actually existed, which was nothing more nor less than abiding by the terms of surrender which had been accepted by General Lee. The position taken by General Longstreet was in full accord with the views of General Lee, so far as he had expressed himself on public matters after the close of the war. From the failure of the South to heed the wise and patriotic advice of General Longstreet, and other great leaders who had fought so valiantly for the Confederacy, we may trace the long train of ills that came with Reconstruction and its consequences. The bitter attack on General Longstreet was the beginning of the revival of sectionalism, race persecution and lawlessness which have so long afflicted the South. It was a part of the propaganda of the provincial and lawless politicians in the interest of the spoilsmen. In *A History of the United States Since the Civil War* (Vol. II, pp. 11-21), Ellis Paxson Oberholtzer says:

At first there was a disposition on the part of the Southern whites to acquiesce in the plans of Congress for the reconstruction of the States. Generals Lee, Johnston, Beauregard, Harden, Hood, Wade Hampton and Longstreet; ex-governers of Southern States, Magrath and Aiken of South Carolina and Joseph E. Brown of Georgia among them, were urging the people to submit as promptly and with as much grace as possible. . . .

Better it would have been, said the *New Orleans Picayune*, if the Southern people had enfranchised the negroes immediately after the surrender, so that they might have been attached in gratitude to the Southern side instead of to the Radicals, who were now to reap the fruits of the policy. They were working "for us in the fields; why should they not do so at the polls?" If the negroes were properly directed, said General Beauregard, the South could defeat its adversaries "with their own weapons." They were Southern born and they could be made to "side with the whites." United States Senator-elect Burnett of Texas addressed a letter to the people of that State. "Teach these ill-informed and lately inducted politicians that their best interests are identical with ours," he said, "that they are Southerners by birth, by residence, in person, in property and in territorial prosperity." In Alabama the conservatives went so far as to ask the negroes to sit in a convention beside the whites, to the end that "Alabamans should rule Alabama." The mothers who had given them birth had been nursed by the whites; they had played in infancy and childhood with the whites."

"Governor Humphreys asked the people of Mississippi 'to offer no resistance to any steps' which might be taken toward reorganizing in that State." Concerning the situation in Mississippi, at the beginning of Reconstruction in that State, Professor James Wilford Garner—*Reconstruction in Mississippi*—says:

The most advanced reconstructionist among the prominent whites was General Alcorn. Inasmuch as there was no hope of escape from the power of the Radicals, he proposed to form an alliance with them in order to secure terms. He proposed to "vote with the Negro, discuss politics with him, sit, if need be, in council with him, and form a platform acceptable to both, and pluck our common liberty and prosperity from the jaws of inevitable ruin." With a platform guaranteeing to the Negro all his rights as a citizen, generous provisions for the education of his children, and the possession of a homestead. Alcorn believed that the white people would be able to hold their old positions as advisers of the Negro race.

Before entering on the subject of Reconstruction in the Southern States and a survey of some of the outstanding occurrences of that distressing epoch in American history, and the ills that followed the events of that period, it is necessary to have authoritative and precise information respecting the relation that existed between the whites and blacks after emancipation and before the beginning of the Reconstruction period. It is also necessary to know the record of the Negro before the beginning of the Civil War and his record during that war. On these two vital points we have better evidence than assertions of the protagonists of sectionalism and race hatred.

Respecting the stamina of the Negro in America before his emancipation, the record is clear; capable and competent witnesses have testified in the Negro's favor. Professor N. S. Shaler, sometime Dean of the Scientific School of Harvard University, was born at Newport, Kentucky. He is the author of scientific works which rank high among scholars and scientists. *The Popular Science Monthly* (March, 1900) published an interesting article by Professor Shaler under the title of *The Transplantation of a Race,* from which I quote the following:

The Negroes who came to North America had to undergo as complete a transition as ever fell to the lot of man without the least chance to undergo an acclimatizing process. They were brought from the hottest part of the earth to a region where the winter's cold is of almost arctic severity— from an exceedingly humid to a very dry air. They came to service under alien task-masters, strange to them in speech and purpose. They had to betake themselves to unaccustomed food and to clothing such as they had never worn before. Rarely could one of the creatures find about him a familiar face of friend, parent, or child, or an object that recalled his past life to him. It was an appalling change. Only those who know how the Negro cleaves to all the dear, familiar things of life, how fond he is of warmth and friendliness, can conceive the physical and mental shock that this introduction to new conditions meant to them. To the people of our own race it could have meant death. But these wonderful folk appear to have withstood the trials of their deportation in a marvelous way. They showed no peculiar liability to disease, their longevity or period of usefulness was not diminished, or their fecundity obviously impaired. . . .

If we compare the Algonkin Indian, in appearance a sturdy fellow, with these Negroes, we see of what stuff the blacks are made. A touch of house work and of honest toil took the breath of the aborigines away. But these tropical exotics fell to their tasks and trials far better than the men of our own kind could have done.

The late Colonel John W. Du Bose, a native of South Carolina, ''a life-long Democrat,'' author of *The Life and Times of Yancey: Political Parties in the United States from 1834 to 1864,* and for many years a contributor to magazines and newspapers, pays the following tribute to the industrial progress and economic stability of the Negro:

With reasonable haste, toward the close of two centuries of bondage in America, the African had become the best plowman, the most expert teamster, the most dexterous hoe hand, the only profitable cotton harvester the agriculture of the world had produced. He was a respectable architect, a good brick mason, cobbler, blacksmith, and the best domestic servant any civilization afforded.

Writing about the remarkable stamina and development of the negroes in America, Dr. A. B. Mayo, distinguished educator and publicist, said:

This people underwent the most rapid and effective transition from the depths of pagan barbarism to the threshold of Christianity and civilization on record in the annals of mankind. The two hundred and fifty years of slavery had, indeed, been in itself a great university, and the history of the world may be challenged to present a spectacle so remarkable.

In the article quoted from Professor Shaler we have the conclusions of a writer who was qualified by education, scientific research and personal observation to testify, not only respecting the progress and actual condition of the Negroes from the viewpoint of the anthropologist, but also from an economic point of view. Concerning the fidelity, moral and physical courage of the Negroes during the Civil War, Colonel Du Bose wrote clearly and forcibly in the words which follow:

Of the thousands of Negro servants who left their families to endure all the privations of the bivouac, on scanty fare of the Confederate Army, there is no record of even one desertion to the enemy. In a whole land, denuded of its arms-bearing, ruling race, there is no record, in the war of the Confederacies, of African insubordination save where the ''party of morality,'' the invading army, instigated it with much labor. The accumulating successes, mental, physical and moral, of the African in bondage were guarantees ample, to the perception of sound statesmanship, that he was working out his own redemption; and that redemption would find him prepared to incorporate his race in the industrial life of a land overflowing with the riches he had created.

As stated by Professor James Elbert Cutler in *Lynch Law*,—

the effects of the discipline of the slave régime were particularly manifest during the progress of the Civil War, when the southern planters were obliged to leave their families with no other protectors than the slaves, and these slaves discharged their trust with uniform faithfulness and loyalty.

The Annals of the War, "written by leading participants, North and South," originally published serially in *The Philadelphia Weekly Times*, contains an article by Edward Spencer from which I quote the following story:

There can be no doubt that the Negroes behaved very well, and that the Confederate people had a lively and very grateful appreciation of the fact. . . . I have before me a curious pamphlet, "Marginolia; or, Gleanings from an Army Note Book," by "Personne," army correspondent of *The Charleston Courier*, published at Columbia, S. C., in 1864, which abounds with instances and recitals of the good conduct of the Negroes. Thus "Personne" relates the story of Daniel, a slave of Lieutenant Bellinger, who was shot to pieces trying to take his master's sword to him, in the fort at Secessionville, during the assault on that post.

Further citations from the articles contributed to *The Philadelphia Weekly Times* furnish cumulative evidence of the fidelity and heroic courage of the Negroes during the Civil War:

When the war broke out, John Campbell, the well-known horse-racer, went to Mobile, leaving his stables in Kentucky in charge of a slave. Four years later, when Campbell returned, a poor man, his Negro had all the horses and their increase waiting for his master, and in the very best condition. There was nothing to prevent this faithful fellow from making away with all of Campbell's property. . . . Lieutenant Shelton's man, Jack, of the 13th Arkansas, fell at his master's side at the battle of Belmont. When Jack was shot, Jack's son took his rifle and went to the field to avenge his "daddy." Major White, of the Alabama battalion that bore his name, had a Negro servant who risked his life to bear off his master's body from the field when he was shot down, and after the funeral he took his master's horse and effects, and rode home with them, over a thousand miles, to the old plantation.

Colonel Du Bose, from whose writings I have quoted in some preceding paragraphs of this chapter, was a gentleman of the "Old South." He was a Democrat but after the war a staunch American, partisan in some respects, but without sectional prejudice or race hatred. Always just and honorable, he found great pleasure in gathering material to support his favorable opinion of the Negroes. I believe my readers will be interested in further testimonials from Colonel Du Bose regarding the fidelity and heroic conduct of the Negroes during the Civil War:

At the battle of Winchester, in 1862, General Jackson discovered the Negro servant of General Taylor exposed to fire and advised him to seek shelter. The Negro replied, if the General please, he would remain near his master, who might need him. On his rounds of the army that night, Jackson found Taylor sitting at one end of a bivouac and his black servant at the other. Advancing to the servant, he grasped his hand warmly, explained to the master the occurrence of the morning.

Colonel Peques, commanding a regiment of Alabama cavalry, C. S. A., permitted his Negro servant to ride away, for an hour, his favorite battle horse. The regiment was suddenly called into action, with the commander badly mounted. The servant learning the facts on his return to camp, dashed into the heavy fire, at imminent risk of his life, and changed horses with his master, all of his own volition.

When Richmond was occupied by the United States Army, in April, 1865, the inhabitants were upon the verge of starvation and without money. The blacks were declared free by the invader, and rations were liberally dispensed to them. Many masters and their families were supplied in this way by their faithful servants with the necessaries of life.

In his testimony before the Ku Klux Investigating Committee, July, 1871, General John B. Gordon, "who used to own several plantations and a great many slaves," spoke in the highest terms of the good conduct of the Negroes before and during the Civil War. He said:

Well, sir, I had occasion to refer just now to a little speech I made at Montgomery, Alabama, where General Clanton also spoke. He and I both struck on that train of thought. I went so far as to say that the citizens of the South owed it to the Negroes to educate them. . . .

In the upper part of the State where I was raised, the Negro children and the white children have been in the habit of playing together. My companions, when I was being raised, were the Negro boys that my father owned. We played marbles, rode oxen, went fishing, and broke colts together; a part of my fun was to play with these colored boys. The Negro girls—those who were raised about the house—were raised very much as a white family was raised. They were raised in the family, and, of course, the intelligence of the family extended, in some measure to the Negroes.

It is plain that the progress of the Negro under slavery in

America was remarkable and his conduct commendable; it is also clear that the Negro's deportment during the Civil War was in many respects heroic and noble. As we have seen, the better class of white people in the South, and especially those who fought the battles of the Confederacy, were practically unanimous in their unstinted praise of the Negro's fidelity and exemplary conduct. In his testimony before the Congressional Committee General Gordon, to whom I have already alluded in this connection, was asked by the Committee:

"Have the Negroes, as a general thing, behaved well since the war?" His reply was:—

They have behaved so well since the war that the remark is not uncommon in Georgia that no race on earth, relieved from servitude under such circumstances as they were, would have behaved so well.

In view of the susceptibilities of the uninformed in all discussions relating to political questions in the South, and all other questions which have any bearing on race relations between the whites and blacks, I shall limit my discussion to actual facts of record and testimony of white men in the South who have been affiliated with the Democratic party. The leaders of the Southern Oligarchy, especially the active protagonists of sectional prejudice and race hatred, usually answer facts with vilification and an appeal to prejudices. My narrative is based on an examination of the record and the testimony of the better class of white people in the Southern States.

An epitome of the Negro's history since his emancipation will show conclusively that his civic and industrial progress has been most remarkable. The truth of this assertion can be proven not only by the records which are available to all intelligent people, who are seeking the truth, but also by the testimony of the most intelligent and reputable white men of the Southern States. If the American Negro were brought before an unprejudiced court he could produce not only the record of his loyalty and patriotism, his character and his achievements, which would be sufficient to make out his case, but he could also introduce the testimony of the better class of white men in the South, who are not only credible but also competent witnesses; because they have been in a position to obtain first-hand reliable personal knowledge concerning the things about which they would testify. The Negro need not introduce the testimony of a member of his race; he can make out his case on the record, and on the testimony of Southern white men and women of the higher and better class.

An investigation of this question will show that, almost without exception, the intelligent, educated, cultured, honorable and patriotic, in short, the better class of white men and women in the South, agree in the statement that the industrial, civic and moral progress of the Negro since his emancipation has been remarkable. And a very large majority of the illiterate whites, with sufficient intelligence and moral stamina to have a definite opinion on any civic or social question, also concur in this favorable opinion of the Negro's conduct and progress. On the other hand, the leaders of the Southern Oligarchy and other pernicious agitators in the South who have condemned the Negro are, with very few exceptions, men who have been engaged in corrupt practices in politics, or have been the direct beneficiaries of the political spoilsmen, or of disreputable practices in the "advancing business," a system of merciless greed on the part of rapacious landlords, so common in the South, by which these agitators and spoilsmen have largely profited at the expense of the poor whites and Negroes.

CHAPTER IV

THE TRUE STORY OF RECONSTRUCTION

Referring to conditions in the South during and immediately following the period of Reconstruction, in his work on *Democracy and Liberty*, Lecky says:

The enfranchisement of the Negroes added a new and enormous mass of voters, who were utterly and childishly incompetent. . . . . For some time after the war the influence of property and intelligence in the South was completely broken, and the Negro vote was ostensibly supreme. The consequence was what might have been expected. A host of vagrant political adventurers from the North, known in America as carpet-baggers, poured into the Southern provinces, and, in conjunction with the refuse of the mean whites, they undertook the direction of the Negro votes. Then followed, under the protection of the Northern bayonets, a grotesque parody of government, a hideous orgy of anarchy, violence, unrestrained corruption, undisguised, ostentatious, insulting robbery, such as the world had scarcely ever seen. The State debts were profusely piled up. Legislation was openly put up for sale. The ''Bosses'' were in all their glory, and they were abundantly rewarded, while the crushed, ruined, plundered whites combined in secret societies for their defense, and retaliated on their oppressors by innumerable acts of savage vengeance. At length the Northern troops were withdrawn, and the whole scene changed. The carpet-baggers had had their day, and they returned laden with southern booty to their own States. Partly by violence, partly by fraud, but largely also through the force of old habits of obedience and command, the planters in a short time regained ascendancy. Sometimes, it is said, they did not even count the Negro votes. Generally they succeeded in dictating them, and by systematic manipulation or intimidation they restored the South to quiet and some degree of prosperity.

There is much truth and some error in the comments of the British historian. The ''refuse of mean whites,'' to whom Lecky refers as confederates of the venal carpet-baggers, or at least a large number of these ''mean whites,'' later became active among leaders of the Southern Oligarchy. The abominable and distressing conditions under rule of the Republican party in the South were clearly stated by *The New York*

Tribune, when, in its issue of June 13, 1874, referring to South Carolina, it said that State was—

lying prostrate and helpless under the foot of the spoiler, her citizens imprisoned, business ruined, enterprise destroyed, lands sold for taxes, her people at the mercy of an ignorant and dishonest rabble, her legislators and her rulers a gang of unprincipled adventurers and shameless thieves.

In the debates of Congress, in political campaigns, in magazines and newspapers, and in many books that have been published, it has been asserted for more than forty years that the people of the North were responsible, the Republican party especially, for the revival of sectional prejudice and racial animosities in the South after the war. It has been charged that carpet-baggers from the North went down into the Southern States and, with the support of the national Republican party, robbed the people and engaged in all manner of corrupt and lawless practices; and that they taught the Negro that he was the social and political equal of the white man and that he could and should rule the white man.

That the rule of the Republican party in the South was as dark as it has been painted there is little doubt. The records show this to be true. That a lot of adventurers from the North pushed the unwilling and innocent Negro to the front, and tried to array him against the native whites, while they plundered the people, there is no doubt. The record shows that such shameful things actually occurred. Those knaves from the North who were guilty of venal and lawless practices were finally driven from the South; at least those who were not allied with the Southern whites were driven away. Some of the carpet-baggers remained and found it profitable to continue their activities under the spoils system of the Democratic party.

It is not true, however, that the North supplied all the rascals, nor even a majority of the spoilsmen who were engaged in venal practices under the Republican régime in the South. A large number of the exploiters were natives of that section, antecedents of some of the leading spoilsmen under the Wilson régime. Nor is it true that all of the so-called carpet-baggers were bad men. There were wise and good men, splendid American patriots and humanitarians, who went from the North to the South after the war, before and during the Reconstruction epoch, quite a number of whom became useful and worthy citizens of the South.

It was the aftermath of Reconstruction that brought forth and gave potency to the un-American Oligarchy which has held the South in its brutal and merciless grasp for more than forty years. The leaders of the better element in the South, the men who in truth represented the manhood and integrity and patriotism of the Southern States, and who had led in discussing the great issues which immediately preceded and directly followed the war, were passing away and a younger, less capable and less worthy class of political leaders came to the front.

Without sufficient ability, courage or patriotism to grasp and successfully deal with the great civic, social and economic questions which immediately concerned the South, this new leadership acquired, and has retained, its political power by appealing to sectional prejudices and arousing bitter racial animosities. Unable and unwilling to promulgate a definite and constructive policy, in state or national affairs, this leadership of the Southern Oligarchy has succeeded in keeping the people in ignorance, relying on political subterfuges and platitudes rather than on an honest discussion of vital questions which affected the liberties, prosperity and happiness of the great mass of the people.

Sectional partisanship and the alleged danger of Negro rule have been the essential propaganda of the Southern Oligarchy since the dark days of Reconstruction, and it has been a most effective propaganda. The South has been isolated, there has been no immigration into that section; it has stood aloof, and remained dormant in social and civic affairs, while the Oligarchy by which it has been ruled was able to perpetuate its power through corrupt practices and an appeal to prejudices of the people. The sad story of Reconstruction has been kept before the people to the exclusion of all other political, social or civic questions. Volumes have been published telling the story of corruption and maladministration under the domination of carpet-baggers. A great deal of truth and an equal amount of falsehood have been published about that shameful régime. The misdeeds and corrupt practices of the carpet-baggers have been narrated in full and in detail, and it is an appalling story. But there is another side to the story of those troublous times in the South about which very little has been written. In *A History of the United States Since the Civil War* (Vol. II, p. 24) Ellis Paxon Oberholtzer refers to the scalawags in the following language:

But viler yet were the blatant, vindictive, unprincipled characters gathered up from the South itself who, cloaking themselves in a pretense of ''loyalty'' to the Union, took up the task of winning office in the reorganized states by base and hypocritical appeals to the new negro voters. For the most part these men were turncoats. They had been small slaveholders, and secessionists. But, failing on the rebel side to gain the prominence they craved, they had gone North to sell their tongues to the Republicans, while the war still had not come to an end, or, if not this, were now ready to do so. Such men soon came to be known to the Southern people as ''scalawags.''

In the absence of an authoritative enumeration of the exploiters, venal politicians, and public officials in the Southern States during the Reconstruction period, it is not possible to state which class was in the majority and exercised the greater power, nor which was the more venal, the carpet-baggers or the scalawags. In some communities the carpet-baggers were in the majority and their venal practices seemed to be the most shameless, while in other localities the scalawags were in the majority, exercised more power and secured more loot than the carpet-baggers. The opprobrious name of carpet-bagger or scalawag was applied indiscriminately to every white citizen or sojourner in the South who did not approve the propaganda and practices of the Bourbon Democracy. This party was provincial, reactionary, intolerant and lawless. With a libelous propaganda against the Negroes and all white opposition, and criminal practices through the agency of secret organizations, this reactionary faction of the Democratic party undertook to set at defiance the terms of surrender made at Appomattox and Durham Station, as well as all provisions of the Federal Constitution and Acts of Congress which were intended to make effective the purposes for which the war had been fought.

In a preceding chapter I alluded to the vindictive and outrageous proscription directed against so loyal and distinguished a patriot as General Longstreet, for no reason except that he had advised the people to show proper respect for the terms of surrender and the Federal laws, and public officials charged with the administration of those laws. There were many worthy citizens of the South who had fought in the armies of the Confederacy who were vilified as scalawags because they endorsed the loyal and honorable admonitions of General Longstreet, and would not follow the reactionary and lawless leaders of the Bourbon Democracy. There were also worthy citizens of the South who were born in the North, some of whom were living in the South at the beginning of the war and who were loyal to the Confederacy and fought with undaunted courage in the armies of the Confederate States. But these men who had been useful citizens and loyal to the South before and during the war were denounced as carpet-baggers and vilified when they failed to support the reactionary policies and lawless practices of the Bourbon Democracy. Numerous cases could be cited in support of this statement, but the point can be clearly illustrated by brief reference to two notable cases, for example, in the two Southern States which, for more than fifty years, have stood at the head of the list in corrupt practices, partisan and sectional animosities, race persecution and criminal lawlessness. I refer to the States of Georgia and Mississippi, and my narrative of the two notable cases in these States follows.

Rufus B. Bullock was born in the State of New York and graduated at Albion (N. Y.) Academy in 1850; a few years later he was sent South to organize the business of the Adams Express Company in the South Atlantic States. He established the Southern Express Company with headquarters at Augusta, Georgia, and was one of the active managers of this corporation which for many years after the war was one of the most substantial and successful corporations in the South. During the Civil War Mr. Bullock was in the service of the Confederate Government in establishing railroad and telegraph lines, and was acting assistant quartermaster-general in the Confederate Army.

In 1867, Mr. Bullock was a delegate to the convention called to form a constitution for Georgia under the Reconstruction laws passed by Congress. He joined the Republican party and was elected Governor. Numerous charges of corruption and malfeasance were made against the administration of Governor

Bullock. It was alleged that gigantic frauds had been committed in the issue and indorsement of bonds in aid of railroads and these bonds were later repudiated. The charges of frauds were directed chiefly against Governor Bullock, and he finally resigned. The story of conditions in Georgia, charges of corruption and counter-charges while Bullock was Governor have filled several volumes. These controversial questions are not pertinent to this narrative. It may be well, however, to call attention to the fact that, after his resignation as Governor, he was president of the Macon and Augusta Railroad, president of the Atlanta Cotton Mills and of the Atlanta Chamber of Commerce, and Government Director of the Union Pacific Railroad.

James L. Alcorn was born in Illinois but he was educated at Cumberland University, Kentucky, in which State he began the practice of law and was elected a member of the Legislature. In 1844, he removed from Kentucky to Mississippi, where he served in the Legislature from 1846 to 1865, when he was elected United States Senator, but was not then permitted to take his seat. He was an elector-at-large on the Whig ticket in the Presidential campaign of 1852 and received the nomination for Governor, which he declined. He was founder of the levee system of the Mississippi and was president of the board; he was a member of the secession convention and had two sons in the Confederate army. After the war, as related in a preceding chapter, he advocated strict compliance with the terms of surrender at Appomattox and Durham Station and respect for all Federal laws.

Alcorn was the first Republican Governor of Mississippi; elected Governor in 1869, he resigned two years later to enter the United States Senate, where he continued until 1877. In spite of his good record as a worthy and useful citizen before the Civil War, and his loyalty to the South during that war, when General Alcorn joined the Republican party he was denounced and vindictively assailed as a corrupt carpet-bagger. Dr. James Wilford Garner—*Reconstruction in Mississippi*— says:

Whether Alcorn's views were the result of honest convictions or of policy there is a difference of opinion. He seems to have been sincere in his professions. Of his attachment to the people of the State, founded on long residence and identification of interests, there can be no doubt. He declared in his inaugural that he was a Southern man in heart and soul.

I have referred to the record of Governor Bullock of Georgia and that of Governor Alcorn of Mississippi as examples of numerous cases of less prominence where useful and worthy citizens who were highly esteemed before they joined the Republican party, suddenly became, after they joined that party, according to popular opinion in the South, very dangerous and unworthy citizens. This popular opinion was the result of the false teachings and libelous propaganda of the spoilsmen.

A story of Reconstruction and Republican domination in one of the States is substantially a story of Reconstruction and Republican rule in every one of the reconstructed States, with this exception. In Mississippi and in South Carolina, where the Negroes outnumbered the whites, the Negroes were more prominent and exercised greater influence with the venal whites than in other States, and there was in these two States a bald depravity and recklessness which was more shameless than elsewhere. The record of Reconstruction in Alabama presents a fair average of all the reconstructed States. I am perhaps better informed touching the details of the history of Reconstruction and Republican domination in Alabama than in other States, and a narrative of some of the outstanding events during that epoch in Alabama will clearly illustrate the more salient occurrences and general practices of carpet-baggers and scalawags during the same period in other States.

During the Reconstruction period one of the many bad laws was that which permitted a voter to cast his ballot at the county seat. That law resulted in attracting a large assemblage of Negro men to the county seat at the time of the greatest political excitement. The Negroes began coming several days before the election, and were usually camped at or near the county seat two days before the election. During the day they were massed by their white leaders and harangued by whites and blacks, and a barbecue was provided with sufficient rations for two days. A vast majority of the poor, ignorant Negroes knew little or nothing about the issues or the candidates in the campaign. They had heard that food would be provided without price, that the supply would be ample and enough to take home. The ignorant, inoffensive Negroes were brought to the county seat by designing and venal white men, and in most cases those white leaders were not the carpet-baggers who came from the North. The antecedents of a number of active leaders of the Democratic party in the South at the present writing were among the active leaders of the Negroes during the Reconstruction period. The world has read the story of the corrupt practices and venality of the carpet-baggers, but there has been very little written respecting the native whites of the South who were allied with the most corrupt and lawless elements.

The community in which I was born and brought up was the home of a large number of leading Republicans, some of whom attained national prominence. It was a locality of active political propaganda and racial conflicts, although it was not in the Black Belt section where the Negroes were in the majority. One of the first, if not the first, institutions for the higher education of Negroes in the South was located at this place. The valuable and extensive property acquired for this institution was owned by one of the leading denominational colleges for the whites before the war, and the fact that the property was purchased at foreclosure sale by a Northern missionary society, for education of colored people, perhaps accentuated sectional prejudices and racial animosities in that locality.

In my native town, under Republican rule, the city council was made up of Negroes, but the mayor was a Southern white man; the juries, petty and grand, were made up of Negroes who could neither read nor write, but the Circuit Judge was a native white man. The County Commissioners, or a large number of them, were Negroes, but the Judge of Probate and ex-officio Judge of the County Court was a Southern white man. He was a native of Tennessee and was prominently identified with the Republican party and very active in controlling the Negroes. One of his sons was County Administrator and there were charges of irregularities during his term of office. Another son of this Republican Judge was an active and prominent partisan Democrat who made a national reputation as one of the most brazen ballot-box stuffers that even the State of Alabama had produced. In running for Congress in a primary of the Democratic party he secured fraudulent returns which gave him a majority greater than the total voting population of the county. The fraud was so palpable and disgusting that it was denounced by the Democratic press; and in a contest before the State Executive Committee the pressure was so strong that he had to withdraw from the race. Notwithstanding his bad record, for many years he was prominent and influential in the Democratic party, holding various high positions.

Of the leading white Republicans of my native section in Alabama, who exercised great influence in State and national affairs, I can recall only two of any prominence who were not born in the South. Lewis E. Parsons, who was appointed provisional Governor by President Johnson, was a native of the State of New York, and he moved to Alabama in 1841. Referring to his record before the Civil War, Garrett (*Public Men in Alabama*) says:

Mr. Parsons was a firm and decided Whig in politics, without any compromise or concession. He had uniformly been a Union man, without disguise. All parties believed him honest and only conservative in his views. He was elected to the House of Representatives in 1859, and in 1860 allied himself with the Democratic party as the best means, in his judgment, to save the country from threatened danger.

Mr. Parsons had two sons in the Confederate army, who were distinguished for their gallantry. After the war, he and his sons were prominent in the Republican party and their record was clean. Neither Governor Parsons nor either of his sons was charged with corruption, though each was a pronounced and prominent Republican during the carpet-bag régime. There were very few native Republicans with so clean and honorable a record. The other prominent white Republican who was not a native of the South located in Alabama many years before the Civil War.

One of the most vindictive and aggressive Republicans in Alabama who attained national prominence during the Reconstruction period and Republican rule in the South, was Alexander White, who was a native of the South and served in the 43d Congress. His father was elected to Congress in 1850 as a Whig. According to Garrett's *Public Men in Alabama*,—

he served only one term in Congress, and was a warm supporter of General Scott for the Presidency, to aid in whose election he exercised the franking privilege quite liberally in the distribution of campaign documents, but on a plan, no doubt, less extensive than that which the Honorable F. W. Bowdon boasted in 1848, while supporting General Cass and acting on the Executive Committee at Washington that he had franked and distributed through the mail more than a million copies of speeches and documents for electioneering purposes.

In the Presidential campaign of 1860, Alexander White supported the Bell and Everett ticket of the Constitutional Union party. He was opposed to secession, but after the ordinance was passed, "he acted with his State throughout the struggle that ensued." White was a famous orator, and at a meeting of representative citizens, at Montgomery, Alabama, he delivered an oration from which the following is taken:

The Bonnie Blue Flag no longer reflects the light of the morning sunbeam or kisses with its silken folds the genial breezes of our Southern climes. The hands that waved it along the crest of a hundred battlefields, and the hearts, for the love they bore it, that so often defied danger and death, no longer rally around it. . . . But dearer to me is she in this hour of her humiliation than she was in the day and hour of her pride and power. Each blood-stained battlefield, each track of her devastation, each new-made grave of her sons fallen in her defense, each mutilated form of the Confederate soldier—Her widow's tear, her orphan's cry, are but so many cords that bind me to her in her desolation, and draw my affections closer around my stricken country. When I raise my voice or lift my hand against her, may the thunders rive me where I stand! Though I be false in all else, I will be true to her. Though all others may prove faithless, I will be faithful still.

Within a year or two after this florid outburst of sectional patriotism and local attachments, Mr. White was one of the most bitter leaders of the Radical element of the Republican party in the South, and he continued his active and partisan connection with the Republican party so long as that party remained in power in the South.

Samuel F. Rice, of Alabama, was a native of South Carolina, and a graduate of Columbia College, with large and influential family connections. He was engaged in the practice of law and was elected to the Alabama House of Representatives in 1840. He was a member of the Southern Right party in 1851 and was an unsuccessful candidate for Congress, but in 1853 he was elected Judge of the Supreme Court. During the Republican and carpet-bag régime in Alabama, Judge Rice was actively identified with the Republicans and was the ablest jurist of that party in Alabama.

Charles Pelham was a native of Alabama and brother of John Pelham, the gallant artillery commander who won distinction in the Confederate army. He became identified with the Radical element of the Republican party in Alabama when that party, with the carpet-baggers, secured control of the State government. He served in the 43d Congress and, later, was elected Judge of the Circuit Court. It was during his term as Judge that illiterate and irresponsible Negroes served on the juries to the total exclusion of white men. Pelham was one of the notorious Radical Republicans of the South. After the Democratic party secured control of the State governments in the South, he went to Washington where he held a position in the Federal Government.

Judge John Pelham, son of Charles Pelham, was elected Judge of the 7th Judicial Circuit on the Democratic ticket in 1904. This was the same circuit in which his father had served as Judge, with Negro jurors, during Republican rule, and the same Congressional district which his father had represented as a Republican. In March, 1911, Judge John Pelham was appointed a member of the Court of Appeals by a Democratic Governor, for a term of six years, and later was elected as the candidate of the Democratic party to the same position and became presiding Judge of the Court, and continued in that office until his death. The fact that he was a son of the Republican who was so actively identified with the carpet-baggers did not affect his standing or influence after he became identified with the Democratic party. It matters not what a man's past affiliations have been, nor very much what his political record has been, after he joins the Democratic party in the South and continues faithful to the policies and practices of the Oligarchy which controls that party.

The door of the Democratic party in the South is always open to penitent enemies, backsliders and renegades. The proselyte is always welcomed into the "bosom and soul" of this

party, especially if he be skilled in the practices of the party,
and his sins of commission and omission are forgotten. According to the tenets of this party, no atonement is required; a mere
declaration of affiliation with the Oligarchy is accepted as complete and satisfactory absolution;

> And sinners plunged beneath that flood
> Lose all their guilty stains.

Thus it is seen that some of the most aggressive and vindictive
leaders of the Republican carpet-bag régime in the South were
native white men, and, later, a considerable number of those
native white Republicans became leaders in the Democratic
party. For the purpose of illustrating this phase of the situation, and in support of my charges against the native white exploiters, I have cited only a few of the outstanding cases which
came under my personal observation. The list could be extended
so as to include every one of the Southern States, and the amplified narrative would furnish cumulative evidence of the prominence and shameless conduct of the native white exploiters during the Republican régime in the South.

A large majority of the best citizens of the South, especially
those who fought the battles of the Confederacy, like General
Longstreet, for instance, accepted the result of the Civil War as
a final settlement of the issues for which the Slave Oligarchy
through the Democratic party had contended from the formation
of the Union. A revival of the dead issues of the Democratic
party received no support from the mass of loyal citizens, North
or South; but the great economic, social and political upheaval
that followed the Civil War in the South presented a new field
for exploitation. The South was prostrate under the brutal
and insolent domination of the spoilers. There was little difference between the alien exploiter from the North and the
native spoilsman of the South. Each was dominated by the
sordid passion of greed; neither had any conception of civic
ideals or American patriotism; each used the most available
agency to carry out his evil designs. The corrupt carpet-bagger
coddled the Negro for the purpose of exploiting the native whites,
while the native spoilsman persecuted the Negro for the same
purpose. In his *History of the United States*, Dr. Rhodes says:

No doubt can exist that, if Negro suffrage had not been forced upon the South, a healthy and respectable Republican party would have been formed, attaining perhaps the power and influence which the Democrats have in New England.

This theory of a distinguished historian may or may not be correct; there has been no opportunity to put it to a practical test. Negro suffrage does not exist, and the elimination of the Negro vote has not strengthened, but rather weakened the Republican party in the South. Mr. Blaine foresaw the collapse of the Republican party in the South when he said that its leaders, as represented in Congress, were not the type of men who would be able to hold their political power in the Southern States:

The representation of the Southern States being complete in both Houses before the close of the first session of the forty-first Congress, an impartial estimate could be made of the strength and capacity of the men who were opprobriously designated in the South as Carpet-baggers or Scalawags. It was soon ascertained that the unstinted abuse heaped upon them as a class was unjust and often malicious. The large proportion, and notably those who remained in Congress beyond two years, were men of character and respectability, in many cases indeed of decided cleverness. But their misfortune was that they had assumed a responsibility which could be successfully discharged only by men of extraordinary endowments. If any considerable number of them had been gifted in a high degree as orators, they would have had great advantage among a people who rate mere eloquence above its true value. If any of them had been men of large fortune (invested in Southern property) and able to make lavish expenditure, they could have produced a deep impression upon a people more given to admiration of mere wealth than the people of the North. But of the entire list of Republican Senators and Representatives from the reconstructed States, there was not one who was regarded as exceptionally eloquent or exceptionally rich; and hence they were compelled to enter the contest without personal prestige, without adventitious aid of any kind. They were doomed to a hopeless struggle against the influence, the traditions, the hatred of a large majority of the white men of the South.

Those who anxiously and intelligently studied the political situation in the South could see how unequal the contest would be and how soon the men who organized the rebellion would again wield the political power of their States—wield it lawfully if they could, but unlawfully if they must; peacefully if that would suffice, but violently if violence in their judgment became necessary.

Every man who went from the North to the South during the

Reconstruction period, and while the Republican party was in power in the Southern States, was classed as a carpet-bagger. Southern politicians have tried to place all in the same class. "The evil they did lived after them; the good was interred with their bones."

Why the Solid South? is the title of a book written, primarily, to justify the seditious talk, and palliate the cruel and corrupt practices of the Southern Oligarchy, but, ostensibly, for the purpose of telling the story of lawless and corrupt practices under the rule of the carpet-bag governments, and to forestall further interference with, or comments on, the policies of the Democratic party in the South. There is another side to the story of corrupt practices in the South, before and after the carpet-bag régime, to which I have alluded; and, fortunately, there are a few books written by Southern authors who were not afraid to tell the truth. The title of a very interesting work by a Southern author is *Reconstruction in Mississippi*, by James Wilford Garner. Dr. Garner is a native of Mississippi, and his book is an important and valuable contribution to American history. Here are a few illuminating excerpts from this volume:

Among the sins charged to the "carpet-baggers" in Mississippi was that after five years of extravagance and plunder they turned over the government to the Democracy with a debt aggregating $20,000,000. According to the report of the Auditor for 1875, the total State indebtedness on January 1 of that year was $3,750,385. . . .On January 1, 1876, two months before Ames surrendered the government, he sent a message to the legislature in which he gave a statement of the condition of the finances of the State. From this statement it appears that the real State debt, that is, its outstanding obligations over and above its ability to pay at once with its currency and available funds, was but a little more than $500,000. His statement agrees substantially with the report of the State Treasurer for 1876, and does not differ greatly from the findings of a special committee of Democrats, who reported that the actual indebtedness of the State three months before Ames resigned was but a little more than a million dollars. The State debt in 1870, when the Republicans took charge of the government was, according to one authority $221,522.75; according to another, it was $653,480, exclusive of the school fund. It is difficult to see how any system of bookkeeping could stretch a debt of half a million or even a million into one of twenty million.

A supplementary foot-note referring to the foregoing general statement contains the following explanation:

A table giving the debts of the Southern States at the close of the Reconstruction period, in which the debt of Mississippi is placed at $20,000,000, appeared first in a speech delivered by Hon. St. George Tucker in the 51st Congress; later, in Hon. H. Herbert's *Why the Solid South?* from which it was copied by Dr. J. L. M. Curry in the *Southern States of the American Union*, p. 231, and has more recently been used in President E. Benjamin Andrews's *History of the United States during the last Quarter of a Century* (Magazine edition, *Scribner's* May 1895, p. 549). Shortly after the publication of President Andrews's article Ex-Governor Ames addressed a communication to him complaining that his authorities had led him into making a "$19,500,000 error in a $20,000,000 statement," so far as the debt of Mississippi was concerned. President Andrews replied that he had been seriously misled, and after procuring the official reports, he was pained to find that his statement as regarded Mississippi was without foundation. The table alluded to was omitted from the book form of his history.

The record of corruption during Reconstruction and Republican rule in Mississippi seems to show that the city of Vicksburg was the headquarters of the spoilers and, consequently, that city was the greatest sufferer from the venal practices of that period. It has been said that nothing can be found in the history of the Reconstruction epoch, or in the history of any other period in any country, that would surpass in lawlessness and venality the record in Vicksburg, and Warren county, of which Vicksburg was the county seat.

The State Senators and Members of the Legislature from Warren county were colored and the sheriff was a very ignorant man. The clerk of the Chancery Court was ignorant and charged with gross corruption; the circuit clerk and every member of the Board of Supervisors, except one, was a Negro, and scarcely one of them could read or write. Four of the eight Councilmen of the city of Vicksburg were Negroes; in fact there were only three white officers in the county. It was stated that the whites paid ninety-nine per cent. of the taxes of the county, "all of which were assessed, collected and disbursed by ignorant and dishonest colored officials." In 1874, Vicksburg had a population of 11,000, of which the blacks were in the majority. The county and city debts before the beginning of the Reconstruction period, in 1869, amounted to $13,000, but during the Reconstruction period and Republican rule the city debt alone increased to $1,400,000. Large sums of money had been squandered by the city governments in grants to railroad companies and in public improvements. It would seem, however, that bad as the carpet-bag record was in Vicksburg, the stealing was not limited to the Republicans. A reference note in Dr. Garner's book says:

Charles Nordhoff is authority for the statement that the Democrats received most of the money spent for public improvements in Vicksburg. He relates an instance in which a Democrat charged the city $500 for moving a safe from the wharf to the Court House.

Another interesting statement in this book is the following:

The colored state librarian during Alcorn's administration was charged with stealing books from the library. The only large case of embezzlement among State officers during the post-bellum period was that of the Democratic State treasurer in 1866. The amount of shortage was $61,962.

Before the beginning of Reconstruction, while the Democrats were in control of the State Government, the State Treasurer stole $61,962; after the beginning of Reconstruction, one of numerous charges against Republican officials was the case of the Negro who stole some books. Writing of expenditures for educational purposes, Dr. Garner says:

The results of the first year of free education in Mississippi were encouraging to the reconstructionists, notwithstanding the undoubted difficulties which they had to confront. State Superintendent Pease reported that more than 3,000 free schools had been opened, with an attendance of 66,257 pupils. Of the 3,600 teachers employed, all except 399 were white. Five hundred school sites had been donated and 200 buildings erected by private subscription. The total expenditures on account of public education for the year were $869,766.76, an amount which exceeded the government expenditures for all other purposes.

This burden might have been much lighter, had it not been for the mismanagement of the school funds prior to the war. More than a million dollars of the sixteenth section funds, to say nothing of the Seminary and Chickasaw funds, were lost through poor management. Few things in the history of the State affords more cause for regret than the manner in which these munificent endowments were administered. Had they been judiciously managed, they would have yielded revenue enough in 1870 to defray the entire cost of the public school system. . . . Nineteen of the sixty-four county superintendents in 1870 reported a loss of $418,765 of the sixteenth section school funds.

The story of Reconstruction in Mississippi is substantially the same as the story of Reconstruction in every one of the Southern States, with the exception noted in a preceding paragraph, that the Negroes in Mississippi and South Carolina were more prominent under Republican rule in these States because they were in the majority.

For the purpose of illustrating the pernicious influence of corrupt practices in politics, especially the train of civic and social evils which followed the spoils system that prevailed in the South before the Civil War, and which was exaggerated and vulgarized after the war, I shall introduce a short review of some of those practices in the ante-bellum South. In his *Life and Times of Yancey*, Colonel John W. Du Bose has narrated the story of corrupt practices in Alabama, with special reference to the management of State banks, and the venal politicians who used their official positions to defraud the State. Excerpts from this shameful story follow:

The banks, being creations of the Legislature, soon learned to corrupt the Legislature, the better to perpetuate their own power. The Legislature elected the President and Directors of the banks—the parent bank at Tuscaloosa, the branches at Decatur, Huntsville, Montgomery and Mobile. A report was prepared by the Legislature, at its session of 1840-41, showing that forty-five Whig members of that body, and Whig Directors and Presidents owed the banks of the State $572,596; and that forty-three Democrats, members of the Legislature and officers of the banks, owed these institutions $149,312. The largest Whig debtor, T. McC. Prince, owed $120,436; the next largest, C. C. Langdon, editor of *The Mobile Advertiser*, the leading Whig journal of the state, owed $89,311. The largest debtor among the Democrats was the President of the Senate, Nathaniel Terry, who owed $46,049. Besides debts on their individual accounts, many of the members of the Legislature, of both parties, were deeply involved, as sureties on the promissory notes of their constituents, held by the banks; some to the extent of $100,000 and over, each. . . . Citizens of Autauga and Coosa counties, regardless of party affiliations, met at Wetumpka to consider measures for relief from a "spirit of speculation and fraud abroad in the land which is destined, unless speedily arrested, to destroy the banks and corrupt the people."

A large meeting of citizens assembled at Vernon, Autauga County, to inquire into bank frauds. A list of citizens indebted to the State bank and its branches, at Tuscaloosa and Montgomery, in sums ranging from $200 to $4,000 was read. Affidavits were read signed by the "mark" of illiterate people, testifying that they had been bribed in sums of ten dollars to lend their names as sureties on promissory notes discounted at the banks. Resolutions were passed declaring State Senator Dixon Hall, Democrat, implicated in obtaining, on worthless paper, large sums of money, from the banks, and demanding his resignation. On complaint of Daniel Pratt and other leading citizens, Mr. Hall was indicted by the grand jury and, by change of venue, his case was sent for trial to Macon County.

Samuel F. Rice, a member of the Legislature, from Talladega, went to the branch bank at Huntsville to borrow $10,000. He was refused. Continuing on his way to the branch bank at Decatur, he met some of the Directors in the parlor of that institution. Denouncing there the conduct of a bank that would not lend money to the people, he avowed his purpose to bring the subject up in the Legislature. At the conclusion of his remarks, he presented his request for the loan of the sum just refused at Huntsville, and it was promptly paid over to him. One of the Commissioners of the Decatur branch, indignant at the transaction, reported it to the Legislature. The complaint was formally investigated, pronounced baseless, and Rice was elected State printer. The State lost heavily on purchases made by the banks of cotton, by advances on cotton in the warehouses in Alabama and at Liverpool and advances made by them on unharvested cotton.

As related in a preceding paragraph, Samuel F. Rice was, after the war, one of the prominent, and one of the ablest of the Southern Republicans. It is also interesting to note that Daniel Pratt, to whom Colonel Du Bose refers as one of the ''leading citizens'' who protested against corrupt practices and bank frauds, was a Northern man who located in Alabama and engaged in the manufacture of cotton gins many years before the Civil War. He was the pioneer in an enterprise which developed into one of the most important industries of the South.

Neither before nor since the war have corrupt practices in America been limited to the Southern States, but such practices were perhaps more common in the South before the Civil War and, unquestionably, they have been more prevalent in the South since the war, than elsewhere. Party divisions, greater liberty of the press and freer discussion of men and measures in the Northern States, before and since the war, have made the fight against corrupt practices more effective there.

While it is not within the purview of this work to describe in detail the corrupt practices prior to the war, brief references have been made to them for the purpose of showing conditions that obtained in the South at that time, and how the same methods have continued since the Reconstruction period, without interruption, under rule of the present Oligarchy. In gathering information on these matters one need not go outside the material supplied by Southern writers. Our indictment is based on the testimony of reputable white citizens of the Southern States and documentary evidence, including the judicial and legislative records in these States.

The repudiation of State debts by the Southern States is a controversial subject respecting which many volumes have been written and published since the period of Reconstruction and carpet-bag rule. A discussion of this matter is beyond the limits of this volume, but in this story of Reconstruction I shall briefly refer to a few outstanding facts in the history of this controversy for the purpose of connecting it with our narrative of corrupt practices in the South.

Shortly after the World War, while the Treaty of Versailles was being discussed in this country, newspapers in the United States published reports from London containing reference to the claims of British bondholders in connection with old debts of the Southern States which were in default. It was suggested that, in a final settlement of international obligations growing out of advances by America to the Allies, British holders of bonds which had been repudiated by several of the Southern States would ask that the United States Government assume the repudiated debts. The following list of debts repudiated by the Southern States is taken from the forty-fifth "Annual Report of the Council of Foreign Bondholders." With the exception of Alabama's debt, of which no reliable information is obtainable, this list, exclusive of interest, is supposed to be correct:

Arkansas	$8,700,000
Florida	7,000,000
Georgia	12,700,000
Louisiana	6,000,000
Mississippi	7,000,000
North Carolina	12,600,000
South Carolina	6,000,000
*West Virginia	15,239,370
	$75,239,370

* ("A settlement of the debt of West Virginia was made in 1919.")

Concerning these debts, the report, signed by the Chairman of the "Council of Foreign Bondholders," said:

It is indeed deplorable that these prosperous and progressive States of the great American union take no steps to settle their defaulted debts, and it seems, to say the least of it, an anomaly that the United States should insist on compliance with its obligations by a country like Santo Domingo when so many of the States within its own borders are not observing their own engagements. The excuses put forward by these States for non-payment are manifold, but they may be generally classed under three heads:

(1) North Carolina pleads that her defaulted obligations were contracted while the State was being administered by the Federal Government after the Civil War. The answer to this, of course, is that the bondholders have nothing to do with differences between the States and the Federal Government.

(2) Louisiana alleges that there were irregularities of some kind or another in connection with the issue of most of her repudiated bonds. It would, of course, put an end to all credit if a State, on discovering that its own officials had acted incorrectly in the course of the issue of a loan, repudiated all responsibility for the money obtained from the public. There is, however, one issue, or part of an issue, known as "Baby" bonds, concerning which not even the foregoing excuse can be pleaded. In this case, in spite of the fact that the bonds are expressed on their face to be issued by the State of Louisiana in accordance with the State's constitution, and although they are specially secured on arrears of taxes collectible by the State, which, it is admitted, were "diverted" to other purposes, payment is denied on the astonishing plea that the bonds were not guaranteed by the State.

(3) Mississippi's excuse for not recognizing her defaulted debt is the worst of all. Between 1831 and 1838 the State issued two loans, for which she obtained full value and the proceeds of which were invested in the establishment and development of two banks. So long as the banks flourished and made good profits the interest on the loans was paid; but when, owing to over-speculation, bad times came and the banks got into difficulties, Mississippi made this the excuse for ceasing all further payments to the bondholders. For a State to repudiate its obligations to its creditors because the investments it chooses to make with their money do not turn out profitably is absolutely indefensible, and as far as the Council are aware, such an argument has never been resorted to by even the most backward of the Spanish-American republics.

On account of the persistent and long-continued agitation of the subject in England, the general impression has been that English investors still hold the bulk of the bonds repudiated by the Southern States. It appears, however, that, with the exception of Mississippi, there are not any large amounts of the repudiated debts held in England. It is perhaps safe to assume that the greater part of these repudiated bonds are held in America, in many cases by the heirs of the original investors. The erroneous impression that the bulk of the bonds were held in England is perhaps due to the activities of the British bondholders, especially the statements contained in the annual reports of the "Council of Foreign Bondholders," with headquarters in London. This association, organized fifty years ago, to protect the interests of holders of foreign securities, has for many years had "eleven foreign States on its black list," but in 1920 the Republic of Guatemala, under pressure from the Foreign Office, "resumed payments after a default extending over fourteen years." As stated in the report (1913), "the elimination of Guatemala from the black list"—

leaves the unenviable distinction of defaulters confined to the Republic of Honduras, and nine States of the United States of America; namely, Alabama, Arkansas, Florida, Georgia, Louisiana, Mississippi, North Carolina, South Carolina, and West Virginia.

As stated by Dr. William A. Scott, in his work on *The Repudiation of State Debts*, Mississippi was the first State to practice repudiation:

As early as the 'forties she refused to pay one class of bonds aggregating in face value $5,000,000, and in the 'fifties another class aggregating $2,000,000 met a like fate.

The first mentioned bonds were issued in June, 1838, in payment of five thousand shares of stock in the Union Bank of Mississippi. This bank was chartered on the 5th of February, 1838, under a law which pledged the State to the issue of bonds to the amount of $15,500,000, for the purpose of supplying the working capital.

A law passed by the Legislature of Mississippi provided that,

as soon as the books of subscription for stock in the said Mississippi Union Bank are opened, the Governor of this State is hereby authorized and required to subscribe for, in behalf of this State, fifty thousand shares of the stock of the original capital of the said bank; the same to be paid for out of the proceeds of the State bonds, to be executed to the said bank as already provided for in the said charter. . . .

Its capital was loaned to insolvent individuals and corporations, and its management resembled that of a gambling concern. In less than two years after the granting of its charter it was hopelessly insolvent. . . .

The first legislature which met after the sale of the bonds passed the following resolution: ''Resolved that the sale of the bonds was highly advantageous to the State and the bank, and, in accordance with the injunctions of the charter . . . bringing timely aid to an embarrassed community.

Needless to say, neither the Negroes nor the carpet-baggers were responsible for debts created by the State of Mississippi prior to the Civil War, on which the State later defaulted and finally repudiated. Twenty years before the beginning of the Civil War, the State of Mississippi repudiated her honest debts; twenty-five years before the beginning of Reconstruction in the Southern States, the Governor of Mississippi sent a message to the Legislature of that State in which he recommended that the State repudiate its debts. Further relating to the repudiation of State debts in Mississippi and the feeling of proscription shown by the citizens who were guilty of repudiation, Dr. Garner, in *Reconstruction in Mississippi*, says:

William Yerger was a man of conservative views and one of the ablest lawyers that ever practiced before the bar in Mississippi. Like Governor Sharkey, Judge Yerger was a native of Tennessee, and a Whig in politics —a fact which practically excluded him from political life before the war. For a while, however, he occupied a seat on the Supreme bench with Judge Sharkey. In the celebrated case of Mississippi vs. Johnson, in which the Court passed upon the validity of the Union Bank bonds, Yerger, in the face of a popular feeling, violent and proscriptive, stood up fearlessly and nobly against repudiation, and declared that the State was legally as well as morally bound to pay the bonds. Although he knew it would cost him his ermine, he could not be deterred from following his convictions.

Other bonds repudiated by the State of Mississippi, issued and sold thirty years before the beginning of the Civil War, were the so-called ''Planters' Bank Bonds.'' This corporation was chartered by the State in 1830 with an authorized capital of $3,000,000, of which $2,000,000 was reserved for the State. Bonds to the amount of $500,000 were issued in July, 1831, and the remaining $1,500,000 in March, 1832. These bonds were sold in Philadelphia at a price which yielded the State a premium of about $250,000.

The bank established branches in several cities of the State; issued large circulation and received large deposits; and continued in active operation until 1839, at which time it had a sinking fund of $800,000. When trouble came, in 1839, and the bank defaulted in interest on its bonds, the State was called upon to meet the deficiency, but the State failed to meet it. At an election in 1852 the question was submitted to a popular vote, whether a tax should be levied to pay the interest on the Planters' Bank Bonds, and a majority of 4,000 against the levy of such a tax was returned.

The 47th annual report of the ''Council of Foreign Bondholders,'' London, contains the following late comment on the Mississippi repudiation:

By far the worst case of all is that of Mississippi, whose debt was contracted many years before the Civil War. With the exception of Russia, there is no similar case on record so far as the Council are aware. The Russian repudiation, however, only took place after the establishment of the chaotic conditions still existing in that unhappy country, and is viewed with indignation by the better class of Russians, while the Mississippi repudiation occurred during peaceful conditions, and is apparently acquiesced in by the citizens of the most prosperous community in the world.

In 1833 the Territory of Florida chartered the Union Bank of Florida with an authorized capital of $3,000,000, which sum was raised, as authorized by the charter, by a sale of Territorial bonds. Lands and slaves of stockholders were hypothecated to the Territory as security. The bonds were sold—mostly in Europe in 1834, 1838, and 1839, at a ''nominal'' discount of from three to ten per cent. The bank suspended specie payment in 1837. In 1842 it failed to pay interest on the bonds loaned it. In 1840 the Judiciary Committee of the Territorial Legislature passed a resolution adverse to the payment of the interest on the bonds by the people of Florida, and the people were advised by the State Government that the bonds issued by the Territorial Government were void, and the taxpayers would not be called upon to pay interest or the principal of the bonds. When Florida was admitted as a State (1845) she had repudiated the bonds authorized by her Territorial Legislature, and it was further claimed that after Florida became a State she was not liable for the obligations of the Territory. The State of Florida also endorsed bonds for $4,000,000 in aid of railroads, which bonds were subsequently repudiated. The aggregate amount of bonds repudiated by the State of Florida was something over $8,000,000.

As early as 1836, the State of Georgia endorsed bonds of the Western and Atlantic Railroad, and in 1856 the State endorsed bonds of the Atlantic & Gulf Railroad. The Georgia Legislature in 1869 and 1870 provided for State endorsements to cover thirty railroads, in the form of bonds issued or endorsed, aggregating about $8,000,000 in face value. These bonds were later repudiated. This was during the period of carpet-bag and scalawag rule. Governor Bullock endorsed bonds of the Air Line Railroad Company "before a foot of the road had been built." Governor Bullock wrote a letter to the State Secretary, directing him to complete the endorsement by his signature as soon as twenty miles of the road were completed. On the strength of this endorsement and letter, the bonds were negotiated. The road was never built, and the Legislature declared the State's endorsement of these bonds to be null and void, and forbade their payment.

In extenuation of their defaults, the States charged with repudiation have asserted that the repudiated bonds were issued by *de facto* Governments without authority to obligate the State, that the bonds were fraudulently put out, and that there was no consideration to the State in the name of which the bonds were issued. These claims are not well founded in truth or in law. As we have seen, a large number of these bonds, especially bonds of the States of Florida and Mississippi, were issued prior to the Reconstruction period. We have also seen that the so-called carpet-bag Governments were composed of the citizens of the several States and a large number of those citizens were natives.

It is true that the States charged with repudiation did not receive full consideration for all the bonds issued during the Reconstruction period and Republican rule, and for some of those issues there was no consideration to the State, and some of the transactions were tainted with gross frauds. But it is also true that corrupt practices, venality and fraudulent transactions of public officials in the South were not limited to the period of Reconstruction, carpet-bag and Republican rule. The carpet-baggers and Republicans of the corrupt and venal classes were coarse and, in numerous ways, brutal in their corrupt practices and thievery, and their stealings were on a more stupendous scale, but those alien spoilers had the active and very efficient support of a large number of trained spoilsmen and thieves who were natives of the South. These white natives of the South, who were confederates and allies of the corrupt carpet-baggers, were actively engaged in corrupt and fraudulent practices before the Civil War. As already pointed out, at the close of Republican rule, a large number of these native corruptionists joined the Democratic party.

The Southern States are not the only States of the American Union which have suffered financial losses from inefficiency and corruption of public officials, from the misfeasance and malfeasance of ignorant and venal politicians. In 1837 the Legislature of Michigan authorized the Governor of that State to negotiate a loan of $5,000,000, the proceeds of which were to be "employed in constructing a system of public improvements." There were charges of irregularities, the financial crisis of 1837 added to the confusion, the State defaulted on interest in July, 1842, and then followed crimination and recrimination. However, as stated by Professor William A. Scott (*The Repudiation of State Debts*),—

the State has always declared her willingness and her obligation to pay every bond for which she had received consideration, although the money was squandered in works for which she received no benefit.

The debt was finally compromised on a basis which, in the opinion of the holders of some of the bonds, was not altogether fair.

In 1858, the State of Minnesota issued bonds in the total sum of $2,275,000 in aid of a railroad which defaulted. It was claimed that the bonds were issued without authority and that the whole enterprise was a fraud, and the suggestion to repudiate the debt met with popular support. After a great deal of legislation and popular discussion, the debt was finally compromised in 1881 on a "comparatively honorable basis," after which the credit of the State improved a great deal.

The States of Michigan and Minnesota are the only States outside the South which have been charged with repudiation. As we have seen, the settlement of the defaulted debts of those two States, while not altogether satisfactory to the creditors, was decidedly more honorable than the action of the Southern States, which deliberately repudiated certain debts that were legal and for which they received consideration. The debt-paying record of Haiti is more creditable than is that of any of the eight Southern States charged with repudiation. The record of Haiti and the Dominican Republic, respectively, in the matter of paying public debts, is far and away more honorable, for example, than is that of Mississippi.

During the Wilson Administration, when the Federal Government was under rule of the Southern Oligarchy, there were gross and stupendous frauds, and, in numerous instances, downright thievery, especially in the matter of war contracts, and yet it has not been suggested that the United States Government should repudiate the bonds which were issued under the rule of an Oligarchy, which openly and shamelessly permitted exploitation and corruption among public officials, because a considerable portion of the money realized from the sale of the bonds was squandered or stolen.

It frequently happens that governments, like individuals, are the victims of unscrupulous money-lenders and traders, and it also frequently happens that governments, like individuals, are forced to pay high prices for commodities when credits are unstable. But such unfortunate conditions never have been held as valid and honorable excuses for repudiating governmental obligations. The Southern States introduced the immoral practice in the United States.

The debt of France to the United States for credits established and cash advanced during the World War amounts to the principal sum of $2,933,405,070. This debt was incurred after America entered the war, while France, Great Britain, and other allies were fighting our battles and we were unprepared. Most, if not all, of the money advanced to France was expended in this country for supplies, and, with a few possible exceptions, large profits were made by Americans in these transactions. However, the attitude of France respecting her debts to the

United States was expressed by M. Stephane Lauzanne, editor of
Le Matin in the noble words which follow:

> Nevertheless, we owe these $3,000,000,000. I believe we can never say
> loudly enough or often enough that we owe them and we will pay them.
> France repudiates neither her signature nor her debts. Having paid with
> her blood on the battlefield, she will pay with her money across the counter.

Not one of the Southern States answered her creditors as
France answered, that she would repudiate "neither her sig-
nature nor her debts." Every one of the Southern States was
in better condition to pay after the end of Republican and
carpet-bag rule, according to actual and potential resources,
than France was to pay after the close of the World War. At
the present time, Russia is under the rule of aliens and carpet-
baggers, some of whom, it has been said, are corrupt; yet, at
the Genoa Conference, April, 1922, about the first thing that
Premier Lloyd George said to the representatives of the Soviet
Government was in the words which follow :

> We will give you all the accommodations you want. What we want is
> that you recognize your financial obligations. The principle is the thing
> that matters. A government which does not recognize its responsibilities
> injures itself.

It is perhaps true that in every country, at some time, honest
citizens and taxpayers have suffered the penalty of inefficiency
or dishonesty in the administration of public affairs, but mis-
fortunes of this character in the affairs of government, national,
state nor municipal, never have been accepted as reasonable
excuses for repudiation of honest debts.

For forty-seven years (at the present writing) the native
white people of the Southern States have been in absolute control of their own affairs; the South has been "solid" under rule
of the Democratic party for nearly half a century. In the
national election of 1880, the first Presidential election after
every one of the Southern States had passed under rule of the
Democratic party, the solidarity of the South was no less pronounced in national affairs than it was in the State governments.
The close of the Reconstruction epoch, followed by the end of
Republican rule, left the eleven States which had composed the

Southern Confederacy under the absolute control of a provincial Oligarchy. In his *Twenty Years of Congress,* Mr. Blaine summarized the actual situation very clearly and forcibly:

The salient and most serious fact of the Presidential election was the absolute consolidation of the electoral vote of the South; not merely of the eleven States that composed the Confederacy, but of the five others in which slaves were held at the beginning of the civil struggle. The leading Democrats of the South had been steadily aiming at this result from the moment that they found themselves compelled by the fortunes of war to remain citizens of the United States. The Reconstruction laws had held them in check in 1868; the reaction against Mr. Greeley had destroyed Southern unity in 1872; it had been assumed with boastful confidence, but at the last miscarried in 1876; and now, in 1880, it was finally and fully accomplished. The result betokened thenceforth a struggle within the Union far more radical than that which had been carried on from the formation of the Constitution until the secession of the South. . . .

Southern men of all parties would unite against the admission of a Northern State, until a Southern State was ready to offset its vote in the Senate, but they never sought to compel unity of opinion throughout all Southern States upon partisan candidates or upon public measures. The evident policy of the South since the close of the Civil War has been, therefore, of a more engrossing and more serious character. It comprehends nothing less than the absolute consolidation of sixteen States, not by liberty of speech, or public discussion, or freedom of suffrage, but by tyranny of opinion which threatens timid dissentients with social ostracism and suppresses the bolder form of opposition by force.

For nearly half a century the Democratic party in the Southern States has been not only in absolute control of the State and municipal governments but, with a few negligible and intermittent exceptions, that party has also maintained a solid Democratic representation from the South in the Senate and House of Representatives of the United States. During this long period of partisan and sectional rule in the South, every Republican Administration, from Hayes to Coolidge, inclusive, has been liberal in recognizing white men of the South, including Confederate veterans and Democrats, in appointments to responsible and high ministerial and judicial positions under the Federal Government.

CHAPTER V

PARTISAN PREJUDICE AND RACE PROSCRIPTION

The Freedmen's Bureau was the first measure on the part of
the Federal Government to control the Negroes in the Southern
States by making them wards of the Nation. It was this interference with the social and industrial affairs of the South, by
Northern representatives of the Federal Government, that
aroused the apprehension and indignation of the Southern people. It also gave vent to a bitter propaganda of sectional prejudice and race hatred which was effectively used—North and
South—for partisan purposes by the Radical and disloyal faction
of the Democratic party.

The "Bureau of Refugees, Freedmen, and Abandoned Lands"
was established in the War Department by an Act of Congress,
March 3, 1865. This Act provided that the Bureau was to be
maintained through the war and for one year thereafter, and
that it should have—

the supervision and management of all abandoned lands, and the control
of all subjects relating to refugees and freedmen, under such rules and
regulations as may be presented by the head of the bureau and approved
by the President.

One important provision of the law authorized the President
to appropriate for use of the freedmen the confiscated and
abandoned lands within the Southern States, not more than forty
acres, and for a period not longer than three years, being assigned to each man thus aided. The administration of the
bureau was placed in the hands of a chief commissioner and his
deputies, and in the actual application of the law much was
done with reference to labor, clothing, fuel, provisions, and
schools for the beneficiaries of the plan.

A second Freedmen's Bureau bill passed Congress, February
6, 1866, but was vetoed by President Johnson and was not
passed over his veto. Later, however, there was passed over

the President's veto the act of July 16, 1866, which extended for two years the term of the Bureau's statutory life, increased its power, authorized the sale for educational purposes of Confederate public property and gave to the Bureau military jurisdiction over infringements of civil rights secured by the act. In June, 1868, another bill was passed, extending the term of the Bureau for one year in unreconstructed States. The Bureau's chief work ended on January 1, 1869; its educational work was concluded a year and a half thereafter.

More than fifteen million dollars was spent by the Bureau, and, in addition to the general relief afforded, it aided appreciably in the movement for higher education of the freedmen, which resulted in the founding of such institutions as Atlanta University, Fisk University, and Howard University, the last being named after the most active protagonist in this work, the Commissioner of the Bureau, General Oliver O. Howard. Widely differing opinions have been, and are, held with regard to the methods used and the results attained by the Bureau, some writers maintaining that its work was almost wholly beneficent, others that on the whole much more harm was done than good. Referring to the Freedmen's Bureau, Professor Burgess, in *Reconstruction and the Constitution*, says:

It would have been a moral outrage for the Government of the United States to have taken the slaves away from the support and protection accorded them by their masters, and to have thrown them upon their own resources without any means of sustenance during the transition into the new status. But there is also no question but that this measure was so administered as to do the race for whose benefit it was intended as much harm as good. When the Government began to furnish them with food, clothing, fuel and shelter gratis, they, like the children that they were, conceived of this, to them, very agreeable state of things as something that was to last forever, as the new Jerusalem. They gathered about the depots of the Freedmen's Bureau and could not be induced to go away in search of work or livelihood. . . .

When, now, the newly reorganized "States" came to assume jurisdiction over matters concerning the freedmen, they found themselves driven to some legislation to prevent the whole Negro race from becoming paupers and criminals. It was in the face of such a situation that the legislatures of these "States" passed laws concerning apprenticeship, vagrancy and civil rights, which were looked upon at the North as attempts to re-enslave the newly emancipated, and served to bring the new "State" governments at the South into deep reproach.

There is no doubt that the Freedmen's Bureau with its powers, jurisdiction and charities, was a far greater source of irritation in the South than was the presence of the United States Army. While its superior officers were generally men of ability and character, a large number of the subalterns were canting hypocrites and outright thieves. They kept the Negroes in a state of idleness, beggary and unrest, and made them a constant danger to the life and property of the whites; and for their veritable tyranny over the white population did more to destroy Union sentiment among the whites and make them regard the United States Government in a hostile light than anything which had happened during the whole course of the rebellion.

The Thirteenth Amendment to the Constitution, proposed by resolution of Congress adopted February 1, 1865, prohibited both slavery and involuntary servitude "within the United States, or any place subject to their jurisdiction," except as a punishment for crime. In order to avoid the provisions of this amendment, several of the Southern States, notably the States of Mississippi and South Carolina, passed laws regulating the employment of labor and providing for the enforcement of severe laws relating to vagrancy. These laws in actual operation appeared to be directed wholly against the Negroes, who were subjected to very harsh restraints. *Black and White in the Southern States*, by Maurice S. Evans, contains a very clear survey of the situation in the Southern States as well as a narrative of the measures undertaken in the South to hold the Negro in subjection after his emancipation. From this interesting volume I take the following:

Laws were passed which could have but one interpretation; they were devised to place the Negro again in a position of servitude, as nearly like that of slavery as it was possible under the Thirteenth Amendment of the Constitution, which had been accepted by the States as they re-entered the Union.

In South Carolina an ordinance was passed at this time, making the provision that "no person of color shall pursue the practice, art, or business of an artisan, mechanic, or shopkepeer or any other trade or employment beside that of husbandry, or that of servant under contract for labor, until he shall have obtained a license from the judge of the County Court, which license shall be good for one year only." The law went on to say that for a license as peddler or shopkeeper a fee of £100 must be paid, while for the rudest mechanical calling it was £10. These license fees were applicable only to Negroes and were not demanded from white men. The object was obvious.

After President Johnson's proclamation of amnesty, May 29, 1865, and the appointment of provisional governors in the Southern States, the legislatures of these States passed laws respecting the Negroes, commonly called the "vagrant" laws, the purpose of which, as pointed out in a preceding paragraph, was to defeat the essential provision of the Thirteenth Amendment to the Constitution. The reactionary provisions of the "vagrant" laws, as indicated by the South Carolina statutes to which I have already alluded, were quite as evident in Mississippi, for instance, where Negroes were prohibited from renting or leasing land in incorporated towns; and, in default of the payment of fines imposed for alleged vagrancy, the sheriff was directed to "hire out said freedman, free Negro or mulatto, to any person who will, for the shortest period of service, pay said fine or forfeiture and all costs." This was the beginning of peonage and the horrible convict lease system to which I shall refer in later chapters. These reactionary and odious measures of the legislatures of the Southern States, in the autumn of 1865, were the "main causes of the passage of the Fourteenth Amendment."

The Fourteenth Amendment was enacted by Congress for ratification by the States June 13, 1866. Under it Negroes were made citizens. Representation in Congress for the Southern States, based on Negro population, was to be reduced unless these States gave the Negro the suffrage with only such restrictions and qualifications as applied to the whites. A sufficient number of ratifications by the States had been obtained for this Amendment; and on July 28, 1868, it was proclaimed a part of the fundamental law. Every one of the States which formed the Southern Confederacy, except Tennessee, and also the States of Kentucky, Delaware and Maryland, during the months of October, November and December, 1866, and January and February, 1867, refused to ratify the Fourteenth Amendment.

Under the original Constitution of the United States, only three-fifths of the slaves were counted in the apportionment of representatives in Congress; under the 14th Amendment all the Negroes are counted as citizens and the representatives in Congress are apportioned accordingly, thus enlarging the representation of the Southern States. That part of the 14th Amendment which recognized all former slaves as citizens, to be counted in fixing the basis for representation in Congress, has been enforced; the provision for reduction in representation on account of the right to vote being denied to male citizens over 21 years of age has been treated with contempt.

It is well to bring out clearly the fact that the attention of the country had been riveted on the Reconstruction policies of Congress, but there soon followed a period of reaction. In the closing paragraph of his life of Charles Sumner, Mr. Storey says:

To Sumner more than to any single man, except possibly Lincoln, the colored race owes its emancipation and such measure of equal rights as it now enjoys.

In honesty of purpose, the Negro had no better friend than Charles Sumner, who, in ability and integrity, stood at the head of the extreme Abolitionists. In the biography from which I have quoted, Mr. Storey further states that Sumner "lived to urge and see enacted every law which Congress had the power to pass in aid of equal rights and against distinctions of color." In his last speech on the Civil Rights bill Mr. Sumner said:

My desire, the darling desire, if I may say so, of my soul, at this moment, is to close forever this great question, so that it shall never again intrude into these chambers, so that hereafter in all our legislation there shall be no such word as black or white, but that we shall speak only of citizens and of men.

Only a little while before his death, after the State of Mississippi had been reconstructed and a Negro senator seated from that State, Mr. Sumner "hailed" the admission of a colored man into the United States Senate as an event "forever setting at rest the question of equal rights." Hiram Revels, the Negro Senator from Mississippi, was born in North Carolina and enjoyed the distinction of being the first colored man to secure a seat in the United States Senate. In his *Twenty Years of Congress*, Mr. Blaine says:

One of the Senators just admitted from Mississippi in advance of the ratification of the amendment (Hiram Revels) was a colored man of respectable character and intelligence. He sat in the seat which Jefferson Davis had wrathfully deserted to take up arms against the Republic and become the ruler of a hostile government. Poetic justice, historic revenge, personal retribution were all complete when Mr. Revels's name was called on the roll of the Senate. But his presence, while demonstrating the extent to which the assertion of equal rights had been carried, served to increase and stimulate the Southern resistance to the whole system of Republican reconstruction.

Thirty-one years after the great Abolition Senator from Massachusetts hailed the epoch-making event which "forever set at rest the question of equal rights," George H. White, the last Negro in Congress, up to the present time, made his farewell speech, in the 56th Congress, on January 29, 1901, from which I take the following:

This, Mr. Chairman, is perhaps the Negro's temporary farewell to the American Congress; but let me say, Phoenix-like, he will rise up some day and come again. These parting words are in behalf of an outraged, heart-broken, bruised, and bleeding, but God-fearing people, faithful, industrious, loyal people—rising people, full of potential force. . . .

The only apology that I have to make for the earnestness with which I have spoken is that I am pleading for the life, the liberty, the future happiness, and manhood suffrage of one-eighth of the entire population of the United States.

George H. White was born in North Carolina in 1852. He was a Member of Congress from the Second North Carolina district, afterward represented by Claude Kitchin, Chairman of the Ways and Means Committee in the 64th and 65th Congresses.

Emerson said that Charles Sumner was "for many years the conscience of the Senate," and Mr. Storey also relates that Emerson said Sumner had the "whitest soul of any man I ever knew." More than a decade after Sumner passed away, Judge Albion W. Tourgee wrote the following comment on the policies of the Reconstruction measures, with special reference to giving the ballot to the Negro, so ardently supported by Sumner:

Those who framed the reconstructionary legislation and exulted in what they had done, seemed not to have accounted this element of citizenship of any importance whatever. The fact that a man was free and had the abstract right to enjoy and exercise the privileges of the citizen seemed to be thought all that was necessary to transform a million of unlettered slaves into an equal number of self-governing citizens to whom the ballot might be safely intrusted. They had forgotten, or they did not know, that something more than liberty is required to enable a man to perform the functions of one of the co-ordinate rulers of a republic. The first element of any task is to know what is to be done. To properly exercise the functions of the citizen a man must first of all things understand the nature and importance of those duties. Sumner exulted too quickly when he declared that by giving the ballot to the freedmen we had ''chained him to the chariot wheel of American progress.'' . . .

The white race of the South rules that region to-day with as little regard to the right or power of the colored citizenship as if its possessor were chattels-real. Whatever the colored man receives of right, whatever he has of privilege, is granted to him simply by the grace of those who were once his masters.

At the present writing it has been nearly forty years since Judge Tourgee wrote the comments which I have quoted from his *An Appeal to Cæsar*, but they are as applicable to the actual present situation as they were to the conditions which prevailed when he wrote. No writer saw more clearly and none wrote more forcibly than Judge Tourgee concerning conditions in the South. An appreciation of his ability and integrity was written shortly after his death by Professor Andrew Joyner, of North Carolina, from which I quote the following:

He was for many years the most thoroughly hated man in North Carolina. The consensus of testimony from these sources shows that he was not a mean man. He was open, bold, determined, fearless and self-reliant. He neither asked nor gave quarter. He never betrayed his party nor sold a friend. He was neither a toady nor a humbug. He had convictions, and with them the courage and the resources with which to proclaim and maintain them. He was clean-handed and clean of life. The bitterest foe in the darkest of those dark hours never charged him with participation in the robbery of our people. . . . His only companions were his faithful wife and his books. His wife was a real heroine in the constancy and the steadfastness of her devotion in her lonely and ostracised life. . . . Unlike the average carpet-bagger, Tourgee was too proud to seek social position on borrowed capital.

Richly endowed by nature, his mind was a marvel in its capacity to grasp, absorb, digest and retain. . . . His name and fame will live longer in connection with his great work in '65 in having enacted and placed in our organic law the code of civil procedure. This was another northern idea, being copied largely from the codes of New York and Ohio, and stubbornly opposed by the older lawyers of the state, but time and experience have vindicated the wisdom of its enactment. . . . As further proof of the sagacity of its author, it may be noted that the reform procedure is now in force in nearly every State of this Union, in England, Ireland, Wales, India, Australia, in several provinces of Canada, and in many other English colonies. To Mr. Tourgee, more than to any other one man, is North Carolina indebted for this new and simpler code of procedure and for relief from the cumbersome and absurd forms of action under the old system.

Even at this late day, nearly sixty years after the close of the Civil War, and nearly half a century after the Reconstruction period, it is only now and then that a man in the South has the courage to acknowledge even part of the truth relating to the Reconstruction epoch, and particularly the actual facts respecting those brave and capable men from the North who, like Judge Tourgee, worked for the civic, educational and industrial advancement of the South, and contributed with their brains, their patriotism and their money to the uplift and progress of the Southern people. Some years ago, Mr. Percy Clark, of Selma, Alabama, writing in *The Birmingham Age-Herald,* said:

Not all carpet-baggers were bad men, in fact some proved themselves friends in need, and at a critical time. I recall the valuable services of Dr. Silsby, a returned from Africa missionary, who came to Selma with the best of intentions. Dr. Courtney J. Clark to whom the city of Selma is indebted for its present splendid school system, for as a member of the city council he separated it from political vicissitudes, securing the appointment of a self-perpetuating board of the very best citizens.

Carpet-bag government in the South closed at the beginning of the Hayes administration. Federal troops were withdrawn from the Southern States, the white people secured complete control of every branch of State government, and the last vestige of carpet-bag rule passed away. White supremacy has been dominant in the South since 1877, and since that time there has not been the slightest cause for apprehension respecting the question of white supremacy. Technically the work of reconstructing the Southern States was completed in 1870, when Senators and Representatives from Virginia, Mississippi and Texas were formally admitted to seats in Congress. Texas was the last of the seceded States to come back, and after its readmission, during the early months of 1870, the work of Reconstruction was completed as well as it could be under the laws made for that purpose. But it was far from termination in the sense of the restoration of law and order in the South. The State governments were more stable in 1866 than they were in 1870. In their relation to the national government the Southern States had been re-organized, and were back in the Union, but re-admission into the Union did not establish law and order, nor did it guarantee government by the people and for the people, white or black. In his inaugural address President Hayes said:

The permanent pacification of the country upon such principles and by such measures as will secure complete protection of all its citizens in the free enjoyment of all their constitutional rights is now the one subject in our public affairs which all thoughtful and patriotic citizens regard as of supreme importance. . . .

The question we have to consider for the immediate welfare of those states of the Union is the question of government or no government; of social order and all the peaceful industries and happiness that belong to it, or a return to barbarism. It is a question in which every citizen of the nation is deeply interested, and with respect to which we ought not to be, in a partisan sense, either Republicans or Democrats, but fellow-citizens and fellow-men, to whom the interests of a common country and a common humanity are dear.

Louisiana was the last of the Southern States that passed from under control of the carpet-bag government and Republican rule. Stephen B. Packard, the last of the carpet-bag governors, was a man of personal integrity, undaunted physical courage and a high order of ability. He was elected Governor of Louisiana in 1876, at the same election and in the same manner, and by the same votes, that gave the Electoral Votes of that State to Hayes. If, as claimed by the Democrats, Packard was not elected Governor, it followed that the Republican Electoral ticket did not carry the State and Hayes should not have been declared elected with the Louisiana vote.

Claiming that he was elected, Packard undertook to assume the functions of the office, but General Nicholls, the Democratic candidate, was recognized as the *de facto* Governor by a large majority of the white people. Shortly after the inauguration of President Hayes, the Federal troops were withdrawn from Louisiana and the Packard government collapsed. So ended, on April 25, 1877, the Reconstruction epoch in the South.

The policies of the Hayes Administration in the Southern States found little favor with the Republicans, especially the Radical faction of that party. In discussing the attitude of President Hayes in his policies and actual practices relating to conditions in the South, Mr. Blaine, in his *Twenty Years of Congress,* stated the case thus:

It was plainly his determination to withdraw from the South all national protection to the colored people, and to put the white population of the reconstructed States upon their good faith and their honor, as to their course touching the political rights of all citizens.

The inaugural address did not give satisfaction to the radical Republicans, but was received with every mark of approbation by the more conservative elements of the party. Many Democrats would have supported Mr. Hayes cordially but for the mode of his election. It was impossible for them to recover from the chagrin and disappointment of Mr. Tilden's defeat. The new President, therefore, began his administration with a bitter personal opposition from the Democracy, and with a distrust of his own policy on the part of a large number of those who had signally aided in his election.

General Burnside and other Republicans who had served in the Union Army urged upon President Hayes the appointment of General Joseph E. Johnston as Secretary of War, but after much discussion the "intention was reluctantly abandoned." After his inauguration the names of several prominent men in the South were suggested to the President by leading Republicans for appointment to important positions in the Federal Government. The President finally decided on the appointment of Judge Key, of Tennessee, as Postmaster General. Judge Key had served in the Confederate Army and voted for Tilden. Never did a President enter upon his duties with more sincere good will for every section of the country. It was said that the kindliness towards the Southern people and the personal interest in the South manifested by President Hayes aroused jealousy in the North, at least to the extent of public confidence being shaken in the wisdom and prudence of the President's extreme policy of conciliation. It was the popular belief, however, that the manifestation of friendship for the South was not affected on the part of the President; it was an honest, patriotic sentiment, and he was slow to acknowledge that his Southern policy was a failure. He seemed to think that a policy of conciliation and real friendship was the only one that would restore peace and prosperity in the South, and he gave it a fair trial before it was pronounced a failure.

General Gordon, of Georgia, defended the Hayes Administration. He was frequently referred to as a warm friend of the President and an earnest advocate of the Hayes policies in the South. But the ingratitude and provincial littleness of the new Southern Oligarchy came out when the Democrats in the House of the Forty-fifth Congress, by refusing to make the necessary appropriations for the support of the army, rendered an extra session necessary. When the Army bill was up, during the first year of the Hayes Administration, it was claimed by Representatives from the South that the Southern States were in danger of intimidation by the army. Senator Blaine showed the absurdity of the charge by giving the exact number of troops at that time stationed in each of the Southern States. He said:

The entire South has eleven hundred and fifty-five soldiers to intimidate, overrun, oppress, and destroy the liberties of fifteen million people. In the Southern States there are twelve hundred and three counties. If you distribute the soldiers there is not quite one for each county; and when I give the counties, I give them from the census of 1870. If you distribute them territorially, there is one for every seven hundred square miles of territory.

It was evident that the presence of Federal troops at the polling-places and seats of justice for the alleged purpose of intimidating the white people, respecting which so many false assertions have been spoken and published, existed largely in the imagination and evil designs of the political schemers of the Southern Oligarchy. But this bogy of Federal interference with State affairs in the South, and the other bugbear of Negro domination, served the purpose of sectional propaganda, and of giving license for corrupt practices which the Oligarchy carried on to perpetuate its power. I have already alluded to some outstanding instances of persecution and proscription by the Southern Oligarchy and I shall now trace some of the salient features of the odious reaction that followed the provincial and proscriptive policies of the Oligarchy.

Some of the most radical leaders of the Democratic party in the South were born in the North, but they were followed and idolized in the South, so long as they supported the provincial policies and corrupt practices of the ruling class in that region. For instance, the Southern people followed to their ruin the irresponsible leadership of John Slidell, a native of New York. They denounced Hinton Helper, a respectable citizen of North Carolina, who had the courage to tell the plain truth and to give the people of his section patriotic and faithful warning. Helper was roundly abused and called a "poor white," the most opprobrious epithet, in the opinion of a Southern Democrat, that could be applied to anyone, and one which they frequently applied to Lincoln. Measures were taken not only to suppress the writings of Helper but also to punish all who had the temerity to read his book. Later events proved the truth of all that Helper had written. The South, on the other hand, accepted and approved the writings of Northern men who defended slavery.

The South rejected and proscribed James Birney, a native of the South, whose career and the career of whose sons was an honor to America; they rejected and vilified Abraham Lincoln, of Southern descent, who was never an extreme Abolitionist, who never spoke an unkind word of the Southern people, and who favored only limited and qualified enfranchisement for the former slaves. With vindictive bitterness the South opposed Grant, one of the bravest, noblest and most faithful friends, who, as we have seen, only a few months after the surrender at Appomattox, visited the South and made a report in which he testified to the loyalty of the Southern people and recommended that the government of the Southern States be restored to the Southern people without further delay or intermeddling. Under the leadership of Carl Schurz, a German-American, who had made a report condemning the South and advising that it be put under military despotism, the South supported Greeley in 1872.

The Southern Oligarchy proscribed and vilified General Longstreet, a native of South Carolina, and one of the most distinguished men that section ever produced. A few years later, with almost fanatical devotion, they followed Grover Cleveland,

who never visited their section of the country until after he
was elected President, and never spoke a kind word in their
behalf when they needed friends With bitterness and injustice
the Southern Oligarchy opposed McKinley and Roosevelt, each
of whom was a devoted and faithful friend, Roosevelt's mother
being a Southern woman and two of her brothers officers in
the Confederate service.

The present situation is no better; indeed, it is infinitely worse
than it was twenty-two years ago, when, in a dissenting report
on the reapportionment bill, before the 56th Congress, Judge
Crumpacker presented some interesting conclusions on this subject. He said:

> The Negro is persecuted and the white man is demoralized. The solu-
> tion of this great problem is one of the burning questions of the hour.
> It is above partyism, it involves the life of this government.

Without reference to the advisability of his proposal to reduce
representation from the South, the words of Judge Crumpacker
are as full of truth as anything that has been said on the
subject. We are approaching a crisis in the continued provincialism and race persecution under rule of the Oligarchy in the
South. So clearly is this the case that it has been observed by
many writers and publicists who have made a study of the actual
situation. For instance, in his interesting work entitled *Black
and White in South East Africa*, Maurice S. Evans says:

> I found that although for fifty years the Negro in the United States
> has had legal political equality guaranteed by the Federal law, his in-
> fluence to-day in politics is a negligible quantity, the white man makes
> the laws as he did before emancipation. I found that although by Federal
> law he is entitled to equal accommodation in all places of public resort
> and entertainment, he dare not enter any theatre, hotel or restaurant and
> he must ride in the Jim Crow car. . . . The racial peace promised by
> some as the result of legal equality of opportunity has not been realized,
> racial animosity seems to grow from more to more. After fifty years'
> experience the position of the United States may be described as tragic.

A general charge against the Negro which is offered as an
explanation for present conditions in the South is that race
prejudice in that section has been greatly accentuated by the

appointment of Negroes to public positions, particularly offices with which the white people come in daily or frequent contact. This, it is claimed, is very offensive to the white people, and is regarded as sectional spite, inasmuch as Negroes are seldom appointed to such places in the Northern States. This is a very strong argument when we consider that race prejudice is so general, and the argument appeals not only to the white people of the South but it is an argument, or an appeal, that has changed, or at least mollified, the policy of a large number of Northern newspapers and periodicals on the so-called race question in the South. And it has cooled the ardor of friends of the Negro in every part of the country.

In the matter of appointing Negroes to office there has been a great change in public sentiment of this country, and this change has made the Southern Oligarchy more secure in its position, and practically closed the question of Negro disfranchisement; and threatened punishment by reduction in representation is no longer considered. Under such conditions the power of the Oligarchy is absolute and nobody presumes to question it, crimes and corrupt practices increase, there is a complete breakdown of the whole system of jurispudence, and the ethical code and moral standard are relaxed.

At no time since the emancipation of the Negroes have Southern political leaders been more dictatorial in their demand that the whole race question, and its collateral issues, be treated as a "peculiar institution," precisely as defined and defended by Mr. Calhoun, the ablest and most earnest defender of slavery. The Oligarchy soon realized that the political work of Reconstruction could be easily undone; they were not concerned about social and economic ills which followed Reconstruction. They experienced little difficulty in trampling the laws under foot; the courts have upheld their construction of the law, and there is now no occasion for entertaining any fear of the law in carrying out their sectional policies and disregarding not only the political but, in a large measure, the civil rights of the Negro. Moreover, public opinion, as represented by the dominating faction of each of the two great political parties, supports the policies and practices of the Oligarchy, and the decisions of the courts, so far as the Negro question is concerned. It is therefore, a waste of time, under present conditions, to talk about relief through the courts, or remedial legislation.

A spirit of intolerance and the absence of free speech have made possible the lawless conditions which have so long prevailed in the South. A large majority of the people of the South are neither more dishonorable nor more dishonest, nor are they less patriotic than the citizens of other sections of the United States. It is in their political affairs that they have permitted an Oligarchy to debauch their institutions, retard their industrial progress, hinder their educational advancement and bring their social system under severe but just criticism. The governmental, social and industrial institutions of the Southern States are under control of an intolerant political party that punishes all criticism of its policies and methods. Under false teachings of their political leaders, the people have become provincial and morbidly sensitive. It has not been considered good form to make unfavorable comments on the propaganda or practices of the ruling Oligarchy.

Difference in political opinion is not tolerated in the South, and the capable and respectable citizens of these States who have had the temerity and fortitude to oppose the Oligarchy have been proscribed and persecuted, and have seldom escaped destruction when they were unwilling to bow to the autocratic will of the Oligarchy. This Oligarchy has ostracised, boycotted and, not infrequently, driven out of the country, robbed or murdered those who were not willing to accept its domination in public affairs and its dictation in private opinions.

William M. Lowe, of Alabama, was one of the early, able and fearless defenders of the civic and political rights of the people of Alabama, after the Reconstruction period, when the Oligarchy was in absolute control of every department of State Government and representation in Congress. Like every other fearless and capable leader who had the ability and fortitude to expose the corrupt practices of the Oligarchy, Mr. Lowe was proscribed and finally defeated, but while engaged in his patriotic campaign against the Bourbon Democrats, he ran for Congress and contested the seat of the Democratic candidate who was given the certificate of election. In that contest Mr. Lowe made a speech in his own behalf, in the House of Representatives, June 2, 1882, from which I quote the following reference to the "Bourbons," as leaders of the Oligarchy were designated at that time:

> The Bourbons are a law unto themselves; and it is a peculiar law of their own making and construing. The term Bourbon, moreover, as commonly used in the South, has no historical reference to that faithful party in France which clung to the Lilies, except perhaps in their common hostility to popular government and democratic institutions. . . .
>
> The Southern Bourbon is an organized appetite. His idea of politics is patronage; his sole conception of party is an organization which acquires and distributes the offices. The Bourbons, as Horace Greeley said of the carpet-baggers, whether many or few, "are a mournful fact." . . . The Bourbons indulge in practices that corrupt the fountain of politics. . . . They teach that opponents in politics . . . have no rights that Christians and patriots are bound to respect; . . . and that any agency, fair or foul, legal or illegal, that makes for the good of their party is just and right.

Some years ago, Mr. Thomas E. Watson, author and prominent politician in the State of Georgia, left the Democratic party; later, he came back in the organization of that party. However, when he was outside the Democratic party and fighting its candidates, *The Atlanta Constitution*, in an editorial comment, referred to a "very cowardly anonymous attack" upon Mr. Watson in the following words:

> *The Constitution* is moved to protest, with unqualified vehemence and indignation, against a cowardly, malignant and unspeakable attack on the private and public character of Thomas E. Watson. . . . So loathsome, so brutal and so utterly unjustifiable is the text of this document that *The Constitution* refuses to stain its columns or to pollute the sanctity of Georgia homes by quoting from those portions that are aimed at blasting the character of a prominent Georgian, who, as bitter as has been our political differences, has never been denied the attributes of honesty and sincerity by *The Constitution*.

For many years Mr. Watson was active and aggressive in exposing the corrupt practices of the Southern Oligarchy, and he was bitter and unrelenting in his attacks on the provincial policies of the leaders of the Oligarchy. Later, however, when he returned to the Democratic party and became one of its most radical leaders in supporting sectional prejudices and racial animosities, he was elected United States Senator, as the nominee of the Democratic party in the State of Georgia. While he was outside the party, attacking its policies and exposing its corrupt practices, Mr. Watson told the story of his experience as a victim of the proscriptive measures of the Oligarchy. From that narrative I quote the following:

If I committed a crime when I left the Democratic party, God knows I have been unmercifully punished for it. Seventeen years have I spent in the valley of political death. Storms of abuse have pursued me, without pity or cessation. Slander has nailed me to her cross, and bitter hatred has broken me on her wheel.

To tell the plain facts about conditions in the South is not considered in good taste, never prudent, and I have known the time and place when and where it was not safe to do so. It is the absence of free speech, an unwritten law against telling the whole truth, that keeps the South in thraldom. Give the people of the South free speech and free schools and the race question will take care of itself, crimes will decrease, peonage and persecution will not be more common in these than in other States. If it were considered proper or prudent, or even permissible, in the South to tell the whole truth in discussing public questions, to discuss frankly and openly the vital questions which concern the people, there would be no serious difficulty in dealing with the race question. Occasionally, some brave, patriotic citizen has had the temerity to tell the truth and to discuss public questions openly, as they are discussed in other parts of the country, and in other parts of the civilized world, but such freedom of speech did not long survive the intrigues and proscription of the Oligarchy. Mr. Lowe, to whose fearless course I alluded in a preceding paragraph, knew the proscriptive practices and provincial animus of the Oligarchy when he said:

I hated, moreover, to antagonize that dominant minority in our politics which finds its definition in Bourbonism and makes its last intrenchment in the Solid South. I hated to arouse that fell spirit which guards its despotism. I hated to invoke upon myself and friends that bitter and proscriptive feeling of personal and political hostility which characterizes its savage warfare.

Some years ago, *Uncle Remus's Home Magazine*, published in Atlanta, Georgia, had the courage to attack the provincialism and lawless practices of the Southern Oligarchy. In one of its several forceful articles, this magazine published excerpts from the speeches and writings of "Mr. Charles S. Barrett, head of an organization of two million Southern farmers," from which I quote the following:

Just as long as we give out the impression that we arrive at our political convictions by tradition and prejudice and not by logic and merit,—and that we absolutely refuse to listen to any save our own side of Presidential campaigns, we can just make up our minds to delay our own development and thwart our progress. . . .

The press of the South, whether sincerely or not, is Democratic. It reflects in the mass Democratic contentions. It suppresses any other contentions. The same thing applies to Southern politicians. They never discuss fairly the tenets of any save one party in the South. . . .

Did you ever think that the Civil War was fought throughout on the Southern side by a rank and file with not a cent's interest in slavery and its perpetuation?

Mr. Clarence H. Poe, a distinguished citizen of North Carolina, native of that State, a Democrat, and editor of *The Progressive Farmer*, understood the situation in the South and he stated it very clearly and forcibly when, in an article in *The North American Review* (October, 1902), he said:

But if the story of Reconstruction makes unpleasant reading for the Northern man, it is no less true that the Southerner finds much to humiliate him in the story of the succeeding epoch. Irregular election methods were adopted, demagoguery encouraged, bullyism condoned, politics corrupted.

Even when there was no real danger of negro supremacy, the race question as *The Baltimore Manufacturers Record* says, was often made a pretext to keep the white vote solid, and almost ostracize those who dared to speak their convictions on economic questions, if against the Democratic organization.

Former Attorney-General Thomas B. Gregory, prominent citizen of Texas, and a Democrat, frankly admitted the truth of the charge that a most unfortunate and serious situation had arisen in the South. In commenting on lawlessness and sectional prejudice, he said:

From the nightmare of Reconstruction and Ku Kluxism two things have been born which have wrought incalculable injury to the South and may continue to do so for a century to come. One of these is the ''Solid South'' and the other is contempt for law. The vicious, unconstitutional laws and our defiance of them left the South with no proper respect for constituted authority, with a disposition to right our wrongs and a contempt for all law not to our liking. This last is our crowning inheritance of woe for which our children and our children's children will suffer.

In support of charges relating to the provincial policies and proscriptive practices of the Southern Oligarchy, I have freely cited the testimony and the opinions of leading publicists and writers in the South who have had the fortitude to speak and write openly and frankly concerning the deplorable situation. Cumulative evidence and amplified opinions could be added from the material I have gathered on this phase of our discussion, but such augmentation would exceed the space to which I must limit this chapter. But let me emphasize the fact that the policies and practices of the Oligarchy have never had the conscientious support of the best intellects, the cultured citizens and most virile patriots of the South. In passing from this phase of our discussion I may add that the first President of the United States elected by the Democratic party, after Buchanan, freely expressed his unfavorable opinion respecting the menace of the Oligarchy that rules the South. Shortly before his death, ex-President Cleveland wrote a series of articles on the political situation, with special reference to conditions in the Southern States, from which I quote the following:

The South has long taken a stubborn, foolish pride in its enlistment under the democracy and has stood like a rock in its partisanship at times when there are now few who would not admit that had its stand been one in the grounds of victory, the consequences to the country, and particularly to the South itself, with her undeveloped industries dependent in their young growth on stable and favorable conditions at large would have been direly unfortunate and productive of injury that cannot be estimated.

It is unfortunate at all times, of course, that a rigid partisan spirit should hold certain sections of the country to whatever course of action is provided for them by the leaders of the party to which they are committed, no matter whether that principle defining the course be some innocent sophistry or some dangerous obsession of a set of blatant demagogues.

A few weeks after the inauguration of President Harding,

leaders of the Oligarchy, and the public in general, in the State of Georgia, were very much agitated over the exposures relating to peonage in that State, especially about the contents of a pamphlet by former Governor Dorsey, in which the writer stated a few plain facts generally known to the public regarding the lynching of Negroes and the prevalence of peonage in Georgia. There were few, if any, categorical denials of the charges contained in the writings of Governor Dorsey, but the fact that he had the courage to tell the truth caused indignation in Georgia, especially among leaders of the Oligarchy.

In letters to newspapers and at public meetings former Governor Dorsey was severely criticised. His successor, Thomas W. Hardwick, a former Representative in Congress and Senator from Georgia, judges of the State Courts and divers other public officials and preachers bitterly assailed the former Governor for no reason except that he had the courage to state a few plain facts relating to the condition of Negroes and the prevalence of crimes, of which the Negroes, in most cases, were the innocent victims. Happily, to the credit of Georgia, there were worthy citizens who had the manhood to defend the former Governor and uphold him in exposing and condemning the atrocities and cowardly lawlessness which had so long disgraced the State of Georgia. *The Atlanta Constitution,* for example, editorially supported Governor Dorsey, and on the same issue Mr. James B. Nevil, editor of *The Atlanta Georgian-American,* commenting on conditions in Georgia in particular, and on the deplorable situation in the South in general, said:

> We rarely can discuss this Negro problem it seems without immediately having our motives, our integrity of purpose and our inherent self-respect challenged—and usually with great vehemence and violence. . . . The very fact that one evokes passionate, bitter and violent replies to every suggestion of the kind he makes is sufficient proof that there is a problem there to discuss—and much unwillingness to discuss it fairly and calmly in the light of reason and common sense and squarely upon its merits.

It has been often stated that the proper thing to do, indeed the one essential thing to solve the race problem and other ills peculiar to the South, is to break the Solid South. This is a consummation devoutly wished for during many years. Wise men and good men have foretold the coming of this happy epoch which would mark the beginning of a new era for democracy and republican institutions in America. It has been the dream of every Republican President since Hayes and the more Republican Presidents we have with timorous and vacillating policies of administration in dealing with questions which are peculiar to the South, the more striking is the evidence of political solidarity in the Southern States.

The South came near the breaking-point during the second administration of Cleveland. Outwardly, it was more solid under the Wilson régime than it had been since 1880, but during the last year of the Wilson Administration there was turmoil beneath the surface. Surfeited with political power and gorged with spoils it had seized in the travail of civilization, ignorant and indifferent to the grave responsibilities it had assumed, the Solid South was not only a menace to the Nation but it had become a menace to itself. The Oligarchy is so well intrenched in economic and political power, the mass of the people are so prostrate, so utterly downtrodden, that they seem to have lost all civic and political initiative; and they have produced no leader with sufficient ability, courage and patriotism to fire them with an incentive.

'As we have seen, every one of the Southern States passed under the control of the Democratic party shortly after the inauguration of President Hayes. In the following Presidential election (1880), fourteen States, including the Border States of Kentucky, Maryland and Missouri, returned a solid Democratic majority, and in every national election down to 1896 these fourteen States gave a solid electoral vote for the Democratic ticket. The first break came in 1896, when Kentucky gave twelve of her thirteen electoral votes for the Republican ticket. In 1900 Kentucky went back to the Democratic party, but Maryland continued with the Republican party with her solid electoral vote; in 1908, Kentucky continued with the Solid South; Maryland gave only two of her eight electoral votes to the Republican ticket, but, for the first time, Missouri gave her solid electoral vote of eighteen to the Republican candidates. In the Presidential election of 1912, the Solid South included the fourteen States with the new State of Oklahoma added, and again in 1916, the Solid South, including Oklahoma, was composed of fifteen States, every one of which cast a solid electoral vote for the Democratic ticket.

The changes which I have cited in the preceding paragraphs have occurred in the Border States of Kentucky, Maryland and Missouri, but there have been no changes in the eleven States which composed the Southern Confederacy, except the change in the electoral vote of Tennessee in the election of 1920. In every Presidential election from 1880 to 1920, inclusive (except Tennessee in 1920), every one of the eleven States which seceded and joined the Southern Confederacy, and which compose the Solid South, has cast a solid electoral vote for the Democratic ticket.

In the Presidential election of 1920, the State of Tennessee gave a solid electoral vote to the Republican ticket, and, from one point of view, that was the first break in the Solid South and was hailed by many enthusiastic Republicans as an omen of the early dissolution of the Solid South. But it was only one of the incidents of the popular protest against the Wilson Administration as expressed in the election of 1920. The Republican party in Tennessee was stronger in organization and leadership than in other Southern States but, withal, it has not been very strong in organization or leadership in any of the Southern States during thirty years last past.

The repudiation of the Wilson Administration in the election of 1920 indicated grave apprehension on the part of the people, and a very decided purpose to get rid of the menace of the spoils system and provincial policies in national affairs. But the leaders of the Southern Oligarchy who dominate the national Democratic party are well trained in the methods which prevail in American politics. They are opportunists, shrewd, crafty, and, in numerous cases, they have been utterly unscrupulous in politics; and they have survived many defeats in national elections.

For nearly half a century the Southern Oligarchy has maintained a policy of proscription of all vigorous opposition to its policies and its rule. When proscription failed, lawless, and frequently criminal, persecution has been used to destroy all opposition. It is as true at the present time as it was when Mr. Blaine wrote the lines I have quoted, in which he charged the leaders of the Oligarchy with "tyranny of opinion which threatens timid dissentients with social ostracism and suppresses the bolder form of opposition by force." No leader of ability and character who has had the temerity to oppose the Southern Oligarchy has long survived; all vigorous opposition has been absorbed or destroyed. Having effectually absorbed or destroyed all white leadership which was capable of successfully opposing the Oligarchy, the next step was to eliminate the Negro so that he could never again be used as an ally or helper in any organization against the power or practices of the Oligarchy.

CHAPTER VI

Since the effectual disfranchisement of the Negro, by methods which will be discussed in our next chapter, the alleged fear of Negro domination, as claimed by leaders of the Southern Oligarchy, has found its most effective and popular expression in bitter and unrelenting opposition to the appointment of Negroes to official position under the Federal Government. Without regard to the fitness, the moral or mental equipment of the Negro for an office to which he may be appointed, this latest proscriptive propaganda has been the shibboleth of the Oligarchy. But it should be observed at the beginning of our discussion of this phase of the subject that it is only when Negroes are appointed by Republicans that such appointments appear offensive to leaders of the Oligarchy. If Negroes be appointed to public offices by Democrats, through the influence or at the request of Democratic politicians, it is not considered objectionable.

In no sort of political chicanery has the Southern Oligarchy shown more craftiness than has been observed in its propaganda against Negroes holding offices in the South. While advertising the worst phases of the situation, the Oligarchy has shown great finesse in educating the people of this country, North and South, to the point of approval, or quasi-assent, to its practices of race proscription; while at the same time, it has been the most active agency in doing those things which it knew would accentuate race prejudice in the South. To illustrate its wicked subterfuges in this matter, it should be observed that the Oligarchy has usually selected only bad Negroes whom it could use in its evil designs and corrupt practices.

I shall allude to only a few of the most striking examples of the abominable practices of the Oligarchy in using the Negro as a political scapegoat for the spoilsman. In this as in other flagrant practices of political corruption and lawlessness, the State of Georgia perhaps supplies the most shameless record.

During a political family quarrel among the leaders of the Oligarchy, plain facts were brought before the public in connection with the appointment of Negroes to official positions by prominent Democrats. *The Milledgeville News,* published at Milledgeville, Georgia, in commenting on the record of Hoke Smith while he was Secretary of the Interior in the Cabinet of President Cleveland, said:

Honorable Hoke Smith appointed Georgia Negroes to high government positions over Georgia white people, as well as those of other States, and appointed these Negroes, too, in preference to Georgia white applicants for positions. The salary of some of these positions amounted to from $2,000 to $3,000 per year, with short hours and agreeable work.

Another Georgia paper, *The Sandersville Progress,* referred to the coddling of Negroes by white political leaders in the Democratic party as follows:

Who does not recall that, right here in Georgia, the Democratic party was fighting its campaigns with hired Negro orators, and with "rope circulars?" Who does not remember that the Populist party was likewise using Negro orators in its campaigns and seating Negro delegates in its county and State conventions? Who disputes the fact that during this entire period all political parties and politicians everywhere were stirring to get the Negro vote by a liberal use of money and the still more liberal use of whiskey?

The Atlanta Constitution stated that David M. Turner, a son of the Negro, Bishop Turner, was appointed to a position in the Interior Department, in spite of the fact that the records showed that he had been dismissed from the service by a Republican administration. In fact, he had been dismissed several times before his appointment by Hoke Smith. *The Constitution* published a list of Negroes who were appointed to positions in the Department of the Interior by Mr. Smith while he was Secretary. This list included, among others, the following:

John P. Turner, son of Bishop Turner, appointed from Atlanta as a clerk in the Department of the Interior; promoted by Secretary Smith by assignment as a special examiner in the field with payment of all traveling expenses as well as salary. David M. Turner, son of Bishop Turner, appointed from Atlanta as assistant messenger in the Pension Office. Cornelius

King, son-in-law of Bishop Turner, appointed from Atlanta as chief messenger, Indian Commission; Mick Mitchell, jr., appointed from Atlanta as clerk in Pension office.

Another article in *The Constitution* relating to the record of Hoke Smith in appointing Negroes to office, contained the following:

The strongly criminating coincidence of the excellent positions given to the members of the family of Bishop Turner following, as those appointments did, the Bishop's strong letter written to President Cleveland in behalf of the appointment of Secretary Smith, has been clearly set forth in the columns of *The Constitution* and of other Georgia papers.

Hardly had he become safely settled in his office before he appointed Dave Turner, the Bishop's son, to the position of messenger at a salary of $840 a year, a far better place than he had been able to secure under the Republican administration. It is a remarkable fact that of the 209 "special examiners" (of all grades) shown by the Register of 1894, John P. Turner is the only Negro. And it is even more remarkable but true, as shown by the Register of 1891, that during the preceding Republican administration not a single Negro was given one of these "special examiner" places. Every man on the list during the Harrison administration was a white man.

In his campaign for Governor, Hoke Smith was running on a platform which favored the disfranchisement of Negroes, and his record in the appointment of Negroes to office was made one of the main issues of the campaign by those who opposed his nomination. Mr. Howell, editor of *The Atlanta Constitution*, published a list of fifty Negroes who had been appointed to offices by Mr. Smith, and at the same time it was charged that Mr. Smith had appointed more Negroes to offices under the Federal Government than had been appointed by any Republican Secretary of the Interior.

In his interesting book, *Our Brother in Black*, Dr. Atticus G. Haygood writes concerning a political campaign in Georgia from which I quote the following comment:

While I am writing this chapter an active canvas is going on in my own county, Newton, for county officers. Our men are patriotic and willing to serve their country in office. There is no lack of candidates; I suppose there never will be. . . . The candidate for Clerk of the County Court has no opposition, and he is the leading Republican in the county. One of the candidates for sheriff was in the old days a slaveholder and he will secure the largest Negro vote, although he is rated as a "stalwart" Democrat. All these candidates are courting the Negro vote. In their eyes, as to this election at least, "a Negro is as good as a white man," if not something better. Nothing is more certain than that every Negro vote deposited in Covington and at other precincts in this county, day after tomorrow, January 5, 1881, will be counted, and on that day the Negro vote will be courted and divided and counted all over Georgia.

A detailed narrative of other instances showing the dubious practices of the Oligarchy in connection with the Negro vote would go beyond the space to which I must limit this chapter. However, in order to amplify my narrative on this phase of the subject, I shall refer to two striking occurrences that came under my personal observation.

Judge James M. Hobson, father of Captain Richmond P. Hobson of Santiago *Merrimac* fame, and later Member of Congress from Alabama, was a native of North Carolina. The day after making his graduating speech at Chapel Hill, he enlisted in the Confederate Army without waiting for his own county to raise a company. He was captured at Spottsylvania in 1864 and was a prisoner of war for eighteen months. He moved to Hale county, Alabama, in 1867, and engaged in the practice of law. In 1892, he left the Democratic party and was a candidate for Judge of Probate on the fusion ticket in the great fight against election frauds and other political thievery so common in that State. He was very popular and was elected by a large majority, but was counted out in one of the most stupendous election frauds in the history of Alabama.

At the time of the war with Spain, Judge Hobson was in feeble health and unable to practice his profession. When news of the sinking of the *Merrimac* reached the world, Captain Hobson was the hero of the hour and numerous articles were published in the newspapers and magazines about the hero of Santiago and his family. Some over-zealous correspondent intimated that Judge Hobson had very little means. Immediately, there was a flood of letters from all parts of the country, offering financial assistance, which, of course, Judge Hobson politely declined. Later on, however, it was suggested that he accept the position of Postmaster at Greensboro, as his friends were quite certain that the President would be glad to appoint him.

Immediately, a Negro who had been private secretary to a Democratic Governor of Alabama, was announced as an applicant for the place. The application of the Negro received the support of leading Democrats.

When these facts were brought to the attention of President McKinley, he immediately appointed Judge Hobson and the appointment was promptly confirmed by the Senate. It may be interesting in this connection to call attention to the fact that the Negro applicant for Postmaster supported the propaganda for a new constitution for the purpose of disfranchising the Negroes; but, as a matter of course, the Negro was only a tool for the leaders of the Oligarchy, not only in his application for the position of Postmaster, but also in his support of the plans of the Oligarchy for disfranchising the Negroes. I am familiar with all the details of the other case to which I refer and which may be briefly stated as follows:

Colonel J— was a native of Talladega county, Alabama. He enlisted in the Confederate Army when he was under twenty years of age, and won distinction for personal courage and good judgment in action, especially at the battle of Chickamauga, where he reformed the line and saved the remnant of his brigade. After the close of the war, he returned to his farm and through years of hard work and good management, at the age of fifty, he owned a good farm and he was regarded as a well-to-do farmer. He was popular with the old soldiers on account of his splendid war record, and he was popular with the young men because he was enterprising and progressive and took an active personal interest in all measures looking to improvement of the condition of the farmers, advancement of education and other measures for the civic and industrial uplift of the people.

Colonel J— had never been allied with the Republican party; on the contrary he was considered a very staunch Democrat, until the corrupt practices of that party became unbearable to a man of his high sense of honor and keen appreciation of the duties of good citizenship. In the conventions of the party he protested against corrupt practices, both criminal and merely unscrupulous. He had never held office nor been a candidate for any office until he was put forward, in response to a popular demand, as the farmers' candidate for Judge of Probate. He ran on an independent "white ticket" and was supported by 80 per cent. of the white voters of the county. He was elected by an overwhelming majority, but counted out in the canvas of returns by Democratic officials in the most lawless and shameful manner.

During the campaign in which Colonel J— was a candidate and active worker, the Democratic Executive Committee hired a most disreputable Negro, who was "very smart," a good talker and had been employed frequently in the service of the Democratic spoilsmen. This Negro went over the country speaking in the interest of the Democratic party and denouncing as "poor white trash" the white people who had organized under the name of the "Jeffersonian Democracy" to resist the corrupt and oppressive practices of the Oligarchy. The Negro was introduced to an audience of white people in the town of Talladega, at the instance and under the personal direction of the Democratic candidate for Congress in the Fourth Congressional District. He was advertised as the "Honorable William—" and spoke in front of the Court House where, a few weeks before, a committee of highly respected white citizens of that county, some of whom were veterans of the Civil War, had been treated with indignity by the Judge of Probate when, in the exercise of their legal rights, they politely requested the appointment of representatives of their party at the polling places. The Negro, who was speaking for the candidates of the Democratic party, was advertised as a speaker of "great force and eloquence" whom the "ladies should go out to hear," and these announcements of the Negro speaker were signed by public officials and leaders in the Democratic party.

The Negro hireling of the Democratic Oligarchy got no respectable Negroes to follow him; his political allies and followers were among the leaders of the Democratic party. At a convention of the white people of Alabama, where there was an audience of more than 5,000 white men, at least four-fifths of whom were Confederate veterans or the sons of Confederate veterans, this Negro forced his way in and insisted on making a speech. He was saved from the fury of a justly indignant audience by the cool courage of Colonel J— and other Confederate veterans who were present and who displayed as much courage on that occasion as they had shown on the battlefield. It was a tribute to the manhood of those people that the Negro was not mobbed when it was well known that he had been going over the State ridiculing and denouncing some of the most highly respected white men in the State who would not follow the corrupt and lawless leadership of the Oligarchy.

Among the splendid articles which have been contributed to the newspapers and magazines, by publicists and writers of the South, who had the ability, the patriotism and the manhood to condemn the provincial policies and the corrupt practices of the Oligarchy, there is perhaps none which contains more truth, and which is more expressive of the high ideals and patriotism of the better class of citizens in the South, than the address to the white people of Georgia, by former Congressman Fleming of that State. Mr. Fleming stated the situation clearly and forcibly; and the warnings and admonitions of that address are as well suited to the present situation as they were applicable to conditions which existed at the time the address was published. Conditions have not improved and Mr. Fleming's words are so patriotic and wholesome that I quote from him at some length:

The controlling factors in the mob spirit are disregard of established law and hate or contempt for those it attacks. How many causes have recently been cooperating in that line from the theatre, the press, and the stump to familiarize us with disrespect for law and to arouse hate and contempt by the whites against the blacks.

Chief among offenders stands a former preacher, the Rev. Thomas Dixon, with his *Clansman*. The day after that play was presented in Augusta, in October, 1905, the Hon. Joseph B. Cumming of this city, a man who had proved his courage and his patriotism on many a bloody field in the late war, and who in the terrible days of reconstruction had been one of our most trusted defenders in the Ku Klux Klan—this gentleman of the old South, and of the best new South, wrote a scathing criticism of Mr. Dixon that deserves to be widely disseminated, both for its literary merit and its moral tone. Here is one paragraph:

"I regard this reverend gentleman's work in *The Clansman* as not only nasty—like all his writings—but fiendish, and worse still, cowardly. I say cowardly because it tends, if, indeed, it does not seek, to incite the more lawless part of our people to deeds of violence and cruelty to a defenseless class of our population who need, and by their general conduct deserve, protection and encouragement. May a blight follow the dirty money which the Rev. Dixon is putting in his pocket by his nasty play." . . .

The Hon. Hoke Smith, in his campaign for Governor on his anti-Negro platform, did conspicuous service in engendering and disseminating a disregard for law and a contempt for the Negro—the two leading factors in the mob spirit that broke out in his home city with such violence. He openly proclaimed upon the stump his purpose to subvert a part of the Federal Constitution on the suffrage question by a fraudulent administration of a proposed State law, and gave his audiences detailed explanations of how the fraud was to be perpetuated—this in addition to his lurid pictures of lynching bees in North Carolina, which seemed to meet his warm approval. . . .

Not only did Mr. Hardwick measure fully up to Mr. Smith in preaching disrespect for law and in advocating its fraudulent administration, but, as reported in the State papers, he repudiated any allegiance to the fifteenth amendment, and openly denied that it had ever become a binding part of the Constitution.

After the provincial and lawless element of the Democratic party came into control of our national affairs, in 1913, the agitation of race hatred was renewed with great vigor and resulted in serious race riots in various parts of the country. There has been a growing disposition on the part of certain leaders of the Oligarchy to push the Negro back and treat him with greater injustice. This is a part of the propaganda which has been used for many years to keep the Oligarchy in power in the South. Through divers corrupt and criminal practices, extending over a period of more than two decades, the power of the Southern Oligarchy had become supreme.

Memory of the dark days of Reconstruction, alleged fear of racial conflicts or Negro domination, were appeals to which the white people of the South listened, and attention to these appeals made possible the methods and practices of the Oligarchy. Finally, however, the leaders of this Oligarchy realized that some new methods must be introduced and that a new phase of their provincial propaganda was necessary in order to retain their power. The whole country was worn out with a discussion of the Southern troubles, precisely as it was worn out with a discussion of the slavery question when the Whig party surrendered to the demands of the Slave Oligarchy and passed into history.

The time was opportune for the effectual and permanent disfranchisement of the Negroes. This step was accepted as correct and wise in theory; it was said that there should be some legal regulations and qualifications for the franchise which would eliminate the illiterate and utterly incompetent Negro. But the plans of the leaders of the Oligarchy were not primarily to shut out the Negro vote. The Negro had ceased to vote. The first and essential purpose of further encroachment on the liberties of the people was to make the Oligarchy more secure in its control of the Government.

Ballot-box stuffing and other forms of corrupt practices had become so common that every branch of State and county administration was notoriously corrupt and, in many places, important official positions were held by corrupt politicians and their incompetent subordinates. Crimes were increasing and the South was prostrated under the rule of a privileged class of spoilsmen whose gain in power was in proportion to the public loss of moral stamina, intelligence, civic virtue and patriotism.

CHAPTER VII

The solidarity of the South, a thorough understanding and a perfect working organization among the leaders of the Bourbon Democracy, immediately followed the Reconstruction period and Republican rule in the Southern States. Under the domination and leadership of this organization, a very large majority of the white people of the South stood together, a political unit, regardless of civic or economic issues in national or local politics. The only question presented to the people and the only question which the ruling class would permit the people to discuss was the real or imaginary issue of white supremacy under rule of the Democratic party. The ruling class seized the opportunity and took advantage of the situation with political subterfuges and partisan astuteness that marked them as masters in political chicanery.

Election frauds had been started in the South for the alleged purpose of eliminating the Negro vote, and securing and maintaining white supremacy. Those who thought it worth while to offer an explanation very wisely said that it was more humane to manipulate the ballot against the Negro than to use brute force to drive him away from the polling-place. In short, election frauds were considered a good substitute for Ku Klux methods. It was generally accepted as the only solution, at that time, of a most dangerous situation.

The political leaders of the new Oligarchy in the South experienced little difficulty in persuading the white people that the Negro was the sole cause of their troubles. Many publicists and writers in the North have said that the enfranchisement of the Negro, so soon after his emancipation, was little less than a crime. The case was well stated by Booker Washington, who said in a public address:

In my mind there is no doubt we made the mistake at the beginning of our freedom by putting the emphasis on the wrong end. Politics and the holding of office were emphasized almost to the exclusion of every other interest, and we accepted responsibilities which our experience and education had not fitted us to perform with success and credit.

On one point all agree, and that is that the ballot has been a curse rather than a blessing to the Negro. Under the law, the Negro had a privilege which he could not exercise, and every attempt to exercise it independently or in opposition to the wishes of the ruling Oligarchy aroused the most bitter and unrelenting animosity of the white man.

The Oligarchy of the South has been so well fortified with what it claimed, and what has been generally accepted, as indisputable evidence in support of all charges they have made relating to corrupt practices during Reconstruction and Republican rule, that it has been taken for granted that they are just as well prepared to prove that ballot-box stuffing and other corrupt practices for the purpose of destroying all opposition to the rule of the Bourbon Democracy were started and continued for the sole purpose of securing white supremacy. But the claim is not true and the record shows that it is not true.

Corrupt practices in elections have been in the interest of the few, whose gain has been in proportion to the public loss, an essential part of the spoils system of the Southern Oligarchy. As Negroes were pushed back, whether by force or corrupt practices, it was soon discovered that election frauds were used quite as freely against white people who had the temerity to oppose the Democratic party as they had been used against the Negroes. The Negroes had ceased to take any interest in politics and they made no effort to vote; but if a division arose among the white people, the party in control, the Oligarchy that called itself the Democratic party, entered the names of Negroes on the polling list and counted them for the "regular Democratic ticket." It mattered not about issues or candidates; all opposition to the Oligarchy was met by election frauds sufficient to defeat it. Dr. Gladden, in his *Yale Lectures*, perhaps unwittingly but forcibly, described the leaders of the Southern Oligarchy when he said:

The man who by corrupt use of money manipulates caucuses and conventions, and debauches candidates and voters, thus poisoning at their source the streams of political power, is the most dangerous man in society to-day, albeit his guilt is shared by those managers of great corporations who furnish him with corruption funds. If our notions of justice were clearer, such men would not be abroad in society.

So much has been written since the Reconstruction period relating to election frauds in the South that the public generally is well acquainted with the details of these corrupt practices. In numerous contested election cases before the House of Representatives, testimony has been submitted time and again showing the general character of these frauds. Ballot-box stuffing was the term generally applied to the corrupt practices in elections. The common practice of those who perpetrated the frauds was to return majorities for the Democratic nominees, both in State and Federal elections, largely in excess of the actual number of votes cast. For instance, in what was known as the "Black Belt" sections of the Southern States, where the Negroes largely outnumbered the white voters, it was the common practice to enter the names of the Negroes on the poll list and count them as voters for the Democratic ticket, even when they never went near the polling-place on the day of election.

For the purpose of illustrating the enormity of election frauds in the South, as they were practiced prior to the constitutional provisions disfranchising the Negro, I shall refer briefly to my experience and observation during two campaigns in Alabama, when the white people had organized under the local name of "Jeffersonian Democracy," and fused in the State campaign with the Populist party.

In the campaign of 1892, and again in 1894, the organization of white people opposed to the Oligarchy and old Bourbon Democracy appealed to the Negroes to stay away from the polls. The Negroes answered the appeal by refusing to register; less than one per cent. of those of voting age actually registered. Reputable white citizens were appointed in practically every precinct in the State to watch the polls on election day. These white citizens, representing the organized opposition to the Democratic party, could not go inside the polling-place, but they could remain on the outside and testify as to the actual number of people who appeared at the polls during the election. After the election, numerous affidavits were made by these white citizens who watched the polling-places as to the number of voters who went to the polls, and in hundreds of cases it was shown that the fraudulent returns gave the Democratic ticket majorities largely in excess of the total number of people who appeared at the polls.

As shown by the affidavits of reputable white citizens who remained at the polls on election day and reported as to the actual number of persons who came there, the total of one county, for example, was only 1,031, but the falsified returns gave the alleged official vote as 6,431. Lowndes county, Alabama, where the Democrats always returned large majorities, was one of the "Black Belt" counties where the Negro population was six or seven times more than the white population. Numerous affidavits were made by watchers at the precincts in that county on election day, showing the actual number of voters who appeared at the polls. The whole story is summarized in an affidavit made by Mr. L. Reese, a highly respected white citizen of that county, as follows:

Affiant further states that he was present at Haynesville, the county seat of said Lowndes county, on the Saturday following said day of election, when the County Board of Supervisors canvassed the vote of said county; and affiant witnessed the canvass of the official vote of the County of Lowndes, at the same time taking down on paper the vote by precincts as called out by the Sheriff of said county, said Sheriff being one of said Board of Supervisors; that the total vote of Lowndes County, as canvassed by said Board of Supervisors, and as called out by said Sheriff, and noted down by the Clerk and others present, was two thousand two hundred and seventy-two (2,272) votes for Oates for Governor, and three hundred and sixty-one (361) votes for Kolb for Governor.

In the official declaration of the result of the State election in the different counties, as made by the Speaker of the House of Representatives of Alabama, the result is said Lowndes County was given as four thousand, nine hundred and ninety-five (4,995) votes for William C. Oates for Governor, and three hundred and sixty-one (361) votes for Reuben F. Kolb for Governor.

In the contested election case of William F. Aldrich vs. Thomas S. Plowman, from the Fourth Congressional District of Alabama (Fifty-fifth Congress), testimony was introduced by the contestant showing the character and extent of election frauds in that election. Like many other Congressional districts in the Southern States, the Fourth Alabama District was "gerrymandered," so as to include one or two black belt counties, where the Democrats could practice their frauds with little or no interference. In the election of 1894, Mr. Aldrich carried the white counties, in which he had a majority of 123. In Dallas County there were over 8,000 colored voters and less than 4,000 white voters. The falsified returns gave Mr. Plowman, the Democratic nominee, a large majority in Dallas County. If Mr. Plowman actually received the votes he claimed, as a matter of course he was elected by the Negro votes.

Two years before Mr. Plowman ran as the Democratic nominee against Mr. Aldrich, the Republican nominee, he was a candidate in the Democratic primary. It was a very bitter fight, but Mr. Plowman was supported by a strong organization with leaders and workers who were well trained in the practices of the Democratic party. There were charges of stupendous frauds in the primary and *The Selma Times*, a leading Democratic newspaper in Alabama, contained an editorial from which I take the following:

The Times is Democratic—warp, woof, and filling. . . . It stands by the nominees of the Democratic party, it gives aid nor comfort to the candidates named by the enemies of our party. But at the same time it raises the red flag of danger and burns the red lights of Democratic peril.

A primary election, so-called, to nominate a Democratic candidate for Congress in this district has just been held. The frauds in that election were patent, gross, palpable, and indefensible. The nominee's best friend dare not try to defend him on the stump; the party's most devoted adherent is powerless to condone them on the hustings.

The nominee may be, and doubtless is, a man of great probity of character and spotless integrity. He may have none of those small vices which are common to humanity; but he is, or hopes to be, the beneficiary of corruption more disgraceful than has ever dishonored the party in this State.

Among the active workers and influential citizens who were leaders in the "Jeffersonian Democracy" which was opposed to the Oligarchy in Alabama, in the great reform movement of 1892-94, was Judge Hobson, of Hale County, father of Captain Richmond Pearson Hobson. Judge Hobson and one of his sons, Mr. S. A. Hobson, testified that in precinct number seven of Hale County, there were 58 voters registered, as officially stated by the Judge of Probate and the Registrar of that County, but that the falsified returns from that beat gave a vote of 504—a steal of 446 votes in the interest of the Democratic ticket. These gentlemen further testified that in precinct number one of said county one of the managers of the election refused to sign the returns because of gross irregularities and falsifications, and "said manager appeared before the Board of Supervisors at the request of witness for the purpose of giving evidence, but the Democratic board refused to entertain a motion to set aside the illegal returns." Another witness from Hale County, a white man of high standing who had distinguished himself in the Confederate Army, testified that he remained at the polling-place of the voting precinct in which he resided from the time the polls opened until they closed, and that 52 voters and no more entered the polling-place; but the falsified official returns from that precinct showed a total of 368 votes, a majority of 360 for the Democratic candidate.

Hale County, where the frauds referred to in the preceding paragraph were perpetrated, was for many years one of the most notorious in election frauds and other corrupt practices under rule of the Democratic party. It is the "Black Belt" county of the Ninth Congressional District, formerly represented by Representative, now Senator, Underwood of Alabama. In the first election in which Mr. Underwood appeared as a candidate for Congress, his seat was contested, and in the contest before the House of Representatives the frauds of which he was the beneficiary were exposed. He was unseated on the last day of the 54th Congress. Since that election, up to the present, no opposition to the Democratic party has developed sufficient strength to make an active fight against the Democratic candidate in that district.

Concerning election frauds in the State of Georgia, an editorial in *The Atlanta Constitution,* of November 8, 1894, two days after the Congressional election, contained the following comment:

The less said about the Congressional election in the Tenth District the better for the good name of the State. The methods which characterized that election reproach the civilization of the day and stigmatize the fair name of Georgia as the most advanced in sentiment and substance of all

the Southern States. . . . We protest in the name of the honesty of our
people and the civilization of our State. If the Legislature of Georgia does
not pass an election law which will guarantee honest elections in every
county in Georgia, those who are responsible for such failure will have upon
their hands the blood of those who might hereafter be sacrificed at the
ballot-box, as in Augusta, as the victims of an incompetent and inadequate
election system. . . .

Richmond County polled 16,000 votes. . . . The census of 1890 gives
Richmond County a population of 45,194. Based on the vote of last Tues-
day its population is shown to be nearly 80,000.

In a speech in the House of Representatives, George White,
of North Carolina, the last Negro Member of Congress, to whom
I have already alluded, some details were given relating to
election frauds in North Carolina. Congressman White said:

The Democrats of North Carolina got possession of the State and local
government since my last election in 1898 . . . and the brother of Mr. Kitchin will succeed me. . . . In the town where this young gentleman was
born, at the general election last August for the adoption of the constitutional amendment, and the general election for State and county officers,
Scotland Neck had a registered white vote of 395, most of whom, of course,
were Democrats and a registered colored vote of 534, virtually if not all
of whom were Republicans, and so voted. When the count was announced,
however, there were 831 Democrats to 75 Republicans; but in the town
of Halifax, same county, the result was much more pronounced. In that
town the registered Republican vote was 345, and the total registered vote
of the township was 539, but when the count was announced it stood 990
Democrats to 41 Republicans; or 492 more Democratic votes counted than
were registered votes in the township.

Comment here is unnecessary. It would be unfair, however, for me to
leave the inference upon the minds of those who hear me that all of the
white people of the State of North Carolina hold views with Mr. Kitchin
and think as he does. Thank God there are many noble exceptions to the
example he sets, that too, in the Democratic party; men who have never
been afraid that one uneducated, poor, depressed negro could put to flight
and chase into degradation two educated, wealthy, thrifty white men.

Election frauds have not been limited to the Southern States.
In Ohio, Illinois and Delaware especially, there have been stupendous frauds, and in the State of New York there have been
corrupt practices in elections, especially where the Democratic
party was in control of the election machinery. Corrupt practices in the Northern States differ from those in the Southern

States in that they are more venal and consist rather in buying the purchasable vote than in falsifying election returns.

There is a marked difference in the methods of corrupt practices in the Southern States and those which have occurred sporadically in the Northern States. In the Southern States the frauds have not been limited to any particular locality; they have occurred in every one of these States, and these corrupt practices have been approved and openly defended. In many cases the beneficiaries have boasted of the frauds and have challenged prosecution. In other sections of the country, outside the South, legislation against corrupt practices, supported by a strong moral sentiment of public opinion, has usually resulted in having the guilty parties punished; while in the Southern States, not only has there not been any prosecution for corrupt practices in elections, but public opinion, so far as it is represented by the leaders of the Oligarchy, has approved these practices.

The latest effort for Federal supervision of elections in the Southern States was in 1890, when Senator Lodge, then a member of the House from Massachusetts, at the request of President Harrison, offered a bill which passed the House on July 2, 1890, but did not reach the Senate until the short session of the 51st Congress, where it was finally defeated after a very bitter and prolonged filibuster by a combination between the Democratic leaders and "free silver" Republican Senators. Senator Arthur P. Gorman, of Maryland, led the fight against the bill for the Democrats. He was a skilled parliamentarian and a very stubborn fighter, and he compelled the Republicans to abandon the contest.

The defeat of the "Force Bill," as this measure was called, was followed by what was known as the "Free Silver Bill," which received the support of the Southern Democrats, and that was the price, it was charged, which the Democrats paid to the "free silver" Republicans for their opposition to the Force Bill. The Democrats urged with their usual political sagacity that if the Force Bill became a law it would give the Federal Government the right to employ Federal troops at the polling-places in the Southern States, and in that way practically insure the election of Administration candidates at all national elections.

The Populist movement in 1892-94 gave the people of the South the first opportunity, after the Reconstruction period, which they could use in an open and organized fight against the Oligarchy. And it was an opportunity which a large majority of the white people seized with avidity and patriotic fervor. The "hill-billies," the poor whites, well-to-do farmers, and a large number of the better and more intelligent class of the old aristocracy, united in a common patriotic cause, without reference to past party affiliations or social positions, for the purpose of destroying the power of the notoriously corrupt Oligarchy. This fusion of the better class of white people gave little heed to the teachings of the platform of the national Populist party; a majority of the fusionists did not approve the Populist platform, but in the agitation they heard the bugle call of American liberty and they recognized the old flag of democracy and they answered the call to arms. They rallied as they have always rallied for the cause of liberty and democratic institutions when they had capable and fearless leaders.

It was a political campaign in time of peace, but in numerous cases such free speech as there was, for those who opposed the Oligarchy, had to be backed up with arms. At the voting precincts, and when the election returns were canvassed before the County Boards, those fearless, liberty-loving patriots were present with their arms, and in that way, for the first time in many years, they were able to secure a measurably free ballot and a fair count. The result was the most serious break which has occurred in the Solid South since the close of the Reconstruction epoch.

During the exciting campaigns of 1892-94, the leaders of the Oligarchy did not limit their spoliations to corrupt practices in elections and jury-fixing. They resorted to every conceivable act of robbery, proscription, violence and murder against their white neighbors who had the temerity to expose the corruption and to protest against the lawless acts of the Oligarchy. In short, they used against the white people the same cowardly, brutal measures which they had so long used against the defenseless Negroes. Moreover, the leaders of the Oligarchy encouraged and supported, openly and shamelessly, a propaganda of racial animosity on the part of the most ignorant and depraved

Negroes against the white people who openly opposed the Oligarchy. Leaders of the Oligarchy and public officials closed the doors of court houses and other public meeting halls where people were accustomed to assemble, to the white people, and opened them to their hirelings, the most disreputable and venal Negroes. They were never able to hire the more intelligent and better class of Negroes. The class of venal Negroes whom the Oligarchy was able to buy were used as tools against the white opposition. Those Negroes were sent over the country to harangue those who would attend their meetings; vilifying the whites who opposed the Oligarchy, ridiculing them as "poor white trash."

In many cases, leaders in the Democratic party hired disreputable Negroes to run for office against intelligent, respectable white men who opposed the nominees of the Democratic party. No carpet-bagger ever engaged in more infamous, cowardly and dangerous practices than the methods employed by leaders of the Oligarchy in using the venal Negro for the purpose of arousing race prejudice against the whites who opposed the Democratic party. In the long list of corrupt practices and crimes which have been charged against the carpet-baggers, there is nothing more sordid, more blatantly felonious, and better adapted to the propagation of race hatred, than the measures instigated and systematically carried out by the Oligarchy in the South for the purpose of destroying all white opposition to its policies and practices.

Fortunately for the whites who opposed the Oligarchy, and greatly to the credit of the Negroes, there were very few Negroes whom the leaders of the Oligarchy could buy at any price. The more intelligent and better class of Negroes voluntarily offered their services to the white people who, without reference to past party affiliations, were organized against the Democratic party. A very large majority of the Negroes were ready and willing to serve in any capacity, without price or the hope of reward, and to meet any sacrifices and dangers in order to serve the white men who were fighting for the preservation of American institutions. But they were told to stand aside and let the fight be among the white people, so that there could not, in fact, be any issue respecting the alleged danger of

Negro domination. The Negroes stood aside and, in spite of the entreaties and inducements of the Democrats, less than one per cent. of the Negro men who were of voting age and legally qualified electors went to the places for registration. They did not register and they did not vote, yet, where they were not carefully guarded by armed men, the registration lists were falsified and the ballot-boxes stuffed in the interest of the Democratic candidates.

I have frequently heard the story of the Negroes' fidelity and fortitude during the Civil War; in numerous cases, Confederate soldiers have testified to the heroic courage of their Negro servants on the battlefield. Their physical and moral courage came under my personal observation after the war. In the political campaigns of 1892-94, I was neither an office-holder nor an office-seeker, but I was in the fight and I know how and where the Negro stood.

An active propaganda for disfranchisement of the Negroes was started by the Oligarchy shortly after the State campaigns of 1892, immediately following the first organized white opposition to the Democratic party, which so clearly and forcibly revealed the numerical weakness of the Oligarchy. The spirit of unrest which was so strikingly shown in the campaigns of 1892-94, followed by the defeat of so many Democratic candidates in the South in the Presidential election of 1896, was a warning to the Oligarchy. In those days there were "free silver" Democrats, "gold-bug" Democrats and a few fiat money Democrats, but the main organized opposition to the Democratic party in the South was found among the white people who had only one plank in their platform and that was a demand for a "free ballot and a fair count"; all other local and national issues were subordinated to this vital question.

The situation was ominous and leaders of the Oligarchy did not fail to see the gravity of those portentous events. They realized that at last the life of their organization was in peril; they awoke to the inescapable fact that the situation demanded desperate measures in order to retain their power. The conspiracy then entered into in order to perpetuate the power of the Oligarchy was carried out in every detail and in the most shameless and lawless manner.

The first corrupt practices carried on by the Oligarchy, in order to destroy all opposition to its rule, were election frauds which consisted, as already stated, in falsifying enumeration lists, stuffing ballot-boxes which came into their possession, and stealing ballot-boxes which had been so carefully guarded that they could not be stuffed. The next step was the enactment of election laws which placed the whole election machinery in the hands of the appointees of the Democratic administration, in both State and Federal elections, and effectually disfranchised all Negroes and a large number of whites who would not vote the Democratic ticket. Concerning the outrageous election laws passed in the Southern States, I am quoting some excerpts from a forcible article by the late Colonel Henry Watterson, commenting on the notorious election law passed in Kentucky, which was a fair sample of the election laws that were enacted by the Democratic party in other Southern States. The article by Colonel Watterson occupied a whole colmun in *The Louisville Courier Journal.* In the course of it he said:

> The people may well stand aghast before the revolutionary election bill which has like some dread monster suddenly emerged from the fastness of passion and error through which the Legislature has been spreading its tortuous way. It is safe to say that annals of free government will be sought in vain for anything approaching its shameless effrontery and unconcealed deformity. The records of reconstruction furnish nothing to compare with it. The Brownlow despotism in Tennessee was considered tolerably reckless and tolerably thorough in its day. But the Brownlow despotism at its worst ventured upon nothing so boldly, wholly bad as this.
>
> In all the force bills meditated by the radicals in Congress during the dark days of reconstruction there were discernible some pretense and pretext some lingering memory of republican instincts and traditions. . . . This force bill gives the voters of Kentucky not a ray of hope. Such measures always react and rebound. The brood of evils they invoke always come home to roost. The suggestion of so reckless a record is a confession of weakness. It is an open declaration that its authors dare not meet the people face to face in the open. It is the reconstruction out of the depths of infamy and disgrace where the people laid them, of wornout and castoff methods and policies, and their application to the supposed exigencies of a faction of democratic politicians who proclaim themselves to be, except for this device, both impotent and bankrupt.

Corrupt practices had become so common, so bald and notorious in the Southern States, that the whole country felt humiliated and besmirched. The rule of the Oligarchy was menaced by the rising tide of outraged public opinion, and the life of the organization which ruled the South was in immediate jeopardy. Some changes were absolutely necessary, and in order to cloud the real issue and preserve the power of the ruling faction, the Negro was again dragged into the white man's fight and made the scapegoat of the white man's sins. New life was injected into the race issue when it was decided that the time was opportune for disfranchisement of the Negroes and extending the power of the Oligarchy by radical and revolutionary changes in the organic law. There is one further point to which attention should be called. It has been emphasized by Maurice S. Evans, in his excellent work under the title of *Black and White in the Southern States,* from which I take the following:

We must remember also that behind all these elaborate legal provisions is the gun. Before the South had begun to legalize the position, the Negro had practically relinquished the rights conferred on him by the Federal Government. He had been made to see quite clearly that if he persisted in claiming and exercising the right, he would be killed, and at the present time if he cannot be kept out by legal enactments he will be kept out by force, which would not, if necessary, stop short of murder.

The story of the methods adopted and the proceedings in connection with the changes that were made in the constitutional provisions relating to the franchise is a disgusting narrative of the abominable practices of the provincial spoilsmen and lawyer politicians. A narrative of the actual occurrences and proceedings will expose the diabolical plans of the instigators of the conspiracy against respectable whites who were not allied with the exploiters, as well as against the Negroes. In wrangling amongst themselves, as usual, the leaders of the conspiracy confessed the wickedness and injustice of their plans and at the same time they exposed the fallacy of the excuses which they had given for their corrupt practices and unfriendly attitude towards the Negro. The story of disfranchisement in one State is substantially the same as that in every one of the Southern States. They differ only in minor details, and as I am more familiar with the details of what occurred in Alabama, I shall narrate the salient events relating to disfranchisement there.

When the propaganda of race hatred and alleged fear of
Negro domination had reached a point where the leaders of
the Oligarchy thought the time opportune, the agitation for
calling a Constitutional Convention was made the main party
issue. At a State convention of the Democratic party, the
Chairman of the State Executive Committee, in addressing the
convention, said:

The Democratic party has been in absolute control of the State government for twenty-four years, almost a quarter of a century. It cannot
be denied that our election laws are defective, and that the punishment
of fraud is difficult if not impossible. . . . Purity of administration must
exist from the office of the chief executive down to the humblest manager of an election. If corruption in one is approved or tolerated, as sure
as night follows day, it will ultimately lead to the corruption of the other,
and I may say of all others. The results of such influence will enter every
branch of society. It will reach your bank cashiers and affect positions of
trust in every department. It will ultimately enter your courts and affect
the administration of justice.

This confession by the executive head of the party brings us
face to face with the actual situation immediately preceding the
calling of the Constitutional Convention, for the purpose, as
stated by the Chairman of the State Committee, "to put the
control of the government in the hands of the intelligent and
virtuous." With full knowledge of actual conditions, the Chairman of the Democratic State Executive Committee further
said at the convention of that party:

Under the able leadership of our present chief executive the party in
the State is stronger in the confidence and affection of the people and
better organized to meet and contend with the enemy than it has been for
a number of years past.

Here was an anomalous state of affairs. First, the party was
"stronger in the confidence and affection of the people than it
had been for a number of years." Second, it had been "in
absolute control of the State government for twenty-four years."
Third, the party was so corrupt that its lawlessness had created
a dangerous "influence" which would "enter every branch of
society, reach bank cashiers and affect positions of trust," and
"ultimately enter the courts and affect the administration of

justice.'' The conditions were as stated by the Chairman of the Executive Committee when a convention was called to make a new Constitution which would effectually and permanently disfranchise the Negroes.

When the convention met, the purpose of the delegates was to make a Constitution that would disfranchise the Negroes. That was the avowed purpose and that was what was done. The proceedings of the convention were not harmonious. Practically all the discussion was on the clause of the Constitution that regulated the franchise. There were a few delegates to that convention who did not hesitate to speak the truth. It is to the record which these far-seeing men left that we must look for the true story of the disfranchisement of the Negroes by constitutional provisions. One of the delegates, Robert J. Lowe, a prominent lawyer of Alabama, and former Chairman of the Democratic State Executive Committee, said:

This convention meets to-day in response to the call of the people of Alabama for fair elections. You may observe the difference between fair elections and elections made possible under the report of the majority of the committee. If there be a difference, Mr. President, I wash my hands of it. I stand here now pleading for fair elections in Alabama, not for white supremacy. . . . White supremacy was established in 1874 and has never been threatened. . . . White supremacy is secure in Alabama. . . . It is a plan that renders possible infamous frauds in Alabama, the most infamous ever perpetrated in Alabama, because they will be written in your constitution.

Captain Frank White, another delegate and distinguished lawyer, said:

By one clause you have formed a group or class who cannot register or vote unless they are of good character and understand the duties and responsibilities of citizenship. By the other clauses you have made a group or class in which you say they shall have the right to register whether they meet the standard or not. . . . Your distinguished Senator, General Pettus, one of the best lawyers in the South, after having investigated it, for the purpose of determining whether or not it was in violation of the Constitution, declared that it was. He investigated it for the Louisiana senators at their request. The provision in the Louisiana suffrage plan is not different in effect from ours, and he gave it as his written opinion that it violated the Fifteenth Amendment. He is now opposed to this clause, and that other distinguished Senator (Morgan) from this State is also opposed to it.

Ex-Governor Oates, who for many years was a member of Congress from Alabama, and later elected Governor on the Democratic ticket was a member of the convention and made a speech from which I take the following:

It has frequently been asserted that the primary object in calling this Constitutional Convention was to completely eliminate the Negro from politics, or disfranchise the Negro. . . . Isn't it in fact a discrimination? If it be a discrimination then it is in violation of that clause of the Constitution. When I feel that this clause is contrary to the oath I have taken I cannot support it. Even if it is a matter of doubt, I would rather not do it. It is not consistent. Such action would not be consistent with my oath to support the Constitution of the United States. . . . We claim a good deal for ourselves, as being Democrats, standing on Jeffersonian democracy, and if we do, ought we to adopt any questionable means here in order to give a white man preference over the Negro? Do you suppose that any white man would be proud of legislation which gave him such an advantage, to keep him out of competition with the Negro for the obtainment of the political rights? If so, the man that seeks such an advantage as that is unworthy of having it.

Ex-Governor Thomas G. Jones, later United States District Judge, said:

There is not a man within the sound of my voice who will not answer in his own mind, if not to the world, if you ask him the question, what is your purpose in this plan of suffrage—that it is my purpose, as far as I can constitutionally, to strike down the suffrage of the black race and uphold the suffrage of the white race.

These expressions of opinion on the real purpose and actual work of the convention are from lawyers who held high positions in the Democratic party, and who never had been affiliated with any other party, and several of whom had served with distinction in the Confederate Army. The Democratic Campaign Committee issued an address to the white people of Alabama which was a part of the propaganda in favor of disfranchising the Negro and in support of the new Constitution made for this purpose. This address contained the following statement:

The party platform pledged that white men would not be disfranchised. To frame a provision that would observe this pledge and eliminate the mass of vicious Negro votes, and yet be constitutional, was no light task, but to it the Democratic members of the convention addressed themselves. . . .

And we unqualifiedly renew our party's pledge that under the operation of the registration feature of the new Constitution no white man who can now vote will be disfranchised. . . . White men insist upon their rights, and will not submit to disfranchisement by any registrars, but if necessary will prove their right to register before a jury of their neighbors. The registrars will know this and will not refuse to register them except for good cause. Besides this, it must be presumed that the registrars who will be appointed by high officials in the party that has always stood for white man's supremacy, will be in sympathy with the best methods yet devised to secure it.

When a man applies for registration, he will not be asked to specify under which class he is entitled to register. The list will not show under what clause he is registered. When the party's pledge not to disfranchise any white man is remembered, it is easy to see that the above plan will effectuate it.

The Honorable S. J. Bowie, a lawyer of prominence, who was later elected a Representative in Congress from the Fourth Alabama District, was one of the leading proponents and he made an active campaign for the new Constitution. In one of his speeches during the campaign Mr Bowie said:

In the counties where the Negroes were in the majority it was necessary to hold dishonest elections. The men who stole these votes were patriots, and though it was revolution, it was necessary to preserve liberty and white supremacy. . . . Under these provisions there are not five Negroes out of a thousand who would not be disfranchised, while not a white man would lose his right to vote.

Mr. Bowie further said that dishonesty had gradually spread from the "Black Belt" counties where it was necessary to the counties where it was unnecessary, and that the evil was becoming alarming, and that a new Constitution had to be made to preserve the purity of the ballot. He also referred to a statement to the effect that in Randolph, a white county, it was necessary to buy Negro votes because they held the balance of power. In commenting on the suffrage clause of the temporary plan for registration, Mr. Bowie explained how a soldier who had served in any war as an American, or the descendant of an American soldier in the Revolutionary War, or any other war in which this country had been engaged, could register in spite of his lack of educational or property qualifications. If there were any white men whom that clause did not reach they could register and vote if of good character and understood the duties of citizenship. In an address delivered in New York City, July 4, 1904, after his election to Congress, Mr. Bowie said:

> This is the philosophy of our new Constitution. No holier purpose, no nobler cause, ever guided the brains or touched the hearts of men than this. . . . It has been alleged that this clause is a limitation upon the suffrage under which all white men could vote and all Negroes be disfranchised. Nothing is further from the truth. The sole effect of the provision was to increase, not to limit the number of voters, both white and black. . . . It has been asserted that the Negro as a race is disfranchised in the South. How untrue is that assertion let the record speak.

Speaking in Alabama, this gentleman tells his audience that "under these provisions there are not five Negroes out of a thousand who would not be disfranchised, while not a white man would lose his right to vote." In New York, he tells his audience that "nothing is further from the truth" than the assertion that under the provisions of the new Constitution in Alabama all white men could vote while practically all Negroes were disfranchised. To say that his position was untenable and illogical would be a very mild criticism of his contradictory statements. I have already alluded to the fact that Mr. Bowie was spokesman for his party and one of the leading proponents of the new Constitution.

The protests of prominent Democrats who were delegates to the convention that made the new Constitution in Alabama, the propaganda published by the Democratic Campaign Committee in urging the people to vote for the Constitution, and the speeches of the protagonists of the Constitution, all justify the conclusion that the laws regulating the elective franchise were made for the purpose of disfranchising the Negro. In the provisions relating to the suffrage the elective franchise is absolutely under the control of registrars, and these registrars are elected or appointed by the party in power. Note the clause from the Campaign Committee propaganda of the Democratic party, in an appeal to the white people:

> The registration will be conducted by three reputable and suitable persons in each county, appointed by three Democratic State officials. When

the party's pledge not to disfranchise any white man is remembered, it
is easy to see that the above plan will effectuate it.

Could language be plainer than this? Would it be possible
for any man to express his purpose in more emphatic words?
Yet time and again we have heard from the lecture platform
and read in the papers and periodicals, that there is no race
discrimination in the laws regulating the franchise, that the
Negro has the same privileges as the white man, and need only
qualify himself as the white man is required to do.

"Only by grace of the registration officials." This is the crux
of the situation; it was so stated in the Democratic propaganda
and acknowledged by the leaders of the Oligarchy that forced
the measure upon the people under the specious plea of preserv-
ing white supremacy. The real purpose of the new Constitution and the reactionary legislation regulating the franchise
was to destroy all opposition to the radical and provincial
faction of the Democratic party then and still in power. The
Negro had already been effectually disfranchised; there had
been some comment on the methods used to effect his disfranchisement, but the result had been accepted, not only by the
white people of the South, but also by the North, and there
was but little complaint from the Negroes. Contests from the
Southern States in Congressional elections had grown so expensive and burdensome and were received with such poor grace,
that they were practically abandoned after Mr. McKinley's first
term.

In an article on *Reduction of Representation in the South*,
which was published in *The Outlook* (New York), January 21,
1905, Mr. John B. Knox, of Alabama, President of the Constitutional Convention, upheld the Alabama Constitution and its
makers on the assertion that there was nothing in that Constitution at variance with the provisions of the Fourteenth Amendment. Mr. Knox said:

I know of no Southern State which has prescribed as a condition to suffrage any other than an educational or property qualification, and am unable to understand how any well-trained lawyer can reach the conclusion
that constitutional provision—whether adopted by a State in the South
or in the North—prescribing an educational or property qualification, can

be considered as an abridgment of the privilege of suffrage within the meaning of the Fourteenth Amendment. Judge Cooley, in his work entitled, *The General Principles of Constitutional Law in the United States of America,* in discussing the Fourteenth Amendment, says: "To require the payment of capitation tax is no denial of suffrage; it is demanding only the preliminary performance of public duty, and may be classed, as may also the presence at the polls, with registration, or the observance of any other preliminary to insure fairness and protect against fraud. Nor can it be said that to require ability to read is any denial of suffrage."

As stated in the editorial comment of *The Outlook,* Judge Cooley is "excellent constitutional authority," but there is a touch of irony in the fact that the strenuous defenders of Jeffersonian Democracy should find it necessary to resort to such subterfuges in defending their attitude and practices in regulating the suffrage. Among the cherished aphorisms of Mr. Jefferson, so frequently quoted by his followers, before they undertook the work of making constitutions to fit their partisan necessities, we find the following reference to popular suffrage:

The influence over government must be shared by all the people. If every individual which composes their mass participates of the ultimate authority, the government will be safe. In a government bottomed on the will of all. the life and liberty of every individual citizen becomes interesting to all. . . . The equal rights of men and the happiness of every individual are the only legitimate objects of government.

In his *Democracy in America,* De Tocqueville says:

There is no more invariable rule in the history of society; the further electoral rights are extended, the greater is the need of extending them; for after each concession the strength of the democracy increases and its demands increase with its strength.

The president of the convention that made the new Constitution for the State of Alabama, and others who have undertaken to defend the action of the Southern States in making constitutions with provisions which would effectually disfranchise the Negroes, should read a little further so that they could get another viewpoint from *Cooley on Constitutional Limitations,* as expressed in the following paragraphs:

All regulations of elective franchise, however, must be reasonable, uniform and impartial; they must not have for their purpose, directly or indirectly, to deny or abridge the constitutional rights of citizens to vote, or unnecessarily impede its exercises. If they do, they must be declared null and void. . . .

The Fifteenth Amendment, it will be seen, does not forbid denying the franchise to citizens except upon certain specified grounds, and it is a matter of public history that its purpose was to prevent discrimination against persons of African descent.

The methods adopted in Georgia differed from those used in Alabama and several other Southern States when new constitutions were adopted for the purpose of disfranchising the Negro. In 1910, Hoke Smith, former Governor of Georgia, was a candidate against Governor James M. Brown, who wished renomination. Mr. Smith had been defeated two years before by Mr. Brown. "It was a fight to get back by Smith and to stay in by Brown." While Mr. Smith was Governor in 1908-9, he secured enactment of laws for disfranchising Negroes, and for drastic regulation of elections, closing the registration books six months before the election. Brown opposed the six months closing, holding that ninety days was enough. It was on these issues that the campaign was waged. The result was a victory for Mr. Smith, and he accordingly became the Democratic nominee for Governor. The Democratic State Convention endorsed all the measures advocated by Mr. Smith while he was Governor; but there were a few good citizens in the Democratic party who had the courage to oppose some of the party policies under his leadership. Among other prominent citizens of Georgia who expressed their indignation over the operation of the registration law, was Mr. J. A. Henderson, who had been a member of the Legislature and a supporter of Governor Smith. After he had "seen the effects of it and studied it," Mr. Henderson wrote a letter to *The Atlanta Constitution,* in which he said:

I am fearful that the great anxiety to disfranchise the Negro has caused us to go into extremes on the registration question, disqualifying thousands of good white men from having any voice in selecting the officers to serve the people.

Further concerning the policies advocated by Governor Hoke Smith in regulating the franchise, *The Atlanta Constitution* published an article by former Congressman William H. Fleming of

Augusta, in which, commenting on the disfranchisement of the Negroes, he said:

> Mr. Hoke Smith's platform: ''I am in favor of passing a state law to disfranchise the Negro.'' Constitution of the United States: ''The right of citizens of the United States to vote shall not be denied or abridged by the United States or any state on account of race, color or previous condition of servitude.'' If the purpose thus avowed by Mr. Smith could be written on the face of the law itself, that law would be held void by its own confession in any court competent to try the case.

Referring to the Georgia registration laws, *The Atlanta Constitution* of March 30, 1910, said:

> It has been freely charged that this new registration law was deliberately devised to disfranchise the country vote—the farmers of Georgia, in other words.

Commenting further on the abominable registration laws in Georgia, in its issue of June 23, 1910, *The Atlanta Constitution* in an editorial said:

> Governor Brown submits reports showing that Georgia stands alone as the one state in the Union requiring so arbitrary a period for ''purging'' its electorate. In some states, rural registration is automatic. In the overwhelming majority, the period runs from a few days to thirty and forty days; in even the latter instances, there are qualifications admitting the belated citizens to the polls. . . .
> These thousands of white Georgians have been robbed of that vote which, next to his home, is the institution dearest to the American citizen; the vote that has been bought with centuries of bloodshed, that is the emblem for which Americans have gone to war, the vote that is the sign manual and the main weapon of defense for that liberty upon which our government is founded.

The leaders of the Southern Oligarchy who advocated corrupt practices not only against the Negro but also against the white man who would not support the candidates of the Democratic party, were as vindictive in their treatment of the whites who opposed them as they were in dealing with the Negroes. When there was organized opposition to the Democratic candidates, the Oligarchy did not hesitate to coddle the Negro, corrupt the colored electorate so far as it was possible to do so, and intimidate the voters or steal the votes, if other plans were not successful in breaking down all opposition to the Democratic ticket. For many years Thomas E. Watson was active and influential in Georgia politics, inside and outside the Democratic party. Commenting on the Negro vote, **Mr. Watson** said:

In 1880, it is well known, the back taxes of thousands of Negroes were paid by white men who wanted their votes. It was rumored that $8,000 was sent to Richmond County alone, and that tax arrears to the extent of fifteen years of default were paid off. Those of us who were in the thick of that fight will never forget the wild enthusiasm, the whoop and hurrah, with which the Negro, roused from his sleep of more than twelve years, rushed back into political activity.

When the Oligarchy was in danger, it rushed to the Negro. Let it be said to the everlasting honor of the Negroes that the large majority did not vote with the oppressors of their race. Nor did they sell their votes. In referring to the record of his own race with special reference to disfranchisement in North Carolina, George H. White, to whom I have already alluded, said:

In the catalogue of Members of Congress in this House perhaps none have been more persistent in their determination to bring the black man into disrepute and, with a labored effort, to show that he was unworthy of the right of citizenship than my colleague from North Carolina, Mr. Kitchin. During the first session of this Congress, while the Constitutional amendment was pending in North Carolina, he labored long and hard to show that the white race was at all times and under all circumstances superior to the Negro by inheritance if not otherwise, and the excuse for his party supporting that amendment, which has since been adopted, was that an illiterate Negro was unfit to participate in making the laws of a sovereign State and the administration and execution of them; but an illiterate white man living by his side, with no more or perhaps not as much property, with no more exalted character, no higher thoughts of civilization, no more knowledge of the handicraft of government, had by birth, because he was white, inherited some peculiar qualifications, clear, I presume, only in the mind of the gentleman who endeavored to impress it upon others, that entitles him to vote, though he knew nothing whatever of letters. . . .

I do not mean to propound theories, nor do I desire, as I have said, "to impress upon my readers views of my own, but to supply them with facts, and (so far as I can) with explanations of facts on which they can reflect and from which they can draw their own conclusions." I have already alluded to the fact that the reactionary policies of the Oligarchy, especially in making new State Constitutions for the purpose of disfranchising the Negroes, met with pronounced and outspoken disapproval from prominent men in the South, including Senators Morgan and Pettus of Alabama and leading publicists in other Southern States. There is one further point to which attention should be drawn. It should be observed that corrupt practices in elections have been severely condemned by prominent men in the South who were Democrats. For instance, Dr. J. L. M. Curry, who was a Member of Congress from Alabama, in 1858, and after the war a prominent citizen of Virginia, appointed Minister to Spain by President Cleveland, and later Manager of the Peabody Fund, was quoted as saying:

He who breaks into a ballot-box will break into a bank; the man who steals an office would not hesitate to steal a horse.

It is perhaps true that not all ballot-box stuffers were criminals, and that there were men of high social position, integrity and honor, who engaged in these immoral and reprehensible practices, but it is also true, as shown by long experience, and the criminal record of the Southern States, that a very large number of the men who engaged in these corrupt practices later became criminals, defaulters and embezzlers. Those sections in the South where corrupt practices, especially in falsifying election returns, have been shamefully flagrant are the sections where homicides, race riots and lynchings have been most frequent. William M. Lowe, to whose writings and speeches I have already alluded, understood the practices of the Southern Oligarchy and he summed up the situation clearly and forcibly when he said:

Bourbonism, like a foul disease, infects the atmosphere. It preys like spotted leprosy upon the minds and characters of men. It tends to corrupt the local courts of justice and to degrade the administration of the law. It has already brought some of these fraudulent officials and much of their proceedings into public criticism and contempt. It taints every man that touches it. It degrades not only the officials who profit by it, but every trickster that steals a vote or stuffs a ballot-box, that uses fraud or force, or that consents to their use, or that conceals these methods for the sake of his party. Every such man has made terms with Bourbonism; every such man has trifled more or less with his better sense of right and truth, and compromised with his conscience and self-respect. . . .

The Democratic party in the Southern States has deliberately subverted the supreme law of the land by an abridgment of the political rights of the Negro, and the Republican party, by inaction, has countenanced this violation of the organic law. The solidarity of the South has been, and always will be, a strong political power, and a dangerous power under the control of designing politicians. Federal and State laws are scraps of paper with the Southern Oligarchy when these laws conflict with its partisan interests.

The Negro has been disfranchised by changes in the fundamental laws of the Southern States, by adopting amendments to the State Constitutions which have effectually eliminated the Negro as an elector in these States. These changes came in the following order: Mississippi, 1890; South Carolina, 1895; Louisiana, 1898; North Carolina, 1900; Alabama and Virginia, 1901; Georgia, 1908; Oklahoma, 1910. These States have qualifications which, as we have seen, are so defined and regulated by Democratic officeholders that they invariably operate to disfranchise the Negro although he may be in truth qualified under the legal requirements for registration.

Under the so-called "grandfather clause," a voter who is not able to meet the educational or property requirements as an elector, if he was a voter in 1867, continues to be a qualified voter, in spite of the educational or property requirements. Another exception to the "grandfather clause" provides that a soldier, or the lineal descendant of such soldier or voter, may continue to vote for life although he may not possess either the educational or property qualifications.

The franchise is a privilege granted by the State to its citizens, under such restrictions as to age, time of residence, and educational or property qualifications as the State may see fit to impose. The Fifteenth Amendment was for the purpose of prohibiting any discrimination "on account of race, color or previous condition of servitude." This amendment was to prevent discrimination against the Negro. In the making and administration of the constitutional provisions and law to which

I have alluded, the Southern States have deliberately violated the provisions of the Fifteenth Amendment. Political rights of the Negro in these States exist only in theory; in actual practice, political rights of a large number of whites are no more secure. Under the rule of the Southern Oligarchy, the political status of the Negro is in truth precisely as it was defined by Chief Justice Taney in the Dred Scott case:

It was too plain for argument that they had never been regarded as a part of the people or citizens of the State, nor supposed to possess any political rights which the dominant race might not withhold or grant at their pleasure.

Disfranchisement was the work of provincial partisans in the South and it made possible the protracted rule of this class of politicians in the Southern States. It has narrowed the vision, warped the soul, and intensified the brutal passions; and the whole country is afflicted with the evils of this civic disorder. It has nourished prejudice where charity should have been cultivated; it has fostered ignorance where education was needed, and it has promulgated falsehood where only the truth was needed to make the people free. It has done greater injury to the white man than to the black man. The plain people, restless under the rule of a lawless and oppressive Oligarchy, have seized every opportunity to rid themselves of the oppression. They have followed every leader who would take up the fight, but they have been unfortunate in not having capable leaders. Thus it is evident that the growing discontent in the South may be traced to the oppressive measures of a corrupt Oligarchy. The situation emphasizes the historic truth as stated by Lord Bryce:

The earlier steps towards democracy came not from any doctrine that the people have a right to rule, but from the feeling that an end must be put to lawless oppression by a privileged class.

From the formation of the United States Government, the Southern States have been the rotten boroughs of America, The compromise on the slavery question in the beginning provided that three-fifths of the slaves should be counted for the purpose of representation in Congress from the Slave States, and added just that disproportion to the representation of the white South. At the present time five-fifths of the Negroes are counted for the purpose of representation, but not one-fifth, nor one-tenth, nor hardly one per cent. of the Negroes are permitted to vote.

The public has been told time and again, especially in Congressional debates, and through the press, that the Negro question is too delicate a subject for public discussion, and that the solution of the so-called race problem must be left in the hands of the men who have been in political control of the Solid South for nearly half a century, and who have quietly and systematically exploited and robbed both whites and blacks, in open defiance of the laws of this country and the moral code of civilization. Bankers, manufacturers, merchants and others in the North who have investments or business interests in the South, have been admonished that even a discussion of the industrial or political situation in the Southern States would hurt business and depreciate values. This assertion, as a matter of course, was not and is not true, because a business that can be injured by a discussion of vital questions that involve the life, liberty and happiness of millions of citizens, as well as the stability of their government, is to say the least a very unstable business. A frank discussion of the actual situation and a comprehensive survey of the deplorable condition of the mass of the people would necessarily involve an exposure of the pernicious practices of the Oligarchy and arouse "the feeling that an end must be put to lawless oppression by a privileged class."

CHAPTER VIII

THE DORMANT BALLOT IN AMERICA

The theory of manhood suffrage as essential to the preservation of democratic institutions, the palladium of human liberty, is not new; it is as old as the struggle for freedom. In different countries, and at different times, there have been various, and sometimes strange and absurd, restrictions and qualifications for the elective franchise. For example, at the beginning of the French Revolution, Jews and actors were among those who were disfranchised on account of race, religion or vocation; and in the early history of the United States some of the States limited the franchise to Protestants while others applied the religious test oath as a qualification for suffrage. There were property and educational qualifications, and down to the present time manhood suffrage exists more in theory than in practice in certain sections of the United States.

In many countries, at various times, autocrats, military despots, oligarchies and plutocracies have found divers and sundry excuses for restricting or suppressing the franchise. But men who valued their liberties and personal freedom have continued to struggle and to die for the right to express their choice of men and measures through the medium of the ballot. Hardly three years before the outbreak of the French Revolution, Marat, in an address to the "unfortunate citizens of the faubourg," urged them to vote, notwithstanding the decree of the Assembly. "No power under the sun," he said, "can deprive you of the right of suffrage, which is inherent in society itself." One of the first radical reforms of the Revolution related to the franchise. Referring to that great reform, in his history of *The French Revolution,* John S. Abbott says:

Among the people every man over twenty-five years of age who paid a tax was allowed to vote. A more sublime spectacle earth has rarely witnessed. Twenty-five millions of people suddenly gained the right of popular suffrage.

Between five and six millions of votes were cast. The city of Paris was divided into sixty districts, each of which chose two electors, and these electors were to chose twenty deputies. The people were also enjoined to send in a written statement of their grievances, with instructions to the deputies respecting the reforms which they wished to have introduced. These statements of grievances, now existing in thirty-six compact folio volumes, present appalling testimony to the outrages which the people had for ages been enduring. With propriety, dignity, and marvelous unanimity of purpose, the people assembled at the polls.

Respecting the reforms which were brought about in France by enfranchisement, Abbott comments in these words:

The offices of honor and emolument in the state thrown open to merit, with but the slightest limitations; religious liberty proclaimed; the Protestant, the Jew, the Negro, and the play-actor enfranchised; law made uniform, criminal jurisprudence reformed, monasteries, those haunts of indolence and vice, abolished, and the military force of the country entrusted to the citizens of the country. Such a transformation from the slavery, corruption, and horror of the old régime, was translation from the dungeon to the blaze of day.

Napoleon declared that he was eager to abolish to the last trace the privileges of the ancient nobility, and to establish a government which, at the same time that it held the reins of government with a firm hand, should still be a popular government. He said:

The oligarchy of every country in Europe soon perceived my design, and it was for this reason that war to the death was carried on against me by England. The noble families of London, as well as those of Vienna, think themselves prescriptively entitled to the occupation of all the important offices in the state. Their birth is regarded by them as a substitute for talents and capacities.

In the United Kingdom there has been a steady but slow progress in extending the franchise. During the Chartist agitation, about the beginning of the reign of Victoria, a pamphlet was issued entitled *The Rotten House of Commons*, in which it was shown from official returns that out of 6,023,752 adult males living in the United Kingdom, only 839,519 were voters. In the petition to Parliament, known as the "People's Charter," it was demanded that the right to vote be given adult men. The charter read: "We perform the duties of freemen, we must have the privileges of freemen."

A series of Parliamentary reform bills—the bill of 1832, the bill of 1867, and the bill of 1884—gradually extended the right to vote throughout England. Hazen, in *Europe Since 1815*, says:

In his introduction of the Reform Bill of 1831, Lord John Russell said "that the theory of the British Constitution was no taxation without representation," and after showing that in former times Parliament had been truly representative, said, it was so no longer.

At the time of agitation for reform in the suffrage under the leadership of Gladstone in 1867, John Bright said:

The men who, in every speech they utter, insult the workingmen, describing them as a multitude given up to ignorance and vice, will be the first to yield when the popular will is loudly and resolutely expressed. If Parliament Street, from Charing Cross to the venerable Abbey, were filled with men seeking a Reform Bill these slanderers of their countrymen would learn to be civil, if they did not learn to love freedom.

Respecting the Reform Bill of 1867, Professor Hazen says:

The Bill as finally passed in August, 1867, closed the rule of the middle class in England and made England a democracy. . . . So sweeping was the measure that the Prime Minister himself, Lord Derby, called it "a leap in the dark." Carlyle, forecasting a dismal future, called it "shooting Niagara." . . . It should be noted that during the debates on this bill, John Stuart Mill made a strongly reasoned speech in favor of granting the suffrage to women. The House considered the proposition highly humorous.

In supporting the reform measure in 1866-67, providing for an extension of the franchise, Mr. Bright and Mr. Gladstone "urged that the wider the basis of representation, the stronger would be the fabric of the Constitution and the more contented the people."

Under the latest franchise law passed by the British Parliament, during the month of February, 1918, more than six million women were given the full ballot, and more than two million men were added to the eligible list. The franchise was extended to men of 21 years who have resided six months in a constituency, and men of 19 years who but for the war would have qualified in other respects and were serving or would have served in his

Majesty's army. The new franchise law disqualified "conscientious objectors" not only for the duration of the war but for a period of five years after the war. As stated by Lord Bryce,—

the United Kingdom has now universal suffrage, and in almost every constituency the labouring class compose the majority, usually a very large majority. . . . Democracy really means nothing more nor less than the rule of the people expressing their sovereign will by their votes.

Comparing the policies of the British Government and the United States, with special reference to actual representation of the people, Lord Northcliffe, in *The Metropolitan*, made the following comment:

The fact is that the British Government to-day represents and includes all classes of the community much better than your American Government does. If democracy means that every different responsible element in the population should have a direct voice and a direct influence in the affairs of the nation, Great Britain is not only as "democratic" as the United States, but more "democratic."

This is a severe but just criticism of democracy in America. There are evidences of the evolution of democratic institutions in all progressive countries, especially in the United Kingdom, the British self-governing commonwealths, in France, in Italy, and other advanced countries, during the past half century, especially since the close of the World War. But the United States is an exception to the general rule of democratic progress in highly civilized countries. The policies of the American Government since the Roosevelt Administration, especially during the Wilson régime, have been reactionary. We are very boastful and self-confident in the United States and believe, or pretend to believe, that we are far advanced in the development of democratic institutions, but the plain truth is that America is very backward by comparison with the more progressive countries. In the extension of the franchise, and in the actual protection that is given the citizen in the exercise of this privilege, the United States is behind every country where the people are supposed to have any voice in the affairs of their government. In the Southern States the methods and policies as well as the actual practices are those that prevailed a hundred years ago. For instance, in his *History of the People of the United States,* John B. McMaster says:

> In the general revision of the old State constitutions, between 1790 and 1800, and in the eight newly made or amended, the rights of men were greatly extended. Pennsylvania cast away her religious test, and put the ballot in the hands of every tax-paying male. In Kentucky and Vermont manhood suffrage for the first time was made a part of the political system of the United States. New Hampshire followed and abolished the religious qualifications once exacted of her Governor and her Legislature, took off the poll taxes, and gave the suffrage to every male inhabitant twenty-one years old. Delaware enfranchised every free white male of age who had lived two years on her soil, and ceased to ask if he believed in the Trinity and the divine inspiration of the Testaments. South Carolina opened the polls to Catholics. Georgia did away with her religious tests for civil office and the property qualifications once required of all voters.

That taxation and representation should go hand in hand, was the popular cry in the early history of America, and there was no principle of democratic institutions under representative form of government that was more frequently asserted and more persistently violated. The privilege of franchise was based, almost without exception, upon a property qualification; so also eligibility to official position depended upon the ownership of property. None but property-owning, tax-paying men could vote or hold office. In the early years of American independence, no citizen could vote who did not pay a property tax, or rent a house, or own land, or have a specified yearly income. While the popular cry was "no taxation without representation," and while this was accepted as one of the leading principles of the American form of government, practically every one of the State constitutions limited the right of suffrage by property qualifications. Moreover, nearly every one of the State constitutions required a religious test of the right to vote. In other words, one who did not believe in the doctrine of Christianity and, in some cases, one who did not accept the Protestant religion, was not qualified as a voter or office-holder.

In the convention that made the Federal Constitution, there was a long and bitter contest over the question of leaving to the States absolute control of suffrage rights. This was one of the contests, it was said, that moved Benjamin Franklin to call for daily prayers over the deliberations. Able members of the convention were earnest and aggressive in their demands for a provision in the Constitution relating to qualifications for voters. In the debate on this question, Mr. Madison said:

The right of suffrage is certainly one of the fundamental articles of republican government, and ought not to be left to be regulated by legislatures. A gradual abridgment of this right has been the mode in which aristocracies have been built on the ruins of popular forms.

The result of the debate in the convention that made the Federal Constitution was a compromise on the question of suffrage, and the Constitution, as originally made, is silent on the question of qualifications for suffrage. The elective franchise was left under control of the States, and the States generally, as we have seen, limited the ballot to white males with educational and property qualifications.

In England the elective franchise has remained under the control of Parliament. In all federated states except the United States (so far as I am informed), the elective franchise is under control of the national government. In other great federations, for example, Switzerland, Canada, and Australia, their constitutions treat the suffrage for the federal offices as a national matter by empowering the federal parliament to make uniform regulations with respect to qualifications for voters. The Constitution of the Australian Commonwealth provides that the qualifications imposed on voters by the States shall remain until the Federal Parliament otherwise provides; and in 1902 Parliament established uniform qualifications throughout the Commonwealth so far as federal elections were concerned, and enfranchised women in spite of opposition in some of the States.

In the United States the control of the elective franchise remained with the States, without any limitations or restrictions by the Federal Government, until after the Civil War. The property and educational qualifications provided by the States in our early history were gradually modified or abolished until we had practically manhood or universal suffrage for white men. The Fourteenth Amendment was the first effort on the part of the Federal Government to regulate or restrict the States in making laws relating to qualifications for suffrage. That amendment, among other things, defined as citizens of the

United States those "born or naturalized in the United States and subject to the jurisdiction thereof." It also provided against the making or enforcing of any law which should abridge the privileges or immunities of citizens, and provided a penalty for any State denying to any male citizen over twenty-one years of age the right to vote. The purpose of this provision was to reduce the basis of representation from the Southern States where the Negro vote was not counted. The Fifteenth Amendment came two years after the Fourteenth Amendment was declared adopted. It prohibits the denial or abridgment of the right to vote on account of race, color or previous condition of servitude. As pointed out in the preceding chapter, the purpose of this amendment was to prevent discrimination against persons of African descent.

The Constitution was made presumably for the purpose of securing liberty to the citizens of the United States. As stated by George Livermore, in *An Historical Research,*—

The Constitution is, and was intended to be, the *people's* document—the palladium of their liberty. It was to defend and to bless the Negro as well as the white man; for Negroes had fought side by side with our white soldiers in the common struggle for liberty; and, in several of the States, they, as citizens, had voted for the delegates to the Convention, and afterwards on the adoption of the Constitution.

In commenting on the assertion that the Constitution was made exclusively by and for the white race, Judge Benjamin R. Curtis, Associate Justice of the United States Supreme Court, stated the case clearly many years ago when he said:

It has been often asserted, that the Constitution was made exclusively by and for the white race. It has already been shown, that, in five of the thirteen original States, colored persons then possessed the elective franchise, and were among those by whom the Constitution was ordained and established. If so, it is not true, in point of fact, that the Constitution was made exclusively by the white race. And that it was made exclusively for the white race is, in my opinion, not only an assumption not warranted by anything in the Constitution, but contradicted by its opening declarations, that it was ordained by the people of the United States, for themselves and their posterity.

When, shortly after the War of the American Revolution, the Legislature of the State of New York passed a bill providing for the abolition of slavery, it was also provided that the franchise should never be extended to any person with even a part of Negro blood. The measure was not approved by the Council of Revision, which then exercised the veto power; but the objection to the bill was not because it would emancipate, but because it would disfranchise the Negroes, and would thus create discrimination between two classes of citizens. The Council held that it would be repugnant to principles of liberty and equality to place the burdens of government on those who have no representation in making the laws. Commenting on the proposed law, the Council of Revision, in a veto message, went on to say that—

this class of disfranchised and discontented citizens at some future period may under the direction of ambitious and factious leaders become dangerous to the State and effect the ruin of a Constitution whose benefits they are not permitted to enjoy. . . . The creation of an order of citizens who are to have no legislative or representative share in the Government, necessarily lays the foundation of an aristocracy of the most dangerous and malignant kind.

Concerning the elective franchise for free colored persons in the State of North Carolina, Judge Gaston, of the Supreme Court of that State, said:

Slaves manumitted here, become **freemen**; and, therefore, if born within North Carolina, are citizens of North Carolina; and all free persons within the State are born citizens of the State. The Constitution extended the elective franchise to every freeman who had arrived at the age of twenty-one, and paid a public tax; and it is a matter of universal notoriety, that, under it, free persons, without regard to color, claimed and exercised the franchise, until it was taken from free men of color a few years since by our amended Constitution.

For more than thirty years, Senator John T. Morgan, a Democrat of Alabama, was one of the most distinguished statesmen from the South. Commenting on the suffrage provisions of the new constitutions made in Alabama and in other Southern States for the purpose of disfranchising the Negroes, he pointed out the menace of those measures in the following language:

The American Revolution was not so much a redress of grievances, as it was a struggle to abolish heredity in government. . . . Heredity disappeared, with its associated rights of perpetuity in the ownership of lands. . . . Political heredity, and all its appurtenances, such as prerogative and titular nobility and primogeniture, and all its protecting laws, such as corruption of blood perished and were placed under the heel of prohibition by our Constitution. Without suffrage, the new system had no possible means of expressing the sovereign will of the people in laws, and their enforcement by executive and judicial authority. . . . The voters as a class, or body, have certain physical conditions, such as age and sex, that are necessary qualifications, and certain moral and political qualifications, that are personal and independent of inheritable blood.

To make blood the medium of transmitting the electoral power from father to son, is to uproot, from its foundations the whole system of Democratic government and to reinstate the system and the form of regal government.

The transmission of electoral power by the blood of inheritance from father to son would destroy all distinction between regal government and democracy, and would throw the door wide open for a return to the system that the American Revolution abolished.

In every country of the civilized world at the present time, except in the Solid South, the people are demanding a larger share in the direction of public affairs. As shown by the official figures presented in the first chapter of this book, for more than a quarter of a century there has been a gradual decrease in the proportion of citizens of voting age who actually vote in the Southern States. The menace of this dormant ballot is found in the growing disrespect for law, the alarming increase of criminal lawlessness, and the gradual decline of the people in civic virtue and virile patriotism. This deplorable situation is not only a vital social and political question in the South, but, in all its ramifications, this peril reaches the civic, social and economic life of every citizen of the United States and our insular possessions. It is a national evil that affects the whole country, and it should be so treated.

As before stated, the Fourteenth Amendment expressly provides that when male citizens 21 years of age are deprived of the right to vote for Presidential electors or Representatives in Congress "the basis of representation therein shall be reduced in proportion which the number of such male citizens shall bear to the whole number of male citizens 21 years of age in such State." This provision of the Constitution has been, and still is, openly, notoriously and defiantly disregarded and violated by an Oligarchy that rules in at least eleven of the Southern States. In contempt of the Constitution, the South continues to enjoy in

Congress and in Presidential elections a representation and consequent power in making laws and in the administration of governmental affairs based on the Negro population. The Negro does not vote in the Southern States and leaders of the Southern Oligarchy defiantly say he shall not vote; yet, in plain violation of specific provisions of the Constitution, these States have representation in Congress and in electing a President based on the dormant Negro vote.

The Democratic party, North and South, has openly and blatantly endorsed this defiance of the Constitution with respect to representation based on the uncast Negro vote. The common practice of the Northern Democrats in supporting sectional prejudice and race hatred, especially in all matters relating to the spoils system and disfranchisement in the interest of the Southern Oligarchy, was clearly shown in the attitude of Mr. William J. Bryan when he was recognized as leader of the Democratic party and the idol of the South. With the usual subterfuges and misleading assertions, Mr. Bryan tried to justify corrupt practices and disfranchisement in the South, when, in a speech at Cooper Union, New York, in 1908, he said:

> The white man in the South has disfranchised the Negro in self-protection, and there is not a white man in the North who would not have done the same thing under the same circumstances. The white men of the South are determined that the Negro will and shall be disfranchised everywhere it is necessary to prevent the recurrence of carpet-bag rule.

The sins of carpet-bag rule in the South, as shown in a preceding chapter, were not the result of Negro enfranchisement, nor has the Negro been disfranchised to prevent a recurrence of carpet-bag rule. The Negro was disfranchised for the same reason that the poor white man was disfranchised. It was to prevent any united and organized opposition to the corrupt and lawless practices of the Oligarchy which rules in the South without regard to the rights of the white man or the black man.

In the former Dutch Republics of South Africa political rights were not enjoyed by persons of color. Racial prejudice was very strong with the Boers and public opinion did not tolerate very much consideration for the native blacks so far as political rights were concerned. When, however, a republican form of government was established in 1853, no color line was drawn in making laws regulating the franchise. In 1892 an act was passed establishing a combined educational and property qualification. There was no discrimination on account of color or race and no inequality of treatment in the regulations relating to suffrage. In his book under the title of *Black and White in South-East Africa*, Maurice S. Evans, C.M.G., refers to the so-called Dutch Republics in these words:

Republics in name, oligarchies in fact; for whilst every white man, as a white man, was a ruler and had an equal voice in shaping the destinies of the country, every black man, because he was a black man, was debarred. The proscriptive measures of the Dutch in South Africa were only a little less severe in their evidences of racial hatred than those found in the Southern States of America, although the criminal record resulting from race antagonism was never so appalling in the Dutch South Africa settlements as in the Southern States.

The population of the Union of South Africa, which embraces the former Dutch Republics of that country, was, in 1911, 5,973,394, of whom 4,697,152 were native or colored. Only a small per cent. of the Negro population have the ballot in South Africa, but those who do not enjoy the franchise are excluded by law because they do not possess the legal qualifications. If the British colonies of South Africa can prosper and live in peace with more than three-fourths of the population made up of Negroes, it would seem that the Southern States, where the Negroes represent not more than 31 per cent. of the total population, could safely extend the franchise to those who are legally qualified without reference to race or color.

The average Negro in the Southern States has never manifested very much interest in the franchise. Unsolicited and uninfluenced by the white man, the chances are that a large number, perhaps a majority, of the illiterate Negroes especially, would never go to the polling-places if they had the legal right to vote and were permitted to exercise that right. In Jamaica, the largest of the British West Indies, there is no color distinction in the suffrage qualifications. ''The qualifications are extremely easy,'' writes Maurice S. Evans—*Black and White in South East Africa:*

The payment of poor rates and taxes of at least ten shillings per annum, or in the case of parish taxpayers of thirty shillings a year, or alternatively the receipt of an annual salary of £50. Yet, in 1906 out of a Negro and mulatto population of 820,437 there were only 3,607 registered voters.

Referring to the situation in America, Mr. Evans says:

The position of the Southern United States is often quoted as a warning, and indeed is, I think, apposite. For between forty and fifty years the Negro has nominally had full franchise rights, and yet to-day has no effective say in the government of the country. Bad enough, but the effect of force and fraud where only reason should prevail is infinitely more disastrous to those who defraud than to the sufferers.

When the Fifteenth Amendment to the Constitution was submitted to the States, the advocates of women suffrage learned that a new class of voters could be created by amending the Constitution. A few months after this amendment was submitted, a meeting was called in New York at which nineteen States were represented and a national women's suffrage association was organized. After half a century of strenuous work and educational propaganda, the Nineteenth Amendment was adopted with the same provision relating to discrimination "on account of sex" as was made in the Fifteenth Amendment "on account of race, color or previous condition of servitude."

On January 10, 1918, the House of Representatives passed a resolution providing for the submission to the States of an amendment to the Constitution prohibiting discrimination on account of sex. This resolution passed the House by a vote of 274 to 136. Of 206 Democrats present and voting 104 were in favor of the amendment and 102 were opposed; of 198 Republicans present and voting 165 were in favor of and only 33 were opposed to the resolution.

It was not until September 26, 1918, more than eight months after the resolution was passed by the House, that it reached a vote in the Senate and was defeated. Of those in favor of the amendment 32 were Republicans and 30 Democrats; of those opposed 12 were Republicans and 22 Democrats. When, in 1919, the Republican Senate finally passed the resolution to submit the proposed amendment to the States, there were 36 Republicans and 6 Democrats who voted for it in the Senate, and there were 17 Democrats and only 8 Republicans who voted against it.

Eight of the States that refused to ratify the amendment for equal suffrage are among the eleven that make up the Solid

South.   Arkansas, Texas and Tennessee are the three States in the South that ratified the amendment.   The eight Southern States which refused to ratify the suffrage amendment are those which have the highest criminal record and the highest percentage of illiteracy, although Arkansas and Texas are not far behind in the criminal record.

Opposition in the South to prohibiting discrimination on account of sex in regulating the franchise was based on the old political claptrap of the Southern Oligarchy—the alleged fear of Negro domination.   "It is for the protection of our mothers, sisters, wives and daughters that we oppose this measure," said some of the political leaders of the South.   This is the absurd propaganda that is always started in the South when the Oligarchy becomes alarmed about some measure providing for better educational opportunities, social or civic advancement, or other wholesome measures which would improve the condition of the people and make them dissatisfied with the rule of the Oligarchy.   The leaders of the Oligarchy have time and again declared that the Negroes shall not vote in the South, and the Negroes do not vote in the States where the Oligarchy rules.   If the Negro men have not voted during the past quarter of a century or more in the South, and if they will not be allowed to vote, how could there be any danger of the Negro women voting?

The Australian Commonwealth was the first country to abolish by law distinctions of sex in relation to the elective franchise. One of the Australian colonies that made up the federation had already taken this step, and another one of the colonies had the matter under consideration when the federal electoral act was passed, but only South Australia had actually conferred the franchise on its female citizens.   The second parliament of the Australian federation was the choice of all persons in the Commonwealth who had reached the full age of twenty-one years, regardless of sex.

Woman suffrage was an accomplished fact in the United Kingdom shortly after the close of the World War.   In the general election in England, shortly after the armistice, more than 6,000,000 women voted.   The enfranchising act passed Commons and Lords with an overwhelming majority, with only formal opposition, and a later act was passed providing that women could sit in the House of Commons. It was one of the greatest revolutions in English history, and like many other great revolutions in the history of Great Britain, it was peaceable. It was stated that 21,000,000 voters went to the polls at the first general election in the United Kingdom after the end of the World War, a vastly larger percentage of the total population of that country than was the percentage of the total population of the United States that voted in the national election of 1920.

Woman suffrage was one of the first things accomplished in Czecho-Slovakia, and eight members of the first National Assembly of that country were women. The new Republic of Poland also abolished all distinctions of sex in qualifications for the franchise. In the first National Assembly of Poland there were 130 peasant Deputies and six women Deputies, and also interesting to note, "there were hardly any lawyers in the Assembly." The Constitution—

guarantees on its territory to all, without distinction, or extraction, nationality, language, race, or religion, full protection of life, liberty and property. . . . The Republic of Poland does not recognize privileges of birth or of estate, or any coat of arms, family or other titles, with the exception of those of learning, office or profession.

Manhood suffrage never has been popular in the Southern States. Prior to the Civil War, it existed more in theory than in fact. The social and political domination of the landed aristocracy tended to discourage the non-slaveholding qualified electors from exercising the privilege of the ballot. The practices of the ruling Oligarchy since the war have not only eliminated the Negro vote but have discouraged the free exercise of the suffrage by the white voters. There is now no democratic government or other form of government selected by the people in any country where the voters are so indifferent to the right of suffrage as they are in the Southern States.

Some years ago, so staunch a patriot and good American as former Congressman Fleming of Georgia stated the feeling and situation in the South regarding the franchise. In an interview published in *The Atlanta Constitution*, commenting on the basis of Congressional Representation from the South, and the Crumpacker proposition to reduce the representation to the proper basis of the vote actually cast, he said:

In the republic of ancient Athens, there was a law placing a penalty on a citizen who neglected to cast his ballot. It is a curious piece of history, also, that in the first Constitution of the State of Georgia, adopted at Savannah, February 5, 1777, there was a provision that a person who absented himself from an election and neglected to give in his ballot should be subject to a penalty not exceeding five pounds.

But there is now no law, state or federal, to compel a free American citizen to vote if he does not wish to do so, nor will our federal laws ever be so amended as to punish a State because its citizens, in enjoyment of peaceful political conditions, have no need to rush to the polls.

Some reference has been made to civic progress in the British self-governing commonwealths. For the purpose of amplifying the subject of the present chapter it may be interesting to cite a reference to regulations of the franchise in one of the most progressive and enlightened of them, as stated by Hugh H. Lusk, in *Social Welfare in New Zealand:*

By the New Zealand law it is compulsory that each person who has the privilege of voting shall either use or lose the privilege. The electoral rolls of persons resident in each electoral district are prepared a few months before each Parliamentary election by the police force in the district, and are confirmed in open court by the magistrate of the district, after public notice to the electors. Every person who does not appear to vote at the ensuing election must either give a good reason for his absence in court, when the next roll is prepared, or must be excluded from the list of persons entitled to vote. It is at least possible that to one or both of these reasons has been due the fact that at the five elections that have taken place since women obtained the full electoral franchise that the women of New Zealand have exercised the right of voting in almost exactly the same proportion to their numbers as the men. In the case of adults of both sexes the proportion of actual voters has been as nearly as possible 80 per cent. of those enrolled.

The menace of the present situation in the United States is found in the fact that citizens who are indifferent or careless about the franchise are usually good Americans. Under the leadership of unscrupulous politicians, especially in the large cities, the vicious and purchasable voters are well organized, and their leaders see to it that their votes are cast. Not only the vicious and venal voter but also the ignorant and mentally unfit, but not legally disqualified, voters are under the control of the beneficiaries of the spoils system in the large cities and they go to the polling-places, "rain or shine," and cast their ballots, while the independent American voter who will neither sell his vote nor cast it under the direction of a political boss, remains away from the polls on account of the inclement weather, indisposition, or other engagements. Herein lies one of the great dangers of our government, democratic in theory but oligarchic in fact.

The Census reports for 1920 give the State of New York, for example, a total population of 10,385,227, including 2,786,112 foreign-born white persons, of whom 2,528,497 were 21 years or over. The native whites of native parentage in New York City, according to the census of 1920, numbered 1,164,834; the foreign white stock element numbered 4,294,629, an increase of 546,785 from 1910 to 1920, while during the same period the native whites of native parentage increased 243,516.

The large number of foreign-born voters, and other voters who do not understand or appreciate American institutions, in the City of New York, who vote under the direction of the spoilsmen who control them, is a continued menace, not only to the City and State of New York but also to the whole country. A coalition of the Southern Oligarchy with the Democratic Oligarchy of New York City is an old story, but it is none the less an ever present and increasing menace to the Nation. Under existing conditions in America, the dormant ballot is as great a menace as the ignorant and venal vote. The situation is clearly illustrated by the following table of statistics, showing the total voting population (1920) in 48 States of the Union, and the number of votes actually cast in the Presidential election of 1920.

VOTING POPULATION AND VOTES CAST IN 48 STATES, 1920.

American citizens, 21 years of age and over, 1920		54,128,895
Total votes cast, Presidential election, 1920		26,674,171
Citizens of voting age who did not vote		27,454,724
Negroes of voting age, 11 Southern States . .	3,953,356	
Illiterates of voting age outside the eleven Southern States	3,010,903	6,964,259
Citizens of voting age, not including Negroes in 11 Southern States or illiterates in other States, who did not vote in Presidential election, 1920 .		20,490,465

As shown in the preceding tabulation, there were 27,454,724 citizens of voting age in 48 States who did not vote in the Presidential election of 1920. From this total of uncast votes I have deducted the Negroes of voting age in 11 Southern States where, as related in the preceding chapter, by constitutional provisions, or by force and intimidation in those States, Negroes are denied the privilege of the elective franchise. From this total of uncast votes I have also deducted 3,010,903 illiterate citizens of voting age outside the Southern States. As shown by the Census reports for 1920, there were 4,333,111 illiterates of voting age, including 1,322,208 Negroes in the 11 Southern States. Not all illiterate citizens of voting age outside the Southern States are denied the privilege of voting. There are very few States outside the Solid South that require a literacy test as a qualification for suffrage, and in the Southern States, as already stated, the literacy and property qualification apply only to Negroes, so far as the effective result of the operation of these restrictions are concerned. However, in making a conservative estimate of the number of citizens of voting age who do not vote we should exclude those who did not vote on account of illiteracy or other mental or moral delinquencies. After making the most liberal deductions for those who were disqualified, there were 20,490,465 citizens of voting age who did not vote in 1920 and for whose failure to vote there is no satisfactory explanation. The actual situation in the Southern States may be illustrated by further comparisons with 11 Northern and Western States, as shown in the tabulation on page 163.

As shown by figures cited in this tabulation, only 21.20 per cent. of the citizens of the eleven Southern States who were of voting age voted in the Presidential election of 1920, while in the eleven Northern and Western States, 60.88 per cent., and in the United States, 49.25 per cent. of the voting population voted in 1920. In Mississippi, 9.46, and in South Carolina, 8.51 per cent. of the voting population voted in 1920. In the Southern States, where opposition to the Democratic ticket developed any considerable strength, the per cent. of the voting population that voted in the Presidential election of 1920 was much larger than it was in those States where opposition to the Democratic ticket was negligible and inactive. For example, in North

Total population, total number and per cent. of voters who voted for President in 1920, 11 Southern States and 11 Northern and Western States, and total of United States.

11 Southern States Solid South	Population	Total voters	Voted for President 1920	Per cent voted 1920
Alabama . . .	2,348,174	1,135,529	241,070	22.11
Arkansas . . .	1,752,204	861,575	183,637	21.31
Florida	968,470	506,660	145,681	28.75
Georgia	2,895,832	1,414,772	154,049	10.89
Louisiana . . .	1,798,509	896,878	126,057	14.05
Mississippi . . .	1,790,618	872,094	82,492	9.46
North Carolina . .	2,559,123	1,207,343	538,758	44.62
South Carolina . .	1,683,724	776,969	66,442	8.51
Tennessee . . .	2,337,885	1,208,219	428,655	35.39
Texas	4,663,228	2,233,854	411,426	18.42
Virginia	2,309,187	1,192,550	230,997	19.37
	25,106,954	12,306,443	2,609,264	21.20
11 Northern and Western States				
Indiana	2,930,390	1,702,652	1,262,398	74.14
Iowa	2,404,021	1,367,212	894,094	65.40
Maine	768,014	421,034	197,530	46.91
Michigan . . .	3,668,412	1,881,597	1,045,388	55.56
Minnesota . . .	2,387,125	1,237,203	730,010	59.00
Nebraska . . .	1,296,372	686,347	382,653	55.75
New Hampshire . .	443,083	235,466	159,092	67.56
New Jersey . . .	3,155,900	1,525,190	908,638	59.58
Ohio	5,759,394	3,228,294	2,019,500	62.56
Rhode Island . .	604,397	288,560	167,386	58.00
Wisconsin . . .	2,632,067	1,341,981	705,686	52.58
	26,049,175	13,915,536	8,472,375	60.88
United States .	105,710,620	54,128,895	26,674,171	49.25

Carolina 44.62 per cent.—more than double the average of the eleven Southern States—of the voting population voted in the Presidential election of 1920, and the Republican ticket received slightly more than 43 per cent. of the total vote of the State. In Tennessee, 35.39 per cent. of the voting population voted and the Republicans carried the State by a small majority.

Of the total voting population in eleven Southern States, only about 11.5 per cent. voted in the Congressional election of 1922, while approximately 49.7 per cent. of the voting population of eleven Northern States voted in the same election. In Louisiana 4.9 per cent. of the voting population voted in the Congressional election of 1922, and in the same election, 4.5 per cent. of the voting population of South Carolina voted, while Arkansas was at the bottom of the list with only 3.8 per cent. of the voters going to the polls to vote for representatives in Congress in 1922.

The figures I have cited are appalling. In a republican form of government, where the people are so boastful of their democratic institutions and talk so much about liberty, and a government by the people and for the people, it seems hardly believable that they would be so indifferent concerning the use of a political privilege without the free exercise of which democratic institutions cannot survive and republican form of government will not continue. When we compare the percentage of qualified electors who actually exercise the right of suffrage in the United States with the percentage of qualified voters, for example, in the United Kingdom, in the British Commonwealths, in France and in Belgium, respectively, who actually vote in these countries, the situation in the United States, by comparison with the more advanced and modern democracies, is deplorable and alarming. We have outgrown the American system which is undemocratic, unyielding and unresponsive to the will of the people. The defects of our system have been demonstrated so frequently, and the menace of the situation has been so clearly perceived that not one of the self-governing nations formed under the new political divisions of Europe that followed the World War adopted the American system or form of government. Every one of these new republics adopted the parliamentary system in preference to the undemocratic system of congressional government in America.

The situation in the United States has developed not only a growing and widespread indifference to the duties and responsibilities of citizenship, but it has also caused a loss of confidence in both State and Federal governments with a consequent spirit of disrespect for law. The teachings and practices of the Southern Oligarchy have accentuated the indifference of the people concerning the men and measures of their government. The people are losing confidence in their government and are showing their lack of confidence by an apathy that increases the menace of this Oligarchy and will, if continued, ultimately subvert the whole system of republican form of government in this country. Our Constitution guarantees a republican form of government, but this guarantee cannot be made effective and permanent if the people fail to use the agencies which have been provided for their own protection.

The amount of discontent among a people living under such depressing conditions has found ominous expression in various manifestations of unrest and civic disorder. This evidence of discontent and lack of confidence in their government has shown no more serious symptoms than is found in the growing indisposition of so large a percentage of the voting population to express their choice of men and measures at the ballot-box.

This increasing indifference to the essential value and sanctity of the ballot in a democracy, under a republican form of government, on the part of so large a number of qualified electors, is one of the evil results of the contempt with which the elective franchise has been treated in the Southern States. The whole country has acquiesced in the corrupt and lawless practices of the Southern Oligarchy, tolerating, if not approving, the disrespect with which that political faction has treated the ballot, and the resultant evil is perhaps the most portentous fact before the American people.

It is perhaps true, as observed by so high an authority as Lord Bryce, that—

party organization is a natural and probably an inevitable incident of democratic governments. It has in itself nothing pernicious. Its evils have sprung from its abuses.

Custom has made party government a fundamental part of the American system, and we can easily perceive that this custom cannot be easily changed, even if it should seem wise to change it. It is clear, therefore, in order to preserve the active principles of democratic institutions, there should be two great political parties; but it is still more important that each of these parties should be representative and responsible.

The representative character and responsibility of a political party can be maintained only through the free and active exercise of the right of suffrage by every qualified elector, or at least by a very large majority of the electors. If the voters abstain from an independent expression of their judgment

respecting party policies, and their choice of leaders or representatives for the party with which they are affiliated, the party
will become irresponsible and corrupt, and in ceasing to be
representative it will become oligarchic. It follows, therefore,
that the voter who fails to exercise the right of suffrage which
the State has bestowed upon him for his own protection, not
only reduces the moral stamina and efficiency of the political
party with which he is affiliated, but he also lessens the efficiency
and weakens the stability of the government of which he is a
citizen.

In theory, we have a government of law in the United States;
in actual practice, we have a government of men. And, on the
whole, it was not a very efficient and patriotic class of men
when the Nation was under rule of the Southern Oligarchy.
All important events in our national history from the beginning
of the Wilson Administration, while the Oligarchy ruled, tend
to show that we had entered upon a period of odious reaction.
The peril of the dormant ballot has appeared in its most pernicious form.

The United States is a republic only in name; our democratic
principles exist only in theory. In the treatment of vital
civic and economic questions we are falling behind other democracies of the world. We were the last, except Brazil, to abolish
slavery; in our failure to recognize civic and political equality
of citizens we are behind other advanced democracies; we are
behind other democracies in recognizing the rights of labor; we
were the last to introduce a budget system in the management
of our public expenditures; and our criminal record is the most
appalling in the world. We give less protection to the exercise
of the right of suffrage,(and we give more protection to peonage
than is given by any other democracy.) America is the only
country in the world where the percentage of homeowners is
steadily decreasing and the passive indifference to the free
exercise of the elective franchise is rapidly increasing.

CHAPTER IX

ILLITERACY AND PUBLIC SCHOOLS IN THE SOUTH

According to reports of the Bureau of the Census, the illiterate population of the United States, 10 years of age and over, numbered 4,931,905 in 1920. The illiterate population represented 6.0 per cent. of the total 10 years of age and over in 1920, the corresponding percentages for the last four preceding census years being 7.7 in 1910, 10.7 in 1900, 13.3 in 1890, and 17 in 1880.

The proportion of illiteracy for the individual States in 1920 ranged from 1.1 per cent. for Iowa to 21.9 per cent. for Louisiana. The greatest percentages of illiteracy appear for States in which the colored population or the foreign-born is relatively large. The largest percentage of illiteracy in the native white population shown for any State was in New Mexico, being 11.9, but the eleven Southern States led the list in illiteracy of native whites after New Mexico. Louisiana with 11.4 per cent. of native white illiterates came next to New Mexico; North Carolina had 8.2; Kentucky, 7.3; Tennessee, 7.4; South Carolina, 6.6; Alabama, 6.4; Virginia, 6.1 and Georgia, 5.5. The percentage of native white illiterates in the United States was 2.5 in 1920, while in 1910 it was 3.7.

The illiterate foreign-born white population in 1920 numbered 1,763,740 and formed 13.1 per cent. of the total foreign-born white population 10 years of age and over, as against 12.7 per cent. in 1910, 12.9 in 1900. 13.1 in 1890, and 12 per cent. in 1880. The highest percentage of illiteracy among the foreign-born white population was 33.8 in Texas. The percentage of illiteracy among the Negroes was the highest in Louisiana, 38.5, and the lowest was in New York; the average of the United States was 22.9, while in 1910 it was 30.4.

In his annual report of 1918, the Secretary of the Interior called attention to the fact that while there were 4,090,000 men in the American army during the World War, of that number there were 1,023,000 illiterates. Of the white soldiers 21.5 per cent. could not read or write, of the colored soldiers 50.6 could not read or write. Prior to America's entrance into the World War, the regular army would not enlist illiterates. At Seagirt, New Jersey, June 17, 1921, General Pershing told National Guard officers and men at Camp Edwards that the illiteracy of the young manhood of the country was a disgrace and that he hoped the nation would never again have to pass through such an experience with untrained minds and bodies as it did in the last war.

As shown in a summary of the "economic cost of illiteracy" (from a Bulletin of the U. S. Bureau of Education, republished in *The World Almanac*, 1924), the loss caused by illiteracy in industrial enterprises is enormous:

Statistics of the United States Department of Labor show that the rate of accidents in the iron and steel industry during a period of eight years was highest among the non-English speaking workers and showed little decrease from year to year.

According to a statement quoted from Marian A. Clark, of the New York State Industrial Commission, estimates show—

that one-half of the accidents in factories, with a resultant loss of $50,000 per day to industries, are due to ignorance of the language.

There are 800,000 factory workers in New York State who cannot speak English. In 1916 $11,500,000 was paid out in that State in accordance with the workingman's compensation law, an amount which would be increased to $35,000,000 if to it were added loss of wages, labor turnover, doctor bills, and the administration of the law.

Under modern forms of industrial employment, where technical knowledge is essential in almost every manufacturing enterprise, and in mining and agriculture, illiteracy is the cause of immense waste, loss and personal injury. For instance, according to a report of Mr. Manning, Director of the Bureau of Mines (1919), 465,000 men in the mining industry came from non-English speaking races and many were illiterates. He says:

The mines that employ numbers of foreigners generally have the precautionary rules printed in the different languages, but if the foreigner cannot even read his own language these safety guides are of no value to him. The best estimates from a number of the larger mining States are to the effect that the non-English speaking foreigners suffer twice the fatalities that the English-speaking miners do.

This means an excess of 930 non-English speaking foreigners killed each year, and I may say unnecessarily. If the average State compensation is $3,000, which is a fair figure, the total economic loss each year to the country through the excess of deaths of non-English speaking miners alone amounts to $2,790,000.

At the present time the educational situation is unsatisfactory in many parts of the country and alarming in some States. This unfortunate condition is of comparatively late development, except in the Southern States, so far as the lack of necessary school buildings and a sufficient number of capable teachers is concerned, but it is an old story in the South, where the lack of proper accommodations and a sufficient number of competent teachers has been and still is a chronic condition.

The evils of illiteracy and near-illiteracy in the South are appalling, not only in the inefficiency and malfeasance shown in the administration of public affairs and in the record of criminal lawlessness, but also in the great economic cost of ignorance. The pernicious results of illiteracy in the Southern States are observed not only in the manifold evils of malfeasance and misfeasance of public administration and in criminal lawlessness, but also in the social and civic disorders that necessarily follow a system of peonage, convict labor, hookworm infestation, child labor, primitive and slipshod practices in the cultivation and marketing of crops, especially the cotton crop, the mainstay of 25,000,000 people, nearly three-fourths of whom are engaged in agricultural pursuits. Illiteracy and near-illiteracy, and the usual concomitants of extreme partisanship, provincialism, race prejudice and religious bigotry are the principal underlying causes of poverty, lawlessness, civic and industrial backwardness in the Southern States. Before reviewing the actual situation in the Southern States touching the matter of educational progress, it may be well to refer briefly to the history of the public school system which is of comparatively recent development there.

Among the early attempts to establish public schools in the South are to be noted the act of the Georgia Legislature of 1783, authorizing the Government to grant 1,000 acres of land to a "free school" in each county in the State. Thomas Jefferson proposed a plan for public education in Virginia, and an act of the Alabama territorial legislature in 1819 authorized county agents to contract for the employment of teachers and the erection of school houses. And there is the record of the development of what might be called the germ of the public school system in Southern cities like Augusta and Savannah, Georgia, Charleston, South Carolina, and Mobile, Alabama. Shortly before the Civil War, Alabama, Georgia and South Carolina passed laws providing for State-wide systems of public schools with State aid, but those laws remained inoperative. As related in a report of the Superintendent of Education of the State of Texas, 1918:

One of the reasons assigned for the establishment of the Texas Republic was the failure of the Mexican Government to establish any system of public education for the people of Texas. The delegates of the people of Texas in general convention at Washington on the Brazos, on March 2, 1836, resolved and declared that:

"Our political connection with the Mexican Nation has forever ended and that the people of Texas do now constitute a free, solvent, and independent republic." In this declaration of independence numerous reasons are set forth for the Texas Declaration of Independence, among which is found the following: "It has failed to establish any system of public education, although possessed of almost boundless resources (the public domain), and although it is an axiom in political science, that unless a people are educated and enlightened, it is idle to expect the continuance of civil liberty, or the capacity for self-government.

The traditions of the Southern people were opposed to free schools. The institution of slavery that dominated in all economic, social and civic affairs of the South was opposed to education except for the privileged class of the social and political aristocracy. In theory and actual practice it was held that parents should provide for the education of their children the same as for food and clothes. Attempts were sometimes made to provide schools for poor children by the gifts of generous friends, but in such cases the suggestion of poverty placed the schools almost on a level with the almshouse. In the few cases where "free schools" were provided they were seldom patronized by those who needed them most.

Referring to the history of the common schools in the Southern States, the late Dr. J. L. M. Curry, manager of the Peabody Fund, and one of the most active and useful workers in the cause of education in the South, said:

It must be borne in mind that under the ancient régime no public school system providing universal education existed in the South. There was no system adequate even to the education at public expense of the white youth. Our peculiar social system forbade the education of the Negroes. That obviously would have been impossible and dangerous. . . . In the course of a few years systems for both races were established. The difficulties were very great. Population was sparse, roads were bad, schoolhouses did not exist, there was an absolute want of acquaintance with the machinery of public schools, no sufficient supply of competent teachers was to be had, and weighing down all spirit of hopeful progress was the dreary poverty of the taxpayer.

The white illiterates of twenty years and more in the South in 1860 were 15.12 per cent., while in the North they were 6.36 per cent. Of the freed Negroes in the South of twenty years and over, the percentage of illiteracy was only 16.52, and in the North it was 6.63 per cent.

The modern idea of public schools for all children was not adopted by the Southern States until after the Reconstruction period, and it has not been fully adopted in every one of the Southern States at the present time, as it is known in the more advanced States. The public school system was one of the wise measures which the Republican party introduced in the South.

The Reconstruction governments in the Southern States established free public schools, but on account of the prejudice against Northern men, commonly known as carpet-baggers, who were identified with these educational measures in the South, they were generally discredited by the Southern white people. Not until 1880 do we find any evidence of appreciation of the public school idea in the Southern States.

An indication of the indifference to public education shown by the Oligarchy that has been in control of the governments of the Southern States since the end of the Reconstruction period, we find in the official report of the State Superintendent of Education of Georgia (1919), the following comment:

When the Constitutional Convention of 1877 occurred the "Fathers" who took part in this were not favorably disposed toward public education.

They believed that the training of children was an individual and private function for each man to look after himself, "if so disposed," as Sairey Gamp would say. They were willing sometimes to educate their own children, but were not at all kindly disposed to the idea of providing for those of the common man. In consequence of this grudging attitude, they tried to make it almost impossible to levy taxes for public schools and succeeded so well that it was 29 years before a single county could be added to Bibb, Chatham, Richmond and Glynn, the only four that in 1877 supplemented the State fund by countrywide tax. As to high school education they would have none of it and there has been little Constitutional authority from that day to this for the building or maintainance of any secondary schools in Georgia outside of the towns in four counties named.

It has been asserted time and again, in the newspapers and periodicals, at educational conventions, and in Congress, that the Southern States have been very liberal in expenditures for educational purposes, and that in this work they have taxed themselves beyond their means. Southern politicians have frequently referred to the "white man's burden," claiming that the Southern people have contributed beyond their means, not only for the educational advancement of the white people, but also for the education of the Negroes. Statistics from official reports do not support this claim.

The first statistics relating to expenditures for public schools to which I shall refer are from official reports for the year immediately preceding the outbreak of the World War when normal conditions prevailed. In some later paragraphs, other figures based on reports compiled during and subsequent to the war will be cited to show that educational progress has been and still is very slow under rule of the Oligarchy in the South.

The report of the Commissioner of Education (1914) contains a table showing "wealth and school expenditures 1912-13." As shown by this tabulation, the eleven Southern States had an assessed valuation of all property subject to ad valorem taxation of $8,073,986,366, while the assessed valuation of all property subject to ad valorem taxation in the eleven Northern States used for comparison was $19,969,689,742. Total expenditures for public schools (excluding debt paid), in the eleven Southern States, amounted to $53,838,031, while the eleven Northern States expended for the same purpose $140,170,831. The average amount expended for public schools on each $100 of assessed valuation of all property was 66.7 cents in the Southern States and 70.2 cents in the Northern States, and the average of the United States was 69.5. The average expenditure per capita of total population was $2.36 in the Southern States; $6.23 in the Northern States and $5.37 in the United States. The Southern States spent less than one-half the average in the United States and a little more than one-third the average of the eleven Northern States.

The total enrollment for the school year 1912-13 in the eleven Southern States was 5,167,874 and in the eleven Northern States used for comparison the total enrollment was 4,392,117. The average per cent. of total population enrolled in the eleven Southern States was 22.11 and in the eleven Northern States the average per cent. of total population enrolled was 18.59. The per cent. of the school population (children 5-18 years of age) in the Southern States was 70.47, while in the eleven Northern States it was 74.62. Notwithstanding the number of children enrolled in the Southern States was about 800,-000 more than the total enrollment in the eleven Northern States, the number attending daily for each 100 enrolled in the Southern States was 66.1, while in the eleven Northern States it was 76.96, and the average of the United States for the same period was 73.2 per cent.

The larger enrollment in the Southern States was due partly to the greater proportion of children of school age, but it was also due in a measure to the fact that the Southern people are as solicitous about the education of their children as are the people of other States. They are more concerned than the people of some other States. Compulsory education obtains in all of the Northern and Western States; there has been no legislation for compulsory education in the Southern States until very recently. The Southern people have done, or tried to do, voluntarily what others have done under compulsion. It has been asserted, more frequently in the South than in the North, that the poor whites of the South are thriftless and without family or State pride sufficient to furnish an incentive for the education of their children. The charge is not true; it is one of the numerous libels against these worthy citizens. The poor whites of the South are not of low strain; they are brave, gentle, loyal and patriotic, and have proven their worth on the battle-field and in the pursuits of peace. They are homogeneous people and come from good stock. Given the opportunity, they never fail to show themselves the equals of any people in personal, racial and national pride.

During many years the Southern people patiently waited for the ruling Oligarchy to give them a chance to vote on educational questions and other measures for their betterment. What they will do when they have a chance to be heard, was shown in Alabama. As the result of very earnest work initiated by the State Superintendent, Mr. Feagin, the Legislature of this State authorized a vote on six amendments proposed for the Constitution. The principal amendment was the one authorizing city and county municipalities to levy a special tax for educational purposes. The number of votes cast for and against the educational amendment totalled 116,884. The majority for this amendment was 21,798, the largest majority given for any measure that was before the people in that election.

The average number of days attended by each pupil enrolled in 1912-13 in the eleven Southern States was 82.7, while for the same year in the eleven Northern States it was 131.7, and the average of the United States was 115.6. The average annual salary of all teachers in the eleven Southern States was $311.27, and in the Northern States it was $542.32, the average for the United States being $511.86. The average expenditure per capita of school population was $7.59 in the Southern States, $25.01 in the Northern States and $20.38 in the United States.

The estimated value of all public property used for school purposes (1914) in the eleven Southern States was $119,558,131, and the value of school property in the eleven Northern States was $369,631,415. The value of all public property used for school purposes in the Southern States was less than one-third the value of all public property used for school purposes in the eleven Northern States, notwithstanding the assessed value of all property subject to ad valorem taxation in the Southern States was nearly one-half the value of all such property in the eleven Northern States. For further comparison between ten Southern and ten Northern and Western States, in expenditures for educational purposes, the following tabulation shows the average per capita expenditure for public schools in 1918:

PER CAPITA EXPENDITURE FOR PUBLIC SCHOOLS IN 1918

Ten Highest States		Ten Lowest States	
Montana	19.14	Mississippi	$2.13
Iowa	13.16	Alabama	2.53
Arizona	12.99	Georgia	2.59
North Dakota	12.50	North Carolina	2.65
Utah	11.81	Arkansas	2.79
Idaho	11.22	South Carolina	2.99
Nebraska	11.09	Louisiana	3.19
California	10.94	Tennessee	3.32
Minnesota	10.66	Kentucky	3.47
Wyoming	10.53	Virginia	3.72
	$12.40		$2.93

During the year 1919, in the rural schools of Alabama, the average salary of each white male teacher was $470 and each white female teacher $312. The corresponding figures for city teachers were $1,345 and $698, respectively. In the case of Negroes, the average salary of rural school teachers was $178 for each male teacher and $180 for each female. In the city districts, the corresponding figures were $602 and $386, respectively. In his annual report for 1919, the Superintendent of Education in Alabama says:

Ten per cent. of the white boys and girls of school age and thirty per cent. of the Negro girls and boys of school age in Alabama did not enter school during the year. . . . More than 500 white schools and a like number of Negro schools could not open during the entire year for lack of teachers.

The State of Florida has made greater progress in education during late years than any other Southern State, due to the fact that a large number of Northern people have moved into this State and they are not willing to bring up their children without the advantages of education. In 1920, the average attendance per teacher in Florida was 22 for whites and 34 for Negroes, while the salary for white male teachers was $119.80 per month, for Negro male teachers it was $61.20 per month. White female teachers were paid an average of $81.00 per month while Negro women were paid an average monthly salary of $43.20. There were 2,609 schools taught in 1920, of which the whites had 1,876 and the Negroes had 733. The whites represented 65.48 and the Negroes 34.52 per cent. of the total population.

In spite of the fact that the value of the school buildings provided for the Negroes was less than 8 per cent. of the value of buildings provided for the whites, and in spite of the great difference in seating capacity of the buildings, and other inequalities cited in the preceding paragraph, the Negroes continued to show an average daily attendance, based on percentage of enrollment, equal to the whites, and in some cases the percentage of Negroes in daily attendance was higher than that of the whites.

Concerning the educational situation in Georgia, before the World War, in the matter of paying teachers, *The Atlanta Constitution* said:

As an inevitable result of the perpetual and petty political wrangling between factions, and the consequent paralysis of legislative action, the common school teachers of more than a third of the Georgia counties are to-day hawking about scrip for salaries earned in March, but not payable until December, AT A DISCOUNT OF TEN PER CENT.

It is of noteworthy significance that in the 64th Congress the Chairman of the Committee on Education and Labor in the United States Senate was a Senator from Georgia, and the Chairman of the Committee on Education in the House of Representatives was Congressman Hughes of Georgia. In 1919, the Board of Education of Atlanta issued a statement in which it declared that conditions under which the schools of that city were struggling were "intolerable," and that the voters should be made fully acquainted with the actual situation. This statement published by the Board of Education contained the following comment:

We found that practically all of the teachers were underpaid . . . found also that the condition of the buildings and equipment therein were in a deplorable state. . . . We merely ask the citizens to visit the Girls' High School and see there the nineteen inside rooms lighted by artificial light and with practically no fresh air. . . . Then visit the Tech High School and note there the tremendous over-crowded condition. Only one-half of the students are able to have seats at any one time, the other half having to work in the shops or drill, or stand up until the expiration of the period in which the students are occupying the seats. . . . There are forty-three basement rooms being used as class-rooms for the children, thirty-seven of which are occupied by white children and six by colored children.

In 1915, the State of Georgia paid to teachers the total sum of $4,385,258.77, of which $695,803.85 was paid to colored teachers. A trifle more than 15 per cent. of the total disbursements for teachers was paid to Negro teachers although the Negro population was 44.24 per cent. of the total population. During the month of May, 1921, the Georgia Association for the Advancement of Education Among Negroes appeared before the Superintendent of State Schools in Georgia and requested that a Negro supervisor for colored schools in the State be appointed. Among other interesting facts presented by the President of this Association were the following:

It is impossible for the State to get value received as long as we have to teach our children in church buildings, lodge halls, rickety and unsanitary school buildings with the facilities such as are provided. . . .

Many of our teachers are paid the small salary of $20.00 per month and $1.05 per capita is paid for the education of the Negro youth while $19.50 per capita is paid for the white youth in the same county and the school term divided up into two or three divisions. . . .

There are twelve agricultural and mechanical colleges in the State providing training for the white youth. The Negro represents between 45 and 50 per cent. of our State's population, yet we have not a single agricultural or mechanical college in the State supported absolutely by State funds for the education of the Negro youth.

Concerning the spirit and ambition manifested by the Negroes of Georgia in their struggle for an education, the Commissioner of Education in this State said:

It is gratifying to state that the Negroes have worked as faithfully as any people could, despite the great number of adult illiterates among them. A compulsory attendance law would affect a small class of white people more than it would the masses of the Negroes, for the Negroes are sending their children to school now. Negro adult illiteracy has been materially reduced in five counties of the State, while it has been well-nigh eliminated in two or three counties.

The per cent. of school population enrolled in Louisiana (1918-19) was 53.69, the lowest in the United States, the average for the whole country was 77.8 per cent. Commenting on scant provision made in the public schools of Louisiana for education of Negroes, the Superintendent of Education of this State said:

> Nor has the school system been able to reach all the Negro school children because we have taken the position that our first duty was to provide good schools for the white race, attacking the problem of Negro education after the performance of that first duty. . . . The Negro schools offer but little of value, and, therefore, the Negro child that fails to attend loses little.

A few years ago, there was another State official in Louisiana who was no less frank than the Superintendent of Education in discussing the question of education for the Negro. The candor of this official, Mr. Leo M. Favrot, State Agent of Rural Schools for Negroes in Louisiana, was seasoned with a sense of justice, humanity and patriotism, when, in an address which he delivered before the National Association for the Advancement of Colored People, at Cleveland, Ohio, June 25, 1919, he said:

> It is not possible to work with these people and not feel for them sympathy, admiration and respect. The sacrifices they are making for the education and enlightenment of their people, their kindly disposition and the sincere appreciation they show for the smallest service rendered them; their patience, the philosophical way they generally take discourtesy and brusque treatment, their cheerfulness even in adversity—all of these things make it a source of never-ceasing wonder to me that for so many years I have lived among these people and knew them not, that for so many years I saw in them only the faults that are bred of ignorance, depravity and neglect and not the inherent good qualities with which our Almighty Creator has endowed them. I am grateful that my eyes have been opened, and that it is my privilege to help open the eyes of others in my State.

The per cent. of school population enrolled in the public schools of Mississippi (1919-20) was 69.8, and the average number of days schools were in session was 122 while the average of the United States for the same year was 161.9. The total number of teachers in Mississippi for this year was 11,962 and the average annual salaries of teachers, supervisors and principals was $291, the lowest in the United States, the average of the United States being $871. The average value of school property per pupil enrolled was $29 in Mississippi; the average of the United States was $112.

Of the total population in Mississippi, the Negroes represented 56.2 per cent. in 1910 and 52.2 in 1920. School statistics for 1919-20 show that the per cent. of the school population was 46.7 white and 53.3 colored. Out of a total of 11,962 teachers, there were 7,673 white teachers and 4,289 colored teachers. With 52.2 per cent. of the total population and 53.3 per cent. of the school population, the Negroes had 35.86 per cent. of the total number of teachers employed in the public schools of the State. As shown by the census of 1920, 59.2 per cent. of all farms in Mississippi were operated by Negroes; yet, as we have seen, scant provision has been made by the State for their elementary education to say nothing of higher education or training in agricultural schools.

In spite of injustice and persecution, and the great difficulties and disadvantages under which the Negroes have struggled for an education for so many years in the South, especially in Mississippi and South Carolina and Louisiana, they have made remarkable progress. For example, *The Manufacturers Record* published in its issue of September 16, 1920, an interesting letter from Judge Charles E. Chidsey, of Pascagoula, Mississippi, from which I take the following:

During the war I had to make out a number of questionnaires and I was surprised to find that the percentage of illiteracy among the white was greater than among the blacks, and some of the finest penmanship that I have ever seen was by Negro men and women who had been educated in the Negro schools. In making out papers for civil service, I have found that there are about four Negro applicants for civil service examination to one white person. The Negroes are most eager to enter the civil service, while very few white men or boys seem to be ambitious in that direction. I have observed, and the school trustees confirm my observation, that the Negroes are more ambitious and are ready to make any kind of sacrifice for an education, while the whites as a usual thing seem to be indifferent to it. A Negro girl in this city, who had been employed by a white family for some two years, lately announced that she would not retain her position, as she had saved up her wages and was going to a Negro college for women in North Carolina. Many such cases may be cited. A member of the Mississippi Legislature at the last session, on the debate on the ''Compulsory Education Bill,'' stated: ''I want to tell you people something. The white people of the South are more in need of compulsory education than is the Negro.''

The late Bishop Galloway, distinguished citizen of Mississippi, in an address before the Southern Educational Association, spoke eloquently and forcibly concerning the educational progress and moral advancement of the Negroes in the South. In answer to the propaganda of race hatred and the assertion that education made the Negro more lawless, he said:

From the declaration that education has made the Negro more immoral and criminal, I am constrained to dissent. There are no data or figures on which to base such an indictment or justify such an assertion. On the contrary, indisputable facts attest the statement that education and its attendant influences have elevated the standard and tone of morals among the Negroes of the South. . . . I have been at not a little pains to ascertain from representatives of various institutions the post-collegiate history of their students, and I am profoundly gratified at the record. I believe it perfectly safe to say that not a single case of criminal assault has ever been charged on a student of a mission school for Negroes founded and sustained by a great Christian denomination.

According to a report of the Superintendent of Public Instruction of North Carolina, during the year 1919, the average annual salary paid to the white teachers in the city schools was $753.66 and in the rural schools $450.01. The average annual salary paid to the colored teachers in the city schools was $445.15, and in the rural schools $262.85. The average length of the school term for the white race was "almost seven months, exclusive of all holidays, it being 136 days." All colored schools increased from 105.6 days to an average of 127.4 days. Before beginning of the great exodus of Negroes from the Southern States (1917), the Superintendent of Public Instruction of North Carolina, in an official report, said:

It is manifest to me that if the Negroes become convinced that they are to be deprived of their schools and of the opportunities of an education, most of the wisest and most self-respecting Negroes will leave the State, and eventually there will be left only the indolent, worthless, and criminal part of the Negro population.

There are but two roads open to him. One is elevation through the right sort of education; the other is deterioration and degradation through ignorance and miseducation, inevitably leading to expulsion or extermination. We must help him into the first if we can. If we do not, our race will pay the heaviest penalty for the failure.

Another prominent citizen of North Carolina, Mr. Clarence Poe, editor of *The Progressive Farmer*, lecturer and author, in discussing the subject of education for the Negro, said:

My answer to the hoary and oft-repeated charge that Negro education is a mistake and will "spoil field hands— . . . ." is that there is nothing else under high heaven that the South needs so much as the "spoiling of field hands" of the type we have had until now. This ignorant Negro field hand is and has been one of the greatest economic curses with which any people has ever had to contend.

The per cent. of school population enrolled in the public schools of South Carolina (1919-20) was 83.9 which was very high and above the average of the United States. In the more important matters of school term, attendance and teachers, however, the situation was not so encouraging. In his report for 1920, the State Superintendent of Education states that—

of every dollar expended during the year eighty-eight and five-tenths cents (.885) was used in the white schools and eleven and five-tenths cents (.115) in the colored schools. Out of every dollar, salaries of white teachers represent fifty-seven and eight-tenths cents (.578) and salaries of colored teachers nine and seven-tenths (.097). For all purposes other than salaries the white schools used 30.7 per cent., and the colored schools 1.8 per cent

Notwithstanding the Negroes receive so small a proportion of public funds for educational purposes, the Superintendent of Education frankly admits that the Negroes have manifested a deeper interest in education than the whites have shown in South Carolina. For instance, in 1920 the—

enrollment increased 22.9 per cent. over last year. The number of white pupils 35,697—18.7 per cent.; the number of colored pupils 53,335—26.8 per cent. . . . The percentage of pupils from both races and both sexes in regular attendance was 69.34. The whites show 67.91 and the Negroes 70.60. Thus, the Negroes exceeded the whites by 2.69.

In considering the statistics on enrollment and attendance in the public schools, as cited by the Superintendent of Education for the purpose of comparison, it should be borne in mind that, according to the census of 1920, the Negroes represented 51.4 per cent. of the total population of South Carolina. Commenting in detail on the record in several counties, the Superintendent said:

A study of the white schools ranks Georgetown County first with an average attendance of 80.89 per cent., and Barnwell County second with an average attendance of 76.90 per cent. Twenty-six counties are above the State average. . . . Curiously enough, Georgetown also ranks first in attendance among colored schools with an average of 87.24 per cent. This is the highest figure reported from any county for either whites or blacks. Though Georgetown is in the black belt, Pickens stands second with an average for its colored pupils of 82.32 per cent., and Lancaster third with an average of 81.56 per cent. Pickens and Lancaster are both distinctively white counties. In 25 counties the colored average exceeded 70 per cent.

According to the report of the State Superintendent, the average salary paid white male teachers was $962.15; white women, $553.74; Negro men, $239.48, and Negro women, $184.58. For both sexes, the average paid white teachers was $601.79, and Negro teachers, $195.72. The following tabulation, showing expenditures for the public schools of South Carolina, 1920-21, for whites and Negroes, respectively, is made up from the figures published in the annual report of the Superintendent of Education:

	Whites	Negroes
Total salaries paid teachers	$5,304,269.35	$779,443.45
Furniture and apparatus	181,804.56	18,027.33
Fuel and incidentals	890,433.69	47,501.74
Grounds, buildings, repairs and rents . .	1,897,396.60	295,574.71
Libraries	3,433.85	50.00
Bonds (white) interest	186,121.87	. . . .
Teachers employed	6,859	3,457
Average salary paid, both sexes	$773.33	$225.47

No comment I could make would add to the pathetic and startling facts revealed in these figures, and yet the report of the Superintendent of Education contains the following gratuitous hyperbole: "The Negro can now secure anything in South Carolina except social and political equality."

According to the biennial report of the Superintendent of Public Instruction of Texas (1918), 88.6 per cent. of the white and 90 per cent. of the Negro scholastic population was enrolled. The length of school term in days for the whites was 154 and for the colored 132 days. As a general rule in the Southern States, the attendance of the Negro children, in spite of the difficulties under which they labor for an education, is about as high as the whites, on the basis of enrollment. The interest shown by the Negroes in getting an education is due in a large

measure to the active and untiring efforts of the leaders of this
race to encourage and stimulate every Negro child in a fight
for education. From a report of the Superintendent of Education in Virginia I take the following significant acknowledgment:

The Negroes in Virginia reduced their illiteracy 35 per cent., 1900 to 1910;
the whites only 29 per cent. Said we not truly in a former paragraph of this
report that the Negro situation would take care of itself if we would keep
the native white statistics constantly before our eyes.

The following tabulation from the United States census reports shows the percentage of white (native parentage) and
Negro illiterates, respectively, 10 years of age and over, in
eleven Southern States and the total of the United States, for
1910 and 1920, and the decrease.

| | White, Native Parentage | | | Negro | | |
	1910	1920	Decrease	1910	1920	Decrease
Alabama . . .	10.1	6.4	3.7	40.1	31.3	8.8
Arkansas . . .	7.1	4.6	2.5	26.4	21.8	4.6
Florida	5.2	3.1	2.1	25.5	21.5	4.0
Georgia	8.0	5.5	2.5	36.5	29.1	7.4
Louisiana . . .	15.0	11.4	3.6	48.4	38.5	9.9
Mississippi . . .	5.3	3.6	1.7	35.6	29.3	6.3
North Carolina .	12.3	8.2	4.1	31.9	24.5	7.4
South Carolina .	10.5	6.6	3.9	38.7	29.3	8.8
Tennessee . . .	9.9	7.4	2.5	27.3	22.4	4.9
Texas	3.3	2.2	1.1	24.6	17.8	6.8
Virginia . . .	8.2	6.1	2.1	30.0	23.5	6.5
	8.6	5.9	2.7	33.2	26.3	6.9
United States . .	3.7	2.5	1.2	30.4	22.9	7.5

Reports from every one of the Southern States show the deep
interest the Negroes have manifested in educational work for
their race. The greater difficulties placed in the way of the
Negro the harder he works for an education, and the official
reports show with what commendable success he has struggled
against great odds. His advancement by comparison with the
whites has been marvelous.

The total investment in public school property for whites in
the Southern States, as compiled in *The Negro Year Book*
(1916-17), was $112,141,942, while the total for the Negroes

was $11,882,954. The average value per child of school age in public school property for the whites was $29.71, and for the Negroes it was $5.07. According to the same authority, the average expenditure per child of school age was $10.55 for the whites and $2.91 for Negroes, while the per cent. of whites of school age was 62.2 and the Negroes was 37.8. In the matter of expenditures for education in the public schools of the South, as respects Negroes, the following is from a book by Mr. Gilbert Thomas Stephenson, entitled *Race Distinctions in American Law:*

It is commonly believed that the Negro has had and is now getting much more than his share of the public school fund. . . . Mr. J. Y. Joyner, Superintendent of Public Instruction of North Carolina, has said: ''Upon the most liberal estimate, it seems that in 1908 the Negroes received for the maintenance of their public schools in North Carolina about twice as much as they paid directly or indirectly for this purpose. . . . My own opinion is that the white people pay, directly or indirectly, for the education of the Negro more rather than less than one dollar for every dollar that the Negro pays, directly or indirectly for that purpose.'' Mr. J. D. Eggleston, Jr., Superintendent of Public Instruction of Virginia, estimates that the public school fund for Negroes in that State is $500,000, of which the Negro pays $87,000, or less than one-fifth.

It is true that the Negro is getting more than his share of the public school funds in the Southern States, if the basis of determining the Negro's share be the relative amount of taxes he pays. There are no official reports which give authentic information on this subject, nor any very definite facts from which one may reach satisfactory conclusions in discussing this subject. In some of the State educational reports definite figures are published which show the actual expenditures for each race, but in the absence of accurate statistics showing the actual proportions of the total revenues which are collected from Negroes, it is not practicable to estimate what proportion of the total sum expended for education of Negroes is actually paid by that race in taxes to the State and municipal governments in the Southern States.

Numerous instances could be cited to show the spirit of self-sacrifice and zeal on the part of the Negroes in the cause of education, and their eagerness to improve every possible opportunity for the educational advancement, civic and moral uplift

of their race. The history of the Julius Rosenwald Fund perhaps furnishes as striking an example as could be found to
illustrate this point. This Fund has aided in building more
than 2,100 rural school houses for Negroes in fourteen Southern
States. According to a "summary statement" as of March 6,
1924, "the present total of completed buildings is 2158; 5266
teacher capacity, 236,970 pupil capacity." Total cost and contributions are shown in the following table.

Public Funds	$4,381,428
Negroes	2,005,614
Rosenwald Fund	1,557,827
Whites	418,424
Total cost	$8,363,293

There are 39 additional buildings now nearing completion or awaiting
final inspection (Alabama 6, Arkansas 4, Florida 4, Georgia 7, North Carolina 13, Texas 4, Virginia 1). These being counted, the total of buildings
as of March 6, 1924, is 2,197.

The construction of schoolhouses with aid of the Julius Rosenwald Fund is directed and the funds administered by the State
Superintendent of Education, and the buildings become public
school property. A condition of aid from the Fund is that the
Negroes raise an amount equal to or greater than that given by
the Fund, securing this from their own contributions of money
or labor, from white friends, and from public funds. The figures
I have cited are taken from the latest (at the present writing)
official report, and these figures plainly show the activities and
liberal contributions of the Negroes in support of this supplemental movement for the education of their race.

In the beginning of this survey of the educational situation
in the South, the first figures presented for comparison were
based on official statistics for the year preceding the outbreak of
the World War (1913), when normal conditions prevailed, but
I stated that later figures from reports during and subsequent to
the war would be cited to show the continued backwardness of
the Southern States in public education. I have already cited statistics from reports as recent as 1921, but in order to amplify
my summary of these reports of State Superintendents in the
Southern States, I have compiled a table showing the average

length of school term and school attendance; total number of teachers employed; average annual salaries; and total per capita cost of public school education in eleven Southern States and eleven Northern States. This tabulation is based on figures contained in *Bulletin, 1922, No. 29, Statistics of State School Systems, 1919-20*, Bureau of Education.

AVERAGE LENGTH OF SCHOOL TERM AND SCHOOL ATTENDANCE

	Average number of days schools were in session		Total number of teachers	Average annual Salaries	Per capita costs of Education
	All schools	Average days attended by each child			
Alabama . .	123.1	58.8	12,558	$484.00	$3.88
Arkansas . .	126.3	73.0	10,476	477.00	4.40
Florida . .	133.1	80.9	6,651	518.00	7.26
Georgia . .	145.0	72.6	15,921	426.00	3.13
Louisiana . .	148.9	68.4	8,966	723.00	6.32
Mississippi .	122.0	53.7	11,962	291.00	3.06
North Carolina	134.0	75.6	16,852	464.00	4.75
South Carolina	109.6	63.7	9,699	464.00	3.94
Tennessee . .	133.5	86.3	13,277	494.00	4.34
Texas . . .	155.6	82.2	29,001	612.00	7.21
Virginia . .	147.0	74.9	14,271	546.00	5.62
	134.4	71.8	149,634	$499.00	$4.90
Indiana . .	155.8	99.9	17,209	$964.00	$12.20
Iowa . . .	174.0	118.0	24,451	827.00	15.53
Maine . . .	169.2	108.7	5,732	603.00	8.34
Michigan . .	172.0	102.8	23,703	911.00	13.00
Minnesota .	160.0	102.6	19,575	882.00	14.97
Nebraska . .	164.0	110.7	14,253	765.00	15.88
New Hampshire	174.0	92.9	2,594	759.00	8.60
New Jersey .	189.0	117.2	16,758	1,282.00	12.96
Ohio . . .	165.0	100.2	31,404	1,088.00	11.71
Rhode Island .	182.1	93.4	2,793	1,070.00	7.89
Wisconsin . .	175.3	94.7	16,210	915.00	10.36
	170.9	103.7	174,682	$915.00	$11.95
Continental United States	161.9	94.3	657,646	$871.00	$9.80

In spite of greater need for expansion, and for more liberal policies and efficient methods in the public school system of the Southern States, than in any other States, the relative progress of the South has been very slow and these States are still very backward. For example, as shown by the figures in the foregoing table, the average number of days all schools were in session, 1919-20, in the Northern States, were 36.5 days more than in the Southern States, and the average of the United States were 27.5 days more than the average of the Southern States. In the Northern States the average days attended by each child were 31.9 days more than in the Southern States, and in the United States 22.5 more days than in the South. In the outlying possessions of Alaska, Canal Zone, Hawaii, Philippine Islands and Porto Rico, respectively, the average number of days all schools were in session were more than the average, and more than any of the Southern States.

The average annual salaries of teachers in the Southern States increased from $311.27 in 1912-13 to $499.00 in 1919-20, an increase of $187.73; in the Northern States the increase during the same period was from $542.32 to $915.00, an increase of $372.68, while the average increase in the United States was from $511.86 in 1912-13 to $871.00 in 1919-20.

In 1912-13, the Southern States expended for public schools $2.36 per capita of total population; in 1919-20, the average expenditures of these States for public education was $4.90 per capita, an increase of $2.54. The corresponding figures for the eleven Northern States are $6.23 and $11.95, respectively, an increase of $5.72 per capita in costs of public education, while the per capita increase in the United States was from $5.37 in 1912-13 to $9.80 in 1919-20. Total expenditures for educational purposes, total outlays for new buildings, sites, and new equipment, and the value of school property per pupil enrolled, 1919-20, of the State school systems are shown in the tabulation on page 188.

The official figures plainly show the continued backwardness of the Southern States in all matters relating to public education. These figures tell their own story and further comment would be a work of supererogation. It may be well to bear in mind, however, that the Southern States have not been taxed for educational purposes according to their means and their ability to pay. In preceding paragraphs of this chapter I cited authoritative reports showing the assessed valuation of all property subject to ad valorem taxation in the eleven Southern States and the Northern States selected for comparison. These figures show that the average amount expended for public schools on each $100 of assessed valuation of all property in the Southern States was less than the average amount expended in the Northern States, on the same basis of wealth and school expenditures in these States. The average of such expenditures in the United States was also higher than it was in the Southern States.

	Total payments, current expenses	New buildings, sites and equipment	Total expenditures for educational purposes	Average value of school property per pupil enrolled
Alabama . .	$7,719,363	$1,399,328	$9,118,691	$33,00
Arkansas . .	5,990,075	1,716,546	7,706,621	35.00
Florida . . .	5,992,950	1,037,983	7,030,933	60.00
Georgia . .	8,369,321	707,132	9,076,453	31.00
Louisiana . .	9,159,395	2,207,539	11,366,934	61.00
Mississippi . .	4,474,796	1,000,000	5,474,796	29.00
N. Carolina .	9,807,856	2,340,000	12,147,856	35.00
S. Carolina .	5,469,525	1,157,492	6,627,017	40.00
Tennessee . .	8,546,521	1,594,853	10,141,374	35.00
Texas . . .	28,337,826	5,268,384	33,606,210	69.00
Virginia . .	10,196,146	2,778,943	12,975,089	44.00
	$104,063,774	$21,208,200	$125,271,974	$42.90
Indiana . .	$28,764,748	$7,000,000	$35,764,748	$120.00
Iowa . . .	32,504,465	4,832,702	37,334,167	130.00
Maine . . .	5,977,300	426,373	6,403,673	110.00
Michigan . .	37,830,588	9,853,175	47,683,763	148.00
Minnesota . .	28,418,954	7,315,142	35,734,096	148.00
Nebraska . .	17,758,883	2,821,186	20,580,069	135.00
New Hampshire	3,628,168	182,501	3,810,669	130.00
New Jersey .	35,420,508	5,489,319	40,909,827	173.00
Ohio . . .	56,860,215	10,566,326	67,426,541	167.00
Rhode Island .	4,545,219	221,114	4,766,333	154.00
Wisconsin . .	22,648,227	4,606,829	27,255,056	126.00
	$274,354,275	$53,314,667	$327,668,942	$140.00
Continental United States .	$882,608,557	$153,542,852	$1,036,151,209	$112.00

CHAPTER X

In the United States Senate, August 6, 1916, the Senate having under consideration the Child Labor Bill, Senator Overman, of North Carolina, said:

I wish to say that the statistics furnished by the Census Office show that North Carolina is increasing as to literacy over a majority of the other States. In a majority of the States illiteracy is increasing, while it is decreasing in North Carolina. . . . There is not a cotton mill in our State which does not have a school, and there is not a child who works in the factories who cannot read and write. . . . While we were a poor State, for a long time we ranked low in literacy; but so far as the facts are concerned, for the past ten years we have been improving in our percentage of literacy as compared with other States; and North Carolina to-day, I believe, stands eleventh in that respect. . . . We put up nice school houses on nearly every hill in the State. That shows the remarkable record we have made in the last ten years, better than two-thirds of the other States.

Official reports do not sustain the assertions of Senator Overman. As shown by the census of 1910, the percentage of illiterates in population 10 years and over, all classes, in North Carolina, was 18.5. This State ranked as sixth in the highest percentage of illiteracy; only Louisiana, South Carolina, Alabama, Mississippi and Georgia being higher. In white illiterates of native parentage, Louisiana was the highest in 1910 and North Carolina was second. These two States occupied the same relative position in 1920 in percentage of white illiteracy of native parentage. The figures in detail were included in tabulations cited in the preceding chapter. In those tabulations I also included some figures showing the ten highest and ten lowest in per capita expenditures for schools by certain States in 1918. In that list North Carolina ranks fourth in the ten lowest. Two years after the Senator from North Carolina addressed the Senate on the matter of educational progress in this State, there were only three States—Mississippi, Alabama and Georgia—

lower than North Carolina in per capita expenditures for public schools. The per capita in North Carolina was $2.65 and, for example, it was $11.09 in Nebraska and $13.16 in Iowa. Later figures, based on the census of 1920, and reports of the Bureau of Education, furnish a complete answer to the assertions of Senator Overman with respect to the educational situation in North Carolina.

As shown by official reports (1914), the amount expended for public schools of each $100 of assessed valuation of all property in North Carolina was 50.5 cents, and the amount expended per capita of total population, in 1912-13, was $1.76. The total population of North Carolina (1913) was 85,337 more than the total population of Iowa; and the white population of North Carolina (1910) was 320,218 more than the white population of Nebraska. The estimated value of all public property used for school purposes in North Carolina (1913) was $8,149,823, while in Iowa the value of such property was $32,964,111 and in Nebraska it was $20,623,819. With a white population over 300,000 less than the white population of North Carolina, the State of Nebraska had school property valued at more than two and one-half times the value of such property in North Carolina. For further comparison, attention may be called to the fact that the school term in Iowa was 173.6; in Nebraska 169, and in North Carolina 122 days. The average number of days attended by every child 5 to 18 years of age in North Carolina was 67.2; in Iowa 110.0; in Nebraska 103.1.

Concerning the qualifications of teachers in the Southern States, in the public schools of Alabama for example, the Superintendent of Education of this State made the following statement:

Eighty per cent. of our white teachers have had no professional training whatever. They are licensed upon examination. One-third of them have never gone further than through the elementary schools, and a great majority of the remainder have gone no further than through the high school.

In 1919, the Legislature of Alabama authorized the Governor to appoint an Education Commission of "five of the most representative men in the State." At the head of this commission appointed by the Governor was the Hon. Sydney J. Bowie. In a preceding chapter (VII) I alluded to the active work of Mr. Bowie in support of the new Constitution of Alabama, made for the purpose of disfranchising the Negroes under the form of law. It is therefore worth while at this point to note the fact that the report of the special commission on education was prepared by Mr. Bowie. In this interesting and illuminating report we find the following frank acknowledgment:

Under the present Constitution, and in fact, since the Constitution of 1875, we have found ourselves more limited and restricted in the matter of local school support than any State in the Union. . . .

The record shows that in the year 1919, fifty-four years after the Civil War, the proportion of illiteracy among our white population is greater than it was in 1860. More than two generations have grown up since the Civil War, more than one-half and perhaps three-fourths of whom have either been totally denied the benefits of education, or else have had access to schools of such limited equipment, and of such short terms, and untrained and inefficient teachers as to leave the great majority of our rural population without adequate equipment for the great competition of life. The figures of illiteracy are startling enough of themselves, but the figures of near-illiteracy, if they could be obtained, or even estimated, would be even more startling, since they would show conclusively that the ''little learning'' which the poet says is a ''dangerous thing'' is all that has been vouchsafed to the great mass of our people.

The most candid and significant admission found in this report of the Alabama Educational Commission, prepared by Mr. Bowie, is the following:

We need not refer to conditions before the war except to repeat that even as far back as 1840 there were proportionately fewer illiterates among the white population than there are to-day. The Constitution of 1868, though enacted by a so-called ''carpet-bag'' government, dealt with the subject of education in a manner far more liberal and infinitely better calculated to promote general intelligence than does either the Constitution of 1875 or that of 1901.

Here, then, we have the acknowledgment of one of the most active and prominent proponents of the present Constitution of Alabama frankly admitting that neither the Constitution of 1875, made by the Southern Oligarchy, after the end of the Reconstruction epoch and Republican rule, nor the latest Constitution, adopted in 1901 for the purpose of disfranchising the Negro, was, by comparison, as able and altogether as wholesome a constitution as the one made under the carpet-bag government in 1868. Indeed, we also find in this interesting report the further frank admission that—

In so far as education is concerned, therefore, the Constitution of 1875 marks a change from a Constitution providing as liberal a method of support for schools as existed in any State of the Union to a Constitution with the most illiberal and inadequate method of support to be found in any State.

During the month of June, 1920, the Russell Sage Foundation gave out reports based on a survey of the educational situation in the United States. Among the interesting results of that survey is the conclusion that the school system of the United States territorial possessions, Hawaii, the Canal Zone, and Porto Rico, have higher ratings than the ratings of many of the States. Hawaii is reported higher than a majority of the States. Ten Southern States have ratings lower than the Porto Rico in educational progress. The State of Montana is at the head of the list, having the most efficient and best all-round public school system in the United States. Next to Montana comes California, then Arizona, New Jersey and Washington. The Southern States are at the bottom of the list. South Carolina is the lowest; the standard in this State, for instance, is 29.4. Next to South Carolina comes Mississippi, then Arkansas, Alabama, North Carolina, Georgia and Louisiana. Florida and Texas are the only two States in the South which may be ranked with Porto Rico.

The first constitution of Hawaii (1840) provided for a school in districts wherever 15 or more children, suitable to attend school, lived close together. School attendance is compulsory for the entire school year for children between the ages of six and fifteen, and tuition is free. Ninety-two per cent. of all children of this class, of school age, attend school, besides a considerable number of pupils under six years, who are in the kindergartens. Eighty-three per cent. of all of those of Hawaiian blood, above six years old, can read and write. Schools are established all over the islands and elementary education has been free since the public school system was established in Hawaii.

The per capita expenditure for public school purposes in

Hawaii was more than the expenditure per capita in any of the Southern States, and it was more than seventy-five per cent. greater than the average of the eleven Southern States. In educational progress Hawaii is not only far ahead of the South in every particular, but it is also ahead of some other States in point of attendance. It has been stated that Hawaii has a record of attendance higher than any State. Every school in Hawaii has a school year of 190 days. Teachers are paid for twelve months of the year, in twelve equal installments, and there is no sex distinction. The women are paid the same salary that the men receive in the same positions.

The deplorable situation in the Southern States may be further illustrated by comparison with the Philippine Islands and Porto Rico in the matter of public schools. From the report (1922) of the "Special Mission on Investigation to the Philippine Islands," I quote the following comment on the educational situation in that country:

The Filipinos are deeply interested in public education. Their enthusiasm, their keenness to secure education for their children, is beyond praise. . . . The progressive development of the school system has been phenomenal. . . . The following table gives an idea of the progress in this department:

ANNUAL ENROLLMENT OF PUBLIC SCHOOLS

	1898	1902	1907	1914	1920
Pupils	4,504	200,000	479,978	621,030	935,678
American Teachers	847	746	658	341	316
Filipino Teachers	1,914	6,141	7,013	7,234	20,691

In 1920 the public owned 4,063 and rented 1,163 school buildings. The total expenditures for administration and instruction were about $6,869,-654.50 for 1920. The university had, in 1920, an enrollment of 4,130, with a teaching force of 379 professors and assistants. The cost of operation was $755,926.57.

As before stated, the self-sacrifice of the parents has been great. They have willingly deprived themselves of many necessities in order that they might aid in the voluntary building of schools and properly equip their children for school attendance.

During the year 1919, as reported in *The American Year Book*, the most important event in the Philippine Islands was the passage of an act—

providing for the spending of $15,000,000 during the next five years (in addition to the regular appropriations) for school purposes. This will mean that free elementary instruction will be placed within the reach of every child of school age in the Islands.

It is plain that citizens of the Philippine Islands are showing a deeper interest in educational progress, and opportunities for the mass of the people, than has been shown in any one of the Southern States under rule of the Oligarchy, during forty years last past. The plain truth is so humiliating, so painfully condemnatory of my native section, that I hesitate to present further evidence of the relative backwardness and delinquencies of the South. And yet I know that a large majority of the Southern people, white and colored, still believe that the whole truth should be published and that it will make them free.

At the time of the American occupation, Porto Rico had a total of 555 schools, including public and private, illiteracy being more common among the white than among the black inhabitants. Only eight per cent. of the school population attended school. Immediately after the American occupation, the school system of Porto Rico was made compulsory. In 1910 the percentage of illiteracy had been reduced to 66.5 per cent. In 1914, with a population of 1,184,489, Porto Rico expended $2,498,584.45, about $2.11 per capita, for educational purposes, being more per capita than the per capita expenditure of each of several Southern States for educational purposes.

In 1913 the total population of South Carolina was about 400,000 more than the total population of Porto Rico, but Porto Rico expended about $100,000 more for educational purposes than was expended by South Carolina during the same year. While expenditures for educational purposes in Porto Rico were on the basis of $2.25 per capita, expenditures for education in the State of Mississippi were on the basis of $1.50 per capita. No State in the South during forty years last past has made the progress in education that Porto Rico has made in twenty years. The colored population of Porto Rico is about 37 per cent. of the total while the colored population of the eleven Southern States is not over an average of 32 per cent. of the total population. Further to illustrate the remarkable educational progress of Porto Rico, I quote from an article by H. P. Krippene, published in *Current History*, January, 1922:

Before the arrival of the Americans scattered Catholic missions furnished a grammar education to the few who could afford it, but the masses had no opportunity of self-improvement. To-day Porto Rico boasts of the most beautiful schools in the West Indies. Fine, large concrete buildings with appropriate play-grounds can now be found in all parts of the Island. The University of Rio Piedras, situated on the outskirts of San Juan, not only offers letters and science, but it also has a Normal Department in which Porto Ricans are trained for grade work on the Island, and efficient commercial, manual training and domestic science departments. The University of Mayaguez, on the other end of the Island, with its modern experimental and agricultural stations, works in conjunction with the University of Rio Piedras.

Compulsory education, a modern curriculum, and a corps of American teachers, who almost without exception have been graduated from colleges and universities in the United States, offer to the young people of Porto Rico opportunities which no other people in the West Indies enjoy. The Normal Department of the University is making teachers of young Porto Ricans with the idea of eventually replacing the American teachers.

In consequence of the disturbed condition of the island and the well-known policy of the Spanish Government to discourage education of the masses, there was very little activity in education in Cuba prior to our war with Spain. In 1899, at the time of the American occupation, 63.9 per cent. of the population were unable to read. The Americans took hold of the elementary schools with vigor, and the schools increased so rapidly that by March 1, 1900, there were 3,099 schools in operation, with 3,500 teachers, and an enrollment of 130,000 children. In 1899, before the Americans began their work, there were only 200 schools with an attendance of 4,000.

Education in Cuba has been obligatory since 1880, but the law was not enforced until after 1899 when the present elementary and secondary school systems were established. Each municipality was required to have a school board, and every town to have schools at which the attendance of children should be compulsory. In 1908, the total enrollment in the elementary schools of Cuba was 210,683; the per cent. of population enrolled was 10.2; total expenditures in 1909, $3,062,507; per capita expenditures to enrollment, $15.62; per capita to population, $1.50. Thus it will be seen that during this period Cuba expended more per capita for educational purposes than the average per capita expended by the eleven Southern States.

The expenditures in Alabama for this period were on the basis of $1.26 per capita; Georgia, $1.49; North Carolina, $1.32; South Carolina, $1.07; Mississippi, $.98 cents.

Within less than ten years after gaining her independence, after passing through an almost continuous period of revolution for thirty years, Cuba was spending more money per capita for the education of her children than the average per capita in eight of the Southern States and more than the average of the eleven States composing the Solid South.

In comparison with the self-governing British Commonwealths, the Southern States make a very bad showing. In 1913-14 the population of Canada was less than one-half the white population and not more than one-third the total population of the eleven Southern States. The expenditures for public schools in Canada in 1913 were more than 65 per cent. of the total expenditures in the eleven Southern States for the same purpose during the same year. The expenditure for elementary education in Australia (1913-14) was $23.75 per capita of enrollment, and $3.51 per capita of population; in New Zealand it was $23.85 per capita of enrollment and $3.59 per capita of population; in the Orange Free State it was $32.00 per capita of enrollment, and $3.49 per capita of population; in the Transvaal it was $35.59 per capita of enrollment and $4.37 per capita of population.

Thus it will be seen that not one of the Southern States has made as liberal appropriation for public education as has been made by every one of the new British States. The population of New Zealand in 1913 was 1,134,506, practically the same as the white population of Arkansas, for example, and yet New Zealand expended in 1913 for educational purposes nearly $3,000,000 more than the total sum expended by Arkansas for the same purpose, and nearly twice the amount expended by Alabama, though the white population of Alabama was 100,000 more than the total population of New Zealand. Education is compulsory in New Zealand between the ages of 7 and 14. In 1916, of the total population (excluding Maoris) over five years of age, 95.0 per cent. were able to read and write, 0.8 able to read only, and 4.2 per cent. unable to read.

As shown by official figures cited, expenditures for educational purposes in the Southern States are less on a per capita basis and less on a basis of taxable values than in other States. These delinquencies of the South are not due to the poverty, nor to unusual financial burdens of these States; nor are these conditions the result of indifference on the part of the great mass of the people, white or colored. The cause of backwardness is found in the antiquated social and economic systems, the gross inefficiency, mismanagement and corruption of an Oligarchy that desires neither liberty nor enlightenment for the people. There is some evidence of improvement and progress in the larger towns and cities, but 75 per cent. of the population of the South is rural, and the most trying conditions are found in the illiteracy and near-illiteracy of these poor people. Statistics relating to higher education, students in universities, colleges and schools of technology show deplorable backwardness in the Southern States.

The total number of pupils in elementary grades in the eleven Southern States (1913) was 5,175,294, while in the eleven Northern States which I have grouped for comparison the number in the elementary grades was 4,478,466. The number of pupils in the elementary grades in the Southern States was 696,828 more than in the Northern States; but the number of pupils in secondary grades in the Southern States was 203,045, while the number in the secondary grades in the Northern States was 410,863.

With practically the same total population, the Southern States had less than half as many as the Northern States had in the secondary grades; and in the higher grades there were only 43,921 in the eleven Southern States while there were 99,057 in the eleven Northern States. In the universities and colleges there were in the Southern States 12,497 in public, and 16,993 in private colleges, making a total of 29,490 students in colleges and universities. In the eleven Northern States there were 30,686 in public universities and colleges, and 26,649 in private colleges, making a total of 57,335 students in colleges and universities. In the graduating classes of 1914, as reported by the Commissioner of Education, there were 17,387 high school graduates in the eleven Southern States, and for the same year there were in the eleven Northern States 57,641. The number of graduates in the high schools of the Northern States was more than three times that of the Southern States.

The number of college preparatory students taking classical courses in the eleven Southern States, 1913-14, was 2,896, while in the eleven Northern States it was 8,863. The total number of students taking scientific courses in the Southern States was 1,462; in the Northern States it was 8,663. The total number of secondary students in college preparatory courses in the Southern States was 4,358 and in the eleven Northern States it was 17,528; so that the number in the Southern States was less than one-fourth that in the eleven Northern States.

There were 1,463 high school graduates in North Carolina in 1914; in Iowa there were 7,019. The total number of under-graduate and graduate students in public universities, colleges and technological schools in North Carolina, 1914, was 1,315; in Iowa there were 5,670. The total population of Iowa (1910) was only 18,484 more than that of North Carolina, but the white population of Iowa was 708,680 more than the white population of North Carolina. The total population of Louisiana in 1910 was 914,017 more than the total population of Maine, and the white population of Louisiana was 201,091 more than the white population of Maine. In Louisiana there were 883 high school graduates; in Maine there were 1,988. In Louisiana the total number of graduate and under-graduate students in public universities, colleges and technological schools was 659; in Maine it was 735. Further respecting the low percentage of attendance at the high schools and colleges in the Southern States, the following comment is taken from the report of the Superintendent of Education of South Carolina, published prior to the World War:

Less than 2 per cent. of our boys and girls ever get to college. Barely 4 per cent. are enrolled in the high schools, while more than 100,000 in attendance in our rural schools go back to their homes without any knowledge of the great, yet simple, laws controlling the materials and surroundings of their every-day life.

According to official reports for the school year of 1920-21, the total number of college students (including university, but excluding independent theological schools and teachers' training schools) who reside in the eleven Southern States was 64,233, while in the eleven Northern States the total number was 128,-730. There were 58,561 college students attending institutions in the Southern States and 121,563 attending institutions in the eleven Northern States. There were 5,299 college students who reside in Alabama, while in Minnesota there were 12,983 who reside in this State. The population (1920) of Minnesota was only 38,951 more than that of Alabama. There were 6,078 college students who reside in Georgia, while there were 18,876 who reside in Iowa. In 1920 the population of Georgia was 491,811 more than Iowa.

Some years ago, Dr. Leonard Gaston Broughton, pastor of one of the leading churches of Atlanta, Georgia, was invited to preach the baccalaureate sermon before the graduating class of the Tuskegee Normal and Industrial Institute. He was so impressed with the things he saw and heard on Sunday that he remained over at Tuskegee the next day, for the purpose of making a personal investigation of the situation and the work of the Negro educational institution at Tuskegee. When he returned to Atlanta, in an address before his congregation he said:

For the industrial training of the white people of the South there is not one-fourth of the money spent on equipment, and there is not one-fourth of the amount of ambition to be trained, and not one-fourth of the willingness to struggle to obtain it, when offered. What is to become, therefore, of the vast armies of young men and women of the white race in the South who are not prepared to do scientific industrial work, when the demand is more and more for trained and skilled workmanship. It seems to me that the answer is very simple. If present conditions are not changed; if in some way industrial training is not made more thorough and more easy for our white people, and if they have not instilled in them more ambition in this direction, it seems to me that the day is not far distant when either industrial progress in the South will stop or the more skilled work will be done by the colored people.

According to a report of the Superintendent of Education for the State of Georgia (1919), "less than ten per cent. of our boys and girls go to college." During the month of April, 1921, an active campaign was started in Georgia for the purpose of raising $5,000,000 for the support of the Georgia Institute of Technology, located at Atlanta, and the leading if not the only modern technological school in that State. A full page advertisement in *The Atlanta Constitution,* under the caption of "Georgia's Shame," contained the following comment:

While Massachusetts Institute of Technology has a plant costing $28,-000,000 and costing $1,250,000 a year to maintain it, Georgia Tech has been forced to exist with a plant costing 1-28th of that of M. I. T.'s, and maintenance cost is but 1-10th, yet Georgia Tech to-day is educating two-thirds as many boys as are attending the Massachusetts Institute of Technology. It has been due to Massachusetts' Institute of Technology that Massachusetts, with none of Georgia's natural resources, has, up to a few years ago, had more factories than all the fourteen Southern States. . . . Georgia has twenty-four natural mineral resources. If Massachusetts had but four of them she would double her wealth within ten years, for she is educating the men to do it for her at her school of technology. . . . Georgia Tech, poorly housed, inadequately equipped, has some 2,000 students and had to turn away hundreds this year from her doors because of lack of money. . . .

Fellow Georgians, do you know New England manufacturers donated thirty to forty thousand dollars' worth of textile equipment to Tech's textile school and that northerners have helped Tech out from time to time with financial assistance? . . . Georgia ranks 43d in educational matters. . . . Georgia produces over 2,000,000 bales of cotton annually, but because of the lack of trained technical men, only spins one-third of the cotton she produces. . . . We rank 22nd in the industrial States of the Union, and yet only six States have natural resources which can compare with ours. . . .

The last statistics show that for every hundred men being given a technical education in this State of Georgia at the time of the report, there were six hundred and thirty technical men being trained in the State of New York and approximately the same number in the State of Pennsylvania. . . . Pennsylvania gave 4,032 men a technical education in the year 1915-16 while Georgia was training only 668.

Through the college years of 1915 and 1916, the citizens of the State of Massachusetts gave private gifts to colleges of that State to the extent of $7,020,775. The citizens of the State of Illinois in the same year gave private gifts totaling $4,292,883 to their schools. Pennsylvania citizens gave $1,741,270. What did the citizens of Georgia give to all the colleges and universities within its State lines? $292,765.

Had the people of Georgia contributed to the cause of education in the same proportion as the people of Massachusetts, Illinois and Pennsylvania, according to their wealth, the amount required for "Georgia Tech" would have been raised without any special campaign for that purpose. In several issues of *The Atlanta Constitution* containing an appeal for "Georgia Tech," there were appalling news items which showed very plainly that Georgia was not behind in its criminal record, but continued to lead not only all other States in the Union but also the world in the number of homicides in proportion to its population. In a report submitted during the month of May, 1921, Mr. M. L. Brittain, Superintendent of State Schools in Georgia, related the following suggestive story:

A gentleman whom I have frequently met at the meetings of the National Education Association some time ago came to the state department and said that he had spent some days in the different parts of Georgia. ''There is this difference between your State and mine'' (Massachusetts), said he. ''In our towns the finest buildings are devoted to training our boys and girls while in Georgia they are generally the courthouses, or even jails. Some of them, I am told, cost more than all the schools of the county put together. Our finest statue at the capitol is to Horace Mann, the educator. Our first citizen is another, Charles W. Eliot. Neither ever indulged in vituperation and would hardly have a hearing if one of your statesmen appeared with abuse for opponents and adroit flattery for the crowd. Your chief heroes for fifty years seem to have been lawyers. Rather a litigation-loving than an education-admiring State, I should say. You will have to change the emphasis before you make great progress.''

While reading the statements published in *The Atlanta Constitution*, showing the situation in Georgia as compared with Massachusetts, it is also interesting to recall that, about 128 years ago, a citizen of Massachusetts, while visiting in Georgia, gave to the world a great invention, contributing perhaps as much as any other to the progress of the industrial age, and one that certainly made possible the wonderful development of the cotton industry. Eli Whitney, while a guest of Mrs. Nathanael Greene, near Savannah, invented the cotton gin. Since the invention of the cotton gin the South has talked a great deal about ''King Cotton,'' but the Southern States have not contributed any invention, achievement in statecraft, or other product of the brain, to perpetuate the dynasty of this monarch. The South has furnished cheap labor and only cheap labor in maintaining the great economic power of ''King Cotton'' and it is not surprising that this labor continues in economic serfdom and political subjection. At this point it may be well to call attention to some comparative figures (1913) relating to the number of public, society and school libraries reporting 1,000 volumes and over.

In the eleven Southern States there were 735 libraries while in the eleven Northern States there were 2,638 libraries; in the libraries of the Southern States there were 5,409,703 volumes, while in those of the Northern States there were 22,472,789 volumes. With about one-fourth the total population, the Southern States had 8.83 per cent. of the libraries and 6.23 per cent. of the total number of volumes in the libraries of the United States.

Of the public and society libraries reporting 5,000 volumes and over in 1913, there were 88 in the Southern States with 2,191,770 volumes, while the eleven Northern States, with practically the same population, had 588 such libraries with 12,331,-652 volumes. Of this class of libraries, reporting 5,000 volumes and over, the eleven Southern States had 4.23 per cent. of the total number of libraries and 4.38 per cent. of the total number of volumes in the United States. In the State of New Hampshire there were 52 libraries, slightly less than 60 per cent. of the total of such libraries in the eleven Southern States, with 767,429 volumes, being 35.01 per cent. of the total number of volumes in such libraries of these States. The total population (1920) of New Hampshire was 2.60 per cent. of the white, and slightly less than 1.77 per cent. of the total population of the Southern States.

After America entered the World War, special favors for the Solid South by the Federal Administration, and the rapid advance in the price of cotton and other products of the South, brought great prosperity to the favored few in the Southern States. In a few years there was great increase in the wealth of these States, but such increase was limited to the privileged class, and it has not been reflected in any great improvement in the public school system or other measures for uplift and progress of the mass of the people. For instance, statistics relating to State school systems in 1919-20, cited in the preceding chapter, show, by comparison with other States, the continued relative backwardness of the Southern States in total expenditures for educational purposes and in providing for elementary schools. This backwardness, however, continues more pronounced in secondary and higher education.

In 1860, so far as higher education was concerned, the Southern States were not behind the Northern States. At the present writing the South is about fifty years behind the North in higher education and a generation behind in elementary education. In this and preceding chapters facts have been presented which show the decline of the South, especially among the poor white people. Many of these poor, illiterate and near-illiterate whites are descendants of men and women of high social position two generations ago. One of the deplorable results of this distressing situation is observed in the steady advancement of the Negro women in domestic positions sought by poor white women, who are trying to get away from the drudgery and unpleasant environment of the corn patch and cotton-field. In many Southern homes of white people Negro women who have had training at school, or have learned by suggestion and example in the homes of educated white people, are supplanting the poor white women who have had no training in domestic affairs. It is not to be deplored that the Negro women are advancing; it is better for them, better for society and government that all men and women be educated and trained in some calling; but it is deplorable, it is pitiable, that the poor white women should be pushed back because they have been denied the opportunity of education and training.

Before the close of the Revolutionary War, in 1779, Jefferson laid before the Virginia House of Burgesses a plan for universal and free public education. He suggested that the counties be divided into sections five or six miles square, called hundreds, in each of which there should be established and maintained by the State a public school which should be free and open for all children, where reading, writing and arithmetic should be taught. The plans of Jefferson for public education in Virginia received little more consideration than did his plans for the abolition of slavery.

The public school system of the United States, at least in all the States not included in the original thirteen, was founded largely on the grant by Congress in 1785 which was in the nature of an endowment. This great land ordinance was the first act of Congress in aid of education. In the Northwestern Territory embraced in the Ordinance of 1787, later divided into the States of Ohio, Indiana, Illinois and Michigan, the sixteenth section of each township was set aside (under the Ordinance of 1785) for the support of public schools. Ohio, Illinois, Indiana and Alabama were the first four States admitted with benefit of land grants by the United States. A large portion of the proceeds arising from liberal Federal land grants made to the States from time to time for educational purposes have been wasted, squandered or stolen by incompetent or corrupt State officials, especially in the Southern States.

In 1857, Congressman Justin S. Morrill, of Vermont, introduced a bill in the House for the purpose of granting public lands in aid of higher education. The measure did not receive the support of the leaders of the Slave Oligarchy who dictated the policies of the Buchanan Administration, but it was finally passed with the aid of Republican votes in 1859 and vetoed by President Buchanan. After the inauguration of Lincoln, Mr. Morrill introduced the bill again and it became a law in 1862. This act gave to each State in the Union 30,000 acres of public lands for each Senator and Representative it had in Congress. Provision was made for States in which there was no public land belonging to the Federal Government by issuing scrip for lands located elsewhere. The Morrill Land Grant Act of 1862 donated to the several States and Territories lands for the purpose of aiding in establishing colleges for the benefit of agriculture and the mechanic arts. The Morrill Art of 1890 was an amendment to the original act and provided for a "just and equitable division of the fund to be received" between white and colored colleges. In accordance with these acts 17 institutions for the Negroes in the Southern States are receiving funds from the Federal Government through the land grants.

In addition to liberal land grants by Congress to the Southern States for educational purposes, there have been numerous donations and bequests by philanthropists for the education of both whites and Negroes. In 1867 and 1868, George Peabody established a fund of $3,500,000 for educational purposes in the South; $1,380,000 of this amount was in Florida and Mississippi bonds and has "never been available"; the remainder was placed in the control of trustees. The first aim of the fund was to encourage the establishment of a public school system for free education of all children. After this was accomplished, the income from the fund was devoted to the training of teachers through normal schools and teachers' institutes.

In 1875, a normal school for whites was established at Nashville, Tenn. This school became a leader in the development of the normal school idea throughout the South. By means of scholarships, worthy students from all the Southern States were enabled to attend this central training school. This Peabody trust was dissolved in 1915, and the residue of the fund was expended in the endowment of the Peabody College at Nashville for the higher education of white teachers.

In 1902 Mr. John D. Rockefeller donated $1,000,000 to a fund to be used for promotion of education in the United States. This he has since increased to much more than $100,000,000. In 1903 the General Education Board was incorporated by an act of Congress, and in 1905 it undertook to provide State Departments of Education in some of the Southern States with trained field workers to arouse a deeper public interest in education. At the present time the Board is coöperating with fifteen States by paying salaries, traveling and incidental expenses of agents dealing with secondary education.

Appropriations made by the General Education Board, from the date of its foundation in 1902 to June 30, 1921, to institutions in the Southern States, were $32,957,478.12. Of this sum, $26,222,075.31 was contributed to institutions for the whites; $5,676,275.33 to institutions for the Negroes, and $1,059,127.48 to "miscellaneous," including appropriations for agricultural work—white and Negro—expenses, rural school agents at Harvard Summer Schools, and surveys in the Southern States. The appropriations for white institutions included $12,635,191.73 for universities and colleges and $12,407,747.11 for medical schools.

In the United Kingdom, as in this country, the imperative need of better and more extensive educational facilities for the mass of the people was realized at the beginning of the World War. England acted promptly and wisely; her statesmen rendered more than lip service in this matter. The curse of medieval landlordism and the survival of the pernicious tenets of toryism, long after the reform measures of 1830-32 had effectually destroyed the political organization of the Tory party as an important power, prevented, until in recent years, any considerable progress in the public education of the masses in England. "We know by experience," writes H. M. Hyndman (*Evolution of Revolution*),—

how difficult it is, for example, to introduce thoroughgoing educational reforms in Great Britain even when they have been admitted to be necessary by all the progressive elements in the community. Fifty years have failed to give the people in our island a decent system of education. Not only have Parliament and the mass of the people to be convinced, and their narrow religious prejudices removed, but the greatest obstacle of all, the bureaucratic spirit of official opposition has to be overcome.

Great Britain, like every other civilized country, except the United States, has passed through a great revolution of democratic reform, social and economic progress, since the beginning of the World War. Late development in the educational situation in the United Kingdom is one of the striking evidences of this progress.

Shortly after the beginning of the World War, the subject of illiteracy demanded serious attention in England. A sweeping National Education Act was adopted, both as a war measure and as a peace measure. In that act it was provided that the new laws should go into effect immediately upon the conclusion of peace. It provided for universal compulsory education. Every English child is required to attend school until he or she is fourteen years old. According to *The Statesman's Year Book:*

Elementary education is free. Attendance at school is to be compulsory between the ages of 5 and 14 years, and by-laws may be made in any area requiring attendance up to the age of 15 years, either for children generally, or with certain exceptions. Provision must be made for courses of advanced instruction for the older or more intelligent children; and for "practical" instruction in cookery, laundrywork, housewifery, dairywork, handicraft, gardening, etc.

Under late laws, provision is also made for—

nursery schools and classes for children between 2 and 5 years of age. Arrangements must also be made for the education of physically or mentally defective children. . . . Provision may also be made for holiday or school camps, centres for physical training, school baths and other facilities for social and physical training.

These late measures will make education universal in England and will abolish the evils of child labor, if the law be properly enforced. Not until very recently, has England taken an advanced position in favor of popular education, but she has now taken a step forward in this matter, as she has in the matter of tenancy, and in the higher and better achievements of progressive legislation and practices for the advancement of democratic institutions.

CHAPTER XI

The tariff question and the so-called Negro problem are the only public issues that are discussed in the Southern States. The subtle acuteness of the leaders of the Southern Oligarchy in keeping these two questions, and only these questions, continually before the people is readily perceived when we recall that the tariff and the Negro have been treated as the main sectional issues in American politics for nearly a century. These issues have been made interchangeable for the purpose of perpetuating sectional prejudice and race hatred, and they have become the fetish of a provincial Oligarchy.

The leaders of the Southern Oligarchy have not only failed to encourage constructive measures for improvement in educational opportunities for the South but, in numerous instances, they have actually antagonized practical measures undertaken for the betterment of conditions. When publicists, educators or humanitarians have undertaken a campaign for improvement in the educational situation, child labor, hygienic conditions, or other vital questions relating to the health, mental development and social uplift of the people, they have usually met with aggressive opposition from Southern Senators and Representatives in Congress. It has been the policy of the Oligarchy to keep the great mass of the people in ignorance and poverty, and to foster sectional prejudices and racial animosities. Such progress as has been made in education and hygienics has been due to the efforts of a few good men and women who had the courage, and I may also say the temerity, to oppose the wishes of the Oligarchy. Added to the work of the men and women of the South who have labored for the cause of education, health and economic freedom of the unfortunate people of that section, there have been not only liberal appropriations of money but also still more liberal service of scientific and well-trained experts provided by the Rockefeller Foundation and a few other institutions engaged in humanitarian work. The work of the General Education Board, the International Health Board and the National Child Labor Committee has been worth more to the South, in moral, mental and economic development, and social uplift, than has all the State and Federal legislation enacted or advocated by the Southern Oligarchy for the past half century.

It is evident that there is a fundamental cause for the deficiencies in the South, to which I have referred in preceding chapters, and which I shall amplify in this chapter, in a brief survey of the hookworm infestation and child labor. I have no theories to propound; I shall present only authoritative facts and opinions which I have gathered in an investigation of this hiatus in the history of a highly sensitive and proud people.

At least one physical cause of deficiency and backwardness in the South was discovered when, in 1902, Dr. Charles W. Stiles, Chief of the Division of Zoology in the Hygienic Laboratory, proved that the hookworm was the cause of the invalidism of the "poor whites" of the Southern States. According to the estimates made by Dr. Stiles the disease was widespread and the number of its victims at least two millions. The individual harboring the disease becomes anæmic, loses ambition, lacks resistance to disease, and is able to perform only a limited amount of work. The Negro is partially immune, "although the hookworm disease increased the death-rate from pulmonary tuberculosis, for example, and perhaps explains the high Negro mortality from the latter malady." As stated in the annual (1920) report of the Rockefeller Foundation (International Health Board):

Hookworm is one of the most serious of the disabling diseases of man. Its control, easily justifiable on its own account, is much more important as a means to a larger end. The disease lends itself readily to purposes of demonstration. It affects fundamentally the welfare of mankind over vast regions, and yet in its cause, its cures, its mode of transmission and means of prevention, it is so simple and tangible that the layman—even the illiterate—may be made to see and understand it. Demonstrations in the control of this one disease, while bringing relief to hundreds of thousands of suffering people and increasing the economic efficiency of communities and countries, are having a more important effect in creating a popular interest in public health and in promoting the development of permanent agencies for the control of this and other preventable diseases.

In *The World's Work*, September, 1912, Mr. Walter H. Page, sometime Ambassador to Great Britain, wrote an illuminating article under the title of *The Hookworm in Civilization*, from which I take the following:

The organization for eradicating the disease in North Carolina is one of the most vigorous and efficient in all the South. The economic gain that has already been made in the State by this work, to take no other measure of it—is simply incalculable; and the very newspapers and politicians who showed such belligerent ignorance, are helping the work with might and main.

False modesty and all differences of rank and fortune are forgotten. So is medical ethics. When a traveling dispensary comes to a neighborhood, the people come great distances to be examined, men, women, children, rich and poor, white and black. The hookworm has no social code, and he uses no ''Who's Who.'' After the people have been treated, they bring their friends to the dispensary.

Mr. Page was a native of North Carolina, and he refers at great length to the work of the Hookworm Commission in that State. One report of an itinerary contains the following story:

Early Friday morning we took the train for Fairbluff, in Columbia County, to see the experiment of the tent hospital and dispensary combined. When the conductor took our tickets for Fairbluff, he said: ''You are going to the right place to-day. They are holding a hookworm convention up there. The State is making a demonstration; it has been running all week; all these people are going there, and the whole damn crowd look as if they've got it.''

Every man who knows the people of the Southern States sees in the results of this work a new epoch in their history, and because of its sanitary suggestiveness, a new epoch in our national history.

Now, for the first time, the main cause of their long backwardness is explained, and it is a removable cause. It is not malaria, it is not the warmth of the climate, it is not the after-effects of slavery, it is not a large ''poor white element of the population''—but it is the same disease that had for centuries made a large part of all tropical and semi-tropical people anæmic, the same cause that has had so much to do with making life and civilization what they are in India, in China, in the Philippine Islands, in Central America. The hookworm has probably played a larger part in our southern history than slavery or wars, or any political dogma or economic creed.

The diagnosis made by Mr. Page explains the distressing situation in governmental affairs under rule of the Southern politicians. Further, by way of example, Mr. Page quotes from an

American "who closely observed the people in the Orinoco region of Venezuela," and wrote to the Rockefeller Sanitary Commission this opinion:

Poorly nourished brains are the natural breeding-places for wild ideas. I believe that the eradication of the hookworm will do more than any other one thing to banish the chronic state of revolution from the countries of Latin America and allow these countries to attain the prosperity to which they are entitled by reason of their natural resources.

It was in 1910-1911 that the Rockefeller Sanitary Commission—

entered into a joint arrangement with eleven States for the relief and control of hookworm diseases. Five years later the unfinished labors of the Commission were taken over by the International Health Board and have been continued to the present.

The eleven States referred to in the 1920 annual report of the Rockefeller Foundation, from which I quote, are the States which compose the Solid South. These are the States with the highest percentage of illiteracy, not only among the colored people, but also among the native whites. According to figures "revealed by surveys made in the period 1910-1914 and re-surveys in the same counties in 1920-1921," as reported by the International Health Board, the State of Georgia had the highest average percentage of hookworm infection and the State of Mississippi came next. In sixteen counties of Georgia, according to the surveys of 1910-1914, of 12,796 persons examined 8,382, or 65.50 per cent. were found to be infected. In four of the sixteen counties the number of infected was over 90 per cent. of all examined; in Mitchell county 99.7 were infected, and of 1,433 in Grady county 99.4 were infected.

Of the total examined in eight counties of Mississippi, 6,962, the per cent. of infected was 63.76; Alabama came next with 62.01 per cent. infected; in Texas, 58.15 per cent. of those examined were infected; 56.31 per cent. in Arkansas; 53.46 in South Carolina, 50.86 in Tennessee; 53.44 in North Carolina; 41.01 in Virginia, and 40.90 in Louisiana. In answer to my inquiry, the International Health Board gave the following summary of its work in the Southern States, in the treatment of hookworm disease:

To obtain a comparison of the percentage of infection, resurveys were made during 1920-1921 of school children in 52 counties in 10 States which had been originally surveyed in 1910-1914. These results are shown by the following tables of infection rates among school children:

Survey 1910-1914			Resurvey 1920-1921		
Examined	Infected	Per cent. infected	Examined	Infected	Per cent. infected
48,456	27,755	57.8	27,524	7,625	27.7

While the rate of infection in school children is much higher than for the adult population, it is assumed that the reduction in the rate in school children from 57.8 to 27.7 per cent. as shown above, is an accurate index of the general reduction in the infection rate for the total population in the States represented in the surveys.

The methods which have proven so successful in treatment for the relief and control of hookworm disease were set on foot by the Rockefeller Sanitary Commission. The total amount of money expended on hookworm work in the South by this Commission, in the years 1910-1914 inclusive, and by the International Health Board of the Rockefeller Foundation, in the years 1915-1920 inclusive, is in round numbers, $1,336,000. The United States Public Health Service and the States have in addition expended large sums in this work.

According to a late report of the International Health Board, interest in public health matters has been stimulated in the Southern States, the people are voting taxes as never before for health purposes, and a sanitary sense is beginning to manifest itself. Ninety-seven counties in twelve Southern States had, at the close of 1920, full-time health departments. There are more than one thousand counties in these twelve States and the ninety-seven with full-time health departments are only about 8 per cent. of the total number of counties. However, this is a good beginning and a great improvement on conditions that obtained before the work of the Sanitary Commission was started. The Southern States have not been "freed of Hookworm. Far from it." As stated by the International Health Board:

The accomplishment of that result, it was understood and stated in the beginning, is a thing that no outside commission could do if it would and that no such organization should do if it could. This is a work for permanent agencies operating over long periods of time. Nevertheless, the object which the Commission set out to accomplish has been achieved. The disease has been greatly reduced in both severity and prevalence; the people have been enlightened as to its importance, its relief, and the means of its final control; permanent agencies rooted in the soil are committed to the task; and a sustaining public sentiment has ben created in the interest of more general measures for the better protection of health. Legislative appropriations for public health purposes have increased during the ten years more than 500 per cent.

My narrative of the hookworm disease and the measures undertaken for its relief and control are based largely, if not wholly, on the reports of the Rockefeller Foundation. A study of these reports brings us face to face with the strange anomaly of the political situation in the Southern States. This is a phase of the subject which the scientist has not discussed, nor have I presumed to comment on the scientific or hygienic aspect of the question. I have simply presented a summary of facts which I have been able to gather from authoritative reports. These authorities concur in the opinion that the "hookworm is one of the most serious of the disabling diseases"; and, as stated by Mr. Page,—

It has, in fact, had a strong influence (nobody can say how strong) in shaping political dogmas and economic creeds. If there had been no hookworm victims in our Southern States, it is certain that our national history would in some way, perhaps in many ways, have been different.

During many years the attention of the country has been rivetted on the Southern States. Economic and social conditions there have been the cause of grave apprehensions, not only to the more intelligent and patriotic citizens of these States, but also to those of other States. With a white population composed of the purest British stock in America, the economic backwardness, civic and social delinquencies have aroused a widespread interest; not only because these conditions are a menace to the whole country, but also because it is so difficult to arrive at a satisfactory conclusion touching the cause of this lapse in the evolution of civilization among an English-speaking people of pure stock. In no other part of the world can there be found such a striking evidence of backwardness and decline among a people of the British race as is found in the Southern States.

It is evident that there is a fundamental cause for this hiatus.

The conclusions to which our brief summary of hookworm surveys seem to point is that the depressing conditions caused by this pestilence have made it possible for a provincial Oligarchy to keep the Southern people in a state of dependence and inaction. The prevalence of this disease will perhaps explain why the South continues solid under the rule of the Oligarchy, and, after all, the problem of the Solid South may be a scientific rather than a political question. Here, for instance, is a curious illustration of the situation when we consider it from a political point of view. It is a remarkable fact that the most overwhelming Democratic majorities in the Southern States are found in those counties where the percentage of persons infected with the hookworm is the highest.

The highest per cent. of infection in Georgia was found in Mitchell County where it was 99.7 of all who were examined. In the Presidential election of 1920, this county gave Cox 930 votes and Harding 144; in Grady County the infection was 99.4 per cent., and the vote was, Cox, 887, Harding, 232; in Telfair County the infection was 97.9 per cent. and the vote was, Cox, 1,069, Harding, 37. In the State of Mississippi, Leake County showed 73.5 per cent. infected of those examined and this county gave Cox 1,082 votes and Harding 121. In Butler County, Alabama, the per cent. of those infected was 70.0 and this county gave Cox, 1,298 votes and Harding, 153. De Kalb County, Alabama, showed the lowest per cent. of infection in any county included in the report of examinations for hookworm. It was only 15.6 in the county, and the vote was, Cox, 3,894, Harding, 4,852. There are a very few notable exceptions, but as a general rule the Republican vote has increased where the hookworm infection has decreased. For example, in Gwinett County, Georgia, the per cent. of those infected was as low as 14.6, and in this county Cox had 1,645 and Harding received 1,140 votes. Wilson County, North Carolina, had an infection of 56.8 per cent.; and its vote was, Cox, 3,496, Harding, 1,374. In Orangeburg County, South Carolina, the infection reported was 54.4 and the vote was, Cox, 2,526, Harding, 284; Leon County, Texas, had an infection of 70.0 and a vote record of 1,175 for Cox and 333 for Harding.

These comparisons could be continued indefinitely, but they

would only show that, as a general rule, the policies and practices of the Southern Oligarchy appeal to the unfortunate people who are infected with the hookworm. In other words, the main numerical strength of this political organization is found among the illiterate and anæmic. Under the leadership of provincial and designing politicians, who subordinate the larger affairs of the national Government to local interests or partisan purposes, we have a large mass of ignorant voters in the South who do not take an active interest in the affairs of their Government and contribute very little to its support. Herein lies the menace of ignorance and license.

Second only to ravages of the hookworm pestilence are the manifold evils of child labor. This is an old and distressing story of greed and inhumanity. In his interesting book, *The Social Unrest*, John Graham Brooks says:

I saw in Georgia and Alabama troops of children, many under 12, working the entire night. I had previously heard every detail of this ugly story, in which Northern capital is implicated as much as Southern, yet nothing but personal observation would have made me believe the extent to which this blunder goes on in our midst.

There has been some improvement in the child labor situation in the Southern States, but it has been intermittent and largely sporadic. Almost without exception, leading manufacturers, and political leaders especially, have opposed all measures for permanent improvement in child labor conditions. In defiance of popular sentiment, child labor continues in the Southern States to an extent that is dangerous to the health and morals of the whole country, to say nothing of the economic menace. The school laws are inadequate and their enforcement ineffectual, and child labor is one of the resultant evils. Writing about national legislation on the child labor question in *The American Review of Reviews*, Dr. A. J. McKelway, Southern Secretary of the Child Labor Committee, said:

The only opponents of the bill before the committee of Congress were certain cotton manufacturers of the cotton-manufacturing States of the South, who had formed an organization for this purpose and secured ex-Governor W. W. Kitchin of North Carolina as their attorney. Members of the House seemed rather to resent the employment of the brother of the majority leader, and Leader Claude Kitchin found an excellent excuse for non-interference with the passage of the bill, which he regarded as unconstitutional, in the fact of his brother's employment. . . . President Wilson signed a second Emancipation Proclamation on September 1, 1916. It goes into effect a year from that date.

When the Southern Secretary of the National Child Labor Committee refers to the " second Emancipation Proclamation" signed by President Wilson, one can hardly fail to recall a few incidents, by way of comparison, in the life of the great man who actually issued an Emancipation Proclamation, as narrated in Herndon's *Abraham Lincoln:*

In New Orleans for the first time Lincoln beheld the true horrors of human slavery. He saw "negroes in chains—whipped and scourged." Against this inhumanity his sense of right and justice rebelled, and his mind and conscience were awakened to a realization of what he had often heard and read. No doubt, as one of his companions has said, "Slavery ran the iron into him then and there." One morning in their rambles over the city the trio passed a slave auction. A vigorous and comely mulatto girl was being sold. She underwent a thorough examination at the hands of the bidders; they pinched her flesh and made her trot up and down the·room like a horse, to show how she moved, and in order, as the auctioneer said, that bidders might satisfy themselves whether the article they were offering to buy was sound or not. The whole thing was so revolting that Lincoln moved away from the scene with a deep feeling of "unconquerable hate." Bidding his companions follow him he said "By God, boys, let's get away from this. If I ever get a chance to hit that thing (meaning slavery), I'll hit it hard."

Lincoln's early protest against slavery came the first time he "beheld the true horrors" of the traffic. That was in 1831, and he fought it unceasingly until 1862 when he issued the Emancipation Proclamation. The so-called "Second Emancipation Proclamation" came as the result of long years of arduous labor on the part of men and women who had devoted their lives to the work. President Wilson's connection with the work looking to emancipation of child labor was only ministerial and perfunctory, and it came at a late day in his life, and then only when the political situation suggested immediate advantage to the party of which he was the head.

In the national political campaign of 1916, one of the campaign documents widely circulated by the supporters of Mr. Wilson was under the title of "No Joker in the Child Labor

Law.'' It later developed in one of the Southern States, when the child labor law which had been so extensively advertised in the campaign literature of the Democratic party was brought before the Federal court for the purpose of testing its constitutionality, that there was in fact ''a joker'' in the law, and that ''joker'' defeated the law.

In a test case brought before the Federal court of the Western District of North Carolina, the court held the child labor law unconstitutional and enjoined the United States District Attorney from enforcing the provisions of the act. This decision was handed down August 31, 1917, the day before the law was to become effective. The Supreme Court of the United States sustained the decision of the Federal District Court of North Carolina, on June 3, 1918, and thus the first Federal child labor law became invalid.

The State of North Carolina, where the Federal child labor law was contested in the courts before it became effective, has been notorious in its inhuman treatment of child labor and in its pronounced opposition to any legislation that would correct this monstrous evil. Meanwhile, not only Representatives in Congress and Senators from North Carolina, but also certain newspapers had persistently misrepresented the actual situation by asserting that North Carolina had properly and successfully regulated the employment of child labor in that State. Answering some of the assertions made by Senators and Representatives from North Carolina, Miss Julia Lathrop, Chief of the Children's Bureau at Washington, called attention to the fact that ''though five-year olds may not be employed, children from 6 to 10 years of age work on eleven-hour shifts, not only in cotton manufacture but in five other industries.'' Miss Lathrop said:

The mills I visited in gathering my statistics constituted about one-tenth of the total number in the State, and they were a fair sample. We therefore gratuitously contribute to *The Charlotte Observer* and to its constituency whatever comfort they can get out of the Government estimate that not more than 910 children between 6 and 10 years of age are working in the five industries investigated in North Carolina, and that those of this number in the cotton mills who were working regularly were on the eleven hour shift. These are the industries presided over by the men who assured Congress that without a Federal law North Carolina would protect her own children.

Following the decision of the Supreme Court to the effect that the child labor law of 1916 was unconstitutional, Senator Pomerene of Ohio introduced a bill in Congress designed "to replace the child labor law declared unconstitutional." This bill, known as the Pomerene bill, was introduced as an amendment to the War Revenue Bill. The vote on the amendment was 50 to 12, with Democrats casting all negative votes. Senators Hardwick of Georgia and Overman of North Carolina led the fight against the proposed child labor legislation. The measure was also opposed by Senators Bankhead, of Alabama; Beckham, of Kentucky; Martin, of Kentucky; Pollock, of South Carolina; Simmons, of North Carolina; Smith of Georgia; Smith, of South Carolina; Thomas, of Colorado; Underwood, of Alabama; and Williams, of Mississippi. Senator Thomas, of Colorado, was born in Georgia.

The revenue act of 1918 provided for a tax of 10 per cent. on the net profits of any mine or quarry in which children under 16 were employed or permitted to work, and of any mill, cannery, factory, workshop or manufacturing establishment in which children under 14 are employed, or children between 14 and 16 are employed more than eight hours a day, or six days a week, or between 6 A.M., or after 7 P.M. This law became effective on April 25, 1919. On May 2, a Federal Judge, James E. Boyd, of North Carolina, made permanent a temporary injunction preventing a cotton manufacturing company in North Carolina from discharging one of its employees between the ages of 14 or 16, or curtailing his employment to 8 hours a day. Judge Boyd held that the law enacted as amendment to the revenue act and laying a ten per cent. tax on the profits of industries employing child labor was—

an invasion of the State's regulatory authority and that it seeks to accomplish the regulation of employment by indirection in the use of the taxing power of Congress.

The second child labor law enacted by Congress was declared unconstitutional by the Supreme Court, May 15, 1922. In spite of opposition from the political party and from the States which had opposed all legislation against slavery before the Civil War, Congress passed a second law. More than two years after this law was passed the Supreme Court declared that it was not a law which could be enforced. It may be well also to note in this connection that the men appearing before Congressional committees against the proposed child labor legislation in 1916 were almost without exception Southern cotton manufacturers. They received the support of Southern Senators and Representatives, and the fight was led by a former Governor of North Carolina, a State which sent more witnesses to Washington for the purpose of defeating child labor legislation than came from any other. The actual situation in North Carolina was clearly stated in an official report from which I take the following:

During the summer of 1918, just after the United States child-labor act had been declared unconstitutional, 53 mills and factories in 12 different localities situated in both the eastern and western districts of North Carolina were visited by the officers of the Child Labor Division of the Children's Bureau. In some instances the officers were detained in the mill or factory office until many of the children had been sent home and in others the children ran or hid as the officer approached, so that all the children employed in the factories visited were not interviewed. Occasionally objection was made by the management to the inspection, and acting under instructions the officers of the Child Labor Division did not press the matter.

Further regarding the child labor evil in the Southern States, Dr. Owen R. Lovejoy, in *The New York Tribune*, June 16, 1918, said:

Down along the Gulf Coast, from New Orleans eastward to Florida, and along the coast of Maryland, the Carolinas and Georgias, stretches a chain of oyster and shrimp canneries, where the longest hours and the most miserable conditions prevail and where the most heart-breaking sights connected with child labor may be found.

Every year in October hundreds of Polish and Bohemian people are herded together and shipped over to the southern coast by train and by boat. They are housed in crowded, insanitary shacks, frequently only a few feet from the marshes. Go out to one of these canneries at 3 o'clock some morning. Here is the crude shed, just off the dock where the oyster boats unload their cargoes. Near the dock is the ever-present shell pile, testifying to the patient toil of little fingers. It is cold, damp, dark. The whistle blew some time ago, and the workers slipped into their meagre clothes, snatched a bite to eat and hurried to the shucking shed. For it is the motto of the padrone, ''Ef day don't git up I go and git 'em up.''

The little children, 6, 7, and 8 years old come stumbling through the dark over the shell piles munching a piece of bread and take their places with the older people. They stand in front of the benches, their pails in front of them, splitting open the rough hard shells and take out the meat. When the pail is full it is a welcome change to carry it off for weighing. Though the oyster shells are painful enough for tiny fingers, the shrimp is worse for the children's fingers and often their shoes are attacked by a corrosive substance in the shells that is strong enough to eat the tin cans they are put up in. They can only work for a few hours on shrimp. Moreover the shrimp are packed in ice and a few hours handling of these icy things is dangerous for any child no matter how hardy he is.

As stated by Dr. Lovejoy, (*The Annals of the American Academy of Political and Social Science*, November, 1921):

In Oklahoma, where children as young as five were found picking cotton regularly, the average daily attendance at school was only 57.2 per cent. of the enrollment, and a study of 174 schools, involving 6,389 pupils, showed that the number of days absent during the year was more than one-third of the total number of days present.

The attitude, and perhaps one could truthfully say the animus, of Senators and Representatives from the South respecting child labor regulation was shown within thirty days after America entered the World War. Reports from Washington, in the early weeks of May, 1917, before the first Federal child labor law had been declared void, stated that "Southern Senators were trying to secure a suspension of the operations of the Federal child labor law during the war." No more reactionary proposal could have been made than that of the Southern Senators who were trying to have the operation of the law suspended during the war.

In England, within less than a year after that country entered the war, some employers returned to regular labor standards. The British Chief Inspector of Factories and Workshops said: "The number of days on which overtime was actually worked tended in many factories to decrease as experience grew to accumulating fatigue and lessened output." In the commonwealths of Canada, Australia and New Zealand the labor standards were maintained during the war with little or no variation from the peace standards. The attitude of France on the subject of child labor during the war was very clearly stated by the French Minister of Munitions as follows:

The experience of war time has only demonstrated the necessity—technical, economic and even physiological—of the labor laws enacted before the war. In our legislation secured in time of peace we shall find the conditions for a better and more intense protection during the war.

After the latest Federal law relating to child labor was declared invalid by the Supreme Court, cotton mill operators in the South boldly renewed their pernicious and shameless practices in the exploitation of child labor. Writing on this phase of the subject, in *The American Child*, August, 1922, Dr. Lovejoy said:

Now that the second Federal act has been declared invalid, Georgia children 12 years of age may be worked ten hours a day, and children 14½ all night long. In North Carolina children of 12 may be worked 11 hours a day during school vacations, and children 14 the same long day the entire year. Reports coming in indicate that a host of children are now going to work who would have been kept out of child labor if the Federal act had remained in force.

In regulating child labor, as well as in some other matters relating to economic progress and social advancement, America is behind the more progressive countries. In regulating child labor, the United States has been held back by the reactionary influence of the mediæval Oligarchy which has ruled in the South for many years. Substantially every country in Europe has recognized the existence of a child labor problem as one of the evils of modern industrialism, and a majority of these countries have attempted to solve it by means of legislation restricting the employment of children. Referring to the employment of children in the United Kingdom, during the early years of the modern factory system, Hazen *(Europe Since 1815)* says:

This monstrous system was defended by political economists, manufacturers and statesmen in the name of individual liberty, in whose name, moreover, crimes have often been committed, the liberty of the manufacturer to conduct his business without interference from outside, the liberty of the laborer to sell his labor under whatever conditions he may be disposed or, as might more properly be said, compelled to accept.

Prior to the World War, the United Kingdom was behind in making provision for the protection of child labor, and in other social and economic reforms in which the self-governing British

Commonwealths, Australia and New Zealand, have led the world. But the British Ministry awoke to the demands of the hour during the World War, and England now ranks with the more advanced States of the North and West, and far and away ahead of the Southern States in regulating child labor. The "monstrous system" for the employment of children in England one hundred years ago is the system that prevails in the South in our own times, and the excuses that are offered by politicians and manufacturers in the Southern States are the same as the excuses that were offered in England one hundred years ago.

Following the World War, there has been a great awakening in the more advanced countries of Europe. Not only in the old governments, but more especially in the newly formed republics, more ample provision has been made for public education, restriction and regulations relating to child labor and, as already noted, the elective franchise has been extended. In most cases, these wise provisions have been made a part of the organic law so that they would not be subject to the caprice or propaganda of political parties. For instance, in the Constitution of the new Republic of Poland the "permanent employment of children and young people of school age for wage-earning purposes is forbidden."

Within a few weeks after the signing of the Armistice, which secured the independence of the new Republic of Czecho-Slovakia, a law was enacted prohibiting the employment of children under 14 years, and it also provides that male workers up to 16 years and female workers up to 18 years shall not be employed on work which is injurious to their health.

CHAPTER XII

SIDELIGHTS ON CORRUPT PRACTICES

Elimination of the Negro vote, by ballot-box stuffing and other lawless acts in the way of falsifying enumeration lists, did not, by comparison with conditions under Republican rule, bring very much improvement. The great blessing that came to the South in the change from Republican and carpet-bag rule to Democratic control of the State and municipal governments was found in the elimination of the alien and Negro office-holders. While corrupt practices were about as bad as they could be under rule of the Republican carpet-baggers and scalawags, very little improvement in the moral standard of party management followed the ascendancy of the Democratic party. The spoils system and corrupt practices continued. There was a vast improvement in the personnel but the power of the spoilsmen was only a little less pronounced in the Democratic party than it had been in the Republican party.

It would be uninteresting to my readers and unnecessary for the purpose of this book, to narrate in detail the story of public embezzlements and defalcations in the Southern States, since the end of Republican rule in these States. The main purpose of this chapter will be accomplished by brief reference to some of the most flagrant and notorious defalcations, embezzlements and other criminal practices, misfeasance and malfeasance, of certain prominent office-holders of the Democratic party in the South. In a survey of corrupt practices during the Reconstruction epoch, it was necessary to introduce brief reference to the spoils system which prevailed in the Southern States before the Civil War. In the present chapter it seems pertinent to follow this precedent for a brief space.

In addition to the sixteenth section grant for public schools, the Federal Government gave the State of Alabama seventy-two sections, or 46,080 acres, for the sole purpose of establishing and maintaining a "seminary of learning." In this grant originated the University of Alabama. It was made a little while before Alabama became a State, but the first Constitutional Convention of the State accepted the grant as a trust and imposed upon the Legislature the duty of careful and honest administration of this trust. Two years after Alabama was admitted as a State in the Union, an act was passed by the Legislature authorizing the sale of these lands at a minimum of $17.00 per acre, payable one-fourth cash and the balance in eight equal annual installments, and the purchasers were given the privilege, at the end of three years, of taking a perpetual lease by paying six per cent. annually on their unpaid balances. The sales were made by seven agents, appointees of the State, in various parts of the State. No bond or other surety for the protection of the State was required of these agents, and they proceeded to sell and lease the lands, each according to his own judgment, and he kept a record, or no record, of such transactions, according to his own election.

In spite of the fact that the grant of lands by Congress was for educational purposes, and for the sole use and benefit of the University, no treasurer was appointed for that institution until 1827. During a period of a little more than six years prior to the appointment of a treasurer for the University, the State Bank acted as treasurer for the institution. Trustees for the University were first appointed in 1821, but so many changes were made in such short time that the trustees had no opportunity to become informed about the University and the management of its assets. It appears that during a period of ten years, from 1822 to 1833, there were 43 different trustees. Under this system, or shameless lack of system, nearly all of the 46,080 acres of land which Congress had granted for educational purposes was sold at the minimum price of $17.00 per acre, though some of the land was valued as high as $60.00 per acre.

The investment of the money realized from sale of the land was made in the Bank of the State of Alabama. The appointment of agents to sell the land was made under direction of corrupt politicians; in brief, the management in every detail was a record of political corruption of the most shameless kind. The State Bank was managed exclusively by politicians, and in their interests. The Legislature was under the influence of corrupt politicians when it passed an act compelling the trustees of the University to invest all the money obtained from sale of the lands. The sum of \$215,977.36 was invested under direction of the Legislature, and it was stated that the funds of the University represented the entire capital stock of the State Bank, but that the University never received any share of profits from the bank.

In 1848, the Alabama Legislature perpetrated its "great act of ungodly robbery," as it was called at that time. The "ungodly robbery" was in the interest of the corrupt politicians who ruled the State, and they were neither carpet-baggers nor Negroes. The Legislature arbitrarily fixed the sum of \$250,000 as the total indebtedness of the State to the University. This amount was fixed in the bill passed by the Legislature in spite of the fact that, at the time the law was passed, the University had \$300,000 worth of bank stock for which it had paid with funds realized from sale of the lands granted by Congress. The Legislature also passed a bill known as the "relief law" under which the original purchase price of a great deal of the land was reduced for the benefit of the purchaser, although a large portion of the total acreage had been sold for less than its market value.

Shortly after the beginning of the Civil War, the State of Alabama converted the University into a military school, and it was destroyed by "Croxton's raid" when the Union Army invaded Alabama. By way of compensating the State of Alabama for the loss resulting from the destruction of the property of the University by the "Yankee army," in 1884, Congress made a second grant of 46,080 acres of land to the University. The acreage of the second grant was the same as the acreage of the first grant. The lands selected under the second grant included very valuable coal property, a large acreage of which is still held by the University. The second grant was made for the purpose of erecting new buildings, and it was provided that if the sum realized from sale of the lands should be in excess of the amount required for construction of new buildings, such excess should be used as an endowment. The actual value of the lands selected under the second grant was greatly in excess of the value of the buildings destroyed by the Union Army.

In practically every one of the Southern States the school

fund, including the "sixteenth section fund," has been squandered and in some cases stolen. In an official letter addressed to the State Land Agent, the Governor of Alabama said:

The public schools of Alabama through the generosity of the national government were the recipients of a most valuable domain, a sixteenth section in every township of the State, which if properly managed and conserved would have furnished a munificent income for the cause of education. While the legislature enacted stringent laws for the safeguarding and protection of this valuable domain, your report conclusively shows that through the failure of the State to exercise proper control, this valuable legacy has been largely dissipated through the grossest neglect and mismanagement on the part of the agent entrusted with its control.

During McKinley's Administration, Congress passed an act granting 50,000 acres of mineral lands in Alabama for educational purposes. This donation was supplemental and in addition to the second grant to the University, in 1884. In this latest grant it was provided that half the acreage should be conveyed to the Tuskegee Institute, of which Booker T. Washington was then President; and one-half to the Alabama Girls' Industrial school for whites located at Montevallo. A commission was appointed to select these lands from any lands owned by the United States Government located in Alabama. So far as the public was informed, the 25,000 acres granted to the Tuskegee Institute were managed with probity and good business judgment. With respect to the 25,000 acres granted to the white girls' school, I quote without comment the following news item published in one of the leading Democratic newspapers in Alabama.

SPECIAL TO THE BIRMINGHAM NEWS

Montgomery, Ala., February 4, 1901

The Governor withdrew the nominations of Messrs. Plowman, Moody, Dortch and Bouldin from the Senate as trustees of the Montevallo school. The opposition is against Plowman on account of his alleged connection with the land deal, it being charged that he was on both sides of the question as seller and buyer. The name of Plowman will probably not be sent in again, and the other nominations will be promptly confirmed.

Corrupt practices by State and municipal officials, and defalcations in various positions of public trust, were distinctive features of Democratic State and municipal administrations before and after Republican and carpet-bag rule in the South. The limits of this chapter will permit only brief reference to a few of the outstanding and most notorious cases of public defalcations under rule of the Oligarchy.

As stated by Dr. Garner, in his work on *Reconstruction in Mississippi*, to which I alluded in a preceding chapter, the Democratic State Treasurer of Mississippi defaulted for $61,962 in 1866, shortly before the carpet-baggers and Republicans gained control of the State government. After the end of the Reconstruction epoch and Republican rule, embezzlements and defalcations among office-holders elected by Democrats were not uncommon, and some of these peculations included large sums of public funds. For instance, in January, 1883, the State Treasurer (Vincent) of Alabama absconded, leaving a depleted treasury with a deficit of about $212,000; early in the same year, the State Treasurer (Polk) of Tennessee "fled from the State, and upon investigation it was found that he was a defaulter to the amount of $374,364.50." The State Treasurer (Burke) of Louisiana, during his term of office (1882-1888), fraudulently issued State bonds and secured large sums of money from fraudulent sale of these bonds. The total fraudulent bonds amounted to $795,535, and "by the unlawful sale of these bonds the ex-Treasurer secured large sums of money, which he converted to his own use."

Defalcations under rule of the Oligarchy have not been so pronounced since the Negroes were disfranchised, at least there have been new methods and new phases of corrupt practices and public exploitations, but the evil has been no less pernicious and immoral under the new system. For example, on March 18, 1913, the president of the State Convict Board of Alabama was arrested on a charge of embezzling the funds of the Board, following the disappearance of the chief clerk, with a shortage of about $115,000 in his accounts.

Speculation, peculation and inefficiency under the spoils system of the Oligarchy have lead to large financial losses to the State and municipal governments in the South. The State of Mississippi perhaps has the worst record in corrupt practices. As I have already stated, Mississippi has the worst record in repudiation of honest debts, and for many years charges of malfeasance and political corruption have been common in that State. For example, *The New International Year Book* for 1911 contained the following comment on public affairs in Mississippi:

Mr. Vardaman, during his term as governor, achieved a national celebrity by his utterances against negroes. . . . In November papers were filed at Jackson in a suit brought by the commonwealth against Senator-elect Vardaman, alleging misuse of public moneys. The suit was brought in behalf of the attorney for the State. Its object was to compel an accounting with respect to the contingent fund of the State, the Spanish-American War fund, and other public moneys, alleged to have been received by Mr. Vardaman during his term of office as governor 1904-1908, and also to recover interest on certain State bonds sold in 1906 and antedated. It was also alleged in the complaint that Mr. Vardaman had made overcharges in connection with his visits to State institutions and that the State moneys were combined with his private funds during his term of office.

Misfeasance and corrupt practices have prevailed so long in Mississippi, and atrocious crimes of the most revolting and loathsome character have been so frequent, that orderly civilized government has practically ceased to function in that State. The campaign of abuse, slander, and persecution, of which poor Negroes have been the victims for so many years, was later directed by political leaders against one another. For example, in commenting on conditions in Mississippi, *The Birmingham Age-Herald,* in an editorial February 9, 1922, summed up the situation in these words:

Charges involving . . . of Mississippi have again brought the lurid politics of that State to national attention. There is probably no other State in the union where political battles are fought with the bitterness that characterizes such contests in Mississippi.

Personalities are freely indulged in and the wonder is that there is not a series of tragedies as the result of every election. Candidates are not content with assailing the public record of their opponents. No man's private life is safe if he aspires to office. He may be as pure as the driven snow, honest and upright, but the newspapers and the politicians will find some weak spot and they don't hesitate to make the most of it.

Narrow provincialism, radical partisanship and a propaganda of race hatred have been the distinctive features of politics in South Carolina under rule of the Oligarchy. Lawless and corrupt practices in this State have also been the subject of numerous comments for more than half a century. In this, as in other States under rule of the Southern Oligarchy, the most radical protagonists of sectional prejudice and race hatred have been those leaders against whom charges have been made.

During the Populist and Free Silver campaigns of 1892-6, Benjamin R. Tillman was elected Governor of South Carolina. His bitter partisanship and racial animosities brought him into national prominence; and after he was elected to the United States Senate, he was one of the leading protagonists of race hatred. While he was gaining so much notoriety by his tirades in the Senate and on the lecture platform, President Roosevelt called attention to some of Senator Tillman's activities in connection with the purchase, or proposed purchase, of government lands. I quote a few sentences from the very complete story of the proposed transaction as narrated by "Raymond," staff correspondent of *The Chicago Tribune*, January 13, 1908:

Mr. Tillman seems to have misconceived entirely the gravity of the situation. He has done little to answer the plain facts in the case and has devoted most of his attention to an attack upon President Roosevelt. . . .

The President submitted to the Senate the original telegram sent from Wausau on October 19, with a deadhead stamp by B. R. Tillman and addressed to the real estate agents who were engaged in exploiting the land mentioned in the circular which Mr. Tillman denounced in the Senate. Further concerning this matter, "Raymond," in *The Chicago Tribune*, said:

If Senator Tillman had completed the transaction before the matter was exposed, as he declared to the agents he was ready to do, he would have acquired color of title for himself and his family to 1,120 acres of very valuable timber lands in the State of Oregon as a result of a cash outlay of only $147.00. . . . It was quite true, as Mr. Tillman's agent stated in his letter of Dec. 7, written on stationery of the United States Senate, that the transaction was "a good gamble." . . . To be entirely fair a middle price might be chosen and from the Senator's own figures it could be assumed that the land in question was worth $10,000 each quarter section, which is an extremely modest price for 160 acres of timber land. On that basis, at any rate, the seven sections, which Senator Tillman sought to obtain for himself and members of his family at a total original outlay of $147.00, would have been worth at least $70,000.

In his *Autobiography*, commenting on the fight in the Senate against the Hepburn Rate Bill, which he heartily supported, Colonel Roosevelt refers to Senator Tillman in the following language:

> The leading Democrat on the committee was Senator Tillman, of South Carolina, with whom I was not on good terms, because I had been obliged to cancel an invitation to him to dine at the White House on account of his having made a personal assault in the Senate Chamber on his colleague from South Carolina; and later I had to take action against him on account of his conduct in connection with certain land matters.

In connection with a propaganda of race proscription by the radical and reactionary leaders of the Southern Oligarchy, Senator Tillman attracted national attention; meanwhile, Governor Blease, of South Carolina, also gained national notoriety. As stated in *The New International Year Book* (1912):

> Governor Coleman L. Blease was much in the public eye during 1912. In his annual message to the legislature he took a strong stand against negro education and urged a law to prevent white persons teaching Negroes. He also indirectly defended lynching and recommended the adoption of a law prohibiting Negroes from secret societies. . . .
> Governor Blease won still more notoriety by addresses delivered before the Governors' conference in Virginia in the first week of December. He made bitter speeches against Negroes and again defended lynching under certain conditions.

While a propaganda of race hatred continued as one of the leading features of political campaigns by the Oligarchy in South Carolina, there were charges of corruption by the contending factions. For example, when Governor Blease was running in the Democratic primary in 1916, Mr. C. M. Stanley, staff correspondent of *The Birmingham Age-Herald*, described the political situation in South Carolina as follows:

> Former Governor Blease and Governor Manning were the highest men in Tuesday's primary for Governor of South Carolina, and will take part in the "run-off" a week from Tuesday. This means some more of South Carolina's famous brand of politics. . . .
> And you can scarcely conceive the number of unprintable stories in circulation about the various candidates. I have talked to scores of good, honest, intelligent South Carolinians who have shaken their heads over these stories, for if half the things were true that have been said about the candidates, they should all be in the penitentiary.

In referring to the situation in South Carolina, following the primary in which Governor Blease was defeated, Mr. Hugh W. Roberts, staff correspondent of *The Age-Herald*, refers to a speech made by Governor Blease as follows:

He declared that the people had been swindled by the political manipulators. Others—not necessarily Blease followers—think likewise. They say, in other words, that if Blease was robbed, God was with the robbers. If Blease was beaten in the count, they say he should have been beaten. "Didn't we rob the carpet-baggers at the polls?" These Carolinians will ask. And indirectly answering their own questions, they affirm: "Yes, we stole Negro votes in those days and are proud of it."

In Tennessee, April 13, 1910, Governor Patterson pardoned Colonel Duncan B. Cooper, who, with his son, Robin Cooper, had been found guilty of killing former United States Senator Carmack. Colonel Cooper and his son were sentenced to twenty years imprisonment. An appeal was taken, and on April 13, the Supreme Court of the State voted, three to one, confirming the judgment of the lower court as to Colonel Cooper, and ordering a new trial in case of his son. Governor Patterson immediately, before reading the opinion and before the Coopers had left the court, pardoned the father, stating as his reason that in his opinion neither of the defendants was guilty. He declared that they had not had a fair and impartial trial, and were convicted contrary to the law and evidence. Colonel Cooper was a close personal and political friend of Governor Patterson, who was at that time leader of the anti-prohibitionist forces, and Senator Carmack had been the leader of the prohibitionist wing. Governor Patterson's administration was notable for the number of pardons issued. In three years and two months he granted 956 pardons, and of these 152 were given to persons who had been convicted of murder.

There was violence and disorder in Tennessee accompanying the attempt to pass a measure for the enforcement of the prohibition law. At a special session of the Legislature it was necessary to station armed guards in the capitol, and a riot nearly resulted from a clash of the partisans. The refusal of the regular Democrats to take their seats and thus make a quorum delayed the formal seating of Benjamin W. Hooper,

Republican, who was elected Governor of the State in 1910, on a fusion ticket, being endorsed by the Independent Democrats. Mr. Hooper was the first Republican Governor in Tennessee in thirty years. Further concerning political affairs in Tennessee, *The New International Year Book* (1915) summarized the story of trouble in Nashville in the following statement:

The City of Nashville was placed in the hands of a receiver in July. This action followed the disappearance of 11 of the cash books of the city which covered a period from 1908-12. The controller and other citizens filed a bill in chancery asking for a receivership to take charge of the affairs of the city. City Treasurer Charles A. Myers was arrested, charged with the appropriation of $10,000 of municipal funds. . . . The grand jury, on June 26th returned indictments against the finance commissioner, the controller, and the assistant city treasurer. The latter officer had left for Australia.

The Atlanta Constitution, May 15, 1921, commenting editorially on corrupt practices and crimes in the city of Atlanta, said:

For more than three years an organized bunco syndicate operated in Atlanta, openly and defiantly, mulcting residents of, and transient sojourners in, this city of hundreds of thousands of dollars and capping its crimes with murder over a division of the spoils. . . . Such a condition could not have existed had not the city detective department been either grossly incompetent or else in collusion with the criminals.

In Texas, on April 11, 1909, Governor Campbell aroused bitter feeling on the part of many members of the House and Senate by an official communication in which he charged that the Legislature was influenced by "the most famous lobby that ever tramped upon the wishes of the people." The newspapers published reports from Austin, Texas, March 5, 1917. to the effect that—

the lower branch of the Texas Legislature adopted, by a vote of 87 to 40, a resolution for an investigation of alleged malfeasance in office of Governor James E. Ferguson. It was a sequel to recent attempts in both branches to secure such an investigation which has failed. . . . Governor Ferguson was indicted by the Travis county grand jury on nine counts, seven charging misapplication of public funds, one division of public funds, and one charge of embezzlement.

The quasi-public corporations in the South have had great influence in political affairs and in some cases they have notoriously aided in corrupt practices. In an investigation before the Interstate Commerce Commission, touching the affairs of the Louisville & Nashville Railroad, it was shown that during 1913 that railroad issued to public officials, and at the request of public officials, free passes to the number of 6,382, representing transportation to the value of $61,727; and the Nashville, Chattanooga & St. Louis Railroad, a majority of whose stock was owned by the Louisville & Nashville, issued to public officials, and at the request of public officials, free passes to the number of 16,580, representing transportation to the value of $164,521.

Reports compiled by examiners of the Interstate Commerce Commission and read into the records of the hearing of charges against these railroads showed that more than 22,800 free passes were issued by them in 1913. These represented a mileage of approximately 7,728,600, with a cash valuation figured at $226,-224. The majority of these passes, according to the testimony of Will H. Carlton, examiner for the commission, were issued to and on the request of legislators in Kentucky and Tennessee.

Seventeen members and former members of the Tennessee Legislature testified in the Interstate Commerce Commission investigation to having received and distributed thousands of passes given by the Louisville & Nashville, the Nashville, Chattanooga & St. Louis, the Tenessee Central, and other railroads in Tennessee. The testimony was brought out in connection with the charges of illegal use of passes, brought by Senator Luke Lea and embodied in a resolution adopted by the United States Senate. It was stated that—

Thomas J. Walsh, a lawyer of Humbolt and a member of the Senate in 1913, admitted that 930 passes was a conservative estimate of his requests and that an estimated value of $7,561 put on these passes might not be too high. Mr. Walsh admitted that it was his understanding that the Louisville & Nashville, and Nashville, Chattanooga & St. Louis are ''showing a little activity in Tennessee politics.''

One witness testified that passes were being requested to influence judges of courts, witnesses, jurors and others. One letter, asking passes for the wife and daughter of a city judge in a Kentucky town, stated that the judge—

had decided practically every case in our favor that has come before him, and we have a great many similar ones and I think perhaps I will be in a position, by getting this favor for him, to get a better class of jurors.

Edwin F. Johnson, an advertising man of Atlanta, Georgia, testified that between $30,000 and $40,000 was expended by the road through his agency in an extensive campaign in Alabama, when a vigorous fight was waged against former Governor Comer. Witness after witness testified to having received without solicitation annual passes from the railroad for personal use immediately after being elected to office. They also told of receiving and distributing hundreds of passes to their county constituents.

To illustrate other phases of corrupt practices on the part of corporations in the Southern States, attention is called to the record of national banks charging excessive and illegal rates of interest. As stated in the report of the Comptroller of the Currency for 1915, the total number of national banks, at the time of that report, in the Southern States, was 1,328, and in the eleven Northern States I use for comparison there were 2,053 national banks. Of the Southern banks there were 546 charging usurious interest while there were only 57 so doing in the eleven Northern States. The number of national banks in the Southern States was less than two-thirds of the total number in the eleven Northern States used for comparison, yet the record shows that there were nearly ten times as many banks charging usurious interest in the Southern States as there were in the eleven Northern States. In the Southern States there were 343 national banks charging 12 per cent. or more, while there were only 30 in the eleven Northern States. Concerning these charges relating to usurious interest, *The Wall Street Journal* said:

A remarkable instance of the .Comptroller's activity during the past year is in exposing the usurious charges of which some of the national banks have been guilty. It should be mentioned, however, that he started out by first attacking the banks of New York City in this particular, in keeping with the general impression prevailing in the interior, but had to capitulate on that score. The principal wrongdoers, he found, after all, were the country bankers.

The Comptroller's annual report recently made to Congress is replete with instances of usurious rates of interest charged. Competing banks in remote sections were found to be paying 7 per cent. on deposits and under-taking to do so by charging from 25 per cent. to 250 per cent. for small amounts of money on short term loans. Sworn statements from national banks in Texas, Georgia, Oklahoma and Louisiana show that they had been lending money at rates of from 20 per cent. to 2,000 per cent. Three banks admitted under oath that the average rates which they charged on all loans were 25 per cent., 36 per cent. and 40 per cent. respectively.

There were five national banks in Alabama which charged an average rate of 26 per cent. interest on loans; the rate in one case was 34 per cent. and in another it was 60 per cent. In Arkansas one national bank admitted making a loan at a rate as high as 120 per cent., another one at 60 per cent., one at 50 per cent.; and another at 25 per cent. In Georgia there were eleven banks where the average maximum rate was about 30 per cent. The maximum rate charged by one was 40 per cent., and the average rate was 15 per cent. In Texas a number of banks reported rates in excess of 100 per cent.

Numerous tables are included in the report of the Comptroller of the Currency, showing usurious charges of interest in the Southern States where these corrupt practices have been most common and flagrant. The Comptroller calls special attention to the complaint of the president of a national bank in Texas, who had criticized the Federal Reserve Board for establishing a $6\frac{1}{2}$ per cent. rate for long term paper at the Federal Bank of Dallas. This bank president characterized the $6\frac{1}{2}$ per cent. rate as unreasonable, exacting, prohibitive and prejudicial to the new system. He also intimated that such a rate was calculated to shake confidence in the members of the Federal Reserve Board. It was discovered that this particular bank was at that time charging to its own customers rates in many cases ranging anywhere from 20 per cent. to more than 100 per cent.

In the State of Oklahoma, according to the Comptroller of the Currency, one bank made a sworn statement that the average rate of interest which it had charged on all loans made between September 2, 1915, and November 10, 1915, was 25 per cent., and the lowest rate charged on any loan was 10 per cent. Another Oklahoma bank reported that the highest rate it had charged was 47 per cent., and that the average rate on all loans made during a certain period was 36 per cent.

These corrupt practices by the national banks were not limited to any particular section of the United States but they largely predominated in the Southern States. The State of Oklahoma has led in the race for loan shark honors, and it is also well to the front in the bad record of some of its public officials and in criminal lawlessness. In that State there were 297 national banks in the loan shark business, charging, as stated in the report of the Comptroller of the Currency, 20 per cent. to 2,000 per cent. Texas had 168 national banks in the same class; Kentucky, 89; Georgia, 85; Alabama, 60; Illinois was the highest among the Northern States; it had 76 loan shark banks while North Dakota had 63.

At the present writing, it has been about twenty-two years since the Chairman of the Democratic Executive Committee in Alabama warned his party against the growing menace of corrupt practices. "It will," said this far-seeing Chairman, "reach your bank cashiers and affect positions of trust in every department. It will ultimately enter your courts and affect the administration of justice." The Democratic Chairman was a wise prophet when he told his party leaders that their corruption would "reach the bank cashiers."

As shown by report of the Comptroller of the Currency for 1919, there were 25 "officers and employees of national banks who were convicted of criminal violations of the national banking laws and sentenced during the year ended October 31, 1919." Of the total number of convictions seven were officers and employees of banks in the eleven States composing the Solid South. If we add the States of Kentucky and Oklahoma, usually included in a grouping of Southern States, there were in these 13 States 9 convictions. The eleven Southern States with 10.85 per cent. of the total resources of the national banks, furnished 28 per cent. of convictions for criminal violation of national banking laws. The 13 Southern States, including Kentucky and Oklahoma, with 13.43 per cent. of total national banking resources, furnished 36 per cent. of convictions for criminal violation of the banking laws. In 1920, the percentage of the eleven Southern States was lower, being only 15 per cent. of the total convictions.

According to a report of the Comptroller of the Currency (1921), there were 41 convictions of officers and employees of national banks during the year ended October 31, 1921, of which 19, a little more than 47 per cent., were in the eleven States composing the Solid South. There were 8,155 national banks in the United States on September 6, 1921, of which 1,406 were in the eleven Southern States. On a percentage basis, according to the figures for 1921, the Southern States had 17.24 per cent. of the aggregate number of national banks, a little less than 10 per cent. of the total deposits, and slightly more than 11 per cent. of the total assets of all national banks. The volume of business and the number of officers and employees, in proportion to the assets and deposits, is relatively less in the Southern States than in other States. Yet, nothwithstanding the relative low percentage of the Southern banks in number and in the volume of business, a little more than 47 per cent. of the criminal violations of national banking laws, in 1921, occurred in the Solid South. Authentic reports showing violations of State banking laws by officers and employees of State banks are not available, but the percentage is supposed to be larger than among the national banks for the reason that governmental supervision of the national banks is more efficient and rigid than is that of the State banks in the South.

According to a report of the Comptroller of the Currency, in June, 1921, there were 1,406 national banks and 4,736 state banks in the eleven Southern States. For the year ended June 30, 1922, there were 126 state bank failures in these States. There were 60 state bank failures in the eleven Northern States, of which 23 were in Nebraska, during the same period, although the Northern States had 5,088 state banks, 352 more than the Southern States. The failures of state banks in the eleven Southern States were more than one-third of the total of the United States. If to the eleven Southern States we add 37 state bank failures in Oklahoma, it will be seen that 163 state bank failures in these twelve Southern States represented slightly less than 45 per cent. of the total state bank failures in the United States for the year ended June 30, 1922.

When, in 1913, the administration of the national Government passed to the control of the Southern Oligarchy, the inefficiency, misfeasance and malfeasance in public affairs, which had prevailed in the South for forty years, were introduced into every department of the Federal Government which the Oligarchy was able to bring under its full control. The cotton crop, which is the leading industry of the South, was utilized in divers ways as a partisan and provincial issue in matters of grave importance, not only in our domestic affairs but also in our foreign relations. Not only during the World War, but after the war, certain leaders of the Oligarchy, in connection with the practices of speculators and profiteers, made the marketing of the cotton crop a matter of international concern, provoking severe criticism from foreign consumers of American cotton.

British spinners who are large buyers of American cotton were very outspoken and caustic in their criticisms of the reports sent out by the Bureau of Crop Estimates in the United States on the crop of 1921. During the cotton-picking season, early in October, the Bureau predicted a crop of only 6,500,000 bales. The final figures in December indicated a crop of 8,340,-000 bales, exclusive of linters, which meant an actual commercial crop of about 9,000,000 bales. In commenting on the American report of crop estimates, *The Manchester Guardian Commercial* said:

It is clear that such estimates are a fruitful source of danger. They only serve to mislead the market and to prevent cotton from finding its economic price level. For some time to come the market will have lost all confidence in the bureau, and it would be better if that body were to confine itself to the publication of no more than the actual acreage figures and the crop condition.

The London Economist was no less severe and just in its criticism of the egregious blunders of our Estimate Bureau. The comments of this influential publication follow:

All people interested in cotton supplies have been very seriously misled by the inaccuracy of the information published. During September there was an important rise in prices on bad crop reports, and it is of interest to mention that even the farmers in the United States did not sell freely at the higher values, as it was believed that rates would go still higher before the end of the season. Lancashire traders are disgusted at the state of affairs, and undoubtedly statistics from the United States Government in the future relating to cotton will be discredited.

The evil of cotton speculation in the South is an old story.

It has been the cause of great suffering and distress to a large number of cotton growers, and it has contributed in no small degree to the development of corrupt practices and the increase of crimes in the South. In nearly every community of the cotton-growing States there is usually one man, occasionally two or three men, who have accumulated fortunes by speculating in cotton, but the men who actually make money in cotton speculation are on the "inside" and their number is very small in the South. While some of the largest fortunes in the South have been made in cotton speculation by men who were in a position to get inside information, at the expense of the producer, a very large majority of those who speculate in cotton lose their money. The National City Bank of New York, in a *Bulletin* issued October, 1920, commenting on the cotton situation at that time, said:

As usual, when cotton declines much is said in the South about the vicious influence of short selling, but the talk among people who are familiar with the market is that the selling orders are mainly from the South, and probably represent hedging operations, that is, sales against new crop purchases.

During the month of March, 1922, the American Cotton Exchange, with headquarters in New York, was under investigation, charged with "operating a big bucket shop business" in violation of the criminal laws of the State of New York. According to the testimony brought out in this investigation, "of the 750 members of this exchange, more than 660 are residents of Southern States and most of them dealers in cotton." Further testimony in this case revealed the fact that 90 per cent of the transactions in the exchange were "cross trades." The method of trading was "so bad, so inaccurate," that it was almost impossible at any time to execute a customer's order, there being no cotton to sell.

Virtually all of the transactions on the floor of the American Cotton Exchange were "cross trades," characterized as bucketing. . . . But little cotton was actually dealt in; clients in the South were unaware their orders were being executed in a fictitious manner, with no intention of making deliveries, and by pre-arrangement the operators balanced dummy entries on the books of the Clearing House Association of the Exchange. Through this method, followed in most cases, the broker made his commission and the exchange received a revenue of $4 on each 100 bales traded in mythically.

The hearing brought out that, whereas the production of cotton in the United States in 1920 amounted to 11,500,000 bales, between 50,000,000 and 60,000,000 bales were traded in on the New York Cotton Exchange alone in 1921.

In the fifth annual report of the Federal Farm Loan Board (January 7, 1922) we find a few paragraphs which furnish further evidence of the inefficiencies and corrupt practices under rule of the Southern Oligarchy:

The secretary-treasurer is the life of the farm Loan Association, and its existence, management and character revolve around his personality. This officer keeps all records, and is, as the title of the office implies, both secretary and treasurer. Upon him are enjoined the duties of properly caring for an accounting for association funds, and of making periodical reports to the Farm Loan Board, and special reports when called upon to do so, and it is made his further duty, under the law, to carry out all duly authorized orders of the Farm Loan Board. . . .

Great difficulty has been experienced from the organization of the system in procuring reports from these officers. The last regular quarterly report was called for as of Sept. 30, ample notice given, and each secretary-treasurer provided with a blank for such report and a self-addressed official envelope for the purpose of forwarding the same to the Farm Loan Board. At the date of this report, two months having elapsed, there are nearly 700 associations from which reports have not been received. This is an intolerable condition. The board has exhausted every resource of which it can think to procure these reports, finally authorizing associations to compensate the secretary-treasurer specially for making the same.

Instances have arisen where examination developed the wilful misappropriation of the funds of the association, and the same was called by an examiner to the attention of the board of directors of such association, and they have refused, notwithstanding such defalcations, to remove the defaulting secretary-treasurer.

There is nothing in the report from which I have quoted to indicate that the delinquencies and defalcations of which the Farm Loan Board complains were more flagrant in the Southern States than they were in other States. Be that as it may, the Federal Farm Loan Bureau was established by an act of Congress in 1916, when the country was under rule of the Southern Oligarchy, and the members of the Board were the appointees of the Wilson Administration. The defects of the law, and the defaults in the administration of the law, are the results of the policies and practices of the spoils system under rule of the Oligarchy.

Corrupt practices are not peculiar to the Southern States. These practices in public affairs and reprehensible methods in private business matters, since the early years of the Great War, have given America a reputation abroad which is not very enviable and of which no patriotic citizen can be very proud. There is, however, this difference between corrupt and lawless practices in the Southern States and like practices in the Northern States. In the Northern States there is an independent and, in many places a fearless and incorruptible press; the people read the newspapers and they get the news. The newspapers in the South are as fearless and incorruptible as those in the North, but the press in the South is essentially partisan and provincial. Public libraries, lecture courses and other modern means of disseminating knowledge and information on current topics, so common in the Northern and Western States, are almost unknown in the Southern States, except in the cities and larger towns, and even there only to a very limited extent.

It is perhaps safe to say that at least 75 per cent. of the white people of the Southern States do not enjoy the means and agencies of acquiring knowledge and getting information that are available to other civilized peoples in the more progressive countries. Public speaking, discussion of public questions before the people by public men, were common before and for fifteen years after the Civil War; but under the rule of the present Oligarchy they have practically ceased and the great mass of the people get only such information as the leaders of the Oligarchy think they should have and which will not weaken the power of the ruling class. The South is falling behind and the people are more backward at the present time than they were twenty years ago. No people could advance under political conditions that exist in the South; under these conditions corrupt practices and criminal lawlessness necessarily increase.

CHAPTER XIII

A narrative of the vile and pernicious fee system in the Southern States is an old and familiar story of greed, corruption and brutality. The fee system is the main support of the execrable convict system and chain gang, which has continued since the Reconstruction period, for the purpose of securing cheap labor, and for the profit of the most venal and brutal spoilsmen of the Oligarchy. The fee system, the chain gang and the prisons furnish a record of venality, brutality and inhumanity more revolting than the most appalling story of the horrors of the slave trade. In the *Sixth Biennial Report of the Board of Convict Inspectors* in Alabama (1904-6), Dr. Shirley Bragg, President of the Board, said:

> The county convict system if anything is worse than ever before in its history. The demand for cheap labor and fees has become so great that most of them now go to the mines where many of them are unfit for such labor, consequently it is not long before they pass from this earth. . . . This system should be wiped out of existence and it cannot be done too soon.

Concerning prisons in Alabama, the report of Dr. Bragg contains the following comment:

> I have not changed my opinion in reference to the jails of the State; in fact, if anything I am more convinced that the ideas of humanity and civilization would be better carried out if the torch were applied to every jail in Alabama. It would be more humane and far better to stake the prisoner out with a ring around his neck like a wild animal than to confine him in places we call jails, that are reeking with filth and disease and alive with vermin of all kinds. . . . I tell no secrets when I say that in many jails of the State men and women remain for months without the means of washing their faces or hands.

There has been some improvement since the date of the report of Dr. Bragg from which I have quoted. New jails have been built and some of the old jails have been improved. However, the general condition of the jails in the South has improved very little during the past forty years. For example, a special report (1914) of Dr. W. H. Oates, State Prison Inspector in Alabama, contains the following:

The buildings were unclean, often vermin infested. . . . Isolation and segregation of prisoners were totally ignored. The hardened criminal, first offender, and juvenile prisoners were confined in the same cells, thus converting our jails into veritable schools of crime, and the constant contamination by association must have been incalculable; while it was not uncommon to find white and Negro prisoners confined in the same apartment.

During the last fiscal year there were confined in the jails of Alabama three hundred and thirty-six white women. . . . Women prisoners, regardless of their color or the crimes of which they were accused, are cared for and under the absolute control of male deputies. There are no matrons in any of the jails in the State of Alabama. Comment would be obnoxious.

The fee system furnishes liberal returns to the Oligarchy. The report of the Prison Inspector deals very clearly and forcibly with this phase of the situation, as follows:

It is a sad commentary on our State, but a fact, nevertheless, that our jails are money-making machines.

The vile, pernicious, perverting, fee system beggars description, and my vocabulary is inadequate to describe its deleterious and baneful effects. It inculcates into the management of our jails greed for the Almighty Dollar; persons are arrested because of the dollar and shame to say are frequently kept in captivity for months, in steel cages, for no other reason than the Almighty Dollar. . . .

As the law is to-day a man can be kept in jail for a year or more awaiting trial for some petty offense, and if convicted the year in jail counts for nothing on his sentence. . . . The law provides that the Sheriffs shall be paid a fee for feeding prisoners. They are not paid money for having fed prisoners; they are not advanced money with which to feed them, but are paid a fee for the performance of an act. . . . Only two meals a day are furnished in a vast majority of the jails throughout the State.

Referring in detail to the Jefferson county jail, Dr. Oates made the following statement:

The feed bill as per the Sheriff's monthly reports to this Department, was $37,688.90. . . . In that the law provides that for each prisoner the Sheriff shall receive 30 cents a day for feeding; and, further, in that the Sheriff fed them for ten cents, it is clear that he made a net profit of

$25,125.94 during the last fiscal year, or at the same rate for his four year term of office, $100,503.76.

In the story of the Bastile we find little that is more suggestive of the sordid, inhuman cruelties of an ignoble prison keeper than is found in the venal practices of some of the keepers of prisons and convict camps in the Southern States. "To the Bastile!" was the cry of the early mobs of the French Revolution. At the time of the destruction of the Bastile, M. de Launay was Governor of the fortress:

He was no soldier, but a mean, mercenary man, despised by the Parisians. He contrived to draw from the establishment, by every species of cruelty and extortion, an income of twenty-five thousand dollars a year. He reduced the amount of firewood to which the shivering inmates were entitled; he made a great profit on the wretched wine which he furnished to those who were able to buy, and even let out the little garden within the enclosure, thus depriving those prisoners who were not in dungeon confinement of the privilege of a walk there, which they had a right to claim. De Launay was not merely detested as Governor of the Bastile, but he was personally execrated as a greedy, sordid, merciless man.

In reading the official reports on prisons and convict camps in the South, one is inclined to believe that it is all a horrible story of the dreadful things that happened many years ago. We try to comfort ourselves with the thought that times have changed, that men have changed, that they are more upright, honest, just and merciful than they were in ages past. But the plain, inescapable truth is that there has been little improvement in prison conditions and in the treatment of convicts in the South during the past half century.

Illustrative of the workings of the detestable fee system, there was the case of three white men who were sent to the convict camp at Flat Top from Anniston, Alabama. The fine in each case was one cent and costs. It was stated that they would have to serve from thirty-eight to forty-four days for an offense "which the Judge evidently considered almost nothing." While the fine was one cent the costs amounted to from $19.00 to $22.00 in each case. There was also the case of one Milly Lee, a Negro woman who had been arrested for "abusive language," and was fined $1.00 and costs. She worked out the fine in two days, but she had to work nearly a year to satisfy the "fee brigade," for the courts got out of the apparently insignificant case $24, the clerks $34, the witnesses $64, the sheriff $10—in all, her costs amounted to $132.   Another case which illustrates the venal and corrupt practices was that of a Negro woman working out a sentence of 286 days because she was unable to pay a fee-bill amounting to $35.

The Montgomery Advertiser published a story of the arrival in that city of seventeen white men and three Negroes, "securely handcuffed and tied together with a rope," on their way to work in a mine in the Birmingham district.   These men were in charge of an agent of one of the Alabama coal mining companies.   As stated in the newspaper story:

Not one of the twenty men has had a trial. They were arrested at the point of the gun, marched to jail, where they were kept four or five weeks, and then without any ceremony they were placed aboard a train and sent to the mines to work there from one to three months. . . .

These men were arrested upon the charge of unlawfully riding upon trains —everyone of them claims to be innocent—by a man who is paid $2.00 for every person he arrests upon that charge. Their treatment under arrest and while en route to Montgomery and the sufferings and privations they have endured recall the tales of cruelty which used to come from Siberia.

Some years ago, *The Mobile Register*, commenting on the sordid convict lease system, said:

Whites and Negroes committed to these camps under the iniquitous leasing system are daily under the lash of foremen, whose business it is to get as much work out of the unfortunates as they can physically stand and to ply the whip if the convicts do not perform allotted tasks, which in many instances they are unable to perform. Convicts have been whipped into insensibility, and have been whipped to death in this State as a result of the traffic in convict labor. . . . Less than a month ago a Jefferson County Negro, convicted of vagrancy, was beaten to death in a mine, and several Escambia County convicts, white men convicted of stealing a ride on a freight train, under the technical charge of trespass, came to Mobile and exhibited marks of the lash inflicted at a lumber camp to which they had been leased.

The United Charities of Birmingham, Alabama, addressed a letter to the Governor of the State and sent a copy of the same to the Sheriff of Jefferson county, demanding "an investigation of the hideous crime committed at Pratt Mines where a Negro convict was beaten to death.'' *The Birmingham Age-Herald* in an editorial said:

Convict whipping is a common practice in this State. The instrument used has a leather handle and a two-foot lash. Presumably, the lash is made of leather. At any rate, it is made of something strong and biting enough to kill its victims.

Concerning the administration of justice in Jefferson county, the richest and most populous county in Alabama, a writer in *The Birmingham Age-Herald* called attention to the fact that four divisions of the City Court, two divisions of the Circuit, and two divisions of the Criminal Court ''stand adjourned and the eight judges were in idleness.'' This adjournment was in order to give ''about twenty-five lawyers out of the 300 that practice in this county an opportunity to argue their cases before the Supreme Court.'' The writer continued:

Lying in a jail which Dr. Oates says is unfit for human habitation, and has ordered torn down, more than 200 men and 18 women, all of whom are presumed to be innocent, and some of whom are so, are awaiting trial. On the docket of the criminal court, up to the first of April are 4,150 pending cases. . . . And yet eight court rooms are empty and eight judges idle. On the docket of the Circuit Court, according to the estimates of one of the deputy clerks, there are 491 quasi-criminal cases, 1,200 civil cases and 250 chancery cases. Many of long standing. And yet there are eight deserted court rooms and eight vacant seats on the bench. . . . The courts all adjourn for three months in the summer and again adjourn two weeks during each term on account of the Supreme Court, and the courts are only in session eight months of each year.

The report of a committee of the Alabama Legislature (July 1, 1919) contains a survey of the convict lease system from which I take the following:

The convict lease system in Alabama is a relic of barbarism; it is a form of human slavery. . . . It is hard to describe the cruelties, woe and misery growing out of such a system. . . .

At one of the turpentine camps, some eighteen or twenty miles from Tuscaloosa, located in a dense forest of several thousand acres almost completely away from civilization, convicts are being worked under lease from the State. The Superintendent of the lessee, who has the charge and control of these men after they are released from the stockade in the morning until they are returned at night, has been found lying out in the woods in a drunken stupor with a bottle of wildcat liquor in his pocket, and the

evidence shows that this same Superintendent has been using the State convicts in the manufacture of liquor and the transportation of the same by
the State convicts to the city of Tuscaloosa.

The report stated that at this camp convicts were required
to rise as early as three o'clock in the morning and walk seven
miles to their work of scraping turpentine and rosin from the
trees and carrying it to wagons 200 yards away at times. The
report also describes the condition of convict workmen in the
mines, as follows:

They start early and are required to walk to their work down through the
rough, wet, dripping slope, and when they have performed their task they
have to walk back up the slopes and in some instances almost climb this
distance of four miles with the result that they seldom see the light of day
except Sundays. . . .

We have found them in mines with faulty tops and roofs, and the records
show conclusively that they are maimed and crippled by falling rocks and
terrible gas explosions which snuff out the lives of scores almost in the
twinkling of an eye.

At one of the mines we found five men who were apparently big, able-
bodied, and strong before they were caught in an explosion and the skin was
almost totally burned from their bodies. They were lying on beds covered
with oil cloth with secretions dripping from their burned bodies, scarcely
breathing, the most pitiful objects of humanity that human eyes could
possibly behold.

According to a statement of Mr. Thomas Orr, Representative
in the Alabama Legislature from Marshall County, published in
an Alabama newspaper,—

eighty per cent. of all convicts in the State prisons, convict camps and
coal mines afflicted with tuberculosis contracted the disease while serving
the State in the mines.

Representative Orr was also quoted as saying that 90 per
cent. of all convict cripples in the mines received their wounds
while working as convicts. Representative George Ross, also
a member of the Legislative Committee "On Convicts and Highways," after an inspection trip to all convict camps, was quoted
as follows:

At one camp I saw a great big man with raw places all over his shoulders
and back made by whippings given him. He had failed to do his task
and for this failure the whipping was administered.

At one of the camps we found the Superintendent drunk and two of the convicts were arrested on the way to town with 30 gallons of whiskey for the Superintendent's brother. The Superintendent, we were informed, operated four illicit distilleries.

At one of the mines we found leads in the scales which robbed the convicts of a big percentage of their work. They made a difference of about 250 pounds in a ton of coal, and they were docked and beaten for loading dirt on cars with the coal.

Out of 3,024 convicts in Alabama, during the month of May, 1923, it was reported that 1,450 were employed in coal mines and "about 150 in a lumber camp." State Senator Walter Bower, of Jefferson county, was quoted in *The Birmingham Age-Herald* as follows:

Men who are charged with very trivial offenses are imprisoned with hardened criminals. Young boys are imprisoned along side of old criminals. Men who are convicted of offenses that do not involve moral turpitude under our laws are sent, in many instances, to the penitentiary and leased out as galley slaves to private individuals whose sole interest in them is the wringing from them as much profit as possible.

The fee system and the convict lease system have the support of many of the office-holders, and their confederates who are the beneficiaries of these inhuman practices in the Southern States. These barbarous usages have not been approved by a majority, nor by any considerable number, of the citizens of these States where such shameful things prevail, but under the rule of a corrupt and merciless Oligarchy the people have been helpless. A few courageous men and women have had the fortitude to expose and denounce these venal and barbarous practices. In Alabama, for example, under the able and courageous leadership of Mrs. Solon Jacobs, second Vice-President of the National League of Women Voters, and her co-workers, the evils of the sordid fee system and the horrors of the convict lease system have been fearlessly exposed and unsparingly denounced. A few public officials (but very few) have also had the temerity to expose and attack these vile practices. Judge William E. Fort, of the Jefferson County Circuit Court, former Representative W. C. Davis, Mr. John C. Arnold and Mr. J. B. Powell, members of the Legislature, and Mr. Irving Engel, lawyer and member of the Junior Chamber of Commerce, have been among the active leaders who have exposed and condemned the fee system and the convict system.

These patriotic men and women, with the courage of crusaders, have received the support of *The Birmingham Age-Herald* —and perhaps of other papers in Alabama which I have not seen—but they have received scant, if any, support from leaders of the Oligarchy. Back of the fee system and the convict lease system is the sordid greed of numerous office-holders, and other beneficiaries of these evil practices, chiefly mining, lumber and turpentine companies, or those engaged in these particular industries that employ cheap labor. As a general rule, in Alabama and other Southern States where the fee system is permitted, the lessees of convicts, and other beneficiaries of these practices, are office-holders and their near kin. Even under the most capable and courageous leadership, slow progress has been made in fighting corrupt and inhuman practices which have so long had the support of the ruling Oligarchy. For instance, following exposures relating to the horrors of the convict system in Florida, to which I shall refer in some later paragraphs of this chapter, at a public meeting held in the city of Birmingham, Alabama, during the month of June, 1923, as reported in *The Birmingham Age-Herald*, that—

Alabama would have a worse reputation than Florida, if the concealed truth were known about the methods of the convict lease system, was not only the statement of one, but the consensus of opinion among several speakers who addressed representatives of civic organizations.

Mr. John C. Arnold, a lawyer of Birmingham, was a member of the Legislative Committee that investigated the leasing of convicts in 1919. In a speech before the public meeting at Birmingham, during the month of June, 1923—

Mr. Arnold exhibited a leather strap, six feet long, two inches wide that tapered off to a lash point, thin, flat and keen. Some of these whips, he said weigh nine pounds.

In describing how the convicts were punished, Mr. Arnold said:

The way the convicts were punished was, the one to be whipped was brought into the middle of the dining-room, a blanket was laid on the floor, the prisoner put face downward on the blanket. A Negro knelt on his head, another on his feet, then the lash was applied. The same treatment was given white women prisoners. As high as 185 blows were given. We were told, under oath, of instances that would make the more or less well known and recent Florida incident seem pale in comparison. The marks given the prisoners by the whip, for a strong man was used to deal the blows, were worn by the convict to the grave. I have seen them marked from shoulders to ankles, scars that will never come off. . . .

Five men were burned to death, convicts, in the . . . mine. Miners, they knew the place where they were to go was unsafe. The day before it had been tested and the eyebrows were burned from the tester's face. They begged not to be sent in. They were sent to their death, their bodies were later taken out, burned to a crisp.

The Birmingham Age-Herald quoted Representative J. B. Powell, of Walker county, as follows:

I have been informed that at certain convict camps in Alabama, prisoners are placed in dungeons in which spikes have been fixed on the floor and walls except a small place on the floor for the prisoners to stand on and that a prisoner is often times placed in such a dungeon and left standing for a day or two in absolute darkness.

During the month of May, 1923, a committee representing the Junior Chamber of Commerce and the League of Women Voters of Birmingham visited the mines where State convicts are worked under a lease. According to *The Birmingham Age-Herald*, Mr. Irving Engel, of the Junior Chamber of Commerce, made the following statement:

I saw one man suspended by his wrists in a coffin-like box, who was pleading to be let down because his arms were swelling. . . . It was not known at the mines we saw what we did, we were told the convicts receiving punishment had been removed from the boxes when it was said we were to visit the place. We would not have known of the men who were being stretched had we not heard the cry of one of them. Three others were found in the "dog houses" being stretched by means of pulleys and ropes, their toes barely touching the ground.

Captain Donald Wood, another member of the Junior Chamber of Commerce Committee, who visited the mines where the convicts were worked, said:

I saw three men, convicts, who had been handcuffed, placed in the "dog houses," in which there is scant room for a human body, and their handcuffed wrists pulled over their heads with ropes and pulleys and held that way on tiptoe anywhere from three to forty-eight hours without food. We were told they had been given this punishment because they had asked for coffee. They were in the boxes when I saw them. I talked to many convicts, all said the men so punished fell unconscious when released.

The history of the fee system and the convict lease system in the State of Florida is a long and tragic story of sordid greed and merciless inhumanity. The limits of this chapter will permit only a brief reference to a few details relating to this appalling record of atrocities. When, during the administration of President Roosevelt, some of the horrors of the convict system were exposed in connection with the prosecution of peonage cases, the deplorable and shameless situation in Florida was disclosed. Ten years after the shocking disclosures resulting from prosecution for peonage by the Federal Government, *The Survey* of May 1, 1915, contained an article by Mr. Marc N. Goodnow, under the title of "Impressions of the Convict Camps of Florida," from which the following:

All the men were in their bare feet; feet, too, that were swelled and misshapen almost beyond recognition. They were spread out, broken down, cut, gouged, blistered and scratched, and the nails of many of their toes were gone. It is hard to imagine what comfort such feet will ever find in the shoes of civilized society when release from prison conditions finally comes.

All prisoners are worked on the task system, and if they finish their work on Friday evening or early Saturday morning they have the balance of the week in which to rest. . . . The captain draws $150 a month; the guard draws $25 per month—$35 if he has a horse. The life they are compelled to lead drives them to excessive drinking as well as to gambling and other questionable practices. One of these captains was part owner of the still and business, and allowed the prisoners to work overtime, for which they were paid. Then, because of his fondness for gambling, he compelled the prisoners to gamble with him, and in that way won back all the overtime he had paid out. These practices exist despite the fact that the warden or captain is an officer of the law, as much as is a county sheriff.

At the time of my visit to this camp, 1,800 or more convicts were leased by the State of Florida to one company for the sum of $323.84 per convict annually and in turn subleased by the company to the individual turpentine distillers operating the 31 convict camps of the State for the sum of $400.00 a year apiece. Thus the Company was collecting the tidy little sum of $76.00 per annum per man upon the labor of between 1,400 and 1,800 convicts—a total of perhaps $125,000 a year. This company paid to the State in 1912 for the use of convicts $307,116.48. The arrangement was so satisfactory and profitable to both parties that the lease was renewed in 1909 for a period of four years more; and on January 1, 1914, a number of leases were renewed for two years. During the 32 years in which the convict has been leased by the State, the State has received a total of $2,722,620.14.

In spite of the shocking disclosures relating to the fee system and the convict lease system in the Southern States, especially in Alabama, Florida and Georgia, at the time of investigations and prosecutions for peonage by the Federal Government, during the Roosevelt Administration, these pernicious and inhuman practices have continued in at least eight of these States. There have been periodic agitations resulting from articles in Northern newspapers and periodicals, but the evils of the fee system and the horrors of the convict system have continued unabated. In Florida, for example, twenty years after the exposures by the Federal Government, during the month of March, 1923, the State of North Dakota made formal protest to the State of Florida against conditions which made possible the tragic death of Martin Tabert, a citizen of North Dakota.

The World (New York) sent a staff correspondent to Florida to investigate the charges that grew out of the protest of North Dakota. This correspondent, Mr. Samuel D. McCoy, remained in Florida several weeks and his daily reports in *The World* relating to the common practice of peonage and the horrors of the convict system attracted national attention. From an editorial in *The World* of April 1, 1923, I quote the following summary of the particular instance of injustice and inhumanity in Florida which attracted national attention on account of the exposures resulting from the formal protest by the State of North Dakota:

Caught in the attempt to ride on a train without a ticket, Martin Tabert was sentenced by a local Judge to pay a fine of $25 or to ninety days imprisonment. The Putnam Lumber Company has leased ''all able-bodied male prisoners for a term of one year,'' and Tabert was taken to one of the company's camps. His family forwarded the money to pay his fine and bring him home, but the Sheriff, T. R. Jones, sent the money back. In the lumber camp Tabert was taken ill and was unable to work, and one Friday night, in the presence of eighty-five convicts he was called out and given from ''thirty-five to fifty licks with a four-inch strap, five feet long, three-ply leather at the handle, two-ply half way down.'' ''The whipping boss,'' according to an eye-witness, ''put his feet on Martin's neck to keep him from moving out of position as he whipped him.'' The next day, sick and blind with fever, he was forced to work. Sunday he lay half unconscious in his bunk. Three days later he was dead, and the doctors pronounced his case ''pernicious malaria.''

There is the record, and no one has attempted to deny a single detail. It is one more hideous tragedy, such as the laws of Florida encourage. For peonage is an institution expressly recognized and fostered by the State. There have been similar abuses and scandals before, and cruelties similar to those practiced at the cost of Martin Tabert's life, and nothing apparently has been done to end them. It is only a short time ago that former Governor Catts was charged with peonage but it was soon forgotten. The case of Martin Tabert is only another glaring instance. Evidently no attempt has been made to clean up the State or to wipe out the long-standing reproach to the people of Florida.

The sad case of Martin Tabert is only one of thousands that have occurred in the convict camps of the Southern States. This case was no more shocking, inhuman, or tragic, in its pathetic details of injustice and cruelty, than have been thousands of other cases in these States. The false and puerile claim asserted by a number of politicians in the South to the effect that the people of Florida were not informed about ''the occasional abuses which have arisen in some of the counties under the system of leasing convicts,'' is the specious plea that has invariably followed exposures of corrupt practices and crimes in the South.

Not only the people of Florida, but the people of the whole country, and the Congress of the United States, were informed about the horrors of the convict camps of Florida in 1902-3, but the ''abuses'' continued unabated. Again, as cited in the article in *The Survey*, by Mr. Goodnow, ten years after the corrupt and inhuman practices were exposed in an investigation by the Federal Government, they continued without abatement or hindrance. Nor did the exposures by *The Survey* mitigate or lessen the evil. In April, 1923, when the State of North Dakota protested, and some of its leading citizens, undertook a personal investigation, the facts revealed a condition in the convict camps of Florida as shocking as they were in 1902-5 or in 1915. Moreover, these investigations in Florida have shown, as similar investigations in Alabama have shown, that public officials and prominent politicians were among the chief beneficiaries of these pernicious and inhuman practices.

In the history of civilization there is no record of venality and atrocities under the form of law more appalling than is the record of the fee system and convict system in Georgia. It would be impossible to conjecture anything more atrocious, inhuman and shocking than some of the tragedies which have occurred in the convict camps of Alabama and Florida, but in a brief survey of the record in Georgia we shall find that the spoilsmen of this State have been as sordid and cruel as those of any other State. Referring to the convict system in Georgia, *The Atlanta Constitution,* in an editorial, July 25, 1908, said:

Such revolting details of convict treatment coming from the lease camps are, in all conscience, appalling enough, but when they are found not only in county camps, but even under the direct and untrammeled administration of the State itself, and entirely separate and apart from any lease contract, all Georgia stands aghast.

Worst of all, the second day's testimony brought to light the death of a convict following application of the lash at the State Prison Farm, an institution where the convicts are worked by the State and for the State and where no private contract intervenes.

Dr. John E. White, of the Second Baptist Church, Atlanta, Georgia, preached a sermon on "The Cross and the Convict" from which I quote the following:

The Georgia convict system has been a subject of almost world-wide notoriety. The good name of the State has suffered, and despite the improvements in the system effected in 1895 and 1903, Georgia is still under a cloud in the esteem of a general judgment. Harsh terms have been applied and the stain lingers; the moral stigma has been laid on, and it is not removed; the finger of reproach has been pointed at Georgia, and it is not yet lowered. . . .

The report does not defend the system which prevailed from 1865 to 1899. It is indefensible. It was barbarous. For thirty years Georgia vacated every moral obligation to the convicts, sold them as one would sell cattle and did not even sell them profitably, sold them to private parties for a penny, who turned around and resold them for a profit, relinquished their custody, abandoned their control and left the, 2,000 of them at one time, to the fluctuations of the slave market, without that ancient southern self-interest in the slave to guarantee the contractor's consideration for the convict who is still a human being.

An investigation of the convict system in Georgia "showed that practically every warden had been receiving extra pay from the lessees." One case cited was that of a "dealer in convicts" who leased to one party for $52.50 a month convicts he had originally secured from the State at $225 a year, making a profit of $405 on each man. *The Ninth Annual Report of the Prison Commission of Georgia* contains some shocking statements from which the following reference to prison conditions:

Your attention is called to the fact that there are a number of women, some white, confined in the county chain gang. The policy of the State, as expressed in the laws, is against the confinement and punishment of females in the same institutions with male offenders, and the policy has not only proven satisfactory but has commanded public approval. No provision, however, has yet been made for the separation of these classes in the chain gangs, and it frequently happens that white women, as well as Negro women, who have been convicted of offences involving no moral turpitude, are confined in chain gangs with white and Negro men who have committed all kinds of crimes.

Two instances within the past twelve months have especially attracted the attention of the Commission, in each of which a white woman had been convicted of selling whiskey illegally, and confined in a chain gang, in which all the other inmates were Negro men, and such cases are liable to occur again.

One of the most revolting stories of the brutal and inhuman treatment of convicts in Georgia was that relating to the beating of a 16-year old white boy with a 6-pound leather strap, from the effects of which cruelty he died. This story was told by R. A. Keith and follows, as published in *The Atlanta Constitution*:

Win was a young white boy, sentenced to the coal mines of Dade for petty larceny. He had stolen two cans of potted ham and the judge said he must be punished. The men at the mine knew he was from Cobb County. What the rest of his name was, or whether he had any, they neither knew nor cared.

One night the convicts at the Durham Coal and Coke Company mine were eating their supper in the yard. This was the main dining room. The men ate breakfast while the morning's program of whippings were being carried out; they had dinner in the mines and ate supper in the outdoor dining pavilion. They made their own coffee, if they had any.

This night young Win spilled some of his coffee on the back of a hog belonging to a herd of swine owned by Warden Goode. The pig set up a terrible squealing, which brought the warden to the scene.

Young Win was forced to strip naked, a number of Negroes held him flat on the ground, and John D. Goode, an officer of the State, who, it is alleged, was also drawing additional salary from the Durham Coal and Coke mine operators, laid 69 lashes upon his body. The child's flesh was cut into ribbons. When released he staggered to the steps of the hospital. Then he entered the building. He did not appear among the men again, but a week later his body was brought out for burial. Dr. J. H. Hendricks attended him during his week's confinement. On the boy's burial certificate prepared by Dr. Hendricks and written by R. A. Keith, the witness on the stand, the cause of death was given as "consumption."

Among other horrible things narrated during an investigation of the convict system in Georgia, was the testimony of J. H. McCroy, a white man who had been pardoned by the Governor and released from the "gang." This man charged that A. N. Luck, the overseer of the camp at Buckhead, was one of several persons responsible for cruel treatment of convicts at that camp. According to his own statement, McCroy was a "dope fiend" and was sentenced to serve five years for forging a name for the purpose of getting money with which to buy morphine. He testified in part, as follows:

When I went to the chain-gang I was crazy, because the morphine was stopped right off sharp. While I was in this condition I lost my left hand. . . . I was taken out and beaten for "shamming" sick, although I was really ill. Seventy-five lashes were laid upon my bare back by the whipping-boss. . . . When they got through I was bloody all over, and the flesh was cut out at every one of those seventy-five blows. . . .

After this, when I was working on the rock crusher, a belt flew off. Although I could do no good with one hand, I was made to try to put on this belt, and my right hand was caught in the chain belt and crushed into a pulp. I was allowed to stay in the hospital thirty days, and then was sent out again, this time, not with white people, but with the Negro squad. As I had no hands at all, I could not work, but I was made to stand in the broiling sun all day long just the same.

On April 1, 1909, the convict lease system of Georgia came to an end as the result of an act of the Legislature in 1908, following an investigation and severe public condemnation of the whole system with its long record of corrupt and inhuman practices. The State had been leasing convicts for forty years. Good citizens who had aided in exposing the corruption and brutality of the abominable system felt that, after the system had been legally abolished by an act of the Legislature, there would follow not only a marked improvement in the treatment of convicts but also a discontinuance of the venal practices of the "fee brigade" in apprehending innocent Negroes and "railroading" them into convict camps or into a state of peonage.

There was some change in the methods but little, if any, improvement in the treatment of convicts, and no abatement of greed by the exploiters. The convict system of Georgia is about as detestable at the present time as it was under the old lease system and peonage has increased. In June, 1915, six years after the convict lease system was abolished by law, there were 3,282 convicts in Georgia, 939 of whom had been sentenced for murder, 476 for manslaughter, 14 accessory to murder and 333 for attempts to murder. The oldest convict was 78 and the youngest was 11 years old.

While, as already stated, the convict lease system was abolished by an act of the Legislature, the pernicious and cruel practices of the system have continued. The fee system continues with all of its sordid and inhuman practices. While the State does not lease its convicts, the poor Negroes, and some of the unfortunate whites, continue to be apprehended on trumped up charges, and in default of fines and costs which they are unable to pay, they are sold into peonage by the county authorities. Fines are imposed which, even if very small, the average Negro or poor white man is unable to pay; but if he were able to pay the fine, the costs are always made so disproportionately large that, in numerous cases, it is impossible for the accused party to pay them. The result is that the defendant who cannot pay the amount of the fine and costs is sold to anybody who is willing to pay the fine and costs, and the purchaser takes his county convict to his mine, lumber or turpentine camp, farm, or any other place where he thinks he may safely keep his peon and work him as long as he is able to work. For instance (as reported in *The Atlanta Constitution*, May 23, 1921), the Rev. John W. Ham, in a sermon at the Baptist Tabernacle in Atlanta, said:

We have beaten, flogged unmercifully and killed men on our chain gangs who were more helpless than the most flagrant case of peonage yet cited. . . . Efforts to inject a racial issue in this particular species of lawlessness and cruelty is for the sole purpose of beclouding the moral issue involved.

When these men, both white and colored, were beaten nearly to death a quick warrant for lunacy was obtained and they were railroaded to Milledgeville to die, this being done to keep down a storm of indignation against a system of barbarism in vogue in the camps. I cite the recent barbarous treatment of a returned soldier who had been gassed in France and his mind affected. He was unmercifully beaten on a chain gang in Chatham county, and had it not been for the A. E. F., they would doubtless have killed him or nearly so and then sent him to the asylum to die.

I appeared before a large committee at the last session of the Legislature to make a speech on the beastly method in vogue in the camps and to show that the whipping bosses were former mule drivers, and what do you suppose they did? By a vote they shut off debate entirely and locked the doors in that session I attended. County commissioners were there up in arms against the abolition of the whipping post. Georgia and Russia to-day use the same methods with prisoners. The cry of the politicians and whipping bosses was "Let us alone." The iniquitous fee system is at the bottom of much of the lawlessness in Georgia. Some of the courts operate in favor of the fee system and arch criminals, rather than the protection of society. Some courts' sentences are made with a view to collecting a fee rather than punishment by confinement and hard labor. Bonds are made of such size as to invite forfeiture and political gluttons continue to fatten on it. . . . Privileged interests do not want reforms if it touches the pocketbook. Sin, whether corporate or individual, has always cried, "Let us alone."

At the State Reformatory, Milledgeville, Ga., according to a statement made by the Rev. D. W. Brannen, before the Sociological Society in Atlanta, boys sent to this institution for reform are—

chained and manacled, and governed according to the convict system. Thus they plow in the fields and do the labor alloted them. In one building limited in size, the cooking, eating and sleeping is done, the white boys in the same apartment with Negroes and lying on the same floor. No training of mind or body is provided for them, no recreation, no religious suggestion; in fact, the conditions described were as hopeless as any that have been told about the worst conducted convict camps.

During the month of May, 1921, the Atlanta Humane Society presented to the Governor-elect of Georgia a petition to abolish whipping in convict camps. It was charged that—

The cruelty in these camps surpasses that reported from Russia. The law requiring that no more than ten lashes can be applied to a prisoner can be easily evaded by calling back a man after he has been beaten ten times, and beating him again.

In an investigation of charges against a prominent white man named Williams for the murder of eleven Negroes on his farm in Jasper county, Ga., it was shown that every one of the murdered Negroes had been taken to the farm to work out fines and costs which Williams paid in Atlanta, or elsewhere. I quote from the reports published in *The Atlanta Constitution* and other newspapers, immediately following this investigation:

Each of the fourteen Negroes alleged to have been killed by the Williamses and their Negro farm boss, Clyde Manning, whose confession led to the recovery of the bodies and the indictment of the planters, were what are known as ''bonded'' laborers. Convicted of crime, they were serving out thir fines in the jails of Atlanta, Macon, or Monticello, when Williams appeared and obtained their release by paying the fines. The Negroes were then supposed to work on his plantation or that of his son until the amount of the fine had been worked out. Charged with his food and clothing and advanced small sums of money from time to time, the Negroes got deeper into debt, and became nothing more nor less than slaves.

Referring to the killing of the Negroes on the Williams farm, the Negro Manning, in his confession, said:

Most of these dead Negroes was originally from Atlanta, Macon, or somewhere else. They didn't come from Jasper county. Mr. Huyler Williams, the son of my boss, would go to Atlanta and Macon and get the Negroes out of the stockade by paying their fines. I used to hear him and his father talking about all that. They brought the Negroes to the farm and put 'em to work, and kept guards over 'em all the time so as not to let 'em get away or talk too much.

According to reports from a special correspondent of *The Atlanta Constitution*, dated Covington, Georgia, April 2, 1921,

Five Negro employees on the ''death farm'' in Jasper County were brought before the Newton grand jury and their bodies bared to show ugly scars of mistreatment. . . . When the Negroes from Atlanta and other places who had worked on the Williams farm were brought before the grand jury, they were made to bare their bodies. Bruises, gashes and scars all disclosed how they had been mistreated. The Negroes were asked how they recived their wounds and replied that Williams and his sons inflicted them.

In an interesting and illuminating article on the convict lease system in Mississippi, published in *The Mobile Register*, Mr. Frank Johnston, of Jackson, Miss., says:

A squad of ten or fifteen State prisoners were brought to Vicksburg by steamboat from a convict camp in the Yazoo-Mississippi delta, on their way to the prison hospital in Jackson, in such a pitiable and deplorable condition resulting from bad treatment, that the city authorities would not permit them to walk across the town to take a train for Jackson, but transported them in covered vans.

The convict lease system was investigated by a committee of the Legislature, in 1888, and the report of this committee, as stated in the article by Mr. Johnston,—

condemned the entire system as brutal and inhuman, and gave a great many instances of the cruelties to which the prisoners were subjected in the sub-lessee convict camps.

They were badly fed and insufficiently clothed. They were housed in contrivances called "shacks" made of logs or poles, low, insufficient in size, with dirt floors, with no ventilation and no warmth, overcrowded and with insufficient bedding. These pens were cold in the winter and suffocating in the summer. The sick and well were all packed together in these death traps.

The committee reported that cruel and brutal punishments were often inflicted for trivial offences. One instance was given of the case of a prisoner in one of the railroad construction camps, who was hung up to a tree by the thumbs and whipped to death. A hole was dug under him, and his body was dropped in it, and covered with the dump from the railroad.

The committee reported that the prisoners were often worked in the water on railroad work, all chained together, and they were forced to drink the water they stood in, with other details that are not necessary to put in print. . . .

The constitutional convention of 1890 promptly abolished convict leasing in Mississippi. And thus ended in this State the most vicious, the most inhuman, the most demoralizing and the most brutal prison system that was ever devised in the history of Christian civilization.

The constitutional provision abolishing convict leasing, adopted by the constitutional convention of 1890, went into effect January 1, 1895.

As related in preceding paragraphs, worthy and prominent citizens of Alabama, including some members of the Legislature, testified that the fiendish atrocities which have continued for many years under the convict lease system were the most appalling and inhuman of which there is any record in the history of civilized countries. Worthy citizens of Florida testified to the same effect concerning conditions in that State, and the same character of testimony concerning conditions in Georgia was submitted by worthy citizens of that State. In fact, prominent representatives of the better class of respectable citizens in Alabama, Florida, Georgia and Mississippi, respectively, have cited the official records to show that the injustice, cruelties and barbarities in these States have been the most atrocious and appalling of which there is any record in the history of civilization.

As stated in the article by Mr. Frank Johnston, to which I have already alluded, the convict lease system in Mississippi ceased on January 1, 1895. Since the lease system was abolished, the convicts have been worked on farms owned and operated by the State. There was great improvement in the treatment of the convicts after the lease system was abolished. They were better housed, better fed, better clothed and received more humane treatment, but the penal farms of Mississippi have not escaped the contaminating evils of political corruption and vice so prevalent in that State. For instance, *The Birmingham Age-Herald*, January 12, 1919, contained the following story:

Governor Bilbo promises the people of Mississippi a real sensation. He has just returned from his annual visit of inspection to the convict farms in the delta and in response to questions put by *The Age-Herald* correspondent, told a story of mismanagement that will prove an eye-opener to the people and public generally. . . .

It was found that one of the sergeants, a man who worked 60 Negro convicts, had drawn about 8,000 pounds of meat from the commissary during the two months of November and December, and that he had slaughtered more than 30,000 pounds of hogs. His record shows, and it was borne out by testimony, that he had weighed out an average of but 60 pounds of meat per day for the feed of the convicts under his charge, and yet there was no meat on the place. The 60 pounds per day for 61 days would account for but 3,660 pounds of the meat. What became of the other 5,000 he drew from the commissary, and the 30,000 pounds of fresh pork? . . .

But these discrepancies sink into insignificance, said the Governor, in comparison with the evidence of immorality permitted on the big farm with the full knowledge and consent of the Superintendent. It is an established fact that scores of Negro women of vilest reputation from Clarksdale, Greenwood, Greenville and other neighboring cities were permitted to come on the farm nearly every Saturday night and remain over Sunday for the use of the convicts. The women were let into the upper stories of the cages, or they were housed in old buildings nearby that had been fitted up with stalls and rough cots for their accommodation, and there they were permitted to remain for weeks at a time, being fed out of the State smokehouse and cribs. A considerable number of the convicts, the Governor says, are now suffering from venereal diseases contracted in this way.

According to *The American Year Book* (1914), the Carolina Prisoners' Aid Association was "making a special effort toward the abolition of whipping," but the "flogging of prisoners is apparently very slow in dying out."

While Chief Justice Clark of North Carolina has handed down a decision declaring that flogging in North Carolina is not reasonable and that it cannot be sustained, we find somewhat earlier in the year the county authorities of Beaufort, N. C., voting as follows:

"The Superintendent shall keep in his possession a lash 18 inches long and more than two inches in diameter, and said lash may be split three times one-half way from the end. No convict may be whipped more than once during two consecutive days, and none shall receive more than 25 lashes at more than one whipping."

Mr. W. O. Saunders, in *The Survey*, May 15, 1915, writing about North Carolina convicts, said:

A convict was not permitted to rise from his bunk at night for any purpose whatever. The horrors resulting may be easily guessed when it is known that the camp diet consisted of boiled beans at least twice a day, every day in the year.

Convicts who complained of the treatment they received were chained with an iron collar at night, the collar being fastened to their necks and padlocked.

Convicts were whipped with a leather strap eighteen inches long, two inches wide, and half an inch thick; this strap being fastened to a hickory stock two feet long. One method of whipping a convict was to stretch him between two trees and bare his back. One of the guards would wrap a heavy blanket about the victim's head and hold him to smother his cries. Another guard applied the lash. Many convicts thus whipped will carry marks for life.

The convicts were chained while at work. Many barbarous devices were employed to shackle them so they could not run. The iron bands on their ankles cut into their flesh, making running sores, that never healed because the iron bands were never removed.

The limits of this chapter will not permit further details

relating to a survey of the cruelties and injustices of the fee system and convict system under rule of the Oligarchy in the South. The distressing situation with respect to prisoners and juvenile delinquents in the Southern States, as shown by the census report of 1910, furnish some interesting figures for comparison. At the present writing, the census figures for 1910 are the latest that are available on the subject. As stated in a Report of the Special Commission on Law Enforcement presented at a meeting of the American Bar Association, San Francisco, California, August 10, 1922:

Up to 1910 the Government, through its Census Bureau, compiled a report of prison statistics. While lacking in some essentials, this compilation still supplied much valuable information. In the census of 1920, just when the study of American criminology could accomplish most, for some unaccountable reason the Government abandoned altogether this most important subject.

Under the Wilson régime, the Government frequently suppressed, withheld, or failed to gather information the publication of which would have been injurious to the Democratic party or the Southern States. These omissions were particularly noticeable in the State Department and in the Census Bureau.

In the eleven Southern States, the total number of prisoners and juvenile delinquents (1910) enumerated was 30,883, but these figures include only 1,157 juvenile delinquents, leaving 29,-726 prisoners enumerated. Very little provision is made for juvenile delinquents in the Southern States; a large number of the white delinquents are never apprehended, and, as a rule, when they are prosecuted and convicted, they are classed as prisoners and criminals with adults. This fact will explain the notable difference in the number of juvenile delinquents in the Northern and in the Southern States. In the eleven Northern States used for comparison, and having practically the same total population as the Southern States in 1910, the total number of prisoners and juvenile delinquents was 27,395, of which there were included 7,665 juvenile delinquents, leaving 19,730 prisoners in these Northern States as compared with 29,726 in the Southern States. The total number in the United States was 111,498.

The prisoners enumerated in the Southern States were considerably more than 25 per cent. of the total of the United States. The total number of prisoners convicted of grave homicides in the Southern States was 3,540; in the eleven Northern States the total was 965, while the total for the United States was 6,904. The eleven Southern States had more than half of the total number of convictions for grave homicides. Of the prisoners who were convicted of lesser homicides there were 3,559 in the Southern States, 648 in the eleven Northern States, and 7,412 in the United States. On the same date of enumeration, the official figures show that there were 39 prisoners who had been sentenced to death in the Southern States and 12 in the eleven Northern States.

In the matter of long term sentences, in the Southern States there were 3,346 prisoners who had been sentenced to life imprisonment, 963 in the eleven Northern States and 6,444 in the United States. With less than one-fourth the total population of the United States, the Southern States had more than one-half of all the life term prisoners. Convicts sentenced to twenty years or more in the Southern States amounted in the aggregate to 1,884, while only 365 were sentenced to twenty years or more in the eleven Northern States, and 3,841 was the total number of prisoners in the United States under sentence of twenty years or more. There were 1,241 prisoners in the Southern States who had been sentenced to the penitentiary for terms from fifteen to nineteen years, and 308 for the same period in the eleven Northern States. The common practice of long term sentence in the Southern States is for the sordid and inhuman purpose of holding the convict in servitude during the period of his earning capacity. The prison records are the best evidence of this practice. Commenting on prison conditions in Alabama, Judge Fort of that State, in a public address, said:

There is no reformatory to send a young man to. He is sentenced to the penitentiary, where he learns only evil and crime. Instead of placing the youth in a curative institution, we herd them with old criminals, from whom they learn all the gaits of crime. In mines, sawmills or turpentine camps, what chance has a boy to become a decent, law-abiding citizen when his term expires? None. He comes out hating the system that put him in these vile surroundings, and with revenge in his heart, no hope of a helping hand from any one, he starts on a downward path.

In his report for 1920, the State Prison Inspector of Alabama called attention to the "youthfulness of many of the offenders." He said:

A distinctly disturbing feature in the report is the youthfulness of many of the offenders. In 37 counties the minimum age of those apprehended was placed between fourteen and twenty years, and in thirteen counties from twenty-one to thirty years. In twenty-one counties the maximum age was given as thirty years, and in fourteen counties as thirty-five years. Nine replies gave the middle age for both minimum and maximum.

Concerning prisons in Georgia and the treatment of juvenile prisoners, Judge Henry C. Hammond, of the Augusta (Georgia), bar said:

The theory of our State seems to contemplate nothing but punishment, and loses sight entirely of the more important question of reforming and restoring to society the criminal and criminally inclined. The greatest handicap to the juvenile court is the fact that there is no adequate place for the boys to be confined and taught useful trades; and also the fact that there is not, so far as I am advised, a place in this State—certainly not in this county—a place where wayward girls or women who are criminally inclined can be detained with any hope of reforming them.

Several of the Southern States, Texas and Mississippi in particular, have penal farms where convicts are worked. According to reports published in the newspapers, the value of crops raised on Mississippi penitentiary farms during 1923 was $726,923. Convicts who work on small farms attached to the main prisons in some of the Southern States usually receive more humane treatment than those who work in the mines, at lumber and turpentine camps, but there has been very little constructive effort to reform prisoners in any of the Southern States. The parole system, the indeterminate sentence, the suspended sentence, the prison school, in fact all modern methods and practices of prison reform are practically unknown in the South.

On most of the prison farms in the South abuse and mistreatment of convicts is about as merciless and notorious as it is in the mining, lumber and turpentine camps under the lease system. From the Texas penal farms, for example, it has been reported that a number of the convicts have been beaten to death. Students of penology, men and women who have had many years' experience in the management of prisons, have agreed that "crimes are more effectually prevented by the certainty than the severity of punishment." The treatment of prisoners in the Southern States is not only at variance with the experience of the most successful prison management, but it is also contrary to the present practice in all other civilized countries.

It has been clearly demonstrated that long term sentences have not decreased crimes in the Southern States; but it has also been shown that long term sentences do increase the profits of the convict lessees and the officers who have control of the detestable business. The longer the term of the convict the greater profit for the venal spoilsmen. About eighty-five per cent. of all convicts in the Southern States are Negroes, many of whom, arrested for trifling offences, have drifted into crimes because of their ignorance and the neglect of the State to educate and protect them. The injustice, persecution and petty thievery of the white man in his dealings with the Negroes, as practiced by so many landlords, merchants and lawyers, is another potent cause of crimes among the Negroes. Concerning lawlessness in America, Lord Bryce, in *Modern Democracies,* said:

As respects the defects of criminal procedure in general, it must be remembered, that an evil which has become familiar ceases to be shocking. The standard custom has set comes to be accepted; it is only the stranger who is amazed. Those good citizens in the States referred to who are shocked and desire reform find it hard to know how or where to begin. The lower sort of lawyers, numerous in the legislatures, dislike reforms which would reduce their facilities for protracting legal proceedings to their own profit, and are apt to resist improvements in procedure.

The "defects of criminal procedure" in the Southern States are not only musty with age, and frequently tainted with political corruption, but they are also burdened with the "lower sort of lawyers, numerous in the Legislature." As pointed out in a preceding chapter, the South is ruled by the lawyer politician. Among a people living under such burdensome conditions, "who are shocked and desire a reform," it is "hard to know how or where to begin," especially without capable and fearless leaders. Every patriotic, self-respecting citizen of every one of the Southern States is sincerely ashamed of the sordid fee system, the inhuman convict system, and other deplorable and outrageous practices which make his State a reproach to American institutions and a byword among all civilized peoples.

The subject of convict labor, in one form or another, has claimed the attention of the Congress of the United States during the past twenty-five years or more. Numerous bills have been introduced in both branches of Congress, and there have been a number of hearings before committees, especially with reference to the important question of prison contract labor. It has been clearly demonstrated that mild punishment by the courts and the honor system in the treatment of convicts, in this and other countries, are not only more humane, but the wiser and more practicable methods of treatment from every point of view.

Perhaps the most noted example of late years in support of the theory of humane treatment in actual practice has been in the State of Colorado, where the convicts were under the control of Warden Tynan, whose practical business management, executive capacity and humane treatment justly won him great praise, to say nothing of the confidence and affection of the great majority of convicts who have come under his control. New Mexico claims to have been the first State to introduce the honor system in the management of convicts, and reports from this State claim that the men are far more efficient without the guards than with them. Experience in this State has shown that "one armed guard is useless and the presence of a gun in the camp is always a menace." Of the 150 men in the honor camps, only about 17 escaped in 1914.

The State of Alabama has produced few better or more useful men than Judge Feagin. He established the probation system in the police court of Birmingham although, as he said, the system "had no law to back or sustain it." Under this system, as inaugurated by Judge Feagin,—

every little Negro 14 years of age, or under, who is arrested and where the evidence shows that he is guilty, is for the first offense released—put on probation. Punishment is suspended with the understanding that if he commits a second offense he is to be punished heavily for the second offense, or he is to be sent to the country on a farm. About 275 little Negro boys or girls, 14 years of age, or under, have been arrested for first offenses, since this plan was adopted. Out of the 275 Negro boys and girls between fifty and sixty have become second offenders; twenty per cent. committed the second offense and were sent to the country. The remaining 80 per cent. are still here on good behaviour, and never come before the police court the second time.

The statistics of France show that 47 per cent. of the first offenders of the criminal laws become second offenders thereafter. In ten years thereafter under the probation plan, the second offenders were reduced to 5.4 per cent. If France can accomplish such marked results under laws passed for such a purpose, is not the City of Birmingham to be congratulated for having accomplished so much in the short time of one year with no law to uphold the system?

In the French Cameroon, a large portion of which was formerly under German control and furnished some of the most revolting records of German injustice and atrocities in her colonial possessions, France has established a system of jurisprudence which insures in a large measure justice to the native population. Under German rule, slavery in its worst form existed; natives were punished without even the form of trial and unmercifully flogged. Under the new French régime, accused natives are given a fair trial in their own districts, and before courts of their own race, presided over by the head officials of each district. The rights of the accused are guaranteed and local customs are respected, and the various races differentiated. According to the administration of the new judicial system and practice, the sentence of a local court imposing a greater penalty than three years' imprisonment is referred to a special court sitting at Douala.

The colonies and dependencies of France have a total area estimated at about 4,000,000 square miles with a population of about 44,600,000.. The population of the French colonial possessions include a vast number of illiterates, semi-civilized and uncivilized people, and more than 60 per cent. of the population of these colonies and dependencies are native Africans. According to *The Statesman's Year Book,* and other standard authorities, most of the French colonies enjoy some measure of self-government and have elective councils to assist the Governor. The older colonies have also direct representation in the French legislature. It is quite evident that natives of the French colonies and dependencies are treated with more consideration, greater respect is shown for their civil rights, they live under a higher standard of justice, and have more voice in the affairs of the government under which they live than the American Negroes have and enjoy in any of the States under rule of the Southern Oligarchy.

CHAPTER XIV

The history of peonage in the Southern States is another story of sordid injustice and appalling horrors, the execrable details of which are beyond the limits of this volume. In detestable and flagrant violation of Federal laws, open and defiant has been the practice of peonage under the protection of the Oligarchy in the South.

A peon is defined in the *Century Dictionary* as " a species of serf compelled to work for his creditor until his debts are paid." The most common form of peonage in the Southern States is found among the tenant croppers, under farming contracts whereby the unscrupulous landlord or merchant, by dishonest practices, manages to keep the tenant continuously in debt for supplies. This form of peonage is sanctioned in some cases by the State laws, in other cases it continues through the maladministration of the law by venal officers of the law, and almost universally, in the cotton and rice-producing States, and in the turpentine and lumber camps of the South. Justice Brewer of the United States Supreme Court, gave the following definition of peonage:

It may be defined as a status or condition of compulsory service based upon the indebtedness of the peon to the master. The basal fact is indebtedness. One fact exists universally; all were indebted to their masters. This was the cord by which they seemed to be bound to their master's service.

It was during the early years of the Roosevelt Administration that the prevalence of peonage in the South was brought to public attention. Through the prosecutions that were started in the Federal courts under that Administration, every effort possible, within the limits of the Federal courts, was made to remove the evil. Among the early prosecutions for peonage under the Roosevelt Administration was the rather notorious case in South Alabama where a white man and his entire family were held in peonage by another white man. There had been a "fake trial" before a Justice of the Peace "specially elected for the business." A fine was imposed which the unfortunate man was not able to pay and he was "turned over to work out his fine." As reported by "Raymond," staff correspondent of *The Chicago Tribune,*—

newly arrived immigrants are in chain gangs in Alabama charged with no crime whatsoever except their unwillingness or inability to pay their debts which may or may not have been just ones. . . . Several instances were cited to show that newly arrived immigrants were made victims of the old-fashioned laws of the Southern States, by means of which a person who makes a contract to labor and fails to fulfill it, or who runs in debt for advances made to him as a laborer or tenant, can be compelled to work by force, or actually be sent to the chain gang.

It was reported that more than 3,000 men were held in a state of peonage in Florida. These men, it was stated, had been induced to accept employment in the South. Further regarding the peonage investigations in Florida, "Raymond" of *The Chicago Tribune* said:

Men have been tried and punished for peonage in Florida, and in other cases, in which the Florida East Coast Railway was concerned, the juries have returned a verdict of acquittal in spite of convincing evidence to the contrary.

Peonage, like the appalling record of the convict system, is an old story of sordid brutalities in Forida. It has been in common practice in this State for forty years or more, with little interference or abatement except, as we have seen, when, during the Roosevelt Administration, the Department of Justice was active in prosecuting cases of peonage in the South.

The appalling record of peonage in Georgia is only a little less shocking than the gruesome story of the convict system. When the Department of Justice was actively engaged in an investigation of the charges of peonage in the South, Judge Emory Speer of the United States District Court in Georgia, on one occasion,—

devoted his entire charge to the grand jury to the matter of peonage. . . . He said there was no doubt that men held in involuntary servitude were really in worse condition than those held in slavery, for the latter had the countenance of law to give it a certain standing, while peonage, under whatever guise it is hidden, is totally ouside the pale.

The investigation of secret service agents in Georgia, in 1903, developed "some horrible cases" of peonage. Among other notorious and shocking cases was that of "three prominent politicians and wealthy citizens of South Georgia." They operated a manufacturing plant and for some years they worked State and county convicts under the lease system; later, they made arrangements with the officers in some of the surrounding counties whereby they paid the fines of convicted misdemeanor prisoners, and the prisoners were turned over to them to work out the fine. But these rapacious landlords did not limit their traffic in human beings to the resources of State and county officials who apprehended unfortunate citizens for minor and frequently for no offense. They resorted to kidnapping, a practice not uncommon in Georgia for many years.

One of the most diabolical and shocking cases against these exploiters was that of a Negro girl, fifteen years old, who, while on her way to visit a sister in Florida, was so unfortunate as to enter the territory preëmpted by these robbers. She was kidnapped while she was at a boarding-house and accused of a crime of which she was wholly innocent, and was threatened with prosecution unless she could pay the sum of $25. She was unable to pay the ransom demanded by her kidnappers whereupon she was told that she would be accused and prosecuted in court for the crime with which she was charged unless she agreed to go to the camp of the exploiters and work until she had paid the sum of $25. She finally accepted the proposition and went to the camp, where she remained at work for three months, until her mother, after employing a lawyer, was required to pay $15 for the release of her daughter, although no criminal charge had been made against her in any court. According to the statement of a United States Revenue Agent, "there were scores of similar cases."

Two special representatives of the Italian Government were sent to Mississippi to investigate the unfortunate condition of twenty-two Italians held in peonage in that State. The efforts of the Italian Government to protect the treaty rights of its nationals in Mississippi were met with the usual refusal on the part of that State to protect the Italians and the assertion that the charges were "an unwarranted attack on the South." With respect to the investigations of the United States Government in Mississippi, among other statements, it was reported as follows:

From evidence obtained by Miss Mary Grace Quackenbos, a woman lawyer, and other federal investigators, Sunnyside plantation is worked by "slaves," who are induced by false promises to go upon the soil there. Once they set foot within its boundaries they are, to all practical purposes, prisoners. If they attempt to leave, debt charges are trumped up against them, and they are arrested. They are brought before a county justice of the peace, who probably has "peons" on his own plantation, and tried.

None ever is acquitted, and outrageous fines are entered against them. Of course, they cannot pay them, and these immigrants, who believed America was a free country are sent to the chain gang, back into prison to work out as a felon the fines assessed against them.

So flagrant and numerous have these crimes against written and human laws become that foreign nations have protested time and again to the State Department in Washington for relief. Secretary Root appealed to Governor Vardaman of Mississippi, asking that he take steps to protect aliens in that State, but to no purpose.

The investigations and prosecutions of peonage during the Roosevelt Administration did not eradicate the inhuman practice in the Southern States, but the activities of the Department of Justice brought relief to many unfortunate victims, and it rivetted public attention on the pernicious evil. It created alarm among the guilty who were not detected and apprehended and there was a marked decrease in the number of violations of the Federal laws against this common and shameful practice. Investigations and prosecutions by the Department of Justice attracted public attention and aroused indignation which resulted in an investigation of the situation by a committee of Congress in 1908. Had the vigorous policy of the Federal Government continued, after the Roosevelt Administration, in a thorough investigation of all charges relating to reported cases of peonage, and an energetic prosecution of all cases where the evidence appeared sufficient to convict the accused parties, the evil of peonage would have been greatly reduced and eventually eradicated. But the leaders of the Southern Oligarchy are well-trained and crafty politicians and expert traders. They have always fought investigations of corrupt practices and law-lessness, and all proposed Federal legislation to punish crimes in the South; and they have usually succeeded in evading all laws which conflicted with their policies and the practices of their agents and confederates. But they were never able to bluff or bamboozle President Roosevelt; their later efforts along this line were more successful.

After the Roosevelt Administration, and prior to the beginning of the Harding Administration, the public heard very little about prosecution of peonage cases. During the Taft Administration the activities of the Federal agents in apprehending and bringing to trial persons charged with peonage declined and the evil increased. Practically nothing was done during the Wilson Administration in the matter of prosecuting peonage cases.

Immediately after the election of Mr. Harding, and the return to power of the Republican party, with some promise of virile Americanism and a suggestion of law enforcement, the newspapers began to publish news items from the Southern States, Georgia in particular, relating to peonage. The situation may be illustrated by comparison. For instance, the annual report of the United States Attorney-General (1920, p. 128) contains the following reference to peonage:

A number of complaints have reached the Department during the past fiscal year, charging that the crime of peonage is being practiced, which complaints, for the most part, have been investigated and found to allege circumstances of a character insufficient upon which to institute prosecutions under the Act. There are several of these complaints, however, in which the investigations have not been completed. No new cases have been instituted and none have been disposed of during the year.

While the Attorney-General was writing this report respecting the matter of peonage in violation of the Federal laws, it is a fact that peonage was more prevalent, widespread and more diabolical than it had been at any time in the history of this country. Within less than sixty days after the publication of the report of the Attorney-General, from which I have quoted, a press telegram from Atlanta, Georgia (January 13, 1921), contains the following statement:

Coincident with the announcement that peonage indictments had been served against a farmer and two of his tenants, one of whom is a Negro in connection with the death of another Negro, United States District Attorney, Hooper Alexander, in a statement to-day said that wrongs were being perpetrated against Negroes in this State that "run all the gamut from the meanest of petty cheating to deliberate and plotted murder." . . . Comparatively little effort is being made by the proper officers to end these conditions. In a large proportion of the cases judicial processes are issued by magistrates that are used in the most shameless manner in the aid of crimes, and the attendant circumstances are such as should call for indictment for malpractice. Cases have occurred in which there is the gravest reason to fear that other officers of the law have been active participants in the gravest kind of wrongs. If the people of the State permit the continuance of conditions that now prevail, sooner or later and in some way we will suffer a dreadful retribution.

It was stated during the month of April, 1921 that there had been numerous investigations in the South in the past ten years in which peonage conditions had been exposed and "countless indictments" had been returned against farmers and planters who were alleged to be holding Negroes in bondage. In only a few cases, however, have verdicts of guilty been returned, and in these few cases light sentences have been imposed. A large number of planters and officials, it was stated, were under indictment and had been under indictment for years, the cases never being called for trial. It was further alleged that Federal agents "who have taken a hand in the case," now charge that the murders on the John S. Williams "murder farm" began as far back as 1910, and cite the killing of three Negroes to support their claims. They produced witnesses to prove that two of the Negroes—one a woman—were killed because they were too old to work and a useless expense to the farmer. Aleck Dyer, a Negro laborer, was knocked on the head with an ax and instantly killed while he worked in the field on the Williams plantation, and Nick and Mamie Walker, aged Negroes, were shot to death after they had lived on the "death farm" for twenty years. These killings "were said by the one-time farm hands" to have occurred in 1910 and 1911.

It was late in February, 1921, that Federal officials first appeared at the Williams plantation to investigate alleged peonage conditions. Immediately after the beginning of that investigation, the "bonded" Negroes began to disappear. It was stated by Federal agents engaged in an investigation of conditions in Jasper County, Georgia, in the matter of alleged peonage in that county, that the Negroes on the Williams farm were taken from the city stockades. For many years it has been a common practice to take Negroes from the city prisons and hold them in peonage as security for the payment of actual or alleged fines and costs imposed by the city courts.

During the month of April, 1921, a few weeks before the expiration of his term of office, Governor Hugh M. Dorsey, of Georgia, published a pamphlet on *The Negro in Georgia* which—

deals with lynching, cruelty, and holding in peonage of blacks. . . . The Governor divided his discussion into four parts—the Negro lynched, the Negro held in peonage, the Negro driven out by organized lawlessness, and the Negro subject to individual acts of cruelty. One hundred and thirty-five examples of alleged mistreatment of Negroes in Georgia were mentioned.

Concerning actual conditions in Georgia and the treatment of Negroes, Governor Dorsey said:

If conditions indicated by these charges should continue, both God and man would justly condemn Georgia more severely than man and God have condemned Belgium and Leopold for Congo atrocities. In some counties the Negro is being driven out as though he were a wild beast. In others he is being held as a slave. In others no Negroes remain. In only a few cases was there any prosecution of white men guilty of attacking Negroes. Acquittal or light fines was the usual result of the trials.

The Atlanta Constitution quoted a "high official" of the State of Georgia as follows:

Since the State of Georgia has failed absolutely in handling peonage, lynching and cruelty to Negroes, I believe the Federal Government should be asked to take complete charge of the situation and remain in control until these violations of the law are checked.

In upholding Governor Dorsey in his attitude respecting the charges of peonage and other criminal offenses of which the Negroes were the victims, *The Constitution* said:

Another fact Georgia must face is that recently the most revolting instance of peonage ever known was brought to light in this State, and with other disclosures that followed, emphasized the seriousness of the situation.

Further respecting the charges contained in the pamphlet by Governor Dorsey, *The Constitution* said:

Strongly defending Governor Hugh M. Dorsey's position in the peonage situation in Georgia, the United States District Attorney, Hooper Alexander, issued a statement Thursday declaring that conditions described in the Governor's pamphlet really do exist in Georgia and offering to furnish names of witnesses who will testify in a number of cases not even listed by the Governor. "The laws of the State of the Georgia are violated and defied in cruel treatment of Negroes with a frequency that warrants inquiry and demands correction. . . . Negroes have been killed on the public highways and their bodies left exposed to the public gaze, and though their slayers are known, no action has been taken to hale them before the jury," the District Attorney stated.

In a preceding paragraph of this chapter, I quoted from the report (1920) of the United States Attorney-General, while America was under rule of the Southern Oligarchy, in which the Department of Justice, in an official report to Congress, asserted that complaints charging peonage had been investigated and "for the most part . . . found to allege circumstances of a character insufficient upon which to institute prosecutions . . . no new cases have been instituted and none have been disposed of during the year." I also quoted from the United States District Attorney of Atlanta, a statement in which he said that peonage existed in the most exaggerated form and that "comparatively little effort was being made to end these conditions," and that "officers of the law have been active participants in the gravest kind of wrongs."

In order to show the shameless neglect of official duty, and also the utter unreliability of certain public officials, State and Federal, under rule of the Southern Oligarchy, in all matters relating to corrupt practices and law defiance in the Southern States, it may be well to call attention to certain statements in the first annual report of the Attorney General under the Harding Administration. This report (December, 1921) contains some comments on the violation of Federal laws relating to peonage from which I quote as follows:

Peonage, or the holding of persons in involuntary servitude, still continues in many of the Southern States. The victims are almost always extremely poor, ignorant and friendless. Many times it appears that county officers conspired with employers to force these unfortunates into bondage, which is worse than outright slavery. Bureau agents have been instructed to make vigorous efforts to put a stop to this vicious practice, and a number of cases have been successfully prosecuted and substantial sentences imposed. Some of the cases reported in the hundreds of reports received have been extremely aggravated and in several instances the poor victims have been murdered when it was discovered by the employer that this bureau was conducting an investigation.

Complaints arising under this act increased during the year, and peonage was found to exist to a shocking extent in Georgia, Alabama, and some parts of Texas.

It will be observed that the Attorney-General under the Harding Administration corroborates and amplifies the charges made by the District Attorney of Atlanta. In most cases where the organization of labor is attempted in the South it is met with bitter opposition and frequently with persecution and violence. By a system of legal chicanery the poor and ignorant whites and Negroes, but more especially the Negroes, are cheated of their earnings, especially on farms, and held in a state of economic dependence, frequently in a state of peonage and a life of serfdom. The report of the Attorney-General (1921) from which I have quoted states the actual situation when he refers to cases of "bondage" in the South as "worse than outright slavery."

In the preceding chapter on the evils of the fee system I referred to the common practice in the South of apprehending poor Negroes (and sometimes poor whites), taking them before petty courts where for misdemeanors, or other minor offences, or no offence, fines and heavy costs are imposed which the poor defendants cannot pay and they are sold to contractors, manufacturers, farmers, or anybody who needs unskilled labor and is willing to pay the fines and fees. This is one method used for making peons; the other and more common practice is to keep farm tenants in debt until they are reduced to a state of peonage.

A system of rapacious landlordism in the South by which tenants are swindled, frequently with the help of public officials, has developed a condition of tenancy more distressing and inhuman than can be found in any civilized country. The condition of the tenant in Italy under the Cæsars was better than the present condition of the tenant in the Southern States. Prior to, and during the early years of the Christian era, the Roman tenant had certain rights which were respected and could be enforced; so long as he paid his rent he could remain a free man and a Roman citizen. In the Southern States the tenant has few civil or political rights that are enforceable. The civil and political rights of which the average American is so boastful exist only in theory, so far as the tenant and the average laborer in the South are concerned. The corrupt and dishonorable practices of the landlord in numerous cases make it impossible for the tenant to pay his rent or other contractual obligations. The tenant is in fact neither a citizen nor a freeman; he is a serf, bound to the soil at the will of the landlord.

In his remarkable book, *The Impending Crisis of the South,* which caused so much excitement throughout the country, and acrimonious discussions in Congress, in 1857-60, Hinton Rowan Helper revealed some plain truths in very plain language. His work was in behalf of the poor white non-slaveholding population of the South. "Poor whites may hear with fear and trembling but not speak," wrote Helper:

They must be as mum as dumb brutes, and stand in awe of their august superiors, or be crushed with stern rebukes, cruel oppressions or downright violence. If they dare to think for themselves, their thoughts must be forever concealed. The expression of any sentiment at all conflicting with the gospel of slavery, dooms them at once in the community in which they live, and then, whether willing or unwilling, they are obliged to become heroes, martyrs or exiles. . . . Never were the poorer classes of a people, and those classes so largely in the majority, and all inhabiting the same country, so basely duped, so adroitly swindled, or so damnably outraged.

The comments of Mr. Helper on conditions in the South a few years before the outbreak of the Civil War could just as well be applied to the situation as it actually exists at the present writing. The poor whites of the South are held in a state of serfdom. Their condition is in fact worse than that of the Negroes, because greater effort is being made by leaders of the Negro race to educate and improve the social and industrial condition of their own people, while the whites are not only neglected, but the ruling Oligarchy continues unremittingly and unmercifully to deceive the poor people, mislead them, exploit and rob them in every possible manner. In an interesting series of articles, published in *The Cosmopolitan Magazine*, in 1909, Mr. Daniel J. Sully, the leader of the "bull campaign" on the New York Cotton Exchange, in 1903, said:

American cotton-planters, proprietors of the greatest gold producing staple in the world, are poor. They are in practical servitude. It is a tragedy of contemporary life that they who produce for the world the commodity without which modern civilization and industrial life could not proceed are themselves absolutely subservient and the poorest paid toilers in the United States. Intellectually the cotton-growers are surrounded and coerced by factors which have no other purpose than to keep them in this benighted vassalage.

Five years after Mr. Sully wrote the plain truth about the condition of the tenants in the cotton-growing States, a practical business man, residing in Atlanta, Georgia, "of large experience with cotton producers," wrote a letter to *The Atlanta Constitution* (September 27, 1914), concerning the practices of the "cotton oligarchy." The writer of this article, Mr. J. T. Holleman, it was stated,—

through years of experience in loaning money on Southern farm lands, has come to intimately know the South's agricultural problems, and he has made what was conceded to be the most searching analysis of the situation.

From Mr. Holleman's article I quote the following:

The South is in the grip of a cotton-growing oligarchy more powerful than the ante-bellum slave-owning oligarchy. Seventy per cent. of the South's farm lands are under control of landlords, largely absentee. Ninety per cent. of the South's agricultural activities are influenced by this oligarchy.

Five years after the publication of Mr. Holleman's article, *The Manufacturers Record*, August 21, 1919, said:

Many of the worst enemies of the cotton growers are men in the South who live by the sufferings of the women and children of the small farmer.

Commenting on the deplorable condition of tenants and farm laborers in the South, in its issue of October 7, 1920, *The Manufacturers Record* said:

There became established an economic serfdom far worse, in many cases, than personal slavery had ever been. Thousands and thousands of Negroes worked their entire lives without accumulating ten dollars worth of property or having at the end of any planting season enough cash to purchase a single suit of clothes. They lived on butts and hominy, and they were thankful to Providence if they could secure enough old clothes and old shoes to keep them going. They were impoverished and the land in which they dwelt was impoverished because the thing they produced and depended on for a livelihood had been manipulated in the world markets so that the manufacturers should take not only the profit legitimately due them, but also the profit morally belonging to the producer. . . . Unless, therefore, the Nation as a whole is reconciled to the idea of maintaining in its midst some millions of serfs, and unless the South itself wants such a population, the time has come when the physical emancipation of the black must be followed by their economic emancipation, which would mean the emancipation also of the white people of the South.

In the story of conditions in France at the outbreak of the Revolution we find a true picture of the social and economic situation in the South at the present time. The historian says that in addition to an indigent peasantry, France was cursed with its usual attendant, a non-resident body of landed proprietors. This was an evil of the first magnitude, drawing after it, as is invariably the case, a discontented tenantry and a neglected country. "The great proprietors all resorted to Paris in quest of amusement, of dissipation, or of advancement." The natural consequence of this was that—

no kindly feeling, no common interest, united the landlord and his tenantry. The former regarded the cultivators in no other light than as beasts of burden, from whose labor the greatest proportion of profit was to be extracted; the latter considered their lords as tyrants, known only by the vexatious visit and endless demands of their bailiffs.

Arthur Young was the greatest of all English writers on agriculture, before the French Revolution, but it is as a social and political observer that he is best known, and his tour in Ireland and travels in France are still full of interest and instruction.

He saw clearly and exposed unsparingly the causes which retarded the progress of Ireland. The soil of France he found in general superior to that of England, and its produce less. Agriculture was neither as well understood nor as much esteemed as in England.

Young, the "Suffolk Squire," rode horseback over the rural

districts of France, his first visit being in 1787, traversing the country in every direction just before and during the first movements of the Revolution. "He has given valuable notices of the condition of the people and the conduct of public affairs at that critical juncture."

The "Suffolk Squire" made a close and careful study of the country and of the people. He found that the French peasants were impoverished and wretched to the limit of human endurance. The king, the nobles, and the priests were literally devouring the common people. Thomas Jefferson had made a study of conditions in France, and in writing about the country and its people, for whom he had great admiration, he said: "A people of the most benevolent and amiable character, surrounded by so many blessings from nature, yet loaded with misery by king, nobles and priests, and by them alone." If in this description of conditions in France, at the time of the Revolution, we substitute for "king, nobles and priests" the words bankers, landlords and lawyer-politicians, we have an exact description of conditions in the Southern States in our own times.

If, as stated by the historian, one-half the soil of France, at the beginning of the Revolution, belonged to the favored rich, those landlords of France did not own so large a percentage of the soil as do those of the South who rent their lands to an impoverished tenantry. In another description of the miserable condition of the French peasantry, as portrayed by Alison, in his *History of Europe,* we find a striking illustration of the present deplorable situation in the Southern States:

Thus robbed under the name of custom and law, the farmer toils joylessly from the cradle to the grave with barely sufficient food and shelter to keep him in respectable working order and when he dies he leaves his children to the same miserable doom.

The major portion of the cotton crop of the South is produced by tenant farmers. As shown by the reports of the Fourteenth Census (1920), in the eleven Southern States, including all cotton producing states except Oklahoma, and a small production in Missouri, more than fifty per cent. of the farms are cultivated by tenants. So far as the question of landlordism is concerned, conditions in the South were better in 1880 than they were in 1920 or are at the present time.   In 1880, the number of farms operated by owners was 62.00 per cent. average for the eleven Southern States; in 1920 the average was 49.8 for these States. The average of farms operated by tenants was 38.01 in 1880 and 50.02 in 1920.   There has been a steady increase in tenancy in the South under rule of the Oligarchy since 1880.

In some of the largest cotton-producing counties of Georgia, South Carolina and Mississippi the percentage of farms cultivated by tenants varies from 70 to 90 per cent.   At the time of the census of 1910 there were 84,242 white tenants in Georgia, which with their families represented a landless, homeless population of 425,000 people.   It has been stated that the average cotton crop of the United States could be produced on the land of the Yazoo Delta in Mississippi.   More than ninety per cent. of the farms of this rich section are operated by tenants. Tenancy in Mississippi increased from 43.8 in 1880 to 66.1 per cent. in 1920; during the same period the increase in Georgia was from 44.9 to 66.6 per cent.   More than eighty-five per cent. of the Negro farmers in Mississippi in 1920 were tenants and 59.2 per cent. of all farms in Mississippi are operated by Negroes.

There are varying forms of tenancy in the South but the share tenants and croppers represent the majority of the farms operated by tenants "under specified forms of tenancy."   As stated in the Fourteenth Census report, on farm tenure in the Southern States,—

A considerable proportion of the tenants in the South occupy a very different economic position from that usually occupied by tenants in other parts of the country. In the North and the West the tenant farmer is normally working toward buying a farm and his tenancy thus represents merely a stage on the way to ownership. In the South, on the other hand, there are large numbers of tenants who do not look forward to ownership and for whom tenancy is the normal economic situation.

The common form of contract between landlord and tenant in the Southern States is so oppressive and unjust in its terms for the tenant, and the landlord, in numerous cases, is so exacting and rapacious that a good deal of friction necessarily arises. Under this form of contract, the landlord not only gets his share which is usually one-half of the crop produced by the tenant and his family, but he also has a prior lien for all advances he makes to the tenant and his family in the way of provisions, clothing, medicines and other things which the tenant must have. A very large number of landlords are also merchants, but if not a merchant, the landlord usually acts as surety for the tenant in order to enable the tenant to get necessary supplies.

The most common cause of friction between landlord and tenant is found in the common and very dishonorable conduct of the landlord or merchant in refusing to furnish the tenant a correct statement of his indebtedness. The tenant being illiterate and poverty-stricken and unable to protect himself, is obliged to accept any settlement the landlord or merchant may offer. In this way the tenants are frequently swindled, but this practice in the South is not always attributable to the dishonesty of the landlord or merchant. In some cases, the landlord, without intending to swindle his tenant, desires to keep him in debt so that he may retain him as a tenant. Out of this practice, as well as the more dishonest practice of charging exorbitant prices for supplies furnished the tenant, a state of peonage has developed in the South which is one of the principal causes of race conflicts and criminal lawlessness, and it is an ever-increasing menace to the peace of the whole country.

The shocking story of the Williams murder farm in Georgia revealed the shameful practice of buying prisoners from the State and holding them in peonage. There have been thousands of cases where prisoners have been bought and held in peonage by their purchasers. But the most extensive and pernicious process of reducing the poor laborer to a state of peonage is through the system of tenancy that prevails in the South. The race riots in Phillips County, Arkansas, in October, 1919, which resulted in the death of five whites and seventeen Negroes, was the outgrowth of dishonest practices and oppression on the part of landlords in dealing with their tenants. The share-croppers were exploited by the landlords and held in a state of peonage. Mr. O. S. Bratton, a native of Arkansas, prominent lawyer of Little Rock and former Assistant United States Attorney, who had prosecuted cases of peonage, made the following statement:

The conditions that affect the colored man to-day in the South are even worse than they were before the Civil War. . . . The system of exploitation which goes on is such that the large majority of the Negroes work year in and year out without receiving anything except a scant bare living. . . . The planters have what is called "commissary stores" from which these supplies are furnished at whatever prices the planters and managers see fit to place on them. . . . He is not permitted to have any statement or bill of the articles purchased.

The Manufacturers Record of June 17, 1920, contained a very illuminating and forcible article by Professor David Y. Thomas, of the University of Arkansas, in which he referred to the evils of the tenancy system in the Southern States, especially as it was practiced by landlords in dealing with their Negro farm tenants. He said:

The crux of the Negro problem to-day is economic. So far as the rural population is concerned—and most of the Negroes live in the country—it revolves around the relation of landlord and tenant. . . .

The most common complaints against the tenant system seem to be that the charges for advances are exorbitant, that accounts are often padded, that the landlord will not render itemized accounts, that the tenant does not enjoy freedom of sale and does not receive the market price for his share when the landlord takes it over for advances, and that often it is impossible to get a final settlement.

The unfortunate condition of the tenants in Arkansas, as described by Professor Thomas, is no worse than the normal condition of the average share-croppers, and other dependent tenants in other Southern States. In every one of the Southern States farm labor, under the tenant system, is being reduced to a state of peonage. This system is an essential and permanent part of the economic policy of the Oligarchy. Without the support of the Oligarchy it could not continue; nor could the Oligarchy continue if the great mass of farm tenants were not held in political subjection and industrial serfdom. Fifteen years after the vigorous efforts of the Department of Justice during the Roosevelt Administration to stamp out this evil, the actual situation, in every one of the Southern States, except Virginia, is worse at the present time than it has been at any time since the Civil War. Sir Horace Plunkett, the leading and perhaps the most effective publicist who has been connected with the great land reform movement in Ireland, in commenting on the condition of tenants in the South, said: "It is the worst of which I have knowledge in any country."

Had it not been for the outlet through her wonderful colonial system, especially in Canada, Australia and New Zealand, the British Empire never could have survived the blight of landlordism as it existed in the United Kingdom and Ireland. At the beginning of the great industrial revolution following the Napoleonic wars, it was said that England was rich only at the top. At that time the United Kingdom had one of the most miserable, demoralized peasantries in the world. Her great industrial class was overworked, underpaid and underfed, uneducated and untrained. Knowing from a sad experience the curse of landlordism in the mother country, the British colonists in Australia and New Zealand made provision against the menace of landlordism in these countries.

In every one of England's self-governing commonwealths, especially in Australia and New Zealand, radical and beneficent reforms were brought about and great changes made in the old English system of land tenure before there was any material progress along this line in the United Kingdom or Ireland. New Zealand was perhaps the first, the most radical and strenuous in its social welfare measures and in providing land for the people and preventing the growth of land monopoly and the old curse of oppressive landlordism. In 1892 a law was passed in New Zealand under which the Government could acquire large estates, either by purchase at an agreed price, or by appraisal, and develop them by laying out roads and dividing the large acreage into farms and villages. These subdivisions were sold to actual settlers at a price sufficient to pay the cost of purchase and development. No person was permitted to acquire more than 200 acres of land in the division of the holdings acquired by the Government, and under the original act it was provided that no person could own or lease from the Government more than 640 acres of first-class farming land, first-class grazing land owned or leased by one person, was limited to 5,000 acres, and second-class grazing land to 20,000 acres, or sufficient to carry 20,000 sheep or 4,000 cattle.

According to authoritative reports in 1921, there had been no rent profiteering in New Zealand. In spite of the great increase in the cost of construction, more houses were under construction in 1920 than ever before in the history of the country. The new homes were sold at cost to the working people in monthly installments. It was stated that there was not a millionaire in all New Zealand, and there were no paupers and no slums in the cities.

In Queensland, the second largest State in Australia, during a period of eight years prior to 1924, the Government expended approximately $16,000,000 in the erection of between 8,000 and 9,000 houses, which were sold to the people. During and after the World War, the housing shortage in Australia was as bad as it was in other countries, but the Government met the situation in a practical and statesmanlike manner. It bought the land, built homes, and sold them to the people on the installment plan, payable weekly; and the installment payments on the purchase price of the homes were no more than the prevailing rent charges for the same class of buildings. In the early part of 1924, it was stated that Queensland would spend $2,000,000 during the year for 1,000 homes to be built and sold to the people on the installment plan.

Australia and New Zealand have made great progress in the settlement of the land question with respect to tenure, and the result is that in these countries there is not only greater distribution of wealth and prosperity, but also a more stable government than in any one of the Southern States; and if we may judge by their contributions in men and money to the World War, there is also striking evidence of greater patriotism in these British Commonwealths than in the Southern States.

In 1870 the first land act was passed which marked the beginning of the new era in the history of landlordism in Ireland. In this land act of 1870,—

for the first time the interest of the tenant was definitely the main object of legislation; and an attempt was made to protect him from eviction.

So far as relieving the burdens of tenancy in Ireland, however, the first Land Purchase Act of the Gladstone Ministry was not worth very much, as under that law provision was made for the Government to advance only two-thirds of the purchase price. Later acts provided that the Government should advance the whole purchase price, giving the peasants the privilege of repaying by installments covering a long period of years. Under the later and present system, the Government buys the land and sells it to the peasant who becomes its legal owner and pays for it gradually. Experience in the operation of this system has demonstrated that the new proprietor pays less this way each year than he formerly paid in rent, and in the end his land is unencumbered.

The Ashbourne Act, passed in 1885, marked the beginning of the real land reform measures for Ireland. The three acts relating to landlordism in Ireland, subsequent to the Ashbourne Act of 1885, are those passed in 1891, 1896, and 1903. Under the Irish Land Act of 1903 State advances are made to tenants to purchase their holdings under the supervision of three "Estate Commissioners." Money for advances was to be raised by the issue of "land stock" bearing interest at 2¾ per cent. According to *The Statesman's Year Book*:

Up to March, 1911, £66,500,000 had been advanced for this purpose, which represented the purchase by Irish tenants of nearly 6,000,000 acres, or little short of one-third the total area of Ireland; while agreements for the purchase of another 4,500,000 acres, at a price of £46,500,000 were pending. By the middle of 1913 the sum of purchase money for transactions fulfilled, or agreed upon, under the acts of 1903 and 1909 was over £96,000,000. Nearly £4,000,000 had been also advanced for laborers' cottages; and the sum of £24,000,000 had in addition been used under the Acts for land purchased prior to 1903. . . .

The total amount of the purchase money of estates for which advances have been made under the Irish Land Purchase Acts, 1870 to 1909, up to March 31, 1919, was £105,496,566, of which £103,723,663 was advanced, and £1,772,903 was lodged in cash by purchasers. In addition, £4,606,156 was advanced to that date by the Land Commission to Rural District Councils, for the erection of labourers' cottages, under the Labourers (Ireland) Acts.

In *Current History*, September, 1920, Lord Bryce said:

As a result of the money voted by Parliament during the last thirty years, and by the large extent to which it has pledged its national credit in guaranteeing loans, Ireland has been made more prosperous and the people better off than they have been for many centuries. Under the provisions of the Land Purchase Acts more than half of the tenant farmers have become, or are now becoming, owners of the land they occupy and cultivate, as the rest of these farmers will be when the process is complete. . . . But the present Irish generation, still brooding over the wrongs of the past, does not realize that the English people have undergone a complete change of heart, and are not only seeking to cure the practical evils brought to their knowledge, but heartily desire that complete reconcilement which the grant of autonomy, or some kind of home rule, is needed to produce.

When we consider the large number of impoverished tenants who have become landowners, we can easily appreciate the magnitude and wholesome results of this great reform in Ireland. For example, in five years after the Land Act of 1891, some 35,000 tenants were enabled to purchase land under provisions of that act; and in five years after the Act of 1903 there were about 160,000 purchasers under this act.

Landlordism and an impoverished tenantry were the curse of Ireland for more than two centuries; the underlying question of land tenure was the vital issue during this long period of unrest and strife. It has been only during the past thirty years that any real progress has been made in solving the Irish land question, but since the work was undertaken in a practical and constructive manner there has been great improvement. The economic and political power of landlordism has been destroyed in Ireland and that unhappy country is no longer menaced by the exactions of absentee landlords. After permitting the wrongs and injustice of rapacious landlordism for centuries in Ireland, the British Government at last took hold of the question in a broad and practical manner and settled it as it should have been settled two centuries ago. The United Kingdom has paid a big price for this reform, but it was necessary and it will be worth more than it cost.

The curse that oppressed and agitated Ireland for centuries left behind it a train of social and political evils which have disturbed not only Ireland but also the Irish people, in a large measure, in every country to which they have migrated. The great emigration from Ireland to America which followed the potato famine of 1846-47 may be traced to the abominable land tenure system that prevailed in that country. Between 1846 and 1851 a quarter of a million of the population of Ireland emigrated each year; between 1851 and 1861 over 100,000 left annually. The total number from May 1, 1851, to the end of 1918 was 4,319,693. Emigration has steadily declined since the beginning of the effective operation of the land reform measures.

In the Southern States, as it was in Ireland, landlordism has been, and still is, the underlying cause of unrest, agitation and crimes of violence. The civic, economic and social ills which continue to afflict the South are the same as those which disturbed Ireland for more than two centuries. Old prejudices, in a large measure justified, which had been handed down from father to son among the Irish tenantry, could not be removed by legislation, nor by belated justice. In spite of the wholesome effects, from an economic point of view, of the late land reform measures in Ireland, that country has passed through distressing civic and political disturbances.

The migration of Negroes from the Southern States finds its parallel in the history of emigration from Ireland. The Irish emigrated to escape the injustice, oppressions and persecution of the landed oligarchy of England; other races have emigrated from Europe to escape the oppressions and persecutions of the land autocracies and oligarchies of that country. The exodus of Negroes from the Southern States was, and is, to escape the injustice, the oppression and cruel persecution of the Southern Oligarchy. The South is not only more backward than any English-speaking country but it is more backward than any other civilized country in its economic policies. The actual situation in the South is worse than it was in Ireland at the beginning of the land reform measures in that country. Tenancy in the South has grown into a condition of peonage, which, as we have seen, is worse than slavery; it is a state of serfdom with all the attending evils of civic decline and increasing lawlessness.

CHAPTER XV

MOST APPALLING RECORD OF CRIMES IN THE WORLD

The limits of this book will not permit a comprehensive survey of the criminal record in the Southern States. The scope of this chapter is necessarily limited to a summary of some of the outstanding evidences of the distressing and alarming result of long years of corruption and lawlessness under rule of the Oligarchy. My narrative is based on authoritative reports. A brief presentation of excerpts from these reports will show that crimes of violence in the South have been the most atrocious and revolting in the history of civilization. This record also shows that crimes of violence in the Southern States are largely the result of the policies and practices of corrupt politicians and pettifoggers.

We have seen that the Negro has been made the scapegoat of practically all civic and political sins in the South. He has been held responsible for the shocking record of crimes; and the corrupt practices of which his traducers and oppressors have been guilty have also been charged to his account. It has been asserted time and again that the deplorable situation in the South is the result of corruption and lawlessness during the Reconstruction period for which the carpet-baggers and Negroes were responsible. But neither the end of Republican and carpet-bag rule, nor the disfranchisement of Negroes improved the criminal record very much. There is no more civil or political liberty, no higher regard for the moral standards of civic responsibilities, than there was when the Negroes had the ballot. Nor has there been any improvement in respect for the law. It may be well also to note the fact that the highest criminal record is not found in those sections of the South where the Negro population is larger than the white population.

Statistics of crimes in the United States, as shown by a special report of the Census Bureau, thirty years after the end of carpet-bag and Republican rule in the South, gave the total number of convicted homicides in the eleven Southern States as 5,144, an average of 26.6 per 100,000 of population, while the number in the eleven Northern States used for comparison, with practically the same aggregate poulation, was 1,266, an average of 5.8 per 100,000. In Illinois, where the criminal record was very high, the average per 100,000 of population was 8.9; in Georgia it was 33.4; in Florida, 52.0; in South Carolina, 24.0; in the State of New York, 6.1. The total number of convicted homicides in the United States for the period designated was 13.3 per 100,000. The number of convicted homicides in the eleven Southern States was nearly one-half the total of the United States. Later statistics show that crimes of violence have continued to increase under rule of the Southern Oligarchy. The record of homicidal crimes in the South, during the past twenty years will be traced by a brief summary of the States in alphabetical order.

The blackest criminal record in Alabama, strange to say, is found in that section where prosperity and enlightenment had, until within the last thirty-five years, made greater progress than in any other part of the State. I refer to the Tennessee Valley, the richest agricultural section of Alabama, especially diversified agriculture, and a most delightful climate. For many years the beautiful and picturesque little city of Huntsville was the educational, social, commercial and political center of the Tennessee Valley. The community was one of the most aristocratic and refined in the South. It was the first capital of the State and seven former Governors of Alabama are buried in the Huntsville cemetery. The record of corrupt practices and homicides in Madison County, of which Huntsville is the county seat, has been very bad under rule of the Oligarchy.

In 1904, two years after the Negroes were disfranchised under provisions of a new Constitution, to which I have already alluded, a mob gathered at Huntsville, ran over the State troops guarding a Negro who was in jail charged with murdering a white man, broke into the jail, seized the Negro and dragged him to a public square where the Daughters of America were holding a festival, and the place was brilliant with lanterns. The women and children were scattered before the mob, the Negro was hung to a tree under an electric light and his body was shot full of holes. The mob cut off his fingers and part of his trousers as souvenirs. Members of the mob were indicted, and on trial the evidence was conclusive, but not one was convicted.

It was stated that within twenty years prior to the lynching in 1904, seven Negroes and one white man were the victims of mobs in Madison County; and in five years before 1904, thirty-three murder cases were tried in the courts and eight murderers indicted but not arrested. The lynching at Huntsville in 1904 attracted national attention. Newspaper and magazine writers who visited the scene of the tragedy and investigated conditions seemed to be unanimous in the opinion that there would not be another lynching in Madison County, that public sentiment was so much aroused on the subject of crimes in that vicinity that there would be a new and better era of law enforcement. Unfortunately, an aroused public sentiment did not remove the cause of the civic malady and the disease of crime continued to spread.

In less than two years after the Negro was lynched in front of the Court House at Huntsville, the body of W. T. Lawler, Judge of the Probate Court of Madison County and a prominent citizen of Huntsville, was found in a slough on the Tennessee River. At the time of the disappearance of Judge Lawler, the grand jury was engaged in an investigation of an election in which he was the winning candidate. As usual, there were charges of frauds and irregularities in the election.

Three days after the body of Judge Lawler was found, Shelby Pleasants, a prominent and highly respected citizen of Huntsville, was found dead in his office. Mr. Pleasants was a nephew of the late David Shelby, Judge of the United States Court of Appeals. Mr. Pleasants had served as Federal Judge pro tem. Three days after the death of Shelby Pleasants, the body of Sheriff Phillips was found in a sleeping-room on the first floor of the county jail. According to newspaper reports, Phillips "killed himself by firing a bullet through his brain." Three months after the death of Sheriff Phillips, the former Chief of Police of Huntsville, and circuit clerk of Madison County, David R. Overton, was arrested on a charge of being connected with the murder of Judge Lawler. Overton had been one of the big political leaders of the local Democratic party and was a candidate for Probate Judge in the Democratic primary against Judge Lawler. David Overton was convicted of the murder of Judge Lawler, and later confessed his guilt. After being sentenced for the murder, he was taken to Birmingham and placed in the Jefferson County jail, from which place he escaped and was killed with two other prisoners who escaped with him.

The number of criminal cases disposed of in the State of Alabama for two years ending September 30, 1908, as shown by the report of the Attorney-General, was 20,672. During the two years covered by this report there were 657 cases of homicides disposed of. The biennial report of the Attorney-General for two years preceding the World War (1912-14) shows that there were 938 homicides in this State, and there were 431 convictions for murder and 239 convictions for manslaughter. In six years there was an increase of 50 per cent. in the number of homicides. This is the period of which the Governor of Alabama, in an address before the General Conference of the Methodist Church South, said:

In all the States you represent, no less than this one, men are killed in the streets, in crowded hotels and stores, shot from horseback and buggy, assassinated from the roadside and from open windows. Unexpected and violent death stalks abroad. . . . Some of the murderers of the well-to-do or prominent class may see the inside of a prison; few go to any further punishment and only now and then does one get the full penalty of the law, whose hardships, in theory only, fall on all alike. And they lynch people— innocent people.

Jefferson is the richest county in Alabama. It pays more taxes, has the largest population, and is the center of the iron and steel industry of the South. Birmingham is the county seat, with a population of about 200,000. Here is one of numerous items published in the Birmingham papers some years ago regarding lawlessness in that county:

Is the mining district north of Birmingham, around Lewisburg, Coalburg and Arcadia, becoming converted into a veritable Dead Man's Gulch? Within the past eighteen months, there have been mysteriously assassinated in that vicinity six white men and eleven Negroes. Within the past ten months two of the six white men have met their doom. Within the past six days six of the Negroes have been killed.

The Birmingham Age-Herald (November 30, 1908), stated that the month of November, 1908, would "leave in the police annals of Birmingham a record without parallel. Account has been given of 21 fatal shooting affairs which have occurred in the immediate Birmingham district during the last thirty days." According to official reports, there were in Birmingham, Alabama, from October 1, 1911, to September 30, 1912, 270 violent unlawful deaths, of which 115 were white. From January 1 to November 1, 1913, there were 105 homicides; and there were 335 unlawful deaths between October 1, 1912, and September 30, 1913, of which 140 were white people.

In a statement made by the Chairman of a Special Committee of Crimes in the city of Chicago, September 17, 1914, the following comparison was made regarding the record of homicides: "Murders—Chicago, 262; New York, 131; London, 36." The aggregate population of London, New York and Chicago was at that time more than six times the population of Alabama, but during the same year (1913) Alabama had more murders than the total of the three cities. These cities gather a large floating population from every race and nationality in the world; there are no large cities in Alabama and the urban population in 1910 was only 17.3 per cent. According to a report of the State Prison Inspector of Alabama (1920),—

there were committed to the jails in the State during the fiscal year ending September 30, 1920, 2,059 more prisoners than for the corresponding period ending September 30, 1917; and 5,500 more than for a like period ending September 30, 1918; and 2,836 more than for a period ending September 30, 1919.

Eleven sheriffs stated that the increase in crime was greatest among the whites, eight among the Negroes, twenty-six that it was among both races alike, thus indicating a tendency toward an increase in lawlessness in forty-five counties.

One of the most atrocious political crimes and cowardly assassinations ever known in the history of the United States occurred in the State of Arkansas fifteen years after the close of the Reconstruction period. Space for the story of revolting crimes in Arkansas cannot be found in this chapter, but it may be well here to remark that the high criminal record of that State has continued unabated down to the present writing.

There were 170 homicides in the State of Florida in 1919, a rate of 17.7 per 100,000. In 1920 it was officially reported that an average of one person a month was killed in Miami and the immediate vicinity. This places that beautiful, prosperous little city about as high, in homicides, in proportion to population, as Atlanta, Georgia. At Miami, Florida, July 17, 1921, eight masked men waylaid the Rev. Philip S. Irwin, white, Archdeacon of the English Episcopal church and head of the work of that church among South Florida Negroes, at the close of the evening service, carried him into the woods and whipped him, and then applied a coat of tar and feathers to his body. He was then placed in a sack and taken in an automobile to a spot near the business center of the city and dumped out on the street. After he had been taken to the police headquarters, Archdeacon Irwin made a statement in which he said:

They told me that unless I left Miami within 48 hours they would lynch me. They tied me to either a tree or a log after stripping me, and applied a strap to my naked body about forty times. The men then poured tar over me and applied feathers to the tar.

There are a number of Negroes from the British West Indies who have found work at Miami and other flourishing towns and tourists' resorts on the east coast of Florida. Some of these British subjects temporarily dwelling in Florida have been flogged, tarred and feathered, and made the victims of other indignities and cruelties of the lawless Ku Klux, night riders and other organizations engaged in law defiance and barbarous practices in the Southern States.

The criminal record of Georgia is worse than that of Alabama or any other State. It is the most appalling in the civilized world; and worse than anything in the uncivilized world so far as there are any records from which comparisons may be made. There is no country where human life is as cheap and where crime so defiantly and unhampered stalks over the earth and tramples down humanity, as in the State of Georgia. According to prison reports published in *The Atlanta Constitution*, May 28, 1921, of 3,076 convicts in Georgia, 947 were sentenced as the result of murders; 222 for attempt to murder; 437 for manslaughter, 597 for burglary. During the month of March,

1921, it was reported that for more than a month the finding
of three Negro bodies in the Yellow River at Covington,
Georgia,—

had baffled State, County and Federal officials, when the confession of a
Negro named Manning that he had knocked four Negroes in the head with
an ax in one week and helped drown others, under the orders of John Williams, a prominent white farmer, brought the first light regarding the
mystery of the dead Negroes.

Within thirty days the dead bodies of eleven Negroes were
found on the Williams farm where they had been killed and
either buried or thrown into the river, and the verdict of the
coroner's jury was that these eleven Negroes had been murdered
by Williams and the Negro, Manning. Several of the Negroes
murdered by the white man and his accomplice, as revealed in
the testimony at the trial, had been forced to dig their own
graves. According to newspaper reports, John Williams, the
white murderer, was a wealthy planter of Jasper County and a
man of "high social position." After Williams had been apprehended, and the confession of the Negro Manning had resulted in finding the bodies of eleven Negroes on the Williams
plantation or adjacent property, it was reported that "startling
disclosures of the merciless killing of two Negroes in addition
to the eleven blacks whose bodies have already been discovered,
were heard in the Newton County Court House." During the
month of May, 1921, Governor Dorsey, of Georgia, was quoted
as saying that—

the Negro has been subjected to mistreatment in Georgia and the time has
come to inaugurate a new policy if we are to retain our own self-respect and
maintain our position as a civilized people before the world.

The disclosures and admonitions from the Governor of
Georgia came after his successor had been elected and only a
few weeks before the expiration of his second term. Moreover,
Mr. Dorsey was Solicitor-General of the Atlanta Judicial Circuit several years before he was elected Governor, and he remained in office as Governor for three years and eleven months
before he discovered that the Negro had been "subjected to
mistreatment in Georgia," or if he made the discovery at an
earlier date he did not make it public.

In the long catalogue of political crimes in the South, perhaps the most cowardly and atrocious—second only to the assassination of Colonel Clayton in Arkansas—was the assassination of William Goebel in Kentucky. Goebel was shot while crossing the State capitol grounds, while a contest was going on to determine whether he or Taylor had been elected Governor. However, political corruption is not the only cause of the high criminal record in a State famous many years ago for its fine horses, good whiskey, productive soil, distinguished men and beautiful women.

Two razor-back hogs, so runs the village story, were responsible for the beginning of the notorious McCoy-Hatfield feud which kept the border country of Kentucky and West Virginia in a state of turmoil and lawlessness for many years. Floyd Hatfield and Randolph McCoy each claimed the hogs; and one "lawed" the other for possession of them. The man who lost at court settled his grudge according to the code of the feudists and the family feud passed from father to son. Twenty-six known deaths and numerous "disappearances" was the record of homicides resulting from this family feud before the Hatfields finally exterminated the McCoys.

The Hatfield-McCoy feud broke out in the early '80s. The Hatfields lived on the State border line, in West Virginia, while the McCoys were on the Kentucky side of the State line. Raiding parties from each side of the line periodically invaded the other side and the family feud almost grew into a State feud between Kentucky and West Virginia. The Governor of Kentucky would not surrender a citizen of his State who was charged with murder in West Virginia, nor would West Virginia show any more consideration for the official requests of the Kentucky Governor.

At Paducah, Kentucky, some years ago, two Negroes were lynched; one for an attack on a white woman, and the other for expressing sympathy for and, it was said, "lauding the accused man." The bodies were burned. After assuring themselves that both Negroes were dead, the members of the mob lowered the bodies from the scaffold and placed them on a blazing pile of brush. It was stated that more than 6,000 people witnessed the execution, hundreds of them mounting a railroad trestle in order to get a better view of the proceedings. On the evening of the lynching, *The Chicago Tribune* received a message signed "Citizens of Paducah," boasting of the lynching and wishing that the bodies might be given over to *The Tribune*.

From Jackson, Ky., November 7, 1921, news came that at the Clayhole voting precinct, near Jackson,—

A quarrel over politics arose and fifteen minutes later six men were dead, their bodies lying within a radius of fifty feet of each other. Five others were wounded, of whom three died later. Some of the fighters died instantly while others thrashed about on the ground until death came. Practically all the fighters were heads of families. The Combses belong to one of the most prominent political factions in the State.

It is the general rule when reporting crimes in the South to state that the person who committed the crime, if a white man, is prominent and of high social position. The total casualties reported from Kentucky on election day, 1921, were 10 killed outright and 7 wounded. A later news item from Jackson, Ky., thirty days after the wholesale killing on election day, stated that "seven masked men attacked the jail and killed a nephew of the jailor and seriously wounded two women."

At Bogalusa, La., November 22, 1919, three white men were shot dead, and a number were severely wounded. One of the men killed was district president of the American Federation of Labor; another was a union carpenter. This murder was the outcome of the arbitrary policy of a lumber company to prevent the organization of its employees in Unions. It was reported that the lumber company was supported by the so-called "Loyalty League"; the main business of this organization was to terrorize Negroes. The following story from Louisiana further illustrates the atrocious record of that State:

When a dissenting juryman yesterday refused to agree to the verdict of guilty in the trial of Alvin Calhoun, a Negro, following the murder of N. H. Arnold, January 20, at Tallulah, La., he was publicly whipped and then dipped in a mudhole.

When the jury returned to its quarters in the court house, escorting the downcast, mud-covered dissenting juror, a verdict of guilty was agreed upon, according to the report. The jury then appeared in the court room, reported its findings which declared Calhoun to be guilty of murder in the first degree.

It was said that the dissenting juryman was later waited upon by a committee and ordered to leave Tallulah.

A coroner's jury at Shrevesport, La., returned a verdict that George Holden, a Negro who was taken from a train near Monroe, La., and shot by an armed mob, came to his death "at the hands of parties unknown." Holden was killed after he had been taken from a stretcher in the baggage car, and was accused of having sent an insulting note to a white woman at Monroe. Here in brief, are the outstanding facts relating to another revolting lynching at Bogalusa, La.:

After being trailed by bloodhounds, caught and identified by a white woman as a man who had attacked her, Lucius McCarthy, a discharged Negro soldier, was lynched by a mob of more than 1,000 men. His body was then tied to an automobile, dragged through the principal streets of the town and finally burned in front of the home of his victim.

At Ellisville, Mississippi, it was publicly announced that officers had agreed to "turn over to the people" a Negro whom they had arrested under a charge of attacking a white woman. The Negro was wounded when captured and a physician who examined his wound stated that the prisoner could not live twenty-four hours. A New Orleans paper announced that the burning of the Negro was scheduled for four o'clock, and carried in big black type across the full width of the first page this announcement: "3,000 will burn Negro . . . Negro jerkey and sullen as burning hour nears." In *The Daily News*, Jackson, Miss., the following notice appeared in display type: "John Hartfield will be lynched by Ellisville mob at five o'clock this afternoon." A telephone message from Ellisville, Miss., confirmed the report that a committee of citizens had been appointed to make the necessary arrangements and the "mob had pledged itself to act in conformity with the arrangements."

It was reported that "more than 5,000 people gathered from all parts of the country" to witness the lynching and burning at the stake of the Negro "scheduled to take place at five o'clock in the afternoon." It was further reported that all roads leading to Ellisville were "choked with automobiles forming a steady stream." Ellisville is located in the timber district and it was stated that—

all lumber mills had closed down in order to permit the employees to attend the lynching. . . . The interurban cars running from Laurel to Ellisville were filled to overflowing.

The Negro was lynched shortly after five o'clock and his body was then burned to ashes. In a story of the legal execution of two Negroes at Starkville, Mississippi, as published in the newspapers, it was announced that a holiday had been proclaimed by the citizens.

They invited their relatives and friends for miles around to come to town, bring their lunches and witness the public hanging of two Negro murderers.

This gruesome story continues:

More than 5,000 men, women and children had gathered before 9 A. M. just outside the town where a scaffold had been erected from which the Negroes were to hang. A double gallows was constructed and the hanging was heralded to occur on Black Friday, so dubbed because several other Negroes were to be hanged in Mississippi the same day, as well as four others across the line in Alabama. Assured there would be something worth seeing, crowds began pouring into Starkville and a steady stream continued until just before the drop.

The practices which have been so successful in maintaining the power of the Oligarchy in the South will be perceived by my readers when they fully appreciate the methods and activities of the Democratic politicians in Mississippi, at all times and under all circumstances, as outlined, for example, in the following supplemental account of the double hanging at Starkville:

Numerous candidates at the primary election for the various county offices grasped the occasion to do a little electioneering. They gathered the white voters under their wings, paraded them to the soda fountains, erected for the day, bought drinks for them, and kept the owners of the booths busy, when they were not engaged in drawing drinks for the children who thronged the grounds.

The gathering was orderly. A casual spectator would have pronounced it a huge picnic. Whole families were gathered about tablecloths spread on the ground. As the people carefully watched the scaffold they munched on sandwiches, hard boiled eggs and pie.

There is no country, civilized or uncivilized, except the State of Georgia, that furnishes so many appalling stories of fiendish crimes as the State of Mississippi. One of numerous stories of savage butcheries that have occurred in Mississippi was narrated in an article by Mary Church Terrell, published in *The North American Review,* June, 1904, and, later, published in an address by President Robert McMurdy of the Illinois Bar Association, May 27, 1914, the details of which follow:

A white planter was murdered at Doddsville in the State of Mississippi, and a Negro named Holbert was charged with the crime. The Negro fled, and his wife, who was known to be innocent, fled with him. They were pursued and captured, and the following account of the ensuing tragedy, written by an eye-witness, appeared in *The Evening Post,* a Democratic daily of Vicksburg:

"When the two Negroes were captured they were tied to trees, and while the funeral pyres were being prepared they were forced to suffer the most fiendish tortures. The blacks were forced to hold out their hands while one finger at a time was chopped off. The fingers were distributed as souvenirs. Holbert was beaten severely, his skull fractured, and one of his eyes, knocked out with a stick, hung by a shred from the socket. Neither the man nor the woman begged for mercy, nor made a groan or plea. When the executioner came forward to lop off fingers, Holbert extended his hand without being asked. The most excruciating form of punishment consisted in the use of a large corkscrew in the hands of some of the mob. This instrument was bored into the flesh of the man and woman, in the arms, legs and body, and then pulled out, the spirals tearing out big pieces of raw, quivering flesh every time it was withdrawn. Even this devilish torture did not make the poor brutes cry out. When finally they were thrown on the fire and allowed to be burned to death, this came as a relief to the maimed and suffering victims."

As shown by the report of the Attorney-General of North Carolina, 1918-1920, the total number of criminal actions disposed of from July 1, 1918, to July 1, 1919, was 7,527; white, 4,014; colored, 3,481; Indians, 29; corporations, 3. From July 1, 1919, to July 1, 1920, the number of criminal actions disposed of increased to 9,285 of which 5,097 were white and 4,152 colored. From July 1, 1918 to July 1, 1919, there were 13 first degree murder cases, 134 second degree murder cases and 73 cases of manslaughter, making a total of 220 homicidal crimes. For the following year, July 1, 1919, to July 1, 1920, the record in North Carolina was 9 first degree murder cases, 170 second degree murder cases and 74 cases of manslaughter, making 253 homicidal crimes for the year.

We read in the papers the story of another horrible crime in the State of North Carolina, where it was discovered that the victim of the savagery of that community was innocent. In brief, here is the story as taken from *The Greenville* (S. C.) *News,* and reprinted in *The Manufacturers Record* of August 19, 1920:

About a week ago a Negro was seized by a mob at Roxboro, N. C., and hurriedly lynched on the charge of attempted assault on a white woman. No opportunity was given him to clear himself of the charge. Now, it appears from the testimony of a white man, a contractor for whom the Negro was working, that he was innocent of the charge. At the time the crime was committed, according to the contractor's published statement, the Negro was at work on his job and didn't get off to go to town until three hours later. If that is true, and it seems to be, the mob not only murdered a man, but it murdered justice.

In the State of South Carolina, as shown by the official report of the Attorney-General, for the fiscal year ending December 31, 1919, there were 242 murder cases and 43 prosecutions for manslaughter. The total number of murder cases for 1920 were 177 and 65 cases charged with manslaughter, making a total of 242 homicidal crimes for the year. In the thirteenth circuit, composed of the counties of Greenville and Pickens, with a total population of 116,827, during the year 1919, prosecutions for murder resulted in 17 receiving the death sentence and 11 persons were sent to the penitentiary for life.

The number of homicides recorded in the State of Tennessee for 1919 was 351, and for 1920 there were 328. In the State of Texas, as shown by the official report of the Attorney-General, from Sept. 1, 1918, to August 31, 1919, there were 1,061 indictments for murder, 551 trials, 380 convictions and 184 acquittals, and during the same period there were 14 death penalties. "Three murders a day" has been the average in Texas. This is slightly more than 1,000 per annum, on a basis of 20 per 100,000 population, a little more than the average of the Southern States but not so high as some of these States.

A few years ago, Mr. John S. Patterson, a highly respected citizen of Texas, State Commissioner of Insurance and Banking, was shot while engaged in his official duties, in a bank at Teague, Texas. A personal letter from a prominent citizen of Texas, who was in a position to obtain reliable information, contained the following statement:

Mr. Patterson, in the discharge of his official duties, had gone to the town of Teague, in this State, for the purpose of closing up a State bank at that place, which, under the reports of the examiners, had been violating the State laws. When he concluded to close the bank, an attack was made upon him by the officers of the bank and he was shot and mortally wounded, a clear case, as we understand it, of assassination.

On March 14, 1912, a band of mountaineers shot and killed a judge, prosecutor and sheriff at Hillsville, County of Carrol, Virginia, just after the judge had pronounced sentence upon one of their number who had been found guilty of a felony. The band dispersed to the hills, but finally all of its members were captured after a search which lasted for months. There were 231 homicides in Virginia during the year 1913. During a period of five years, 1915-1919, Virginia had 1,204 homicides.

For some years, *The Spectator*, a weekly insurance journal, has published annually statistics of homicides, compiled by Frederick L. Hoffman, LL.D., Third Vice-President and Statistician of the Prudential Insurance Company. According to Dr. Hoffman, as shown by figures published in November, 1920:

Of thirty-one major cities of the United States listed according to their respective homicide ratings, the first six in order are Memphis, Savannah, Atlanta, Charleston, Nashville and New Orleans. The rate of human killings in Memphis is 55.9 per 100,000; that in Savannah, 42, and in Atlanta— third on the list—40.8. Buffalo, N. Y., has the same rating as that of New York City with five homicides per 100,000. Rochester 4.5; Dayton, Ohio, 2.7; Milwaukee, 2.5; Spokane, 4.8.

As shown by the figures compiled by Dr. Hoffman, and published in *The Spectator*, New York, Dec. 2, 1921, four cities in the United States had over 36 homicidal deaths per 100,000 for the year 1920. These cities are: Memphis, Tenn., with a rate of 63.4; Savannah, Ga., 44.0; Atlanta, Ga., 40.9, and Charleston, S. C., 36.5. According to the same high authority, in the geographical distribution of homicides in the registration States, the average rate per 100,000 population in 33 States was 6.6, distributed according to geographical grouping in the following order:

New England States, 2.8; Middle Atlantic States, 5.1; Southern States, 10.8; Central States, 6.1; Rocky Mountain States, 9.4; Pacific States, 9.2. In this geographical grouping Delaware and Maryland are listed with the Southern States, while Alabama, Arkansas, Georgia, Oklahoma and Texas, where there is no official registration, are not included, although the homicidal record of each of these States is very high. The homicidal record in Delaware and Maryland, respectively, is much higher than it is in any of the New England States, or the average of the Middle Atlantic States, and also higher than the Central States; but the homicidal record of Delaware and Maryland is much lower than any of the eleven Southern States included in the Solid South. In political affiliation and lawlessness Missouri is usually classed with the Southern States, but in the geographical grouping it is placed with the Central States. The homicidal rate in Missouri is the highest of the Central States and largely increases the average of this group.

As we have learned from other sources, especially the reports of the Attorney-General, each of the four States not included in the compilations made by Dr. Hoffman, has a very high criminal record, among the highest in the United States. If these four States were added to the group of Southern "registration" States, it would greatly increase the average homicidal rate of the Southern States. In Alabama, for example, the figures cited in preceding paragraphs of this chapter show a rate of 32 per 100,000 for two years ending Sept. 30, 1908, or 16 per 100,000 for each year; and for two years preceding the beginning of the World War (1912-14) the rate had increased to 44.70 for the two-year period, or an average of 22.35 for each year. For the five years 1914-1919, the average number of homicides for the eleven Southern States was not less than 18.5 per 100,000, not including the victims of mobs and other man-killings of which there is no official record.

Before the World War, the highest criminal record, outside the Southern States of America, was in Hungary where, in 1901-1910, the rate of homicides per 100,000 of population was 7.70, which was less than one-half the rate per 100,000 of population in the South. During the same period, the number of homicides in Italy was 3.99 per 100,000 of population; in England and Wales it was 0.88; in Australia (1910-11) it was 1.90; and in New Zealand it was 0.79 per 100,000 of population. It will be observed that no other country even remotely approached the appalling record of the Southern States.

A report submitted to the American Bar Association, by the Special Commission on Law Enforcement, August 10, 1922, contains for comparative purposes some startling statistics relating to crimes in the United States. For instance, in comparing the criminal record in Canada with Chicago, attention is called to the number of prisoners charged with murder in the penitentiaries of Canada and Cook County, Illinois, respectively. The number charged with murder in the penitentiaries of Canada was 57, while the number of prisoners in the Cook County penitentiaries charged with murder was 212. These figures are for 1921 when the population of Canada was about 9,000,000 while the population of Cook County was about 3,000,000. With a population of one-third the population of Canada, Cook County had nearly four times as many murders.

Our story of the appalling situation may be amplified at this point by including one of the Southern States in the comparison of criminal records in Canada and Cook County, Illinois. Take for example the State of Georgia which boastfully—and perhaps correctly—claims to be the most prosperous and advanced State in the South. In 1920 the population of Georgia was 2,895,832 which was less than one-third the population of Canada and over 100,000 less than the population of Cook County. In 1921 (same date as the figures for Canada and Cook County) there were in the Georgia penitentiary 947 convicts sentenced for murder and 437 for manslaughter, making a total of 1,384 convicted for homicidal crimes; more than twenty-four times as many convictions for murder in Georgia as there were in Canada with three times the population of Georgia, and nearly seven times as many as there were in Cook County with a population of 100,000 more than the population of Georgia.

In addition to the prisoners convicted of murder, there were in the Georgia penitentiary 222 convicted for attempt to murder. During the same year (1921) there were "in all Canada's penitentiaries, 1,930 prisoners; in the Joliet penitentiary, one of the Illinois State prisons, 1,930 prisoners." In the Georgia penitentiary there were 3,076 convicts. Statistics of crimes in other Southern States cited in preceding paragraphs reveal a comparative record only a little less revolting than that of Georgia. The criminal record in the South is appalling; a blight upon civilization before which Christendom stands aghast.

It is true that a great "crime wave" spread over the whole country after the end of the World War. Reports from Washington during the month of October, 1921, stated that "crime is on the increase throughout the United States, Government reports show, at a rate never before equalled. Criminal indictments against more than 100,000 persons are now awaiting trial in Federal courts." The increase of crime in America was not the result of the World War. In France, in England, and in other countries where social conditions, economic and civic affairs were more disturbed than in America by the war, there was not an increase of crime such as we had in America. Crimes decreased in several countries that were engaged in the World War. According to official reports, the total "number of persons for trial" in England and Wales (Assizes and Quarter Sessions), in 1914, was 11,408, convicted, 9,277; in 1917 the figures were, respectively, 4,697 and 4,567. In Scotland the total number for trial (High Court of Justiciary and Sheriff Courts), in 1914, was 1,292, convicted, 1,012; in 1917 the figures were, respectively, 997 and 826. During the month of April, 1922, it was stated in press reports from England that—

No fewer than eight prisons in various parts of Great Britain are being closed down. The fact is that there has been a remarkable decrease in the number of habitual criminals. In 1914 there were in England and Wales 17,800 prisoners, but to-day the total is 6,000 less.

Concerning the increase of crime in the United States, in comparison with the criminal record of Great Britain and France, during and subsequent to the World War, the report of the "Special Commission on Law Enforcement of the American Bar Association," submitted during the month of August, 1922, contained the statement which follows:

The criminal situation in the United States, so far as crimes of violence are concerned, is worse than that in any other civilized country. Here there is less respect for law. While your committee cannot obtain the exact figures, from all available sources of information we estimate that there were more than 9,500 unlawful homicides last year in this country; that in 1920 there occurred not less than 9,000 such homicides, and that in no year during the past ten years did the number fall below 8,500. In other words, during the last ten years, no less than 85,000 of our citizens have perished by poison, by the pistol or the knife, or by some other unlawful and deadly instrument. . . .

Crime and lawlessness in the United States have been steadily on the increase and out of proportion to our growth, and there has been a steady and growing disrespect for law. In our opinion this is not the result of the war. We do not find the proportional increase in crime from 1916 to 1922 greater than from 1910 to 1916, and we have not been able to discover that crimes of violence have materially increased in France, England or Canada during or since the war, although the effects of the war naturally must be more marked in those countries.

According to official reports, covering the "death registration area"—about 85 per cent. of the total U. S. population—the homicide rate per 100,000 population increased from 5.9 in 1910 to 8.5 in 1921. Commenting on "the frequent failures of criminal justice," and "the practical impunity accorded in many States to violent crime," and the "indifference of the public to so grave an evil," in his last work, *Modern Democracies*, Lord Bryce says:

Recently the Bar Association of New York has bestirred itself to secure reforms; but there are States where the conditions are far worse than in New York, and where the frequency of homicide and the feebleness of the law in coping with it rouse little comment. This is especially the case in the Southern States where the habits of violence formed in the days of slavery have not died out, and where racial feeling is so strong that it is just as difficult in many districts to secure the punishment of a white who has injured or even killed a negro as it has been to obtain justice in a Turkish court for a Christian against a Muslim.

While America was under rule of a provincial and lawless Oligarchy there was introduced into our national affairs the low standard of civic obligations which had made the States where this Oligarchy had ruled for forty years notorious as the most criminal in the civilized world. Naturally, the crime disease spread over the whole country when the country was under rule of the Oligarchy. While the increase of crime has not been limited to the South, the proportionate increase has been greater in the Southern States than elsewhere.

Crimes have increased under every Democratic administration from Jackson to Wilson inclusive. During the second Jackson Administration a great crime wave swept the country, and the same thing occurred under the administrations, respectively, of Van Buren, Polk, Pierce and Buchanan. The Wilson Administration was no exception to the long-established record of the Democratic party. Beginning with the administration of Andrew Jackson, corrupt practices, the spoils system and law defiance have been more persistent and pernicious under Democratic administrations than at other times. This perhaps is due to the fact that the policies of the Democratic party, from the time of Jackson's second administration, have been essentially sectional and defiantly partisan. Slavery developed a spirit of intolerance and lawlessness and this was reflected in the national government when the Slave Oligarchy was in control of the Government.

The South may be called the nursery of crimes in America. The migratory criminal population of the United States may be traced from the Southern States to every part of the country. The highest record of defalcations and embezzlements is found in those sections of the South where election frauds, and other corrupt practices, have been notorious. In the same communities, peonage has prevailed in the most aggravated form; lynchings, race riots and the most appalling crimes have occurred in those communities where corrupt practices and vice have been most flagrant.

The situation in the South forcibly illustrates the truth of the statement that crime is a disease, the result in a large measure of economic conditions, but due more perhaps to social causes. Unfortunately, both social and economic conditions in the South are conducive to the propagation of crime. Punishment alone will not prevent crime; so long as the economic and social causes remain, in some cases, punishment tends to increase crime.

CHAPTER XVI

LYNCH LAW AND THE KU KLUX KLAN

Various theories have been advanced respecting the origin of lynch law in the United States. It has been erroneously stated that the term originated in Ireland in the action of James Fitzstephen Lynch, Mayor of Galway, who, in 1493, is said to have executed the law on his own son. However, there is no authority for ascribing the origin of this term to the alleged action of the Mayor of Galway. Numerous cases of lawless outbreaks in the early history of this country have been cited as evidence of the beginning of lynch law, but the accepted opinion is that summary procedure in the lawless punishment of a person charged with crime, to which the term lynch law is usually applied, originated in Virginia, during the early part of the War of the American Revolution.

Lynch law owes its origin to one Charles Lynch, a Virginia planter, who, strange to say, was a non-resistant. He was opposed to war and did not believe in capital punishment by process of law nor in a lawless summary manner. Yet, like Robespierre, and a few other radical pacifists, his name has been associated with some of the most atrocious crimes in the history of civilization. Charles Lynch had a Quaker brother whose name was John Lynch, a man of some prominence and ability, and the founder of Lynchburg, Virginia.

Charles Lynch was a resident of Bedford County, Virginia, and in that mountainous district there was very pronounced opposition to the patriots of the American Revolutionary War. A number of the Virginia mountaineers were either Tories or so influenced by their prejudice against the landed aristocracy that they availed themselves of the opportunities during the war to commit depredations and aid the British forces by attacking all their neighbors who were friendly to the American patriots.

Charles Lynch was friendly to the cause of the American patriots and became very much incensed at the depredations of

Tories. After conferring with his neighbors, Robert Adams and James Galloway, they decided to "take the law into their own hands" and punish all disaffected persons who were accused of acts unfriendly to the revolutionary government. Mr. Lynch was at the head of the court of inquisition which he formed in conjunction with his three neighbors, Robert Adams, James Galloway and William Preston. Accused parties brought to his house were tried with this informal court and were "often, hung up by their thumbs until they cried, Liberty forever; but the penalty of death was never inflicted." After the close of the Revolutionary War, as narrated by Professor Cutler, in *Lynch Law,*—

the Tories who had suffered at the hands of Colonel Lynch and his associates, threatened to prosecute Lynch and his friends. To avoid law suits and as a means of finally settling the affair, Lynch brought the whole matter before the Virginia Legislature. After a lengthy debate, the Virginia Legislature passed an Act in October, 1782, the title of which, was "An Act to indemnify certain persons in suppressing a conspiracy against this State." The Act recited that the measures taken by Lynch and his associates to suppress conspiracy against the State of Virginia were timely and effectual but not strictly warranted by law. The Act further recited that Lynch and his associates were fully justified in all they had done and if any suits or prosecutions were instituted against Lynch or his associates they could plead in defense the provisions of that Act.

The proceedings in Bedford, which the Legislature thus pronounced to be illegal, but justifiable, were imitated in other parts of the State and came to be known as Lynch's Law. In justice to Colonel Lynch, it should be remembered that his action was taken at a time when the State was in the throes of a hostile invasion.

From the foregoing brief summary of the origin of lynch law, it is clear that the evil is peculiarly an American form of summary lawlessness and that it originated in the South. From its beginning in this country, the evil of lynching has been more prevalent and persistent in the Southern States than in other sections of the United States, not only since the emancipation of slaves in the South but before the Civil War. As stated by Cutler,—

for more than a century the principle laid down by the Legislature of Virginia has been appealed to as a justification for recourse to lynch law. In Revolutionary times it was held that the immediate urgency and imminent danger of the situation justified the summary and extra-legal measures that were taken to suppress conspiracies against American patriots.

The justification or excuse for the summary and illegal measures introduced and practiced by Lynch and his self-appointed court, as we have seen, was accepted by an Act of the Legislature of Virginia. The extenuating circumstances justified the method of procedure. In other words, almost any steps were justifiable in order to save the American colonies from further depredations of the Hessians hired by the German King of England for the purpose of holding the American colonies in subjection. At that time the independence of America and the liberty of the American patriots was paramount to all other questions.

Unfortunately, the excuse accepted by public opinion and by the law-makers of Virginia in the early history of lynch law have been put forward as valid excuses for the practice of this lawless procedure down to the present time. The excuse for lynching in the South prior to the Civil War was that summary measures were necessary to prevent insurrection of the slaves. The utter falsity of this excuse is clearly shown not only by the history of slavery in the United States but also by the testimony of the most distinguished citizens of the South, who, after emancipation of the Negroes, voluntarily testified concerning the exemplary conduct of the Negroes before and during the Civil War. Brief reference to this testimony was cited in our Chapter III. As stated by Cutler,—

before about the year 1830, then, lynch law was confined almost entirely to the border settlements, and was generally excused and justified on the ground of necessity. It was not regarded as a serious menace to law and order but was adopted merely as a temporary expedient which was expected to fall into disuse when the civil government and the judiciary became firmly established.

As pointed out in the preceding chapter on crimes, there was a marked and portentous increase in lawlessness, especially in crimes of violence, at the beginning of Jackson's Administration. There were two causes for this increase in crimes. The first and principal cause was economic. The invention of the loom, the spinning-jenny and the cotton gin; and other inventions and

discoveries which added to the value of cotton, made the producers, the landed aristocracy of the South, who owned the
major portion of the land on which the cotton was produced,
and the great bulk of slave labor by which it was produced,
more avaricious and domineering. Negro labor was not only
the best labor for cultivation of cotton, but it was the cheapest
and only available labor for that purpose. The growing world
agitation for abolition of slavery could not be met with legal
or moral argument and, in desperation, the narrow and provincial leaders of the Slave Oligarchy resorted to violence. The
unfortunate slaves and the protagonists of abolition who were
so unfortunate as to fall, defenseless, within the reach of the
vicious and lawless element of the Slave Oligarchy, offered the
least resistance and were the first victims of their wrath.

The second cause for the sudden increase of crimes of violence
under Jackson's Administration was subsidiary or incidental
to the first cause. In order to maintain their position against
the agitation of the Abolitionists of the North and the growing
unrest among the non-slaveholding whites of the South, it
was necessary to sustain a strong national political organization
and for this purpose the spoils system was used to gain the
support of unscrupulous politicians, and this system was maintained not only through corrupt practices but also by crimes
of violence.

A great change took place during Jackson's first Administration. The anti-slavery agitation was met by a revival of lynch
law. The Nat Turner insurrection in 1831 added fuel to the
flame, although Turner and his accomplices were given a fair
trial; some were acquitted and all who were convicted and
executed, except Turner, were given a decent burial. Beginning with the second administration of Jackson, the spoils system, accompanied with corrupt practices in every department
of government, gave license to a spirit of law-defiance which resulted in lynchings and other crimes of violence more shocking
and extensive than had been known in the United States before
that time. During the year 1835 *Niles's Register* referred to the
lawlessness of that period in these words:

Anti-gaming societies have been introduced in a number of cities and
towns. Executions by ''Lynch-Law'' have been numerous. Acts of personal

violence, on other accounts, some of which are terrific, also abound. Society is in an awful state. What is the cause of it?

This is the period of which Cutler (*Lynch Law*) wrote:

The years of Jackson's Presidency, 1829-1837, have been distinguished by political writers as the Jacksonian period—a period in which there was an unusual amount of turbulence and violence. It has been repeatedly suggested that Jackson's own arbitrary temperament and example did something to set this fashion.

Cutler quotes the following comment from *Niles's Register:*

During the last and the present week we have cut out and laid aside more than 500 articles, relating to the various excitements now acting on the people of the United States, public and private. Society seems everywhere unhinged, and the demon of ''blood and slaughter'' has been let loose upon us. . . . An awful political outcry is about to be raised to rally the ''poor against the rich.'' We have executions, and murders, and riots to the utmost limits of the Union. . . . The character of our countrymen seems suddenly changed, and thousands interpret the law in their own way, sometimes in one case, and then in another, guided apparently only by their own will.

As stated by Professor William Graham Sumner, in his *Andrew Jackson—(American Statesmen),*

Niles, in August, 1835, gathered three pages of reports of recent outrages against law and order. A month later he has another catalogue, and he exclaims in astonishment that the world seems upside down. The fashion of the times seemed to be to pass at once from the feeling to the act. That Jackson's character and example had done something to set this fashion is hardly to be denied.

In 1835, the citizens of Madison County, Miss., arrested five slaves and put them to death without any sort of trial. At Grand Gulf, Miss., in 1836, a Negro was—

burned over a slow fire; the fire was pulled away from him when he was about half dead, his head cut off and stuck on a pole at the corner of the road in the edge of the town.

In his journey from Tennessee to Texas, where he died as one of the heroes of The Alamo, David Crockett stopped at Natchez, Miss., where he witnessed some of the shocking crimes of that period in that State. The following story is found in his autobiography:

There exist throughout the extreme South, bodies of men who style themselves Lynchers.   When an individual escapes punishment by some technicality of the law or perpetrates an offense not recognized in courts of justice, they seize him, and inflict such chastisement as they conceive adequate to the offense.   They usually act at night and disguise their persons.   This society at Natchez embraces all the lawyers, physicians, and principal merchants of the place. . . .

Foster, whom all good men loathed as a monster unfit to live, was called into court, and formally dismissed.   But the Lynchers were on hand.   The moment he stepped from the court-house he was knocked down, his arms bound behind him, his eyes bandaged, and in this condition he was marched to the rear of the town, where a deep ravine afforded a fit place for his punishment.   His clothes were torn from his back, his head partially scalped; they next bound him to a tree; each lyncher was supplied with a cow skin, and they took turns at the flogging until the flesh hung in ribands from his body.   A quantity of heated tar was then poured over his head, and made to cover every part of his person; they finally showered a sack of feathers on him, and in this horrid guise, with no other apparel than a miserable pair of breeches, with a drummer at his heels, he was paraded through the principal streets at midday.   No disguise was assumed by the Lynchers; the very lawyers employed upon his trial took part in his punishment.

It was during the second term of President Jackson (1836) that a mulatto was lynched at St. Louis, described as "the execution of lynching upon a yellow fellow by means of a slow fire."   It was for denouncing the burning of this colored man that E. P. Lovejoy had his printing office destroyed by a mob in St. Louis.   He moved his paper to Alton, Illinois, where, after his press had been destroyed three times, he was killed by a mob.   In an address on "The Perpetuation of Our Political Institutions," delivered before the Young Men's Lyceum, Springfield, Illinois, January 27, 1837, Abraham Lincoln referred at some length to the lawlessness, especially crimes of violence in the Southern States.   He said:

Thus went on this process of hanging, from the gamblers to the Negroes, from Negroes to white citizens, and from these to strangers, till dead men were literally dangling from the boughs of trees by every roadside, and in numbers almost sufficient to rival the native Spanish moss of the country as a drapery of the forest.

In the fall of 1837 nine slaves and three free colored men were lynched on the Red River in Louisiana.   In 1838 the following advertisement appeared in a North Carolina newspaper:

Twenty Dollars Reward: Ran away from the subscriber, a Negro woman and two children; the woman is tall and black, and a few days before she went off I burnt her with a hot iron on the left side of her face; I tried to make the letter M.

It was authoritatively reported that there were at least 118 similar cases of branding or maiming Negroes clipped from Southern newspapers during three years of Van Buren's Administration, 1837 to 1839. In 1839 *The Southern Literary Messenger* referred to the spirit of lawlessness and crimes of violence at that time prevailing, in the words which follow:

Forty years ago the practice of wreaking private vengeance, or inflicting summary and illegal punishment for crimes, actual or pretended, which has been glossed over by the name of Lynch's law, was hardly known except in sparse, frontier settlements, beyond the reach of courts and legal proceedings.

Whittier's poem, *The Branded Hand,* is based on the following story:

Captain Jonathan Walker, of Harwich, Massachusetts, was solicited by several fugitive slaves at Pensacola, Florida, to convey them in his vessel to the British West Indies. Although well aware of the hazard of the enterprise, he attempted to comply with their request. He was seized by an American vessel, consigned to the American authorities at Key West, and by them taken back to Florida, where, after long and rigorous imprisonment, he was brought to trial. He was sentenced to be branded on the right hand with the letters "S. S." (Slave Stealer), and amerced in a heavy fine. He was released on the payment of his fine in the sixth month of 1845.

When compared with some of the tortures of recent persecutions and atrocious lynchings in Florida, the punishment of Captain Jonathan Walker was very mild. He was guilty of an overt act which he knew was in violation of the penal laws, although he was moved by the noblest motives of humanity. Respectable white men have been flogged, tarred and feathered in Florida during the last few years, charged with no breach of the law, or other offense, except that of teaching and trying to improve the civic and industrial condition of industrious, law-abiding Negroes.

The state of unrest and lawlessness continued during Van Buren's Administration and there was no improvement until after the election of Harrison. During the administrations of

Pierce and Buchanan, respectively, there were other epidemics of horrible crimes in the Southern States. The following editorial appeared in *The Liberator* December 19, 1856:

A record of the cases of Lynch Law in the Southern States reveals the startling fact that, within twenty years, over three hundred white persons have been murdered upon the accusation—in most cases unsupported by legal proof—of carrying among slave-holders arguments addressed expressly to their own intellects and consciences, as to the morality and expediency of slavery. If this figure be accepted as reliable for the whites, it is within the truth to say that a considerably larger number of Negroes met with summary capital punishment during the various insurrection excitements which occurred.

The "cases of the Lynch Law in the Southern States," cited in the editorial which I have quoted from *The Liberator,* include twenty years, from the beginning of Van Buren's Administration to the end of the Pierce Administration. It does not include either of the Jackson Administrations when, as we have seen, lynchings were very frequent in the South. There are no authoritative statistics showing the number of lynchings during Buchanan's Administration but during the four years immediately preceding the Civil War the most radical and virulent leaders of the Slave Oligarchy were in control of the Federal Government, and crimes of violence were of frequent occurrence in the Southern States.

Before entering on a brief survey of the record of lynching in the South after the Civil War, we should bear in mind the inescapable and potent facts cited in our Chapter III relative to the conduct of the Negroes before and during the war, and the cordial relations that existed between the whites and blacks immediately after the war and before the beginning of Reconstruction. It has been asserted time and time again that the lynching evil in the South was necessary to protect the women of the South. This base, spiteful libel on the Negro has been proclaimed in Congress, in political campaigns, on the lecture platform, written in books and dramatized. For example, in a speech in the city of Boston, in 1919, former Governor Emmett O'Neal of, Alabama, said:

The lynching evil in the South had its origin in the revolutionary conditions created by Reconstruction..

The assertion quoted from the former Governor of Alabama has been the rallying shibboleth of the leaders of a provincial and lawless Oligarchy for more than a half century, and it is the most wicked and pernicious slander that ever misled the American people. It was started and it has been continued for the sole purpose of accentuating racial prejudice and, so far as possible, to tolerate or excuse the mob spirit of the South.

We know that the record of the Negro during slavery was good. We know that the South was "stripped of its white men" during the Civil War; especially was this true in the rural districts where practically every white man who was "able to carry a gun" joined the army. For nearly four years the white women of the South were left with the Negroes and absolutely at the mercy of the colored population. During that ordeal the Negroes were loyal, faithful and honorable. On this point a Negro woman, Mrs. Ida B. Wells, in her pamphlet entitled *A Red Record*, has with great earnestness and eloquence paid this just tribute to her race:

> The Negro may not have known what chivalry was, but he knew enough to preserve inviolate the womanhood of the South which was entrusted to his hands during the war. The finer sensibilities of his soul may have been crushed out by years of slavery, but his heart was full of gratitude to the white women of the North, who blessed his home and inspired his soul in all these years of freedom. Faithful to his trust in both of these instances, he should now have the impartial ear of the civilized world, when he dares to speak for himself as against the infamy wherewith he stands charged. . . .
>
> During all the years of slavery, no such charge was ever made, not even during the dark days of the rebellion, when the white man, following the fortunes of war went to do battle for the maintenance of slavery. While the master was away fighting to forge the fetters upon the slave, he left his wife and children with no protectors save the Negroes themselves. And yet during those years of trust and peril, no Negro proved recreant to his trust and no white man returned to a home that had been despoiled.

There was no friction between the whites and blacks at the close of the Civil War. The men who had fought the battles of the Confederacy accepted the liberal terms of surrender and they acknowledged the fidelity and good conduct of the Negroes. Representative men and women in the South advocated all possible aid for education and moral uplift of the Negroes. There were very few schools for the whites and none for the Negroes, but in the white churches where the white people worshipped in the forenoon, the Negroes were invited to assemble in the afternoon where they were taught by the better class of white men and women. Some of the white churches were provided with "galleries" which were occupied by the Negroes during service for the whites, and the whites and Negroes entered the church through the same door. Negroes employed as domestic servants traveled with their white employers and it was the common practice for a Negro man to occupy a single-seated buggy with a white woman by whom he was employed when it was necessary for the white woman to have a male servant "to drive and take care of the horse." There was never any charge of attempted assault or even "impudence" or "familiarity" on the part of the Negro employed by the white woman as servant or attendant. Nor was there any occasion for the least apprehension on the part of white women who found it necessary to travel with their Negro male servants. This amicable relation of confidence continued for nearly two years after the "surrender" in every one of the Southern States.

The sudden and radical change in the relationship between the white and black races in the South, which turned mutual confidence into distrust and hatred, was brought about by the same cause and the same agencies that started the propaganda during Jackson's Administration that resulted in lynchings and other crimes of violence. As pointed out in some preceding paragraphs of this chapter, the first and principal cause of the lawlessness which began during Jackson's Administration was economic. The anti-slavery agitation alarmed the slaveholders and they resorted to violence which they thought would frighten not only the slaves but also the whites who were not friendly to the institution of slavery.

The revival of lynching after the war was caused by economic conditions; the claim that it was for protection of the white women was an afterthought. In order to nullify the effect of the Thirteenth Amendment to the Federal Constitution, laws were passed by the Southern States for the alleged purpose of regulating the employment of labor, and the provisions of those laws relating to vagrancy were very severe. The enforcement of the laws regulating labor was, if possible, more severe than the spirit of the law contemplated. Many of the former slave-holders still held to the theory that free labor could not be successfully used on the farm; they also decided that free labor would be more expensive than chattel labor. They undertook to meet the situation by the enactment of summary State laws which, if administered under their direction, would keep the Negroes in a state of peonage. It was necessary to disguise the actual operation of the laws regulating labor and in order to do this a propaganda was started which appealed to the pride and racial sensibilities of the poor whites, and methods were adopted which aroused the superstitious fear of the Negroes. Every self-respecting white man was ready to support any sort of law, society or organization, necessary for the protection of the white woman.

The Negroes committed no assaults on the white women before the war, during the war, nor for several years after the war; but designing and unscrupulous politicians were able to persuade the ignorant whites that a great change had taken place in the feeling and disposition of the Negro. Secret societies of white men appeared in all parts of the Southern States for the alleged purpose of protecting the white women of the South and guarding the country against the alleged evils of Negro domination. It is clear that the principal, if not the only purpose of these societies, which were finally merged into the organization known as the Ku Klux Klan, was to regulate and terrorize the Negroes. These societies were active in their vandalism and crimes of violence before there were any specific charges of assaults on white women by Negroes and before the Negro exercised any political power.

When the carpet-baggers invaded the South, the vicious and evil-disposed among them started a propaganda of social equality among the Negroes and the disreputable scalawags of the South were no less active than the carpet-baggers in poisoning the Negroes against the whites. The Negro was slow to accept the theory of social equality. Respect for the white man was a part of his nature. He had never known freedom, and respect for the superior race that had held him in slavery was a part of his being. The Negro's respect for the superior race and his reverence for the white women of the South held him in check and it was not until he was brought face to face with the vices and corrupt practices of the disreputable politicians who coddled him that the Negro lost respect for the white man.

The secret societies among the whites of the South organized for the purpose of intimidating and terrorizing the Negroes operated under divers names, some of which were State organizations and many only local and without name. One of these societies was organized in Pulaski, Tenn., during the month of May, 1866, under the name of the Ku Klux Klan. The details of the origin of this society are not pertinent to the purpose of this chapter, but concerning these various organizations and societies in the South for the purpose of intimidating the Negroes it is true, as stated by Dr. E. Benjamin Andrews in his *History of the United States,* that they—

sprung from the old night patrol of slavery times. Then every Southern gentleman used to serve on this patrol, whose duty it was to whip severely every Negro found absent from home without a pass from his master.

When, in 1867, Congress passed the Reconstruction Acts, the Ku Klux organization was utilized for the purpose of establishing a band of regulators in substantially every community of the Southern States. From a burlesque fraternity, it was quickly and effectively transformed into a systematic organization of regulators for the purpose of intimidating the newly emancipated and enfranchised Negroes. A convention of the Klan was held at Nashville, Tenn., in May, 1867, at which time General Nathan B. Forrest was placed at the head of the organization with the title of Grand Wizard. The "prescript" or constitution was amended and revived, and plans were made for an extensive propaganda for the purpose of extending the influence and increasing the membership throughout the South. As stated by Dr. Andrews,—

its awful mysteries and grewsome rites spread utter panic among the superstitious blacks. . . . In their hideous masks and long white gowns they frightened all but the most hardy.

The original organization known as the Ku Klux Klan, in the beginning, had among its membership a few good citizens and brave men who, in those troublous times, were misled by designing agitators; but as a general rule the organization was made up of a band of outlaws and it continued in its lawless and cowardly practices until it was finally destroyed by the enforcement of Federal statutes of 1871 and 1872. It has been stated that the original organization was officially disbanded in 1869, but the activities continued several years later. Before it was officially disbanded, it had absorbed—

all the horse thieves, cutthroats, bushwhackers and outlaws of every description. It had degenerated into a mob of rioters and marauders who plundered and abused friend and foe alike, sparing neither party nor sex.

Dr. Andrews refers to the final collapse of the original Ku Klux Klan as follows:

The very violence of the order which it at last turned against the old Southrons themselves brought it into disrepute with its original institutions, who were not sorry when Federal marshals put up to it by President Grant hunted den after den of the lawbreakers to the death.

As shown by the testimony taken by a Congressional Commission in 1872, and printed as public documents in 13 volumes of about 600 pages each, in Alabama alone not less than 107 murders had been committed by the Ku Klux in that State and more than 100 persons had been cruelly whipped and beaten. It was reported that over 2,000 persons were assassinated, or murdered, or maltreated in Louisiana during a few weeks in 1868, and it was also reported that 120 corpses were found in the woods or taken out of Red River after a "Negro hunt" in Bosier Parish, Louisiana. Governor Alcorn of Mississippi stated that 124 murders had been committed in that State from April, 1869, to March, 1871, and there were more than 60 murders in three months prior to April, 1871. During a period of eighteen months, ending on June 30, 1867, there were reported in North and South Carolina 197 murders and 548 cases of aggravated assault. According to reports of the Congressional investigation, in the State of South Carolina, in the nine counties covered by the investigation, for a period of approximately six months, the Ku Klux Klan lynched and murdered 35 men, whipped 262 men and women, otherwise outraged, shot, mutilated, burned out, etc., 101 persons.

In 1868, it was reported on "partial returns" from the counties that 1,035 men had been murdered in Texas since the close of the war. For the two years ending May, 1870, according to the report made to the Texas Senate by the Secretary of State, there had been 905 homicides. According to a statement made by the Freedmen's Bureau of Tennessee, 162 persons had been murdered in that State during the year ending July 1, 1868. Commenting on the cruelties and horrors of the Ku Klux atrocities in the State of Louisiana, James G. Blaine said:

These Klans and organizations hesitated at no cruelty, were deterred by no consideration of law or humanity. They rode by night, were disguised with masks, were armed as freebooters. They whipped, maimed or murdered the victims of their wrath. Over 2,000 persons were killed, wounded and otherwise maimed in Louisiana within a few weeks of the Presidential election of 1868.

Reverdy Johnson, of Maryland, distinguished lawyer and publicist, was a warm friend of the South. He had sympathized with the cause of the Confederacy, and after the war he opposed the Fourteenth Amendment and the Reconstruction measures of Congress. He was retained as associate counsel by some citizens of South Carolina who had been indicted in the Federal court as members of the Ku Klux Klan. After hearing the testimony of a number of witnesses, and confessions of some of the accused, Mr. Johnson denounced the organization and its members in the following language:

I have listened with unmixed horror to some of the testimony that has been brought before you. The outrages proved are shocking to humanity; they admit of neither excuse nor justification; they violate every obligation which law and nature impose upon men; they show that the parties engaged were brutes, insensible to the obligations of humanity and religion.

Benjamin Hill, of Georgia, was one of the most loyal, able and eloquent defenders of the South during the dark days of Reconstruction and Republican rule. Commenting on the Ku Klux Klan organization and its work he said:

The Ku Klux business is the worst that ever afflicted the South. Every day that we let it continue we cut our own throats. . . . It is a curse upon our land, a blight following slavery and the greatest blunder our people ever committed.

Neither the orders of the Grand Wizard, nor Federal or State laws, succeeded in completely destroying the Ku Klux

Klan for a number of years. A large number of local organizations, "dens," as they were called, continued to hold meetings in secret and engage in night raids on Negroes, sometimes only to intimidate or terrify, but frequently to mutilate or murder the unfortunate Negroes. From the work of the original Ku Klux organization came divers local societies and clans. "Knights of the White Camelia," the "Pale Faces," the "Constitutional and Union Guards," the "White Brotherhood," and the "White League" were among the numerous secret societies that followed the Ku Klux in lawless and criminal practices.

The Night Riders, White Caps, and various other lawless societies and organizations continued their criminal practices in the Southern States and, as pointed out in a preceding chapter, neither the disfranchisement of the Negro under the form of law nor the long uninterrupted rule of the Oligarchy has improved the situation. In the preceding chapter on crimes I referred to the lynching of a Negro in front of the court house at Huntsville, Alabama. In a public address, Governor Jelks of that State said:

When I had been in the Governor's office three years I carefully inquired into the facts of every one of the five lynchings that had taken place. It would astonish you to know that out of the five who had met violent death at the hands of a criminal mob, three of them were without offense before the law.

Here is another story told in a public address by former Governor Jelks:

Some time ago, in a county in this State, a poor old crippled Negro in a justice court swore to a statement differing from the sworn statement of a young white woman in the same court. This was his whole offense. It is not an unusual occurrence to have witnesses in the court differ in their testimony. A trifling little case in a justice court. A complacent constable on his way to the jail turned over the cripple to a small mob of regulators, or allowed him to be taken without serious opposition, and the cripple that night supped in another country. I have often wondered if that figure summoned to another court, ever comes back to sit at the humble feast of his murderers as did the ghost at the great Macbeth's table.

In Montgomery, Alabama, the latter part of September, 1919, one policeman and four Negroes were killed. Three Negroes were taken from a deputy sheriff by a small band of masked men and lynched. One of the Negroes "was dressed in regulation uniform of the United States Army. Two of the Negroes who were lynched had been in the army." One of the Negroes was shot "about 15 times and severely clubbed. The third victim was shot to death in a hospital where he had been taken after a battle with a Montgomery policeman."

On August 19, 1916, five Negroes, two women and three men were taken from the jail at Newberry, Florida, and lynched. The crime with which they were charged was that they had assisted another Negro, Boise Long, to escape after he had killed an officer of the law, and wounded another man who was assisting the officer in an attempt to arrest Long who was charged with hog stealing. Another Negro, Jim Dennis, was killed by a posse who were hunting Long. It appears that the total number of Negroes lynched was six, including two women and a preacher.

At Pensacola, Florida, in July, 1918, a mob stormed the jail and lynched a Negro. Two men were killed and over twenty wounded in the attack on the jail. A general exodus of Negroes from Ocoee, Fla., was reported during the month of November, 1920. The immediate cause of the new migration of Negroes from Florida was a fight which occurred between whites and blacks in which ten or twelve persons were killed. It was also reported that several buildings in which Negroes had taken refuge were burned. More than twenty buildings in the Negro settlement were burned and one of the houses destroyed by fire is said to have contained eight Negroes. The trouble started when a Negro man attempted to vote. During the first week of January, 1923, a mob of white men at Rosewood, Florida, killed five Negroes and burned a Negro settlement of eighteen dwellings and a church. A Negro woman was killed as she was leaving her burning dwelling.

The houses were fired one at a time, while the crowd of between 100 and 150 looked on. The burning of the houses was carried out deliberately, and, although the crowd was present all the time, no one could be found who would say he saw the houses fired. . . . Two white men were killed and four wounded in the fight with the Negroes.

According to reports from Washington, Georgia, October 5,

1919, one Negro was shot to death, two others were whipped and five were reported as being held by a mob that—

has been scouring the swamps for Jack Gordon, a Negro who shot and killed Red Freeman. A later telegram from Washington, Georgia, announced that Jack Gordon, Freeman and Will Brown were burned near Lincoln. Brown was charged with aiding Gordon in escaping after he had shot Freeman. The third Negro to lose his life, Moses Freeman, was killed yesterday because he attempted to throw the pursuers off Gordon's trail.

From Valdosta, Georgia, it was reported that Lowndes and Brooks counties—

were "in a state of great excitement" because a mob of 500 white men aroused by the brutal murder of Mrs. A. A. Simmons took James Cobb, Negro, from his cell to the scene of the crime and hanged him. . . . Later, Sidney Johnson was killed by the police and he was the sixth Negro who met violent death as the result of the murder of Hampton Smith.

During this particular "crime wave in Georgia," at Ocumulgee, a Negro was shot to death by a mob; "the church was then burned, and other churches and a lodge in the vicinity were burned." At Gray's Station, the county seat of Jones, twelve miles from Macon, Georgia,—

a mob was formed for the purpose of lynching four Negroes who had been in jail for some time, and who were charged with assault with intent to murder, but when the mob arrived at the jail they found every door open, and the cells empty, whereupon the mob proceeded to set fire to two Negro churches and a big wooden building for lodge meetings. Two colored churches and a Negro school building were completely destroyed.

A report from Albany, Georgia, stated that there was "a reign of terror" among the Negro inhabitants of Calhoun, Baker and Miller counties, Georgia,—

as the result of a raid by "Night Riders," the trail of the outlaws being marked by the blackened ruins of thirteen Negro churches and school houses. The "Night Riders" first made their appearance at a point three miles east of Kestler where the first church was fired. They galloped away toward the east and before the glare of the first fire had reached its height another was being kindled a few miles away. Fire followed fire and the destruction of every building to which the torch was applied was complete.

From *The Atlanta Constitution* of May 18, 1919, I quote the following:

A mob stormed the jail at Vicksburg, Miss., the other day, battered down the doors, overpowered the sheriff and twelve deputies, dragged out a cowering Negro prisoner who was awaiting court trial for a revolting offense, poured oil on his head, hanged him by the neck from the limb of a tree, set fire to the oil, and while the struggling wretch was burning, riddled his body with bullets.

The next day a Georgia Negro was arrested in Johnson County. He, likewise, being charged with a heinous offense—an offense for which the law would have hanged him if a fair, orderly trial had established his guilt. An officer of the law had the prisoner in charge and was hurrying him to jail for "safe keeping," pending his trial.

The prisoner was taken from the officer—from the hands of the law, from the people of Georgia—bound to a tree, and, according to *The Constitution's* Dublin correspondent, "literally shot to pieces"; and there in that condition the remains of the Negro were found by passers by.

Brutal business; barbaric business; dangerous business; intolerable business! And it is a type of business which must be stopped by the States which now permit its practice if they expect Uncle Sam—the American people as a whole—to keep hands off and continue to respect their sovereignty. In other words, if the States do not put a stop to it, the time is inevitably coming when the Federal Government will.

The "States," especially the State of Georgia, have not "put a stop to it." Time and time again, for thirty-five or forty years, *The Atlanta Constitution* has admonished, pleaded with, and warned the people of Georgia concerning the horrible crimes which have been perpetrated in that State, but the admonitions, pleading and warnings have accomplished nothing. Crimes of violence continue and neither Georgia nor any other Southern State will "put a stop to it" so long as it continues under the rule of a provincial and corrupt Oligarchy.

Two years after publication of the editorial I have quoted from *The Atlanta Constitution,* Governor Dorsey of Georgia published a pamphlet in which he called attention to the criminal record of Georgia to which I have already alluded. In defending his position he gave out a statement in which he said:

Since 1885, mobs in Georgia have shot, hanged, burned, or drowned 415 Negroes, some of them women. Since these figures were compiled in the last sixty days a mob has taken a helpless old Negro woman from her home and drowned her by night. . . . In neither of these cases, men burning human beings, nor in any one of the 413 other cases, has a member of the lynching mob been punished in Georgia.

The "Georgia Committee on Race Relations" is composed of

prominent citizens of Georgia, men and women, including seventy-five whites and twelve Negroes. A report on the *Progress in Race Relations in Georgia,* issued by this Committee, eighteen months after publication of the charges by Governor Dorsey, shows very clearly and shockingly that conditions have not improved in that State. Although this report states that "no attempt has been made to collect all the cases of injustice in the State," the few "typical cases" which are cited are shocking almost beyond description, and if such appalling cases had not occurred so frequently, they would be beyond belief. The "typical cases" include murder, brutal assaults by masked men, peonage, kidnapping, proscription and persecution of industrious, innocent law-abiding Negroes, against whom no sort of criminal charges had been made. In this report we also read the most shocking story of extortion and pettifoggery practiced against the poor Negroes that ever disgraced the legal profession or blackened the annals of civilization. The appalling climax of this report states that—

for the 37 years preceding 1922 there were 430 lynchings in Georgia. During the four years from 1917-1920 there were 57. In these cases we have been unable to locate the record of more than one indictment.

Following every shocking exposure relating to the appalling conditions in the Southern States, the public has been informed through the press and, occasionally, through a few worthy citizens, that the situation is being investigated and that public opinion will be more exacting in its demands for law enforcement. After publication of the pamphlet by Governor Dorsey, to which I have referred, there was a great hue and cry. Southern newspapers and a number of worthy citizens declared that they were shocked to learn of such appalling conditions, although conditions described by Governor Dorsey were no worse than they had been for forty years. The same perfunctory protests and gentle admonitions were published that had been exploited in the South for more than forty years. It came to naught, as usual. Conditions did not improve; they grew worse, especially in Georgia.

The inhumanity and barbarity of race persecution and criminal lawlessness under rule of the Oligarchy in the South since the end of carpet-bag and Republican domination are more cruel and revolting than anything that was ever charged against the institution of slavery. I have made an abstract of all specific and implied charges against slavery found in the writings and speeches of Harriet Beecher Stowe, Henry Ward Beecher, Wendell Phillips and William Lloyd Garrison. For the purpose of comparison, I have also made an abstract of articles printed in *The Atlanta Constitution,* containing accounts of race riots and lynchings, cruelties and outrages against Negroes, including some outstanding cases of peonage or other forms of illegal bondage, in the Southern States, especially in Georgia, during twenty-five years, 1896 to 1921. After a careful comparison of the indictments against slavery by the four leading Abolitionists with the reports of lynchings and the barbarous treatment of Negroes held in peonage or other form of unlawful servitude, as published in *The Atlanta Constitution,* I find that none of the Abolitionists ever described or remotely referred to anything so atrocious and diabolical as the appalling crimes of the past twenty-five years described in *The Atlanta Constitution* and, frequently, reported in other newspapers published in the Southern States.

Two generations in the South have been taught that *Uncle Tom's Cabin* was a wicked libel on the Southern people; and yet nothing related in the writings of Mrs. Stowe is as horrible and as atrocious as numerous crimes that have been committed in the Southern States every year for the past forty years. Compared with some of the exploiters, taskmasters, landlords and public officers who have persecuted, robbed and tortured Negroes in the South during the past forty years, Simon Legree was a very kind-hearted man. History furnishes no record of savagery and barbarities more fiendish and revolting than those which have occurred in the South.

Beginning with the year 1885, the Department of Research of the Tuskegee Institute has kept a consecutive record of lynchings. This record shows a total of 3,889 lynchings from 1885 to 1918. Of the total, 1,008 were white and 2,881 Negroes. From eighty to ninety per cent. of the total number of lynchings were in the South. Less than one-fourth of the lynchings of Negroes were due to assaults on women. The largest number of lynchings were for murder. Sixty-three Negroes, five of them women, and four white men, were lynched in 1918, and in no case was any member of the mobs convicted in any court, and in only two instances were members of the mob brought to trial. There were 82 lynchings in 1919, of which 77 were in the South and 5 in the North and West; of those lynched 75 were Negroes and 7 whites. Sixty-one persons were lynched in 1920; 18, or less than one-third of those lynched, were charged with attacks on women. In 1921, of 64 victims of lynching, 19 were charged with attacks, or attempted attacks, on women. In his statement relating to "135 examples of the alleged mistreatment of Negroes in Georgia in the last two years," published in April, 1922, Governor Dorsey called attention to the fact that "in only two of the 135 cases cited is the usual crime against white women involved."

The ascendancy of the Southern Oligarchy in full control of the Federal Government presented the moment of opportunity for the unrestrained activities of spoilsmen, manifestations of racial and provincial animosities and criminal lawlessness in the South. The opportunity was not neglected by the lawless element that worked under the cover of darkness and the criminal fellowship of secret societies and mysterious symbols. These secret organizations assumed the authority of regulators and dispensed with the processes of civil government by exercising in the most cruel and barbarous manner all the functions of investigation, prosecution, trial and punishment without the slightest regard for justice or forms of law.

The latest organization engaged in lawless practices under the name of Ku Klux Klan established executive headquarters in the city of Atlanta, where it claimed legal domicile under a Georgia charter as a fraternal organization. The head of this secret fraternity with its weird ceremonials, grips and signs, was "Colonel" William Joseph Simmons, organizer and "Imperial Wizard." According to newspaper reports, "Colonel" Simmons had been an itinerant Methodist exhorter and his title of Colonel was obtained from the Order of Woodmen of the World. It has been stated that this latest Klan was organized in 1913, but the first definite public information about its existence was when it became a corporate body under the laws of Georgia, where it secured a charter July 1, 1916. Inasmuch as peonage, racial animosities and criminal lawlessness increased after inauguration of President Wilson, March, 1913, it is perhaps true that the renaissance of the Ku Klux Klan dates from the ascendancy of the Southern Oligarchy in the Federal Government. The State of Georgia was wisely and properly selected as the community in which to revive the Ku Klux Klan. In no State could such a diabolical and lawless organization more securely carry on its wicked and proscriptive practices.

This organization engaged in the same insidious and misleading propaganda that was circulated by the original society, organized for the avowed purpose of protecting the white women of the South and maintaining white supremacy. There never was a more contemptible libel published against an unfortunate and helpless people. As pointed out in some preceding paragraphs, the conduct of the Negroes before and during the Civil War was orderly and commendable. Nor was there any cause for complaint respecting the conduct of the Negro after the war until he was contaminated by corrupt politicians. The wicked libel against the Negro was promulgated in order to justify and palliate the corrupt practices and criminal violence of the spoilsmen. As stated by James Weldon Johnson, Secretary of the National Association for the Advancement of Colored People:

When Negroes have protested against lynching, Southern newspapers have called upon them to condemn the crime which leads to lynching. Such editorial sentiments are intended to foster in the mind of the public at large the idea that rape and the lynching of Negroes in the South bear the relation of cause and effect.

In the single county of New York there were more indictments for rape in the first degree in one year than there were lynchings of Negroes in the whole country on the charge of rape in the last five years. From 1914 to 1919, 325 Negroes were lynched in the United States and only 28 of these were charged with assault. In 1917 in New York County the grand jury indicted 37 persons for this offense. Among these 37 rapists indicted by the New York County grand jury, where the evidence must be convincing and conclusive (something that does not prevail where mob law reigns), there was not a single colored American.

I have already alluded to the fidelity and good record of the Negro before and during the Civil War, and it is a remarkable fact that less than one-fourth of the lynchings of Negroes since 1884 were due to assaults on women. Neither lynch law nor a lawless secret society was necessary to protect the white women of the South. The so-called knightly champions of Southern womanhood, under the guise of the Ku Klux Klan, usually worked at night. Their organization was secret and their deeds, with few exceptions, were cowardly and inhuman. They committed every conceivable form of brutal outrage. The knights-errant in the age of chivalry openly championed the cause of the ignorant and oppressed, while this secret, lawless band, under the name of the Ku Klux Klan, invented every form of terrorism that could be used to alarm an ignorant and defenseless people. In the romances of mythology, ancient and medieval history, the knights-errant who were the champions of women fought in the open. Neither in the Iliad, nor the Æneid, nor in the narratives of Plutarch, or the Chronicles of Froissart, do we find the record of a gallant knight prowling around after dark and unmercifully beating some poor, unfortunate serf.

In the early history of the original Ku Klux Klan it is undoubtedly true that some prominent citizens of the Southern States joined the organization. These worthy citizens believed that a secret society would afford the most humane and effective agency for dealing with the portentous situation that followed the Civil War. The better class of citizens who supported the organization in its formative state soon withdrew and the lawless and criminal element secured control of the Klan.

A great social and economic cataclysm followed the Civil War in the South; the orderly processes of civil government were inoperative, and the deplorable situation was complicated by corruption and disorder under the rule of former slaves, alien adventurers and native spoilers. There was, therefore, some excuse for the organization of societies for self-protection. No such conditions existed in the Southern States, or in any other part of the United States, when, in 1913, the Ku Klux Klan was revived. Every Southern State was under control of the Democratic party; the Federal Government was also in the hands of the dominant party of the South; the Negroes had ceased to attempt to exercise any political power, and their civil rights were more restricted in the Southern States than they had been at any time since their emancipation. The rebirth of this secret and lawless organization was conceived in the interest of the spoilsmen and demagogue under the form of mediæval bigotry. In order to broaden the field of its exploitation, the new organization included Catholics and Jews with Negroes as subjects for its proscriptive propaganda and criminal practices. This propaganda and the lawless practices of the Ku Klux Klan are utterly and dangerously at variance with the principles of democratic institutions and the religious freedom and political independence of American citizens.

Referring to present conditions in the South in general and Mississippi in particular, Mr. Howard Snyder, "a native of Illinois," who "has lived for some years on a plantation in Mississippi," contributes a very interesting article to *The North American Review* (January, 1924), in which he says:

Add to all this the horrible lynchings, the burning at the stake of many Negroes whose names never get to our larger papers, and also consider the fact that the field Negro of the South is a primitive creature desperately afraid of the dreaded Ku Klux, and we have another reason for the vast migration of Negroes. Nowhere on the earth among civilized nations are such atrocious outrages committed against human beings as are committed in the South against the Negro. Almost any day we can read of some benighted Negro peasant being hunted down with hounds, or shot by a posse of men, or burned at the stake amid the multitudinous cheers of a vast concourse of people. That the South could expect these same benighted people to remain with her and uncomplainingly endure all this, when a twenty dollar bill will carry a man beyond its occurrences, passes my understanding.

My narrative is based to a large extent, if not wholly, upon conditions in the Southern States, the policies and practices of an Oligarchy by which these States have been ruled for many years. A survey of the activities outside the Southern States, of the late organization calling itself the Ku Klux Klan, would surpass the limits of this volume. However, there are certain historical parallels and some outstanding events of a national character which are pertinent to the present subject and to which I should refer before passing from this phase of our discussion.

It is a remarkable fact that the most insidious and dangerous enemies of democratic institutions in America have usually worked through secret organizations. In summarizing some outstanding facts in American history relating to the record of the Tories, Know Knothings, Copperheads, Ku Klux and a certain class of Pacifists, I have in mind the observation of Macaulay that "in proportion as men know more and think more, they look less at individuals and more at classes." Not all the enemies of this country and misguided zealots who have joined secret societies engaged in a propaganda of race proscription, religious bigotry and sedition have been found inside the Democratic party, nor located in any particular section of the country. But it is an historical fact that the Democratic party has been a sort of refuge or cave of Adullam for the most seditious propagandists and traitorous schemers in the history of the United States. It is also true that the numerical strength and political power of these secret, seditious organizations have been more persistent in certain sections than in others. For example, the present Ku Klux organization has its main strength, outside the Southern States, in those localities where the Copperheads were strong during the Civil War.

At the beginning of the Revolutionary War, the American colonists were divided into three groups, designated by historians as patriots, neutrals and loyalists. The patriots were called Whigs but some of the Whigs stood for independence while others favored aggressive opposition to British policy but not independence. The neutrals, as usual, were pacifists, "always wavering," neither for the king nor against him, but always doing something to injure the cause of the patriots. These neutral pacifists gave Washington more cause for apprehension than the open enemy. Washington's retreat from Long Island was due more to the secret work of the neutral pacifists than to the military skill of Lord Howe or the valor of his Hessian troops.

As the Revolution progressed, the neutrals were forced into the ranks of the patriots or loyalists and every one was later classed as either Whig or Tory. The loyalists were bitterly attacked as Tories and the patriots were known as Whigs. The City of New York was the great stronghold of the Tories, and after the City and Long Island were occupied by the British it was the place of refuge for loyalists and non-resistants.

Next to New York, Pennsylvania contained the largest Tory element.   There was a large German population that was unfriendly to the patriots and there were other elements in Pennsylvania that were opposed to the Whigs.   The Tory element was also strong in New Jersey, Delaware and Maryland, but they were not strong in the New England States.   The Tories had little or no influence in Massachusetts, New Hampshire, or Rhode Island, but they had some following in Connecticut.   In the South, Virginia was dominated by the Whigs and the patriotic feeling was strong and active.   North Carolina was about equally divided between Tories and Whigs.   In South Carolina and Georgia the Tories were very strong.   According to George Livermore—*An Historical Research:*

In Georgia and South Carolina, however, where there was the most urgent call for more troops, and where the slave-holders were backward in enlisting, the case was different.   These States, it will be remembered, contained so many Tories, whose sympathies were with the enemy, that it was impossible to obtain from them enough soldiers for a ''home guard.''

Colonel John Laurens, cavalier and patriot, Moultrie, Rutledge, Gadsden, Pinckney, Marion, Jasper, and Sumter (native of Virginia) were among the distinguished exceptions in South Carolina who supported the cause of the patriots.   Charleston was the Boston of the South, but it was dominated by the Tories and, in 1779, it was saved from surrender to the British by Laurens, Moultrie and the gallant Polish knight, Pulaski.

The political activities of the Know Nothing party were first observed in the State of New York, about the year 1852.   It was organized in opposition to foreign immigrants, who were coming to the United States in large numbers, and was also opposed to the Roman Catholic Church.   It held a National Convention in 1855, when it adopted the name of the American party.   Concerning the Know Nothing movement, in his *History of the United States,* Rhodes says:

The methods of the Know-nothings were more objectionable than their aims.   The party was a vast secret society with ramifications in every State. Secret lodges were instituted everywhere, with passwords and degrees, grips and signs. . . .

The Know-nothing movement, born of political unrest, augmented the ferment in the country.   This was a year of excitement and lawlessness.

Riots were frequent. . . . Most of the disturbances, however, grew out of
the Know-nothing movement. A mob forced their way into the shed near
the Washington monument, and broke to pieces a beautiful block of marble
which came from the Temple of Concord at Rome, and had been sent by
the Pope to the memory of Washington.

The Know Nothing movement was very active in Maryland
where there were numerous outbreaks and some atrocious crimes.
There were riots in New York and Philadelphia and in Kentucky nearly a hundred poor Irish and Germans were ''butch-
ered or burned and some twenty houses burned to the ground.''
Increasing crimes in connection with the renewed activities of
the lawless element of the Slave Oligarchy and revival of the
Fugitive Slave law during the Pierce Administration contributed in a large measure to the lawless practices of the Know
Nothing party. According to George W. Julian, as related
in his *Political Recollections*, the ''career'' of this party ''was
as remarkable as it was disgraceful.'' . . .

Its birth, simultaneously with the repeal of the Missouri Compromise, was
not an accident, as any one could see who had studied the tactics of the
slave-holders. It was a well-timed scheme to divide the people of the free
States upon trifles and side issues, while the South remained a unit in
defense of its great interest. It was the cunning attempt to balk and divert
the indignation by the repeal of the Missouri restriction, which else would
spend its force upon the aggressions of slavery; for by thus kindling the
Protestant jealousy of our people against the Pope, and enlisting them in a
crusade against the foreigner, the South could all the more successfully push
forward its schemes. . . .
In November of the year 1854 the Know-nothing partly held a National
Convention in Cincinnati, in which the hand of slavery was clearly revealed,
and the ''Third Degree,'' or pro-slavery obligation of the order, was
adopted; and it was estimated that at least a million and a half of men
afterward bound themselves by this obligation.

On February 19, 1856, the Know Nothing party held a ''secret
grand council''; three days later, February 22, an open convention was held in the City of Philadelphia, at which there were
227 delegates present, but the delegates from the Northern
States refused to be bound by the action of this convention. It
was clear that the influence of the Slave Oligarchy predominated
in the ''secret grand councils'' of the Know Nothing party. On
this point Nicolay and Hay *(Abraham Lincoln)* allude to the
Philadelphia meeting in the following language:

Its national council had in February at Philadelphia nominated Fillmore and Donelson as a presidential ticket; but the preponderating Southern membership forced an indorsement of the Kansas-Nebraska act into its platform, which destroyed the unity and power of the party, driving the Northern delegates to a bolt.

Abraham Lincoln was not misled by the propaganda of the Know Nothing movement, nor did he fail to perceive the menace of this seditious organization. In a letter to Joshua F. Speed, written at Springfield, August 24, 1855. Mr. Lincoln said:

The slave-breeders and slave-traders are a small, odious, and detested class among you; and yet in politics they dictate the course of all of you, and are as completely your masters as you are the master of your own Negroes. You inquire where I now stand. . . . I now do no more than oppose the extension of slavery. I am not a Know-nothing; that is certain. How could I be? How can any one who abhors the oppression of Negroes be in favor of degrading classes of white people? Our progress in degeneracy appears to me to be pretty rapid. As a nation we began by declaring that "all men are created equal." We now practically read it "all men are created equal, except Negroes." When the Know-nothings get control, it will read "all men are created equal, except Negroes and foreigners and Catholics." When it comes to this, I shall prefer emigrating to some country where they make no pretense of loving liberty—to Russia, for instance, where despotism can be taken pure, and without the base alloy of hypocrisy.

In the turmoil and confusion of political parties immediately preceding the outbreak of the Civil War, the Know Nothing party was absorbed by other parties, but its pernicious practices soon appeared under a new guise. The leaders of this secret and seditious organization were swept aside when the virile American spirit was aroused by the new party of Abraham Lincoln. Concerning the political influence and menace of secret societies "appearing at recurrent intervals" in American history, Professor William Starr Myers, in a very forcible article, published in *The North American Review* (January, 1924), says:

Our national history shows phenomena of a more or less identical type appearing at recurrent intervals, and with astonishing regularity. This is especially the case with the present phenomenon known as the Ku Klux Klan. With the possible exception of masks, robes and other like paraphernalia, it is an almost complete replica of the old Know-nothing movement of the 'fifties of the last century. It professes the same objects, and uses nearly the same methods. Pessimistic citizens of the present day, who look upon our country as going fast and straight to destruction, should remember this fact and take courage.

The evil purposes of the malcontents and political schemers appeared in new form shortly after the beginning of the Civil War. These seditious societies and other organizations of the exploiters during the Civil War were variously known as the "Knights of the Order of the Sons of Liberty"; "Order of American Knights"; "Knights of the Golden Circle"; "Circle of Honor"; "Mutual Protection Societies," and divers other bombastic and misleading names. These societies and other organizations of the Pacifists and Copperheads were strong in the City of New York, and in the States of Indiana, Illinois and Ohio.

At the head of one of these pacifist organizations was Clement L. Vallandigham, who was a good lawyer and an orator. He was a pro-slavery Democrat and was elected to Congress in 1852. In December, 1862, when the cause of the Union was in the decline, Vallandigham advocated "peace by mediation," and called for "union and constitutional liberty through an honorable peace." In 1863 he was the Democratic candidate for Governor of Ohio. He united the Copperheads and made seditious propaganda of the growing discontent, and a revolution was forming with him at the head. In 1864, Vallandigham stated that there were in his order 300,000 members, of whom 85,000 were in Illinois, 50,000 in Indiana and 110,000 in Ohio. Seditious gatherings called "peace meetings" were held in Springfield, Illinois, and plans were made to take possession of the State Governments of Illinois, Indiana and Ohio. Lincoln referred to Vallandigham as "the person who, more than any other," was responsible for the wholesale desertions in the Northern armies in 1863, and for the disturbances and threatened revolution in the Northwest and in New York.

Vallandigham was finally apprehended by the Commissioner of the Department of Cincinnati, who sent a squad of soldiers to arrest him and put him inside the Confederate lines, telling him if he wished to advocate the kind of propoganda he had been preaching and circulating he should go beyond the Confederate lines. Be it said to the credit of the Confederacy, whose military leaders were men of courage and honor, the Copperhead was not well received inside the Confederate lines and he was not trusted there.

The Copperheads were strong and very aggressive in Indiana. Among the most active and boldest leaders was Colonel E. E. Bowles, who owned a health resort, French Lick Springs, about seventeen miles from Indianapolis. Colonel Bowles and four other conspirators were tried and convicted as traitors in connection with a plot of the "Sons of Liberty" to make a concerted attack on Camp Chase, Camp Douglas, Camp Morton, and Johnson's Island for the purpose of releasing about thirty-five thousand Confederate prisoners and arming them, so that they would form the nucleus of an army to which would be added about sixty thousand members of the "Sons of Liberty," making an army of 100,000 with which to make war on the United States. Colonel Bowles and three other leading conspirators were sentenced to death, but after the assassination of Lincoln they were reprieved by President Johnson. From the time that Colonel Bowles made French Lick Springs headquarters for the Copperheads, down to our own times, this beautiful health resort has been a sort of trysting-place for some of the prominent leaders of the Democratic party. The late organization of the Ku Klux Klan has received its most active support, outside the Southern States, in the old haunts of the Copperheads, especially in Indiana, Illinois and Ohio.

The rowdies and misguided zealots who were engaged in a pacifist propaganda during the Civil War, were, with few exceptions, in sympathy with the States in secession against the Union. They availed themselves of every opportunity to befriend the cause of the Southern Confederacy when they thought they could safely do so. Enlistments in the Union army were discouraged, draft resisted, deserters helped, seditious literature disseminated, and every possible effort made to communicate news to the Confederacy and to aid the enemy in the destruction of Government property.

The Copperheads were active and unscrupulous in their efforts to weaken the cause of the Union in the Northern States but they did not go South to fight for the Confederacy, although the armies of the Confederate States were sorely in need of more fighting men. When the present Ku Klux Klan was organized, in 1916, and boastfully proclaimed its fraternalism and quixotic knight-errantry, the Allies who were fighting the battles of civilization needed men and supplies. For more than two years after the birth of this society the cataclysm of civilization continued, but there is no record of the Ku Klux Klan fighting for the cause of the oppressed or downtrodden. Their belligerency was restricted to operations against poor, defenseless Negroes and whites who were so unfortunate as to incur the ill-will of the Klan.

The Copperheads of the North, even those who were honest and sincere in their belief, were looked upon with contempt and suspicion, while the open enemies in the South who had taken up arms against the Union were regarded with respect, inasmuch as they had the courage openly to declare their purpose and to make their deeds, so far as possible, conform to their words. The passions excited by wars pass away, enemies are forgiven, but this country has not forgotten, nor will it ever forget, the pernicious teachings and evil practices of the Tories, the Know Nothings and the Copperheads. The same feeling of contempt will be the final judgment of this country concerning a secret society that has contributed nothing to the defense of the country nor the progress of its institutions. Monuments have been built in marble to commemorate the memory of the soldiers of the Union army and those in the Confederate army; still more lasting monuments are found in the hearts of the people who revere the memory of those who fought for the North and those who fought for the South. There are no monuments in marble, nor in the hearts of the people, in memory of the Copperheads of the Civil War. The memory of the American soldiers who served in the World War will be revered for all time. The rebirth of the Ku Klux Klan, which added to our racial perplexities with its pernicious propaganda, and increased our civic and social disorders with its criminal practices, will have its place in American history as a thing of evil, like the Know Nothings and the Copperheads, a menace to government and society.

CHAPTER XVII

With a population of more than 25,000,000, of which 17,000,-
000 are whites of the purest British and French stock in
America, and 8,000,000 of the most advanced, highly developed,
industrious and patriotic people of the African race, the Southern States are held in a condition of industrial slavery and
political subjection. These States are not governed; they are
ruled with an iron hand by a corrupt and provincial Oligarchy.
In no other part of Christendom can there be found a people
with such civic and economic potentialities so easily held in
subjection.

There has been industrial progress and wonderful development in certain localities in the South, but it has been in spots
and it has contributed very little to the civic and material
progress of the mass of the people. This development has been
under a mediæval and iniquitous system of land tenure, peonage,
cruel and unjust contract labor laws, inhuman convict system,
and merciless practices in the exploitation of child labor.

A large amount of capital has been invested in certain localities and in many cases it has brought large returns to the
investors, but the great bulk of the bonds and stocks of both
private and public-utility corporations, and State and municipal
bonds, are held by non-resident investors. The wealth of the
South is owned by non-residents and a very small privileged
class of citizens. The small deposits in savings banks, the very
small per cent. of the total population who have savings deposits,
or other investments, increasing tenancy in the agricultural
sections, the tumble-down farm houses, and the abandoned
farms show the wretched condition of the great mass of the
people.

In a preceding chapter I cited some figures relating to the
condition of farm tenants and the oppressive practices under

the land tenure system in the South. Further information concerning the backwardness and impoverishment of the people may be gathered in a study of certain outstanding facts relating to bank statistics. The problem of arranging material covering so many phases of the civic, social and economic situation among a people living under such depressing conditions as those which prevail in the South is a task which cannot be successfully accomplished without adhering strictly to my original purpose. My narrative is based on authoritative facts of record. It is necessary, therefore, at this point to introduce a summary of some bank statistics which bring us face to face with the actual situation.

The figures submitted for comparison in the following tabulation are taken from the report of the Comptroller of the Currency for 1913, the latest report prior to the World War, and at the beginning of the domination of the Southern Oligarchy in national affairs. This summary of bank statements, as of June 4, 1913, includes National, State and private banks, loan and trust companies, in eleven Southern States and the eleven Northern States used for comparison and with practically the same total population as the Southern States:

SUMMARY OF BANK STATEMENTS, ALL REPORTING BANKS, JUNE 4, 1913

	Capital Stock	Surplus & Undivided Profits	Individual Deposits	Per capita Deposit
Northern States	$463,029,816	$381,109,097	$3,993,158,255	$171.62
Southern States	315,483,166	189,322,332	1,208,183,972	51.66

The capital stock of the Southern banks (June 4, 1913) was about 68 per cent., the surplus and undivided profits were slightly less than half, and the individual deposits in the Southern banks were only about 30 per cent. of those of and in the Northern banks. On a per capita basis, the individual deposits in the Southern banks were considerably less than one-third of those in the Northern banks and less than one-third of those of the United States. The per capita deposit in the Southern States was less than that in Hawaii.

During five years (1913-1918), the Southern banks were as prosperous as the banks of the eleven Northern States, perhaps more prosperous, so far as their prosperity, in the aggregate, may be determined by official reports. The following tabulation, based on statements of all reporting banks in the eleven Southern States and eleven Northern States show the increase in capital stock, surplus and undivided profits and individual deposits during the period of inflation and profiteering:

SUMMARY OF BANK STATEMENTS, ALL REPORTING BANKS, JUNE, 1918

	Capital Stock	Surplus & Undivided Profits	Individual Deposits	Per capita Deposit
Northern States	$551,795,000	$494,537,000	$6,313,106,000	$259.24
Southern States	334,083,000	241,734,000	2,197,230,000	88.29

In the five years period of inflation (1913-1918), the Southern banks increased 27.60 per cent. while the Northern banks increased 29.76 per cent. in their surplus and undivided profits. In the matter of individual deposits the Southern banks increased 81.86 per cent. while the increase in the Northern banks was 58.10 per cent. During the same period individual deposits in the United States increased 58.66 per cent., an increase from $179.04 per capita in 1913 to $267.06 in 1918.

During eight years of the Wilson régime, the individual deposits in the Southern States increased from $51.66 per capita in June, 1913, to $114.33 in June, 1921; in the Northern States during the same period the increase was from $171.62 per capita to $310.77, and for the United States it was an increase from $179.04 to $335.43 per capita. The increase in the Southern States was 137.61 per cent.; in the eleven Northern States used for comparison it was 102 per cent., while for the United States it was 103 per cent. In every one of the Southern States the increase in deposits was over 100 per cent., while in six of the Northern States the increase was less than 100 per cent. In South Carolina the increase was 182 and in North Carolina it was 175 per cent., while in Iowa, for instance, the increase in individual deposits was 77 per cent. during the Wilson Administration.

So far as an increase or decrease of individual deposits may be treated as an index to prosperity or depression, it is clear that the Southern States received larger returns from the profiteering of the war period than was received by the eleven Northern States used for comparison and more than the average of the United States. The manufacturing interests of the Northern States are more extensive and diversified than those of the South but the Wilson Administration found opportunities for special favors to the Southern States in the profligacy of war expenditures.

Comparative statements relating to savings deposits are a better index to the actual financial condition of the mass of the people than are the commercial deposits. In a classification of families by tenure of homes, especially in an agricultural country, we find the best evidence of the actual condition of the mass of the people. In comparative statistics relating to savings deposits, especially in industrial centres, we also find evidence of the social and economic condition of the mass of the people. From a report on *Savings Deposits in Savings Banks, other Banks, and Trust Companies of the United States, on June 30, 1922 and June 14, 1912,* compiled by Mr. Leo Day Woodworth, Deputy Manager, American Bankers Association, Savings Bank Division, I have prepared a table showing per capita deposits and number of savings accounts, in eleven Southern States and eleven Northern States. This tabulation follows:

SAVINGS DEPOSITS

In Savings Banks, other Banks, and Trust Companies:

Southern States	June 14, 1912		June 30, 1922	
	Per capita deposit	Savings accounts	Per capita deposit	Savings accounts
Alabama	$12	45,485	$25	161,994
Arkansas	7	9,873	23	23,586
Florida	26	32,308	75	94,777
Georgia	19	75,284	37	125,380
Louisiana	23	70,147	53	26,894
Mississippi	11	17,091	32	17,819
North Carolina . . .	15	67,835	43	120,740
South Carolina . . .	19	51,768	54	75,375
Tennessee	19	63,194	50	116,576
Texas	8	33,995	22	148,479
Virginia	32	104,478	72	507,176
	$17	571,458	$44	1,418,796

Northern States	June 14, 1912		June 30, 1922	
	Per capita deposit	Savings accounts	Per Capita deposit	Savings accounts
Indiana	$57	68,487	$96	222,536
Iowa	114	373,622	202	1,064,024
Maine	191	376,532	297	563,792
Michigan	97	279,966	172	1,805,495
Minnesota	89	192,374	191	1,090,469
Nebraska	64	49,336 (Est)	108	66,929
New Hampshire . . .	253	227,460	352	332,939
New Jersey	105	480,937	220	1,643,168
Ohio	86	433,309	143	637,345
Rhode Island . . .	270	212,702	377	311,016
Wisconsin	79	187,907	130	1,001,583
	$128	2,882,632	$208	8,739,296
United States . . .	89	12,584,316	158	30,323,320

Only about 2.56 per cent. of the total population of the Southern States had savings accounts in 1912. while savings accounts in the eleven Northern States represented 12.89 per cent. of the population of these States, and in the United States it was 13.68 per cent. of the total population. In 1922, the savings accounts in the Southern States represented 5.65 per cent., in the eleven Northern States, 33.55 per cent., and in the United States 28.69 per cent., respectively, of the total population. Of the total number of savings accounts in the eleven Southern States, 35.76 per cent. were in the State of Virginia.

At the beginning of the World War, in August, 1914, the savings deposits of Canada were nearly three times those of the Southern States, although the population of Canada was hardly one-third the total, and less than one-half the white population of those States. On a per capita basis, the savings deposits of Canada were more than five times those of the Southern States. Further comparison of savings deposits in the Southern States with those of other countries may be made from the following tabulation:

SAVINGS DEPOSITS IN OTHER COUNTRIES

Country	Date of report	Average deposit per inhabitant
New Zealand . . .	March 31, 1921	$151.93
Australia	December 31, 1921	118.03
Norway	December 31, 1920	124.02
Denmark	March 31, 1920	81.46

The losses of Australia and New Zealand in the World War

were greater than those of the Southern States, in proportion to population and resources, not only in casualties but also in property and economic disturbance, yet within three years after close of the war, these British Commonwealths had per capita savings more than three times the per capita savings of the Southern States. On June 30, 1922, the per capita savings deposit in Vermont was $394 while in Georgia it was $37, less than ten per cent. of that in Vermont, in spite of the fact that Georgia is richer than Vermont in natural resources and potential wealth. On the same date, the per capita deposit in Connecticut was $359, and in California it was $307, while in North Carolina it was $43 and in Alabama it was $25. It should be borne in mind, however, that strict governmental supervision of savings banks, which usually obtains in other States and countries, is not customary in the Southern States. The statistics of reporting banks which I have cited are the most authentic and complete that are available.

By comparison with other States and other countries, the per capita savings of the Southern States are small, but the most deplorable phase of the situation, as revealed in bank statistics, is found in the fact that a very small per cent. of the total population in the South have savings deposits. The bank deposits, savings and checking accounts, like the land and substantially all other property in the Southern States, is in the hands of the ruling class, and this class, as we have seen, is a very small per cent. of the total population. In order to make it clear how small a percentage of the total population have savings deposits in the Southern States, for comparison, I have prepared a tabulation showing the per cent. of total population having savings deposits in eleven States and eleven foreign countries.

The figures relating to eleven States, in the following table, are based on statistics of savings deposits as of June 30, 1921, compiled and published by the Savings Bank Division of the American Bankers Association, and the 1920 census figures as to population. The figures relating to foreign countries are based on a tabulation contained in the report of the Comptroller of the Currency, December 4, 1922, and the date of each report is indicated in the table which follows:

PER CENT. OF TOTAL POPULATION HAVING SAVINGS DEPOSITS, IN ELEVEN STATES AND IN ELEVEN FOREIGN COUNTRIES

American States	Per cent. of total population, Census of 1920	Foreign countries	Per cent. of total population	Date of report
Massachusetts	88.15	Switzerland	65.44	Dec. 31, 1918
Vermont	87.97	Norway	64.78	Dec. 31, 1920
Connecticut	79.33	New Zealand	61.96	Mar. 31, 1922
Maine	71.70	Australia	60.40	Dec. 31, 1921
New Hampshire	67.06	Japan	58.47	Mar. 31, 1920
California	54.00	Germany	56.42	Dec. 31, 1919
Rhode Island	50.09	Sweden	49.85	Dec. 31, 1921
Michigan	49.78	Denmark	47.52	Mar. 31, 1920
Minnesota	44.10	France	40.12	Dec. 31, 1920
Wisconsin	37.96	United Kingdom	39.47	Dec. 31, 1918
Washington	18.12	Netherlands	36.71	Dec. 31, 1920
	58.94		52.83	

As shown by the figures in the preceding tabulation, the average number of savings accounts was 58.94 per cent. of the total population in eleven Northern and Western States selected for comparison, as of June 30, 1921, while, as cited in a preceding paragraph, the average of the eleven Southern States one year later, June 30, 1922, was 5.65 per cent. of the total population of these States, which was slightly more than ten per cent. of the average in the eleven foreign countries cited for comparison. Further comment on these comparative figures would be superflous and painful.

It is the common practice in the South to hold the Negro responsible for all civic, social and economic delinquencies. The Negro has been made the scapegoat of political corruption and crimes of violence and his traducers are always ready to explain their economic and financial difficulties with the general charge that the Negro is thriftless. This threadbare excuse for the deplorable situation will not bear investigation. The census figures on tenure of homes in the Southern States show that the Negroes have made remarkable progress in acquiring homes under great difficulties, and in spite of injustice and persecution. If the figures showing the number of Negroes who have savings accounts in the South were available, they would undoubtedly show great progress for the race in accumulating savings. As will be seen in a later chapter, the record of the Negroes in

subscribing for Liberty bonds, war savings stamps, and to the
Red Cross and other war work activities will fully sustain this
assertion.

Further statistics relating to economic and financial conditions in the South are found in the census reports (1910) on
the value of farm lands, buildings and equipment, and the
value of farm products. The backwardness and the impoverishment of the South are not due to a lack of the natural
advantages of productive soil and favorable climate, nor to the
indolent habits of the people. The figures shown in the following table illustrate the point:

| | Average Acres per farm | | Average value per farm | | | |
	All farm land	Im-proved land	Land	Buildings	Implements and Machinery	All Live Stock
Northern States	128.6	80.9	$5,502	$1,706	$293	$897
Southern States	103.0	42.0	1,640	421	90.5	368
United States	138.1	75.2	$4,476	$994	$199	$774

The average value of the farm in the South is hardly 37 per
cent. of the average farm value of the United States; however,
the total average acreage of the Southern farm is 25 per cent.
less than the average of the United States, while the average
of the improved land on the average farm in the South is about
56 per cent. of the average in the United States. The marked
difference appears in the value of buildings, implements and
live stock. But in spite of this great difference in the value of
buildings and equipment, the industry of the Southern people,
and their natural advantages of soil and climate, are observed
in the value of the products, as shown in the following table:

| | Income per farm from all crops | Value of all crops per acre of improved land | |
	1910	1910	1900
Northern States . .	$982.75	$14.18	$8.49
Southern States . .	627.57	15.53	8.59
United States . .	$862.40	$11.45	$7.24

The value of all crops per acre of improved land was more
in the Southern States than it was in the Northern States, and
more than the average of the United States. The income per
farm from all crops was more in the Northern States because

the acreage of improved land per farm was larger, and the value of the live stock was more in the Northern States than it was in the Southern States. For the same reason the average income per farm for all crops in the United States was higher than it was in the Southern States.

Cotton is usually second in commercial value of all crops produced in the United States, and it is the most important export product. The acreage and production of cotton in the United States, 1909 and 1919, are shown in the following table:

COTTON CROP

	Acreage	Production, bales	Production per acre	Cotton seed, tons
1919	33,740,106	11,376,130	0.34	5,327,721
1909	32,043,838	10,649,268	0.33	5,324,621
Increase	1,696,268—5.3%	726,862—6.8%	.01	3,100

Concerning the value of leading crops in the United States, the Census Bureau says:

The twenty leading crops of the United States in 1919, arranged in order of value, were corn, hay and forage, cotton, wheat, oats, potatoes, tobacco, apples, barley, sweet potatoes, rye, rough rice, grapes, peaches, kafir and milo, oranges, sugar beets, peanuts, dry edible beans, and sugar cane. The total value of these twenty crops was $13,754,290,926, which represents more than nine-tenths of the total value of crops shown by the Fourteenth Census.

Corn heads the list, with a value of $3,507,797,102, or almost $1,000,000 more than hay and forage, which stands second on the list with a value of $2,523,050,224. Cotton ranked third, with a value (including cottonseed) of $2,355,169,365, and wheat ranked fourth, with a value of $2,074,078,801. These four crops combined represented a value amounting to $10,460,095,-492, or 70.9 per cent. of the total value of all crops harvested in 1919.

On 33,740,106 acres the cotton-growers produced a crop total market value of which was $2,355,169,365, while on 73,099,421 acres the wheat-growers produced a crop the market value of which was $2,074,078,801. On less than one-half the acreage, to be exact, on 46.15 per cent., the cotton-growers produced a crop worth $281,090,564 more than the wheat crop. The market value of the land on which the cotton is grown is considerably less than the market value of the wheat land, and the price paid for labor in producing cotton is less than the price paid for labor by the wheat-growers. But the acreage market value of the cotton crop was greater than the value per acre of the wheat crop, and it was also greater than the acreage value of the corn crop.

In 1909, the eleven Southern States expended for commercial fertilizer the total sum of $69,574,361; in 1919, these States expended the aggregate sum of $205,258,317 for fertilizer, an increase of 195 per cent. in ten years. In South Carolina expenditures for fertilizer in 1919 amounted to $52,546,795, which was $31.21 per capita; during the same year North Carolina expended $19.07, and Georgia expended $15.96 per capita for fertilizer. The total expenditures for fertilizer by the eleven Southern States in 1919 represented 62.88 per cent. of the total of the United States; on a per capita basis it was $8.18 for the Southern States and $3.08 for the United States. In spite of the enormous increase in expenditures for fertilizers, in the cultivation of cotton, the average yield per acre has decreased.

No country has been blessed with greater advantages of soil and climate, waterways, minerals, and other things supplied by nature, which, so far as natural resources and advantages go, have made the South a very rich country. Under the false teachings and provincial policies of the Oligarchy by which they have been ruled, the Southern people have unwittingly, or indifferently, assumed that their natural resources would insure their industrial progress and high civic attainments. They seem to ignore the historical truth that the greatness and stability of a country are not due to its natural resources but to the inherent qualities and educational attainments of its people.

Notwithstanding the importance of the cotton crop in our international trade, and the dependence of at least one-fifth of our population on this product, it is a distressing and shameful fact that for many years the marketing of this crop has been notoriously slipshod and frequently tainted with corrupt practices. Time and time again have British spinners and other foreign consumers of raw cotton complained of the primitive methods in packing and marketing the American cotton crop. The warehousing, ginning, baling and compression of cotton are problems that were solved in other cotton-producing countries long ago. The only country in which these questions remain unsolved is in the cotton-producing States of America,

where the bulk of the world's cotton supply is produced. Mr.
A. B. Treland, Director of the Manchester Chamber of Commerce and Manchester Cotton Association, England, and a delegate to the World's Cotton Conference, New Orleans, October,
1919, said:

The condition of American cotton landing in Liverpool is not better than
it was fifty years ago, while the Egyptian cotton, weighing 200 to 300
pounds per bale more, is landed in perfectly neat condition.

Primitive methods and slipshod practices, due largely to
ignorance and the absence of efficient governmental supervision
and direction in preparing for the market, and in marketing the
cotton, entail a great deal of unnecessary loss and many hardships on the cotton-growers of the South. Sir Charles Macara,
President of the English Federation of Master Cotton Spinners'
Association, has spoken very pointedly on this subject. He said:

If the American cotton were properly packed and compressed, it would
occupy much less space than at present, and the reduced cost of freight and
carriage together with the preventing of immense waste caused by the present
slovenly packing would mean an enormous annual saving estimated to
amount to millions of pounds sterling.

It has been stated on high authority that "American cotton
is more barbarously baled and handled than any other cotton
produced in the world. It is a lamentable fact that even in
India and Egypt the cotton baling and handling methods are
far and away above the methods used in the South." Writing
in *The New York Tribune*, May 8, 1921, respecting the presence
of American representatives at the World Cotton Conference
in England, Mr. William Whittam, formerly special agent,
United States Department of Commerce, in Great Britain, said:

These men will hear in blunt language that while their fibre with its
products is far and away the most valuable commodity dealt with in international commerce, the business of American raw cotton production, packing
and merchandising constitutes the most shameful example of waste in twentieth century commerce.

Mr. Whittam also said that if the American cotton-producer
could—

set afoot any plan that will deliver the American bale to the spinner in as
respectable shape as he gets, say, his Egyptian, the South might well keep

the date on which the breath of life was put into such a reform, as an annual gala day. . . . One is led to wonder when the cotton grower will learn that he can never be carried to prosperity on a flood of words.

In Egypt, India and other cotton-growing countries, the cultivation and marketing of the cotton crop is under governmental supervision, and the cotton reaches the mills in good condition, clean and properly packed. The value of the American cotton crop is found in the natural advantages of superior staple and production; without these natural advantages, inefficiency and slipshod practices in handling the crop would exclude America from successful competition with other cotton-producing countries.

For further illustration of inefficiency and lack of system in the South, we may take the story of the boll weevil. It has been nearly thirty years since this plague appeared in the cotton-producing States. About 1893, it crossed the Rio Grande and started from Brownsville, Texas, on a slow but destructive journey through the cotton-growing section of the United States. Within a few years the pest had spread over the State of Texas, and in the years 1900 to 1905, caused an annual average loss of $15,000,000. It crossed into Louisiana in 1903 and has continued its eastward journey during the past quarter of a century.

At the close of the year 1922, it was reported that 97 per cent. of the cotton-producing territory had been devastated by the boll weevil during that year. The Department of Agriculture estimated that the loss for the four years 1917 to 1920 inclusive, approximated $300,000,000 annually, or a total loss for those years, from devastations of the boll weevil, of about $1,200,000,000. The total loss for 1921 was estimated all the way from $400,000,000 to $700,000,000. This brings the total of the five years period prior to 1922 at from $1, 600,000,000 to $1,900,000,000. Commenting on the decline in production of cotton in America, *The Wall Street Journal* said:

The situation calls for serious study in the United States, where the principal loss has been sustained. . . . The present production is down to the level of thirty years ago, while consumptive demand has been increasing.

In 1914 the average yield of lint was 209.2 pounds to the acre. Since that date it has been growing less and in 1921 was only 124.5 and 139.2

pounds in 1922.   The time has passed when low producing lands can be cultivated profitably in cotton unless the price is inordinately high, and a high price will encourage foreign competition that in the end will break our monopoly.

The ravages of the boll weevil, added to the increasing scarcity of labor resulting from continued migration of Negroes from the cotton-producing States, present the most serious economic problem with which this country has been called upon to deal for many years.   The economic situation in the South is a matter of grave concern not only to 25,000,000 people in the cotton-growing States who depend on this crop for their main support, but also to the industrial and commercial interests of the whole country.   The far-reaching consequences of the boll weevil pest in the South were summarized by Mr. Whittam, in an article published in *The New York Tribune*, January 7, 1923, as follows:

There is nothing in the history of American agriculture to compare with the Mexican cotton boll weevil as a costly blight upon those engaged in farming, neither has any other living thing made its pernicious influence felt by such a large proportion of the human race.   Every person on earth, except the utter and naked savage, has been involuntarily taxed to pay for the mischief wrought in the United States by this noxious thing.

It would be impossible to estimate the actual damage and the enormous loss in dollars that the cotton-growing States have experienced from the ravages of the boll weevil during the past twenty-five years.   Although this pest has been slowly moving in an eastward direction through the cotton States for more than twenty-five years, there has been no practical, organized effort in the South to eradicate it, and no concerted, effective plans have been undertaken to rid the country of this great menace to one of its most important industries.   Commenting on this phase of the subject, the Secretary of Agriculture said:

The cotton boll weevil could have been eradicated any time during the first five years of its invasion of the United States for a relatively small sum if the cotton growers had only realized the danger that was impending and been willing to conform to the control measures recommended by the department's scientific staff.   On the other hand, the eradication of a pest of long standing which the people have come to consider a necessary evil may be very difficult, owing to the lack of faith in the possibility of the program and a consequent lack of co-operative endeavor.

Further concerning the need of enlightenment and "coöperative endeavor" among the farmers of the boll weevil infested States, Mr. W. E. Hinds, entomologist, Alabama Experiment Station and Extension Service, Auburn, Alabama, was quoted as follows:

The first requirement is educational—a better informed farmer, industrious and open-minded, willing to try some at least of the measures which have given the best results wherever they have been given a fair and continued test.

With their proverbial self-confidence, under rule of a provincial and reactionary Oligarchy, the cotton-growers of the Southern States have relied too much on their natural advantages of climate and soil. Already our production has fallen from around 70 per cent. to about 55 per cent. of the world crop of commercial cotton. Concerning production of cotton in other countries, Mr. Whittam, in *The New York Tribune*, November, 1921, said:

It is, of course, simple nonsense to say, as many Southern enthusiasts do, that they have "a permanent, God-given monopoly of cotton production," when they produce less than two-thirds of the world's commercial crop and are seeking to more than cut that quantity in half. It has been demonstrated in very practical fashion that cotton of American upland variety can be grown as cheaply in some other regions, and in still others at considerably lower cost than in the South. Africa has vast areas of virgin land of the right sort, a climate eminently suited to cotton culture and a population the forbears of the American Negro.

The British Empire Cotton Growing Corporation under a royal charter, with a grant of £1,000,000 from the Government, represents a late Government movement of English spinners to develop new fields of cotton production so that they may be less dependent on the American producer. The Government grant to this corporation is supplemented by a fund raised by the spinners. Not only Great Britain, but also France and Belgium, are engaged in a systematic effort to develop great cotton production in their African colonies.

The shortage of American cotton for English mills, following the small crop of 1921, resulted in the British Government undertaking extensive plans for increasing the Sudan production. It was reported that the Government had decided to grant a loan to construct an extension of 217 miles of the Sudan Railway to Kassala, in order to develop cotton-growing in the River Gash delta; and a further loan for the building of a dam at Makawar, on the Blue Nile, and also irrigation works for the development of a cotton area in El Gezira extending over 3,000,000 acres.

While production in the South is not commensurate with its natural advantages, the people do not enjoy the prosperity which they should have from the commercial value of the things which they actually produce. A large majority of the people have very few of the comforts of modern life; they are not able to educate their children, and the percentage of home-owners has steadily decreased during the past thirty years. In view of these deplorable facts, it is an interesting question as to what disposition is made of their earnings. This question was answered many years ago, as quoted in *Southern Sidelights* (Edward Ingle), by a South Carolinian, "in the midst of the turmoil of 1852," who said:

If all the money which is spent in political conventions and caucuses, stump-speeches and elections, controversies and office-hunting, which demoralize the Southern mind, and is preparing it for everlasting subjugation, was devoted to improvement at home, the encouragement of Southern art and Southern industry, the division of labor, and the diversity of employment, we would be a more united people.

The threadbare excuse or explanation, so long offered in the South, to the effect that the South's backwardness is due to the disasters of the Civil War and racial troubles, is no longer effective. I have already cited some facts of record with respect to the Negro as an industrial factor in the South. It goes without saying that the Southern States suffered, not only in the loss of property, but also in the greater loss of many of its splendid citizens during the war. But it has been nearly sixty years since the end of the war, and other peoples have passed through more disastrous wars, made greater sacrifices than the Southern people made, and suffered greater hardships during and after war than the South has experienced.

Six years after the close of the Civil War in America, France passed through a shorter but more disastrous war. France lost valuable territory and paid a heavy indemnity; the South lost no territory and paid no indemnity. Subsequent to the war of 1870-71 and prior to the World War, France passed through several trying periods. In addition to political changes, revolutionary in effect, she was called upon to deal with a most serious and delicate religious question. Yet in ten years after the war of 1870-71, France made greater progress than the South has made in fifty years. And three years after the Great War, in 1921, the economic and financial situation in France, the condition of the mass of the people, was almost immeasurably better than was the condition of the people in any one of the Southern States. Commenting on the wonderful recovery of France, M. Jules Cambon, French Ambassador in London, in a speech on May 27, 1920, said:

France, a nation pre-eminently of peasants and small holders, had already taken up the work interrupted by the war. The demobilized soldiers who had formed at least 75 per cent of the army—had returned to cultivate the fields. Out of 6,400 schools at work before the war, 5,300 had been re-opened either in the repaired buildings or in hutments. Out of nearly 9,000,-000 acres of farm land, 7,000,000 had been cleared of explosives on May 1, nearly 6,000,000 of barb-wire and over 4,000,000 had been cultivated.

Figures of the staple crops in France for the years 1913 and 1921 show that more wheat was raised in 1921 than before the war, and that the rye and barley crops almost equaled those of 1913. The potato crop was only about 70 per cent. of the pre-war production. As compared with 1913 in live stock production there was a loss of about 25 per cent. of horses and other draft animals, but only a small decrease in the number of cattle. Mr. Frank A. Vanderlip, writing for *The New York Tribune*, February 16, 1922, made the following statement:

The French investing public is unique. . . . Practically everybody in France is an investor. . . . The work that has been accomplished in the reconstruction of the devastated districts has been little short of marvellous. France is at work. The total of idle workers receiving government aid in the fall of 1921 was only 35,000. Contrast this with England, where 1,600,000 industrial workmen are receiving unemployment doles.

The zone of French territory invaded by the Germans had 4,700,000 inhabitants in 1914, of whom 2,700,000 abandoned their homes to enter the army or to become refugees. In a hundred towns not a single building remained standing; 2,600 towns were damaged; 300,000 houses were destroyed and 360,000 injured. The work of reconstruction was begun before the Armistice was signed and it followed the retreating German army. The new homes which were built with the help of the Government, as well as those that were built by the railroads, coal companies and other industrial enterprises for their employees, are modern in convenience and comfort and artistic in design. The roads and grounds have been made attractive and these new homes for working people which have been built in the territory laid barren by the Germans are veritable palaces compared with the tumble-down boxes, huts and shambles used for habitation by a large majority of the industrial workers in our Southern States.

Since the Revolution of 1793, when the large estates were subdivided into small farms and placed in the possession of peasant proprietors. France has been a nation of home-owners and these peasant proprietors have been the main source of the economic strength of that marvelous country. The remarkable recuperation of France after the fiasco of Napoleon III and the hard terms imposed by Germany in 1871 was regarded as an economic and financial wonder. The explanation was found in the independence and thrift of the French peasants and working people who owned their own homes. In a ''survey . . . of the conditions under which democracy was born in France . . . the salient economic facts and the most potent intellectual and moral influences that were affecting the political life of the nation when the storm of war broke suddenly upon it in 1914,'' Lord Bryce, in *Modern Democracies*, says:

In most parts of the country the land was in the hands of peasants who owned the soil they were tilling, who were intensely attached to its possession, and who shared with most (though not all) of the bourgeoisie an almost timorous conservatism. . . .

Through all these changes of government and various forms of strife the French nation has remained intensely patriotic, united, when everything else tended to divide it, by its pride in France and its love of the sacred soil.

The aristocracy of landlordism in France was destroyed during the Revolution and it has not been revived. One great point of difference between France and the Southern States is found in the matter of tenancy. France has the lowest percentage of tenancy, and consequently the highest percentage of home owners, of all countries in the world, except Denmark. "Every Frenchman," writes M. Stephane Lauzanne, Editor-in-chief of *Le Matin,*—

believes profoundly in the equality of citizens. It was to win this equality much more than liberty that the French fought the great Revolution, and he is fiercely tenacious in the preservation of this equality.

In *The North American Review,* October, 1920, this distinguished Frenchman said:

The Frenchman, who, it must never be forgotten, belongs to a people a large majority of which are peasants, is imbued above all by two sentiments; that of property and of equality. Every Frenchman is proprietor of something, if not of a field it is of a bond or a saving bank book. M. François Marsal, Finance Minister, mentioned the other day that at the time of the last national loan there were almost 10,000,000 individual subscriptions, that is to say, one out of every four Frenchmen owning some money came to bring it to the State.

Two years after the end of the Great War, the savings deposits of France were held by more than forty per cent. of the population of that country, while less than six per cent. of the population of the Southern States had savings deposits. After four years of war, as stated in the article by M. Stephane Lauzanne, from which I have quoted, one out of every four Frenchmen was able and willing to invest his savings in the bonds of his Government, while in the Southern States of America only one out of every twenty-six of the total population was able and willing to subscribe to our Victory loan.

When the World War began America was not immediately involved to the extent of participating in the war, while Canada, as a British commonwealth, was among the belligerents and began at once to furnish men and supplies; and she continued to furnish them to the end. At the beginning of the war Canada was in a state of depression and financial difficulties; there was a crop failure and widespread unrest, especially in the western part of the Dominion; but in spite of the depression and demands for men and supplies in the war, Canada increased her acreage. The total population of the three British commonwealths, Canada, Australia and New Zealand, is nearly 2,000,000 less than the total white population of the eleven Southern States. The South was far advanced in civilization and industrial development before Australia or New Zealand was colonized, and before there was any considerable industrial development in Canada.

The three British self-governing Commonwealths, with less than the white population of the South, paid more taxes, subscribed more for government loans, contributed more money and more in commodities to war relief work, furnished more soldiers, fought longer, lost more in killed, and had more wounded in the World War, and, in short, they made greater sacrifices and suffered more than the Southern States. And yet at the present time each of these English-speaking States, of the same race as the Southern white people, is far ahead of each of the Southern States in industrial progress, financial strength and general prosperity of the people, and these British States are also ahead of the Southern States in education, and all other things relating to human progress and civic advancement.

While the Southern States have been in a condition of dependence and backwardness, Australia, New Zealand and Canada have produced statesmen able to deal with the great social and economic questions that concern the people of these countries. When the World War menaced civilization and the great crisis called for statesmen of a high order, these British States produced men who were intensely patriotic and wise in leadership. The South produced no statesmen who were able to grasp the great issues of the World War. The political leaders of the South during the World War were never able to rise above their partisan provincialism.

The explanation of the advantages and better condition of the people in the British commonwealths is not found in the difference in the people. They came from practically the same stock; the Southern white people are not inferior to Canadians, Australians or New Zealanders. The reason for the difference in present conditions is found in the fact that these British commonwealths have democratic institutions and representative forms of government. They have not been during the last forty or fifty years, and they are not now, governed by a corrupt and provincial oligarchy. In *The Annals*, January, 1921, an article by Julian Korski Grove contains a frank statement about conditions in the South which I quote without further comment:

All attempts to direct Polish immigration to the States south of the Mason and Dixon line have been unsuccessful. The number of Poles in Texas, although they began to immigrate there long before the Civil War, never reached thirty thousand, while in Wisconsin, where they started to settle about the same time, their number crossed the 300,000 mark. Moreover, the Poles in the Northwest produced many professional men with University training, while the Polish settlers in the "Rice and Cotton Belt" during the seventy years of residence in that uncongenial climate have produced not one representative either in science or politics.

A century ago the Danes were among the poorest people of Europe, but at the beginning of the World War they were very prosperous. The remarkable progress and prosperity of Denmark has been due to the education of the people and the interest which the Government has taken in wisely directing and protecting its producers. It has not only aided in financing industrial enterprise, especially the agricultural interests, but it has supplied for the benefit of the people educated and well-trained experts, in every line of business and industrial enterprise in which the people are engaged.

Denmark is a country in which the people actually rule. There is no other country where the Government is more quickly and positively responsive to the will of the people. By comparison it may be interesting to note that there is no civilized country in the world where the people have as little voice in their government as in the Southern States. The results are observed in the civic and economic condition of the people and in the educational situation in the two countries. The dominating class in Denmark is the small farmer, owning from twenty to sixty acres of land, and the leaders are men and women of education and culture. The ruling class in the South is the small lawyer and the rapacious landlord. There is no illiteracy in Denmark and the standard of living in that country is above the average of Europe. Illiteracy and poverty are the outstanding features of existing conditions in the South.

The population of Denmark in 1914 was only about 25,000 more than the population of Georgia, and at that time more than 60 per cent. of the population of Denmark had deposits in savings banks, with an average of $66.01 per inhabitant. In 1914 not more than 2 per cent. of the population of Georgia had deposits in savings banks. Another point adds interest to the story. Denmark voluntarily abolished slavery more than sixty years before Georgia was coerced into emancipation.

CHAPTER XVIII

The omissions and blunders of the Wilson Administration, in failing to make adequate provision for taking care of the enormous cotton crop produced in 1914, and ready for the market within sixty days after the beginning of the World War, resulted in a loss of not less than $30.00 per bale, or a total sum of $475,000,000 in round figures. The Southern Oligarchy was in full control of the administrative and legislative branches of the Federal Government, and it could have carried through any economic or financial measure of legislation or administration that it desired to put into effect. But there was not a statesman in the Democratic party, and certainly not one in that provincial faction of the party that dictated its policies, who was broad enough to grasp the situation and big enough to deal with the great questions of that crisis in our history. The result was disastrous to the whole country, but particularly harmful to the cotton-producers who, according to a frequent practice under rule of the Oligarchy, were reduced to the necessity of asking for public charity when they had in their possession the most stable basis of credit produced in this country.

Within a few months after the beginning of the World War, the country was startled by alarming and distressing stories from the cotton-producing States. A large portion of the South was represented to be in a state of distress and dependence. "Buy a bale of cotton," was a popular cry; it became a fad and for a little while there seemed to be more concern about the alleged distress in the Southern States than the actual suffering in Belgium. According to newspaper reports, New York bankers formed a pool of $100,000,000, to which the Southern bankers undertook to add $35,000,000, as a credit fund to enable the South to carry the cotton which it could not sell. But it was all unnecessary, as shown in later developments in the cotton market. The patriotic undertaking of providing $135,000,000 to save the South from bankruptcy, by assisting in carrying the cotton crop, dwindled to the aggregate sum of $18,000, all of which was used in one county in Alabama.

By comparison with the policies of other countries we may forcibly illustrate the blundering and pathetic inaction of the Wilson Administration in connection with the vital economic and financial questions which arose at the beginning of the World War. Take for example Brazil, a country that produces four-fifths of the world's supply of coffee. State supervision of the coffee crop in Brazil runs back at least to 1901-02, when the State of Sao Paulo produced its abnormally large crop of more than 10,000,000 bags, which with the Rio crop raised the total production of Brazil 15,000,000 bags, a larger crop than the average world total up to that time. During the month of June, 1920, *The New York Sun and Herald* called attention to the financial situation in Brazil, with particular reference to the measures adopted in that country for taking care of the coffee crop. It said:

There was an almost exact analogy between the predicament of Brazilian coffee growers in 1917 and our own cotton growers at the outbreak of the war in 1914. In 1917 the withdrawal of tonnage because of submarine conditions prevented the shipment of Brazilian coffee. Brazil is more of a one-product territory than even our own cotton States and the stoppage of coffee exports meant widespread paralysis to general business. The Brazilian Government extended a loan of $27,500,000 to the State of Sao Paulo to enable the growers and merchants to finance their coffee until the market should reopen.

There was a great shortage of coffee at the end of the war and Brazilian coffee was sold at a high price. The Brazilian Government received not only the principal amount of the loan, but more than $500,000 profit, and there remained 600,000 bags of high grade coffee on which the Government would receive a further profit. The Brazilian Government looks after the coffee crop and controls the market. It limits the shipment from the Government warehouses to such amounts as will not depress prices unduly, and all shipments on private account are checked by heavy export duty. In controlling conditions under which coffee is accepted at the warehouses, the Government is able to regulate production and keep it within bounds.

In his interesting work entitled *Egypt in Transition,* Sir Sidney Low calls attention to "some recent reforms" for the protection of cotton-growers in Egypt. For instance, the Government found it necessary to supervise the selection of seed:

More careful selection of the plant was found to be requisite; and as the poorer cultivators often found it difficult to obtain good seed from the merchants, who sold them inferior varieties at high prices, the government now supplies the fellah with the article he requires at a reasonable price.

Another great reform is the establishment of halakas, or official markets, in which the cultivators can sell their cotton. . . . Halakas have been established throughout the cotton-growing areas of Egypt, with a view to protecting the small cultivator from fraudulent practices, and in order to bring into closer contact buyers and local sellers. . . . The official weighing machines placed in them are periodically inspected and tested by inspectors attached to the Department of Weights and Measures. . . .

In a prominent position, a notice-board is placed, on which is daily marked up in large figures the opening price of ginned cotton, received by telegram from an agent in the Bourse in Alexandria. . . . In addition to this a circular is dispatched every afternoon by the National Bank of Egypt at Alexandria giving the latest prices of all the various kinds of cotton and seed.

Thus it is seen that greater protection is given the cotton-producers in Egypt, under supervision and direction of the Government, than has been provided for the cotton-producers in America. But the greater protection for the cotton-producer in Egypt is described by Sir Sidney Low as follows:

A more important reform is that which is called the Five Fedden Law. It is intended to protect the small cultivator, the man who farms five Egyptian acres or less, from having his land, house, or farming utensils seized for debt. . . . The protection of the poorer peasants in this manner was rendered necessary by the action of the small foreign usurers who, scattered throughout the country in the villages, and financed by various banks, were able, with the support of the Capitulations, to lend money on mortgage to the fellaheen at exorbitant rates of interest. Not even a country as agriculturally prosperous as Egypt can stand such a burden indefinitely, and the inducements held out to the fellah to take the first step into debt were temptations few could resist, with the inevitable consequence that, once in the clutches of the moneylender, there was no escape for the victim until the whole of his property became so involved as to bring about his expropriation.

It is the standing evil which attends on peasant proprietorship everywhere, in Ireland, in Hungary, in Roumania, in Bengal, and all wise governments do their best to guard against it by making it difficult or impossible for the peasant to expropriate the holding without which he cannot exist. But with five acres free of debt it is considered that the fellah can live in comfort and bring up his children properly; and gradually he may learn to do without the local usurer, put his money in the savings bank, and raise funds when he needs them by getting advances on his crops from the Agricultural Bank of Egypt, which lends under government restrictions, and is not allowed to exact extravagant interest.

It is plain that the farmer in Egypt has more protection than has been afforded the farmers of the South. In the wise provision made for the protection of the farmers in Egypt, as cited by Sir Sidney Low, there is evidence of a broad, humanitarian statesmanship which does not obtain in any of the Southern States. I have already alluded to the merciless exactions of the rapacious landlord and moneylender to which the poor farmers in the South have been subjected for many years without any semblance of protection by the local, State or national government.

Another fact which illustrates by comparison the dependence, lack of enterprise and progress in the agricultural sections of the Southern States is found in the reports issued by the Bureau of the Census (1920) relating to "coöperative marketing and purchasing through farmers' organizations." As shown by these reports, the total of farms in the United States reporting sales through farmers' marketing organizations was 7.9 per cent. of all farms, and the average per farm was $1,412. In Minnesota, for example, 43.9 per cent. of all farms reported sales through farmers' marketing organizations; and 16.6 per cent. of all farms reported purchases through farmers' organizations, an average of $224.00 per farm. In Iowa, 20.3; in Nebraska, 26.2 and in Kansas, 20.4 per cent., respectively, of all farms reported sales through farmers' marketing organizations. The farms reporting purchases through farmers' organizations in each of these three States were 15.2 in Iowa; 22.0 in Nebraska, and 19.6 per cent. in Kansas. The three leading States in coöperative marketing and purchasing by farmers in the South are Florida,

Louisiana and Virginia. The fruit and truck growers of Florida, a large number of whom went thither from the Northern States, are perhaps the most progressive in the South, yet only 2.5 per cent. of the farms in that State reported sales and only 0.7 reported purchases, through farmers' organizations. In Louisiana, 3.2 per cent. of all farms reported sales, 1.2 per cent. reported purchases through farmers' organizations; in Virginia, the figures were 2.1 sales and 2.8 per cent. purchases through farmers' organizations. Outside the States of Florida, Louisiana and Virginia, the average of the Southern States was less than one per cent. in sales and purchases through farmers' organizations. According to the *New International Year Book:*

The farmers' coöperative associations in New Zealand have steadily developed until they are now important factors in the business life of the dominion, and are very rapidly gaining strength. These associations have taken up different lines of development and trade and formed plans for building and operating their own flour mills, establishing hydro-electric plants for the benefit of members of the association, as well as using their influence for better roads throughout the Dominion. They are also interested in fertilizer and cement plants, and, in the aggregate, control a large portion of the business of the country.

The War Finance Corporation was a belated measure on the part of the Federal Government "to assist in the task of reconstruction and readjustment." This agency for financial relief of the agricultural interests was created after the election of the 66th Congress. The Corporation was empowered by Congress, in March, 1919, to make advances not exceeding $1,000,-000,000 for the purpose of financing the exportation of domestic products. This authority was exercised until May, 1920, when the activities of the Corporation were suspended. By joint resolution of Congress, in January, 1921, the activities of the Corporation were resumed. The following figures, for illustration, show the advances approved by the War Finance Corporation from January 4, 1921, to November 15, 1921:

Export advances:

Cotton	$47,527,598.00
All export advances exclusive of cotton	21,437,109.00
Total export advances	$68,964,707.00

Advances for agricultural purposes:

Cotton	$13,025,214.50
All advances for agricultural purposes, exclusive of cotton	37,092,861.71
Total advances for agricultural purposes . . .	$50,118,076.21
Total of all advances for cotton	$60,552,812.50
Total of all advances exclusive of cotton . . .	58,529,970.71
Grand total of all advances	$119,082,783.21

Of the total advances for export purposes the cotton interests received 68.91 per cent.; for agricultural purposes 25.98 per cent.; and the cotton interests received a little more than 50 per cent. of all advances made by the War Finance Corporation, for relief of the agricultural interests, prior to November 15, 1921. In view of the export value of cotton, perhaps the making of liberal advances on this product was the proper thing to do; not only for the immediate relief of the cotton-producing section but also for the improvement of our foreign trade relations. According to the official report of the War Finance Corporation, "as raw cotton is our greatest agricultural export product, attention was directed first to this important factor in the problem."

The decline in the price of corn and wheat from the average of 1919 was considerably more on a percentage basis than the decline in the price of cotton. Notwithstanding this fact, and the further fact that for eight years the Federal Government was under control of the cotton-growing section, and all possible legislation and administration help, within the limits of provincial statecraft and partisan practices, that could be given the cotton-producing States was freely and lavishly given by the Government, the cotton-producers have been the most aggressive in their complaints and the most insistent in asking for governmental help. Although the percentage of decline in the market value of cotton was less than that of corn or wheat, the earlier and greater relief by the Federal Government, after the Republican party came into power, in 1921, was extended to the cotton-producers. Federal appropriations and special legislation for relief of the cotton-producers have been as freely granted under Republican as under Democratic administrations, but the relief has seldom reached the men and women who actually labor to produce cotton. It is usually absorbed by the cotton factors, bankers, speculators and other allies of the Oligarchy before it reaches the unfortunate people who cultivate the soil and gather the crops.

It has been the long-established custom for the States composing the Solid South to go to the Federal Government for special favors and donations for actual or alleged distress. When it comes to paying taxes, furnishing men to fight in defense of the Nation, or maintaining a status of respect for the Government by observing its laws and respecting its institutions, the Solid South is usually delinquent. In asking for Federal grants and special legislation for partisan or sectional interests, the Solid South is never derelict. Moreover, almost without exception, Senators and Representatives in Congress from the eleven Southern States, affiliated with the Democratic party, have opposed all measures for defense of the country; and legislation conducive to the prosperity of the country and for insuring the stability of the national Government have seldom received the support of Southern Senators and Congressmen when introduced by Representatives from the North or West.

During the month of July, 1916, Senator Underwood of Alabama introduced a joint resolution appropriating $540,000 for relief of flood sufferers in the States of North Carolina, South Carolina, Georgia, Alabama, Florida and Mississippi, and for other purposes. In support of this resolution, among other things, Senator Underwood said:

In Alabama there are 23,000 destitute people. . . . Unfortunately, a large proportion of the 23,000 people in Alabama who have been driven from their homes, are the Negro population. They are unable to take care of themselves.

In the debate pending adoption of this resolution, Senator Penrose, of Pennsylvania, said:

It would seem to me, Mr. President, that the Governor of Alabama should call a special session of the Legislature of that State, and show some willingness on the part of the local authorities to remedy the dreadful conditions prevailing.

A few years ago we had in Pennsylvania the Johnstown flood, a rather famous disaster, in which thousands of people lost their property and many hundreds lost their lives; but the Legislature appropriated the many hundreds of thousands of dollars that were necessary to meet the disastrous conditions arising from the breaking of that dam. A few years afterwards the Susquehanna River rose, as it frequently does, until it forced through the streets of Williamsport, a large and thriving town in Pennsylvania, a wall of water from 12 to 20 feet high, as indicated by appropriate inscriptions on the buildings to-day, with the consequent destruction of a vast amount of property; but no one came to Congress, or, even in that case, to the Legislature to ask for relief.

There was practically no opposition to the resolution asking an appropriation for relief of the flood sufferers in the Southern States, but in the course of the debate some things were said which well illustrate conditions in the South, and the increasing menace of the narrow and extreme partisan policies of the leaders of the Southern Oligarchy. For instance, Senator Newlands of Nevada, Democrat and native of Mississippi, supported the resolution, but in giving his support he said:

I think this relief ought to be given. I wish to say, however, that I deem this not an unfitting moment to call attention of the Senator from Mississippi and other Southern Senators to the fact that for ten years a bill has been urged in this body providing for river regulation and flood control. . . .

I wish to call the attention of the Senators also to the obliviousness of the members of Congress from the South to the principal economic need of the time, and their failure to respond to the sentiment which exists elsewhere throughout the entire country in favor of a broad and comprehensive measure that will take care, not simply of the lower Mississippi or the lower Sacramento, but will embrace every watershed in the country in a system of plans and works which will ultimately secure control over these waters, mitigating their destructive effects, and at the same time putting them to use as creators instead of destroyers of wealth. I feel that the South has been singularly oblivious to this great menace, and to the economic demand of the time, that all waters should be controlled and beneficially utilized.

A delegation of Southern bankers and allied interests visited Washington within two weeks after the inauguration of President Harding, and from that city, April 14, 1921, came the news that Senator Hardwick, of Georgia, had personally called upon the President, suggesting that the United States ask the allied governments to underwrite German bonds which would be accepted in payment of cotton exports from this country and would be held as securities against war debts due the United States. This suggestion, it was reported, came after the visit of Southern bankers who were asking for relief for the actual or alleged distress of the cotton producers. At this point it may be well to call attention to some outstanding facts relating to the true value of property and the payment of Federal taxes in the Southern States.

According to statistics published by the Bureau of the Census, the estimated true value of all property in 1900 and 1912, in the eleven Southern States and eleven Northern States, respectively, and in the United States, is shown in the following tabulation:

ESTIMATED TRUE VALUE OF ALL PROPERTY, 1900 AND 1912

	1900	Per capita	1912	Per capita
Northern States	$24,791,264,070	$1,292	$49,661,380,823	$2,132
Southern States	9,592,177,149	498	25,126,759,247	1,050
United States	$88,517,306,775	$1,165	$187,739,071,090	$1,965

The true value of all property in the eleven Southern States in 1912 was more than one-half the true value of all property in the eleven Northern States. We have seen, by comparison with other States, how little the Southern States have done for the education of their children, and how much they have relied on outside help instead of taxing themselves, like other States, according to their means; and we have seen how the South frequently appeals to the Federal Government for aid when that section is disturbed by industrial depression or public calamities. In this connection it is well to bring out clearly the fact that the sectional prejudices of the Southern Oligarchy predominated in manipulating Federal taxes when the Democratic party was in power.

While the 64th Congress was considering a new revenue bill for increasing the income of the Government, it was stated that Congressman Kitchin, of North Carolina, Chairman of the Ways and Means Committee, advised his fellow citizens of the South that practically all of the new inheritance and excess profit tax would ''go north of Mason and Dixon's Line. The preparedness agitation,'' he said, ''had its hot-bed in such cities as New York''; and he later repeated that ''the North reaped all the harvest of gold and silver when the nation underwent the preparedness mania. It is right, therefore, that the North, having profited, pay for its fun." In August, 1916, *The Rochester Chronicle* summed the matter up when it said:

It is an old story how that the income tax was manipulated, that the bulk of the tax was saddled on four prosperous Northern States. Nearly one-third of that tax is paid by New York State alone. The tax paid by this State for this fiscal year which ended June 30, 1915, was $17,417,-537.60. On the other hand, the States of Alabama, Arkansas, Florida, Georgia, Kentucky, Louisiana, Mississippi, Missouri, North Carolina, South Carolina, Tennessee, Texas and Virginia, all combined paid less than $5,-000,000.

The total income tax from individuals under the Democratic law of October 3, 1913, and total emergency or "war taxes" under the Democratic law of October 22, 1914, collected for the fiscal years ended June 30, 1914, 1915 and 1916, for the eleven Southern States, eleven Northern States and the total of the United States, respectively, are shown in the following table:

ADDITIONAL TAXES LEVIED BY DEMOCRATIC LAWS

	Individual income tax	Emergency or war tax	Total tax collected
Northern States	$21,605,713.06	$33,185,753.23	$54,291,466.29
Southern States	4,991,080.59	9,792,999.69	14,784,080.28
United States	$137,033,387.46	$136,084,323.61	$273,117,711.07

Of the total tax collected, the per capita basis was $2.72 for the United States, including Hawaii and Alaska; $2.24 for the Northern States and $0.622 for the Southern States. The total tax collected in Hawaii was equivalent to $2.04 per capita, and in Alaska it was $0.636 per capita. Hawaii and Alaska, respectively, paid a larger per capita tax than was paid by the Southern States. With about one-fourth the total population and fourteen per cent. of the estimated value of all property in the United States, the Southern States paid 5.40 per cent. of the total Federal revenues collected as shown in the preceding table. According to statistics already cited, the estimated true value of all property in the eleven Southern States, in 1912, was in round figures a little more than one-half that in the eleven Northern States, and the per capita wealth of the Southern

States was also one-half that of the Northern States. But in paying taxes the Southern States paid considerably less than one-third of the amount paid by the eleven Northern States. Delinquencies of the Southern States in paying Federal taxes may be more fully illustrated by statistics contained in the following tabulation, showing internal revenue collections in these States and in the eleven Northern States.

INTERNAL REVENUE COLLECTIONS, FISCAL YEARS 1917 AND 1918, INCLUDING MISCELLANEOUS TAXES FOR 1918, ELEVEN NORTHERN AND ELEVEN SOUTHERN STATES

| | Income and Excess Profits | | Per capita | Miscellaneous | Per capita |
	1917	1918	1918	1918	1918
Northern States .	$63,699,245.03	$571,405,034.53	$23.46	$196,295,042.04	$8.07
Southern States .	18,171,240.61	165,691,984.15	6.66	99,283,730.16	3.98

The per capita income and excess profits tax for 1918 was $27.40 for the United States. The per capita paid by the Southern States was less than one-fourth of the United States and less than one-third of the eleven Northern States. The number of persons making income tax returns and the amount of net income reported for the year 1917, and the per capita basis of the estimated population for that year, for the two groups of States used for comparison, and the United States, are shown in the tabulation which follows:

INCOME TAX, 1917

	Number	Amount	Per person making return	Per capita
Northern States	921,669	$3,225,435,869	$3,500.00	$132.45
Southern States	351,086	1,278,154,066	3,640.50	51.03
United States .	3,472,890	$13,652,383,207	$3,931.13	$131.73
Alaska . . .	4,570	10,549,506	2,308.43	62.52
Hawaii . . .	3,131	21,868,755	6,984.59	99.60

The State of North Carolina, which for eight years wielded so much power in making revenue laws and levying taxes in this country, furnished (1917) 22,977 citizens who made income tax returns. In 1917 the total number of income tax returns in New Zealand was 30,230 and this was after New Zealand had been engaged in war for three years and had contributed in men and treasure as much as, if not more, in proportion to her population, and wealth, than any other country. The total population of North Carolina (1917) was 2,434,381; whites, 1,673,443; Negroes, 760,938. The total population of New Zealand (1916) was 1,099,449, about 65 per cent. of the white population of North Carolina, and about 45 per cent. of the total population of North Carolina.

Subscriptions to Liberty Bonds and other war loans furnish interesting figures for comparison. The following tabulation tells the whole story of the four Liberty Loans, the Victory Loan, War Savings and Thrift Stamps:

SUBSCRIPTIONS TO WAR LOANS

	Total 1,2,3 & 4 Liberty Loans	Per capita	Victory Liberty Loan	War Savings & Thrift Savings	Per capita
Northern States	$4,009,459,100	$164.64	$1,149,634,450	$308,187,776.55	$12.66
Southern States	1,407,302,250	56.55	383,616,100	182,366,181.63	7.33
United States	$18,828,399,350	$181.21	$5,249,908,300	$1,015,067,471.80	$9.64
Alaska	6,003,300	92.48	1,428,850		
Hawaii	19,893,000	90.60	5,005,650		

The figures in the foregoing table are from reports of the War Loan Organization of the Treasury Department, as published in 1919. The figures on war savings and thrift stamps represent total sales from the beginning of the campaign to December 31, 1918. Each of the five war loans was oversubscribed, especially the first, second and Victory Loans. I have used as a basis for my comparisons the maximum original subscriptions, as reported by the War Loan Bureau, which give the best showing that can be made for subscriptions in the Southern States. Figures are not available for a full comparison of final allotments for the reason stated by the Treasury Department which was that "the Federal Reserve Bank at Richmond did not maintain records showing allotments by States for the first and second loans." The allotments, however, were about on the basis of the subscriptions, and the net result for comparative purposes would be approximately the same whether the comparison be made on basis of subscriptions or allotments.

Bulletins "prepared by the War Loan Organization, U. S. Treasury Department," and published from the Government Printing office, contained statistical information relating to subscription to the war loans according to estimated number of subscriptions and "per cent. population subscribed," third and fourth Liberty Loans and Victory Loan. This information relating to the number of subscribers and per cent. of population that subscribed was not available in reports on first and second loans. The percentage basis of population subscribing to third, fourth and Victory Loans is shown in the following table:

WAR LOANS: PER CENT. POPULATION SUBSCRIBED

	Third Loan Per cent. of population	Fourth Loan Per cent. of population	Victory Loan Per cent. of population
Northern States	20.78	27.2	13.96
Southern States	7.01	9.57	3.83
United States	17.7	21.98	11.3

This tabulation from the official record tells its own story and further comment would be superfluous. I shall amplify the figures presented in this table only to the extent of calling attention to two or three specific cases for the purpose of comparing the records of subscriptions in certain States. In the State of North Carolina, for example, where, as pointed out in the preceding chapter, bank deposits increased 175 per cent. during the Wilson Administration, the per cent. of population that subscribed to the Third Liberty Loan was 3.3; to the Fourth Loan, 6.2; and to the Victory Loan, 2.08. In each of these three loans, of which there is a record of the number of subscribers in each State, the lowest percentage of population that subscribed was in North Carolina. In Mississippi, where there are more Negroes than whites, the per cent. of population that subscribed to each of the loans was larger than in North Carolina. For comparison, on a per capita basis, total subscriptions to the four Liberty Loans in Minnesota amounted to $149.50; in New Hampshire, $146.42; in Nebraska, $139.10; in Georgia, $48.31; in North Carolina, $45.06; in Arkansas, $38.82; and in Alabama, $35.91.

The patriotic feeling in the South was as strong with the

great mass of the people as it was in other parts of the country, but the patriotism did not reach the privileged Oligarchy that rules the South.   In subscriptions to war savings and thrift stamps made by the mass of the people, the Southern States came up to the full measure of their ability, and comparison in this respect, either with the eleven Northern States, or with the average of the United States, is most favorable to the South, especially when we consider the large per cent. of Negroes, as well as a considerable number of white people who were absolutely penniless and could not have subscribed to any fund for any purpose which required cash payment.

It is well known that the Negroes, according to their means and limited earnings, subscribed very liberally to war savings stamps, and those who were able to pay for Liberty and Victory Bonds subscribed more liberally than the whites in many cases. Take for example the State of Mississippi, where the colored proportion of the total population is larger than in any other Southern State.   The per capita subscription to war savings stamps and thrift stamps in this State amounted to $7.35, while in Georgia, where the whites are in the majority, it was $4.78. The poor whites of North Carolina subscribed liberally, an average of $8.66 per capita; also in Tennessee and Texas the subscriptions reached $9.49 and $9.94, respectively, per capita. In several of the Southern States the per capita subscriptions to war savings stamps and thrift stamps ran ahead of several of the Northern States and in Tennessee it was a little ahead of the per capita of the United States.   The total amount subscribed to war savings stamps in the Southern States was considerably more than fifty per cent. of the total for the same purpose in the eleven Northern States.

Our story of delinquencies in the South during the World War would not be complete without some reference to collections for the American Red Cross, Young Men's Christian Association, the Salvation Army, and other war work activities.   In order to present a clear abstract of the facts in the fewest possible words, I have made a summary of the official reports of the Red Cross (first and second drives); Young Men's Christian Association (first and second campaigns, 1918); and United War Work campaign, November 11-18, 1918.   The sum of all collections, during the period stated, is shown in the following tabulated abstract:

	Total collection, war relief funds	Per capita
Northern States	$120,848,885.95	$4.96
Southern States	41,568,734.02	1.67
United States	$498,191,935.64	$4.80
Hawaii	449,971.80	2.05

This little table of large figures well illustrates by comparison the delinquencies of the Solid South in a work that should have touched the hearts and opened the purses of the citizens of these States whose representatives made the laws and ruled the country during the war. It will be observed that the per capita subscription in Hawaii was far ahead of the South. The citizens of North Carolina contributed to all war relief funds the sum of $1.23 per capita, while Iowa gave $5.32 and New Hampshire $4.75 per capita. Georgia subscribed $1.15 per capita, the lowest in the United States, except Mississippi, where with a large Negro population, the people contributed on the basis of $1.10 per capita. As stated in *The Negro Year Book:*

The Negroes of the country, according to their means, contributed very liberally to all of the war activities, and especially in subscribing for Liberty bonds and War Savings Stamps, to the Red Cross and the Y. M. C. A. work. Investigations and estimates are that the Negroes of the United States to the several Liberty Loans, the Thrift Stamp Drive and the War Work activities, contributed more than two hundred and twenty-five million dollars.

Numerous instances were reported where the Negroes in the South subscribed for more bonds and stamps than they were asked to buy and in some places they subscribed more liberally than the whites. The Negroes did not falter in the World War, nor did they engage in profiteering.

CHAPTER XIX

DEFAULTS OF THE SOUTH IN THE WORLD WAR

Writing about the brave Americans who volunteered for service in the cause of the Allies, before America entered the World War, in *Collier's*, July 29, 1916, ex-President Roosevelt referred to a memorial service held in Trinity Church, New York, in honor of the—

gallant young Victor Chapman, a corporal of the American Flying Squadron in France, who was slain fighting in the air over the trenches.

This body of young American aviators, of which Victor Chapman was a member, included, among others, Elliott Cowdin, Norman Prince, Larry Rumsey, Clyde Baisley, Wm. K. Thaw, Kiffen Rockwell and Bert Hall. Every member of this American Aviation Corps was decorated or promoted for "feats of signal gallantry." Commenting on the heroic service of these volunteers from the United States, Colonel Roosevelt said:

The American nation has had scant cause for pride during the last two years, and much cause for bitter shame and humiliation. We are therefore all of us indebted to these young men of generous soul, who showed not only that they were not "too proud to fight," but that they were proudly willing to die for their convictions. To the extent of their power they have partially redeemed us as a nation from the twin curses of gross materialism and silly sentimentalism.

Not only in urging the great need of preparedness in the United States, but still more in proclaiming the higher and nobler ideals of civic virtue and virile patriotism, Colonel Roosevelt was an inspiration for all loyal Americans before and after this country entered the World War. His earnest patriotism had little patience with the prattle and practices of weaklings and mollycoddles. Concerning some public manifestations of weakness and utterances of indifference to the vital issues of the war, he said:

About the time that Victor Chapman was dying, one of the great political parties was holding its national convention at St. Louis. The convention worked itself up to a pitch of bellowing enthusiasm; but not about heroism, nor righteousness, nor national honor, nor the display of courage nor self-sacrifice. None of these things interested that convention, nor could the mention of them draw a single plaudit. But the convention went frantic with delight whenever one of its "key-note speakers" uttered sentiments praising the peace of cowardice, the peace obtained by refusing to help the weak to whom we were pledged, and by refusing to protect our own women and children who were murdered on the high seas or in Mexico. One of these key-note speakers recited the fact that not an American widow nor an American orphan existed because of our having gone to war, and the convention with frantic enthusiasm responded by shouts of "Say it again." It was said again. It was not true, of course; for widows and orphans have been made by the deaths of our soldiers who have fought in the inglorious little wars which we have inefficiently waged in Mexico. But aside from this that audience knew at the bottom of its shallow heart that the "widows and orphans" had been saved the necessity of moaning about the deaths of fighting men, merely because these same fighting men had been made to sit idle while the "widows and orphans" themselves lost their lives by the acts of German submarines and Mexican banditti. The crowd roared in delighted sympathy with the men who had not dared to fight; but they uttered not a word even of regret for the women and children who had been killed because able and brutal foreigners were convinced, and as the sequel shows rightfully convinced, that the American nation could not or would not protect the lives of American citizens, and demanded of the American Government only adroit elocution, as a substitute for straight-forward and efficient action.

Shame is ours as a people that feelings as base as these should obtain among any of our people. High honor is due to men like Victor Chapman who have shown that courage and idealism are not dead among us.

Every true, patriotic American, with pride of family or country, was proud, and every true American always will be proud to know that men like Victor Chapman, Norman Prince, and others of equal courage, volunteered to fight for the cause of humanity and civilization. These men went to the front in the spirit and with the heroic courage of the Crusaders. They went to France with the same noble spirit that brought Lafayette to America, and they helped pay the debt that America owed to France. The deeds of these American volunteers in the Foreign Legion, before an aroused and indignant public sentiment forced the Wilson Administration into war against Germany, are among the most glorious achievements in American history.

The humiliation of this great nation by an administration that had manifested no concern about the sufferings of humanity and the peril to civilization; that had failed to appreciate the highest ideals of the American people, created an unfavorable impression which could not be effaced by the fancied security of isolation and commercial prosperity. The great comfort that came to the wounded pride of patriotic Americans, before the United States entered the World War, was found in the splendid record of the young Americans who volunteered for the cause of humanity and fought in the armies of the Allies.

The indisposition and indifference of the leaders of the Southern Oligarchy, as shown by their unwillingness to support essential measures for preparedness in order to defend American institutions and territory, was the cause of serious trouble when, after three years of "watchful waiting," the President finally found it necessary to call out troops to protect the Mexican border from Mexican raiders. During the months of May and June, 1916, the President issued orders calling into the service of the United States the larger part of the National Guard of all the States, and of the District of Columbia. Shortly after the second call about three-fourths of those called out were sent to the border; and the rest of those included in the call remained at their mobilization camps for various reasons, the principal one being lack of requisite legal number of men, lack of supplies and slowness of preparation.

It was stated that troops from New York and Pennsylvania constituted a well-organized division. The others were more or less imperfectly organized into eight divisions. The organizations turned out were short of their peace strength over 4,000 men and of their war strength 97,000 men. Of those responding, about 29 per cent. had to be discharged for physical disabilities. At the end of the year the number of National Guard troops on the border was approximately 110,000 officers and men. Of this total number of troops on the Mexican border, called by the President to protect the country from invasion, the Southern States sent 2,000 from Virginia, 500 from Louisiana and 3,000 from Texas. On August 1, 1916, the State troops included 16,000 from New York, 9,000 from Pennsylvania, 7,000 from Massachusetts, and 11,000 from Illinois. The Southern States did not furnish their full quotas of men for service on the Mexican border, but when the United States entered the World War the defaults of these States were more glaring.

The report of the Provost Marshal General (December 20, 1918), contains statistics relating to selective service which show, by comparison with other States, the defaults of the Southern States. A curious phase of this matter, as revealed by this report, is found in the figures relating to the population arbitrarily fixed as a quota basis for draft. These figures in detail are shown in the tabulation on page 381.

The percentage of aliens (who were exempted from military service) was less in the Southern States than in other States, yet the reduction in population, for draft purposes, was the largest in these States. For the purpose of determining the quota of men to be drafted, the population of the Southern States was reduced 2,838,752, and for the same purpose the population of the eleven Northern States was increased 1,908,-248. This change was made in spite of the fact that the Census Bureau estimates for July 1, 1917, place the total population of the Southern States as 534,315 more than the total population of the Northern States. When it came to a matter of fixing the quota basis for the selective service the basis of the eleven Northern States was placed at 4,212,685 more than the eleven Southern States. Commenting on the draft regulation in the Southern States, *The New York Tribune* (October 12, 1920), editorially said:

In executing the conscription act of 1917 the War Department nullified the law which ordered the draft apportionment to be based on population. It was apparent at the time that the apportionment enforced by Secretary Baker was scandalously unjust and discriminatory, but the inequalities went uncorrected. . . . This system worked out to the exclusive benefit of Democratic States where registration was conducted slackly. . . .

These extraordinary sectional over-drafts and under-drafts vitiated the purpose of the universal service law, which is based on equality of obligation. The law couldn't have been administered any more effectively toward the end secured if it had contained a clause giving Democrats exemption and compelling Republican States to make good the deficits.

TOTAL POPULATION AND QUOTA BASIS OF POPULATION

Total population, 1920, population estimated by Bureau of the Census, as of July 1, 1917, and population as basis for quotas enforced in draft apportionment, in eleven Southern and eleven Northern and Western States.

States	Population 1920	Estimated population July 1, 1917	Quota basis of population	Decrease	Increase
11 Southern States:					
Alabama	2,348,174	2,363,939	1,946,536	417,403	
Arkansas	1,752,204	1,766,343	1,594,835	171,508	
Florida	968,470	916,185	925,641		9,456
Georgia	2,895,832	2,895,841	2,486,544	409,297	
Louisiana	1,798,509	1,856,954	1,688,862	168,092	
Mississippi	1,790,618	1,976,570	1,501,345	475,225	
North Carolina	2,559,123	2,434,381	2,146,266	288,115	
South Carolina	1,683,724	1,643,205	1,384,203	259,002	
Tennessee	2,337,885	2,304,629	2,024,893	279,736	
Texas	4,663,228	4,515,423	4,397,097	118,326	
Virginia	2,309,187	2,213,025	1,951,521	261,504	
	25,106,954	24,886,495	22,047,743	2,848,208	9,456
11 Northern and Western States:					
Indiana	2,930,390	2,835,492	2,738,893	96,599	
Iowa	2,404,021	2,224,771	2,327,079		102,308
Maine	768,014	777,340	646,588	130,752	
Michigan	3,668,412	3,094,266	4,015,053		920,787
Minnesota	2,387,125	2,312,445	2,377,938		65,493
Nebraska	1,296,372	1,284,126	1,270,301	13,825	
New Hampshire	443,083	444,429	403,884	40,545	
New Jersey	3,155,900	3,014,194	3,255,407		241,213
Ohio	5,759,394	5,212,085	6,074,771		862,686
Rhode Island	604,397	625,865	573,583	52,282	
Wisconsin	2,632,067	2,527,167	2,576,931		49,764
	26,049,175	24,352,180	26,260,428	334,003	2,242,251

From figures contained in the report of the Provost Marshal General (December 20, 1918), I have compiled a summary which shows the total registration, enlistments and inductions, in eleven Northern States used for comparison and the eleven Southern States, April 2, 1917, to October 31, 1918. This summary is shown in the following table:

REGISTRATION, INDUCTIONS, ENLISTMENTS AND INCREMENT ARMED FORCES

	Total registration	Total increment, armed forces	Inductions, national army	Enlistments Army	Navy	Marine
Northern States . .	5,994,247	995,280	651,946	236,028	94,067	13,239
Southern States . .	5,026,390	851,762	638,501	137,770	68,954	6,537
United States . .	24,234,021	4,034,743	2,666,867	877,458	437,527	52,891

With slightly more than 24 per cent. of the total population, the eleven Southern States furnished less than 21 per cent. of the total registration and slightly more than 21 per cent. of the total increment of armed forces. Exclusive of the Negro population, the South also fell behind in its proportion of enlistments. The total enlistments of the eleven Northern States, including army, navy and marine corps, amounted to 343,334, while the total enlistments of the eleven Southern States were 213,261. The white population of the eleven Southern States was slightly more than two-thirds of the total population of the eleven Northern States, and on this quota basis the Southern States should have furnished at least two-thirds as many enlisted men as were furnished by the eleven Northern States.

Further details relating to defaults of the South in the World War were cited in an editorial of *The Chicago Tribune* which follows:

The failure of Democratic States to furnish their share of volunteers is shown by War Department records made public early in April, 1918. These public official records show that all but eight States had filled their quotas in the regular army recruiting. Six of those eight States were Southern and two Northern. . . .

These six States, of course, had a total representation of twelve votes in the Senate. *The Congressional Record* shows that when Senator New's amendment for universal service was brought up for passage not one of these twelve Southern Senators voted for it. Six voted against it and six failed to vote.

Reference to manipulation to save the Democratic States from their fair quota under the draft is based in part upon the Surgeon General's records showing the number of physically incapacitated men passed by the Southern draft boards and credited to their quotas. In this connection we have at hand a letter signed by Hugh S. Johnson, of Moline, Ill., which, while protesting that as Deputy Provost Marshal General he must have known of manipulation had there been any, admits that ''it is true that large numbers of the quotas furnished by Southern States were composed of Negroes who were not incorporated into fighting divisions, but were sent to France in labor battalions.'' They were unfit to fight, but they counted in the draft quotas as soldiers.

Our statement that Illinois and Indiana boys in large numbers were used to fill up the ranks of Southern outfits is substantiated by the records of the Blackhawk division and the Blue Ridge division. Three hundred soldiers of the Blackhawk division were sent to Camp Lee as replacements for the Blue Ridge division, and served with them until discharged. Instead of coming home with their Northern buddies they were sent to Newport News and thence to Virginia, and were the last on the discharge list. . . .

The soldiers know that the Democratic States did not furnish volunteers for the war. They know also that the draft law was manipulated by the Democratic Administration to spare the Southern States from furnishing their quotas of troops. They know that boys from Illinois and Indiana were sent to fill up the divisions accredited to the Democratic States.

When the United States entered the World War, the problem of using the Negro as a soldier was freely discussed. Leaders of the Oligarchy in the South insisted that the Negro should not be used at all; that he should be excluded from the draft, or if drafted, he should be mobilized for work only. The Southern newspapers were filled with stories relating to the probable uprising of Negroes and the alleged danger of placing arms in their hands with which to fight for their country. Serious race conflicts in the South were prognosticated if the Negroes were drafted. It matters not what question may arise, whether industrial, social or political, or even the vital matter of saving the life of the Nation, there always comes the same old provincial and racial prejudice from political leaders of the South, and, without exception, their prophecies of evil come to naught.

In spite of the objections it was felt that the Negro would be needed in the army, and when the law was passed the draft regulations were applied to Negroes the same as to whites. The white man and the black man were required to register at the same place and at the same time. There was a great deal of discussion with reference to where the Negro troops should be trained, whether they should be placed with the white troops, or in separate camps, whether they should be trained in camps nearest the place where they were drafted, and particularly whether those drafted in the South should be sent to camps in the South. Respecting the race question in the army, after

America entered the World War, the second report of the Provost Marshal General says:

Color and race were, of course, not material under the law and the regulations for the purpose of the classification (except so far as non-citizen Indians were exempt from draft). But the organization of the army placed colored soldiers in separate units; and the several calls for mobilization were, therefore, affected by this circumstance, in that no calls could be issued for colored registrants until the organizations were ready for them.

In comparing the colored and white classifications, the Provost Marshal General made the following statement:

In the first place, enlistments depleted the white Class 1 in the South of a large proportion of its eligibles, enlistments not being available for colored registrants, except to a negligible degree. (Only 1.5 per cent. of enlistments were of colored men.)

Cumulative evidence of the loyalty and patriotism of the Negroes, and their eagerness for active service in the army, is found in the very full reports of the Provost Marshal General:

The records of appeals from rulings on dependency show that in the South, as a whole, the average annual income of those making dependency claims is surprisingly low, and the average for the colored race is undoubtedly lower than for the whites. . . . After making all these special allowances, it should be noted that the numbers selected for full military service were, respectively: Colored, 342,277, White, 1,916,750, and that these figures represent respectively 31.74 and 26.84 per cent. of the total colored and the total white registrants (of the first two registrations), thus leaving them only five per cent. apart. . . . Now the same Table 53 shows that, for every one hundred men examined physically, the ratio of colored men found qualified physically for general military service was substantially higher than the ratio for white men, by just five per cent., viz: 74.60 per cent. as against 69.71 per cent.; this difference in physical qualifications therefore accounts for this remaining excess (five per cent.) of colored registrants over white registrants accepted for full military service.

His race furnished its quota, and uncomplainingly, yes, cheerfully. History, indeed, will be unable to record the fullness of his spirit in the war, for the reason that opportunities for enlistment were not open to him to the same extent as to the whites. But enough can be gathered from the records to show that he was filled with the same feeling of patriotism, the same martial spirit that fired his white fellow citizens in the cause for world freedom. . . .

That the men of the colored race were as ready to serve as their white neighbors is amply proved by the reports from the local boards. A Pennsylvania Board, remarking upon the eagerness of its colored registrants to be inducted, illustrated this by the action of one registrant who, upon learning that his employer had had him placed upon the Emergency Fleet list, quit his job. Another registrant, who was believed by the board to be above draft age, insisted that he was not, and, in stating that he was not married, explained that he "wanted only one war at a time."

In dealing with the Negroes, Southern boards gained a richness of experience that is without parallel. No other class of citizens was more loyal to the Government, or more ready to answer the country's call. The only blot upon their military record was the great number of delinquents among the more ignorant; but in the majority of cases this was traced to an ignorance of the regulations, or to the withholding of mail by the landlord (often himself an aristocratic slacker) in order to retain the man's labor.

It was charged that, despite the objections which the "white South made to the enlistment and conscription of colored men, every means was used to exempt as few possible from military service." It was further charged that in many sections of the country exemptions were granted white men who were single, with practically no dependents,—

while Negroes were conscripted into service regardless of their urgent need in agriculture, or the essential industries, and without considering their family relations or obligations.

The total colored registrants in the eleven Southern States were 1,595,698, which was 31.78 per cent. of total registrants in these States. The total white registrants in these States were 3,425,726, which was 68.22 per cent. of all registrants. The per cent. of colored population in the eleven Southern States, as of July 1, 1917, as estimated by the Census Bureau, was 34.06, the white population being 65.94 per cent. of the total population. When we take into consideration the migration of Negroes from the South during 1916 and 1917, a per cent. of 31.78 colored registrants is an excellent showing for the Negroes.

An example of the willingness and eagerness of the Negroes to fight for America and civilization is found in the fine record of a local draft board in the "black belt" district of Chicago containing 30,000 persons, of whom 90 per cent., at the time America entered the war, were colored. This district registered upward of 9,000 and sent 1,850 colored men to cantonments. Of these 1,850 there were only 125 rejections. On November 11, 1918, when the armistice was declared, this district had 7,832 men passed by examiners and ready for call to the colors.

The beneficiaries of the spoils system and corrupt practices under the Wilson Administration, who have held Negroes in peonage, robbed and murdered them, are not the men who fought the battles of their country in the World War or any other war. But the Negro harbored no revenge; he did not take advantage of the opportunity that came to him during the Civil War to injure the white man; and he was loyal to his country, open and honorable, during the World War. Not one of the eleven States composing the Solid South can show a record of so large a percentage of the white population being inducted into the service as was the percentage of Negro population in the Chicago district to which I alluded in a preceding paragraph.

From Bunker Hill to the Argonne, the Negro has carried the American flag with dauntless courage and with honor and glory to the flag. When the German propagandist and spy went among them with tempting offers, the Negroes continued loyal and steadfast; when the draft came the Negroes did not skulk. They refused to follow the white propagandist of pacifism and non-resistance, and they were not among the spoilsmen. Those who know the Negro, who can understand and appreciate the simple folklore and plaintive songs of this oppressed race; and those who have seen with a sense of justice the marvelous civic and educational progress of this race, have an abiding faith in the patriotism, civic and economic worth of the American Negro. Through many hardships and great suffering the Negro has continued to advance. Often he has stumbled when there was hardly a friendly hand extended to lift him up; often he has been wrongfully accused when no advocate appeared to plead his cause. But never in a crisis has he faltered.

A summary of casualties among members of the American Expeditionary Forces during the World War (Report of The Adjutant General, December 15, 1919), from the eleven Southern and eleven Northern States under consideration, is shown in the following table:

SUMMARY OF CASUALTIES, OFFICERS AND MEN, AMERICAN EXPEDITIONARY FORCES

	Deceased	Prisoners	Wounded	Total casualties
Northern States .	19,738	854	54,391	74,983
Southern States .	14,799	452	34,805	50,057
United States .	76,789	4,420	220,183	301,395

The State of North Carolina, for example, that exercised so much influence in the affairs of government during the Wilson Administration, had a total of 5,799 casualties, while the State of Minnesota had total casualties of 7,323. The population (1917) of Minnesota was 121,936 less than the population of North Carolina. The population of Michigan (1917) was 198,-425 more than that of Georgia; there were 10,369 casualties among the soldiers from Michigan and 4,425 casualties among those from Georgia. In 1917, the white population of Nebraska was, in round figures, the same as the white population of Arkansas, but the total population of Arkansas was 482,217 more than Nebraska. The total casualties among the soldiers from Nebraska were 3,041, while the casualties from Arkansas were 2,658. But these outstanding facts relating to the record of the Southern States in the World War, as expressed in statistics, lose their significance unless we consider the strange anomaly of the whole political situation in America during the World War. It was clearly and forcibly expressed in an editorial of *The Chicago Tribune*, February 9, 1919, from which I take the following:

With almost unanimity the families of those in supreme authority stayed far away from the battlefield. One conspicuous young man was the son of a father who could have placed him anywhere in the war. He went to the Naval Academy during the war, which incidentally was the safest place in America, and resigned upon the dawning of peace. Other conspicuous young men joined the marines, but not the marines of Chateau Thierry. We read of them on moonlight excursions along the Potomac at a time when other young men were doing their night life to the illumination of star shells. . . .

American soldiers walked through the snows of wintry France without socks on their feet and wearing paper shoes. American soldiers manned their guns in the deadly fumes of poison gas with ill-fitting masks. American infantry charged without support of artillery. Americans who had not been taught how to fight machine guns marched against machine guns, and they marched never more.

In a great crisis of American history the Southern Oligarchy failed to uphold the dignity and honor of the United States. The absence of virile patriotism and broad statesmanship during the World War strikingly and pathetically revealed the sad truth concerning the gradual decline of the South.

By their narrow and provincial policies, the political leaders of the South who dictated the policies of the Government under the Wilson régime misled the constituency whom they were supposed to represent until a large majority of the Southern people, uninformed regarding the actual situation, failed to come up to the full measure of their patriotic duty as American citizens, and they fell far behind the splendid record made by their forefathers in the early history of America. A people living under such depressing conditions as have prevailed in the South for many years could hardly produce leadership capable of dealing with great questions of a world crisis.

It is safe to say that ninety per cent. or perhaps a larger per cent., of white and colored people in the Southern States were sincerely in sympathy with the Allies before America entered the World War. Yet, strange to say, a majority of leading Senators and Representatives in Congress from these States were opposed to the Allies, Great Britain in particular, before the United States declared war against Germany.

The Wilson Administration, if not pro-German, was anti-British before America entered the war. In support of this charge there is cumulative evidence based on official records and the statements of those in high positions. It was difficult to explain the actual situation, but our Ambassador to Great Britain, Mr. Page, understood the crisis in the United States, and he possessed the patriotism, ability, patience and fortitude to deal discreetly but courageously with a very delicate situation.

CHAPTER XX

THE ERA OF PATRIOTISM AND STATESMANSHIP

In the early history of America, especially during the formative period of the Union, the South produced men of great ability who were able not only to take a prominent part in making the United States a free and independent nation, but also to grasp and deal with great international questions of that troublous period in world history. One vitally important episode relating to our foreign affairs in the early history of the United States well illustrates the high order of statesmanship and intense patriotism of distinguished men from the Southern States.

The French Revolution soon followed the War of the American Revolution. Then came the protracted period of Napoleonic wars which tested the strength of every government in Europe. During this world crisis there came from the South some of the greatest men of this important epoch in the history of civilization. One of the most interesting and important events in our early history, which brought great honor to the South and gave evidence of the high class of statesmen who represented the Southern States, was our experience with France under the Directory.

The Directory was the name given to the French executive government from October 28, 1795, to November 9, 1799, that followed the dissolution of the National Convention, by which the first republic of France had been governed during the stormy period after the overthrow of the Bourbon dynasty.

As stated by Dr. Willis Fletcher Johnson, in *America's Foreign Relations:*

The Minister for Foreign Affairs was Bonaparte's close friend, Talleyrand, one of the shrewdest but most unscrupulous and dishonest of men. The French Government had already begun a course of arrogance and oppression toward all European States which were weak enough to make such a policy safe. . . . Chief among the practitioners and beneficiaries of this sordid scoundrelism was Talleyrand himself, and since France was already practicing oppression against America with impunity, he determined in addition to try blackmail and extortion.

For the purpose of adjusting the differences with France, and, if possible, reaching a peaceable settlement of matters in controversy, three commissioners were appointed by President Adams. Two of these commissioners, John Marshall and Charles Cotesworth Pinckney, were distinguished citizens of the South. The third member of the commission to France was Elbridge Gerry of Massachusetts.

Prior to the appointment of the commissioners, there was a feeling of great friendship for France in the United States. Adulation of everything French had been the popular rage. French cockades were mounted on every hat; French flags adorned public and private buildings; orators vied with one another in eulogizing France. Even the title "Citizen" was substituted for the ordinary modes of address.

John Marshall was a Federalist, the most distinguished of American jurists, and for 34 years he was Chief Justice of the United States Supreme Court. He was a native of Virginia and had distinguished himself before his appointment on the French commission, not only as an able jurist but also as a patriot and soldier. At the outbreak of the American Revolutionary War he entered the army as a volunteer and soon rose to the rank of first lieutenant, and by 1777 he was a captain. He was at Valley Forge during the memorable winter of 1777-78. It was through the efforts of Marshall and Madison that Virginia was induced to adopt the Federal Constitution, but the greater credit perhaps is due to Marshall because he was particularly effective in refuting the arguments of Patrick Henry against adoption of the Constitution. As stated by Colonel Allan B. Magruder in his *John Marshall—(American Statesmen)*:

The great fame of John Marshall, as Chief Justice of the United States, has so far over-shadowed the remembrance of his other services to his countrymen, as to render many of them oblivious of his public career as a soldier, legislator, envoy, historian, and statesman, both previous to and after his elevation to the first place on the Supreme Bench.

Charles Cotesworth Pinckney, of South Carolina, the other Southern member of the French commission, came from a distinguished South Carolina family. He was educated in England, at Oxford and the Middle Temple, where he studied under Blackstone himself. After studying for a time at the Royal Military Academy at Caen, France, he returned to America. He served with distinction in the Revolutionary War and was promoted to be a Brigadier General, and he was also on Washington's staff. Pinckney was a prominent member of the Constitutional Convention in 1787. On his return to the United States, a war with France seemed imminent, and he was appointed a Major-General. He was the Federalist candidate for Vice-President in 1800 and for President in 1804 and 1808, and he was the third President General of the Society of the Cincinnati.

Thomas Pinckney, brother of Charles Cotesworth Pinckney, served with distinction in the Revolutionary War. He was Governor of South Carolina, and he was sent on a special mission to Spain, where he negotiated the important treaty guaranteeing to the United States the free navigation of the Mississippi river and the right of deposit at New Orleans for at least three years.

Elbridge Gerry was an anti-Federalist and was conspicuous as an opponent to the Society of the Cincinnati, and he was also very active in his opposition to the Federal Constitution as finally adopted. He was appointed on the French mission as a recognition of the opposition party. His record was not such as to inspire confidence, but he was supposed to be a warm friend of France; moreover, it was a custom in our early history, and continued a custom down to the administration of Wilson, to recognize the two leading political parties in appointments on matters relating to the settlement of troubles with foreign nations, especially in making treaties. Gerry was one of the ardent Republicans who had welcomed Talleyrand to America. His appointment as one of the commissioners to France was also a concession to the radical friends of France in America.

Shortly after their arrival in France, the American Commissioners were informed that a "gratuity" would be necessary before beginning negotiations on the matters in dispute between America and France. In other words, it was suggested that a gift of money was a necessary preliminary to any conference with Talleyrand. The negotiations were brought to an abrupt and dramatic end when Monsieur Bellamy, speaking for Talleyrand, pressed the American Commissioners for an immediate and categorical answer to the French demands for money.

"What is your answer?" demanded Hottinguer for his principal, Bellamy. "We have already spoken to that point very explicitly," was Pinckney's response. "No, you have not," protested Hottinguer. "What is your answer?" "It is No, and No; and again No; not a single sixpence. We will spend millions for defense," said Pinckney, "but not one cent for tribute."

Marshall and Pinckney conducted the negotiations with Talleyrand and very justly received all the honors of that early and dramatic experience in American diplomacy. Referring to Gerry's record on the French mission, Colonel Magruder says:

His conduct provoked severe criticism at home and lowered his character with his countrymen, though he was generally accredited with fair intentions.

When the first dispatches from the American Commissioners in Paris were received in the United States, March 5, 1798, President Adams sent a message to Congress, advising that news had been received from the Commissioners. The dispatches had not been fully deciphered, but enough of their contents was known to justify him in warning the people not to expect good news, and later, on March 19, the President announced the failure of the mission and recommended that steps be taken immediately to defend the seacoast and protect the commerce of the country. Friends of France, led by Jefferson, denounced the President's warning as a subterfuge designed to create prejudice against our former friends and sister republic, and demanded the production of the official documents themselves. It seems that President Adams had anticipated what the friends of France would do in America.

The opposition of Jefferson gave Hamilton the opportunity he so much desired. He induced some of his followers in Congress to propose a resolution, which was adopted, demanding to see the original correspondence relating to the negotiations with Talleyrand. This was precisely what the President desired; and concealing the names of Talleyrand's agents, designating them as Messrs. X., Y., Z., he submitted the whole story of the Commissioner's experience in Paris. This revelation startled the whole country. As related by Dr. Johnson, in *America's Foreign Relations:*

A tidal wave of amazement, indignation, and wrath swept over the country, against the venal French Government. Adams was the hero of the hour. Republicans and Federalists alike rallied to his support. Only Jefferson himself and a few extreme Republicans held aloof. The National Anthem, ''Hail Columbia,'' was written as a war-song against France, and was sung on every hand; as was also ''Adams and Liberty,'' set to music now known as the ''Star Spangled Banner.''

During the excitement and preparation for war with France, Marshall and Pinckney returned from Paris and their arrival produced another outburst of patriotism; parades, public receptions, congratulatory addresses and complimentary dinners. Marshall and Pinckney were the heroes of the hour. Meanwhile, however, Captain Stephen Decatur became the greatest hero of that time by capturing a French privateer preying on American commerce, which he brought into port as a prize.

In the War of 1812 the South furnished some of the most distinguished commanders, among whom were Harrison and Scott, of Virginia, and Jackson of Tennessee; and in the Mexican War of 1846-7, Generals Taylor and Scott, the two military leaders, were natives of Virginia. Of the fifteen Presidents from 1789 to 1861, eight were from the South, and a ninth, William Henry Harrison, was born and educated in Virginia. During the seventy-two years between 1789 and 1861 Southern Presidents occupied the executive chair forty-eight years, or two-thirds of the time.

In the early history of this country, and during the formative period of the Republic, the Southern colonies, and later the States, were as emphatic, and perhaps more emphatic, than were the Northern colonies and States, in their opposition to slavery. Virginia was the first State to prohibit the further importation of slaves. In 1772, the Virginia colonies addressed a petition to the King in which they said:

We implore your Majesty's paternal assistance in arresting a calamity of the most alarming nature. The importation of slaves from Africa hath long been considered a trade of great inhumanity and under the present encouragement, we have too much fear will endanger the existence of your Majesty's American dominion.

As related by Bancroft, "Virginia resisted the British commercial system from abhorrence of the slave trade. The Legislature of Virginia had repeatedly shown a disposition to obstruct the commerce." Substantially every great leader of that period in Virginia was outspoken in opposition to slavery. Washington, Jefferson, James Madison, Patrick Henry, George Mason, Richard Henry Lee and John Randolph were opposed to slavery. Mason denounced the slave trade as an "infernal traffic." In the Virginia Convention, called to ratify the Federal Constitution, Mason opposed ratification and his objections were stated in these words:

The augmentation of slaves weakens the States; and such a trade is diabolical in itself, and disgraceful to mankind; yet, by this Constitution, it is continued twenty years. As much as I value a union of all the States, I would not admit the Southern States into the Union, unless they agree to the discontinuance of this disgraceful trade, because it would bring weakness, and not strength, to the Union.

Richard Henry Lee, descended from one of the oldest families in Virginia, was educated in England; his "first recorded speech was against slavery, in behalf of human freedom." As stated by Rhodes—*History of the United States:*

On many pages of Virginia history may one read of noble efforts by noble men toward freeing their State from slavery. But the story of the end is a repeated tale; the seed sown fell among thorns, and the thorns sprung up and choked them.

Georgia, the last of the thirteen original colonies to be settled, prohibited the importation of slaves. Oglethorpe, the founder of the colony, said: "Slavery is against the Gospel as well as the fundamental law of England. We refused, as trustees, to make a law permitting such a horrid crime." After his great work in Georgia where he had observed the evils of slavery, John Wesley said:

Men-buyers are exactly on a level with men-stealers. . . . American slavery is the vilest that ever saw the sun; it constitutes the sum of all villainies.

In the early history of South Carolina there was pronounced opposition to slavery. In 1764, a tax of 117 pounds was placed on the importation of a slave. This import tax, supposed to be prohibitive, continued until the Revolution, and after the Revolution, in 1787, South Carolina passed an Act prohibiting the importation of slaves. Two years before the Declaration of Independence, a convention of South Carolina citizens resolved,—

that his Majesty's subjects in North America (without respect to color or other accidents) are entitled to all the inherent rights and liberties of his natural born subjects within the Kingdom of Great Britain.

John Laurens of South Carolina was one of the most distinguished officers of the American army in the War of the American Revolution. He was a gentleman of polite education, a fearless patriot and a gallant officer. In the language of George Livermore, Laurens was "one of the most patriotic and brave of the Southern officers, and has not improperly been called the 'Chevalier Bayard of America.' " He tried to persuade his native State to authorize him to levy and command a regiment of Negro troops. He had seen the colored soldiers in service in the Northern States and he knew the splendid record they had made and he proposed to offer freedom to all slaves who would fight for the cause of liberty in America. The Legislature of South Carolina would not heed the recommendations of Congress nor the entreaties of Laurens. In a letter to Washington, written only a few months before he was killed in battle, Colonel Laurens wrote:

The plan which brought me to this country was urged with all the zeal which the subject inspired, both in our Privy Council and Assembly; but the single voice of reason was drowned by the howlings of a triple-headed monster, in which prejudice, avarice, and pusillanimity were united. . . . Some hopes have been lately given me from Georgia; but I fear, when the question is put, we shall be outvoted there with as much disparity as we have been in this country.

Like other great leaders of the South in our early history, prior to the ascendancy of the Slave Oligarchy, in his early public career Calhoun was distinctly nationalistic in his politics, laying himself open to a charge of inconsistency when he later became a leader of the strict constructionists. In 1816 he was in favor of a national bank, advocated the strengthening of the navy for defense, and favored as a means of binding together the widely separated States not only permanent improvements in the shape of public roads but also a protective tariff. In 1820 he favored the Missouri Compromise. He was the first to announce the change of sentiment in the South on the slavery question, and he became the recognized leader of the new economic theories and political policies of that section.

One-half of the delegates to the American abolition conventions between 1794 and 1809 were from the Southern States, and it has been stated that the earliest American publications advocating emancipation were published in the Southern States. In 1827, a year before Jackson was elected President, and only nine years before Calhoun came forward with his doctrine of the "peculiar institution" that put slavery above the Constitution, there were 106 anti-slavery societies in the South to 24 in the North, or more than four to one. The Southern societies had 5,150 members to 920 in the Northern societies, or more than five to one. It is perhaps true that the change in the South which came with Mr. Calhoun's doctrine was not so much a change of public sentiment as a change of political policy for partisan purposes, in order to strengthen the hold of a privileged class on a section of the country that was rapidly developing an economic power which, with slavery, could be so easily controlled by an oligarchy. Because of that change, leading and influential citizens of the South who opposed slavery found it necessary to leave that section and continue their work in the North.

Among the earliest and most earnest advocates of abolition in the United States were the Grimke sisters; Sarah More and Angelina Emily. They were both born in Charleston, South Carolina, where their father, John F. Grimke, was a prominent lawyer and large slave-holder. After their father's death, the two sisters freed their slaves and removed to Philadelphia; Sarah going first in 1821 and Angelina following in 1828. These two

sisters, noble patriots and humanitarians, were among the leading spirits of the American Anti-Slavery Society, delivering
public lectures and writing pamphlets. Sarah Grimke wrote
an *Epistle to the Clergy of the Southern States,* and Angelina
wrote *An Appeal to the Christian Women of the South.*

James G. Birney was the leader of the conservative abolitionists during the early history of the abolition movement, and
he was earnest, fearless and able. Born in Danville, Kentucky,
graduated at Princeton in 1810, he removed to a plantation in
the vicinity of Huntsville, Alabama, in 1818, where he engaged
in the practice of law. He was a member of the Alabama Legislature and the leader of the Constitutional Abolitionists and
was a candidate of the Liberty party for President in 1840 and
again in 1844.

A decided change occurred in the attitude of the South after
the administration of Jackson. The manhood and patriotism of
the Southern States declined and consequently this section of
the country which had furnished so many notable men in the
early years of American history ceased to produce men of the
high standard of ability and the intense patriotism that had
formerly marked the distinguished careers of the representative
men of the South. The most notable exceptions to this decline
were found in the Confederate generals of the Civil War. The
splendid type of manhood, the prowess, military genius and fortitude of Lee, Longstreet, Jackson, Johnston, Bragg, Albert Sidney Johnston, Admiral Semmes and others, won the admiration
of the world. Friend and foe have paid tribute not only to
the valor and fortitude of the Confederate soldiers, but also to
the great commanders under whom they fought.

Nor were the men from the South who fought in the Union
Army less distinguished for their valor, fortitude and ability.
A very large number of representative citizens of the South not
only refused to follow the leadership of the Slave Oligarchy
into secession, but also went further by offering their services
to the cause of the Union, and in this list of Southern patriots
we find some of the most distinguished men who served in the
Union Army and Navy.

Admiral Farragut, who attained the highest rank in the Navy
during the Civil War, was a native of Tennessee. Rear-Admiral

Winslow, commander of the *Kearsage,* who, in one of the most important naval engagements of the war, defeated and sank the Confederate cruiser, *Alabama,* off Cherbourg harbor, was born at Wilmington, North Carolina. Rear-Admiral Samuel P. Lee, grandson of Richard Henry Lee, was a native of Virginia. He was in the blockade off Charleston, in the expedition against New Orleans, commanded the advance division below Forts Jackson and St. Phillip, and commanded the advance position in attacks on Vicksburg. Later he commanded the North Atlantic Squadron, engaged in blockading the coasts of North Carolina and Virginia.

General George H. Thomas was born in Virginia. He commanded the Fourteenth Army Corps in the campaign of Middle Tennessee; he was the ranking officer in the field at Chickamauga, and for his distinguished service in that battle he gained the title of the "Rock of Chickamauga."

John C. Fremont, first candidate of the Republican party for President, and later a Major General in the Union Army, was born at Savannah, Georgia, and educated in Charleston, South Carolina. Major General John L. Pope was a native of Kentucky, as was also Major General Rousseau, who commanded the Fifth Division of the Army of the Cumberland at Stone River, and at Chickamauga.

William Birney, a son of James G. Birney, was born at Huntsville, Alabama. He took an active part in the Revolution of 1848 in France; entered the Union Army at the beginning of the Civil War and rose to the rank of Brigadier General. He served with conspicuous gallantry and commanded a division at the close of the war. David Bell Birney, another son of James G. Birney, was born at Huntsville. He practiced law in Philadelphia before the war and entered the Federal Army as a lieutenant colonel in the 23d Pennsylvania Infantry. He served with gallantry at Fredericksburg and Chancellorsville and, in May, 1863, he became Major General of Volunteers, and during part of the battle of Gettysburg he commanded the Third Army Corps. After July, 1864, and until his death in October, 1864, he was in command of the Tenth Corps of the Army of the James. Birney's and another division formed the first line in the attack on the Bloody Angle, Lee's center, at Spottsylvania.   According to Charles C. Anderson, in *Fighting by Southern Federals,*—

Twenty Southern men commanded infantry corps. . . . There were many Southern generals of divisions. . . . There were 160 Southern Federals who commanded brigades of battle, fighting with distinction. . . . About one-half of the Southern graduates of West Point, numbering 162, took the Federal side.   The number of Confederate Generals was 425.   The Federal Generals totaled 680; thus about one-fourth of the Federal generals were born in the South.   There were a great many Southern officers of other inferior ranks. . . . There were 4,000 commissioned officers from Kentucky in the Federal service.   Three hundred and twenty-one Southerners left the United States Navy; three hundred and fifty remained.   There were eighty naval commanders of Southern birth who were actively engaged on the Federal side with distinction.

There were 296,579 white soldiers, 137,676 colored soldiers, living in the South, and approximately 200,000 men living in the North who were born in the South, making 634,255 Southern soldiers who fought in the Union Army.   The Union sentiment was strong enough in Kentucky, Maryland and Missouri to prevent these States from going with the Confederacy.   A large part of the population of East Tennessee was opposed to secession, but the Confederacy succeeded in getting control of the State.   In the mountain regions of Alabama, Georgia, North Carolina and South Carolina, a very large majority of the people were opposed to secession.   The Union sentiment in the South was strong and it was only through the coercive measures of the radical secessionists that the eleven States were finally forced into disunion.   As related by Nicolay and Hay—*Abraham Lincoln:*

It is a significant feature in the secession proceedings of the six Cotton States which first took action that their conventions in every case neglected or refused to submit their ordinances of secession to a vote of the people for ratification or rejection.   The whole spirit and all the phenomena of the movement forbade their doing so.   From first to last the movement was forced, not spontaneous, official not popular; and its leaders could not risk the period of doubt which a submission of the ordinances would involve, much less their rejection at the polls.   To this general rule, Texas, the seventh seceding State, formed an exception.   Governor Houston opposed secession, and as long as possible thwarted the conspirators' plans.

In the State of Georgia the secession resolution was rushed through under the previous question, 166 yeas to 130 nays. On the following day an inquiry into the election for delegates was throttled with similar ferocity, 168 to 127.

Writing about the "Hill People of the South" of the Appalachian upland, Professor Shaler says:

These mountaineers—they may be better termed the "hill people of the South"—were an eminently peculiar people. They are not to be compared with the poor white trash. . . . If the Confederacy had won its independence, its plantation districts, with a relatively small voting population, would soon have had to settle an acccount with the people of the hills. As it was, the existence of this folk in the great ridge of country extending from the Northern States to within two hundred miles of the Gulf of Mexico was an element of weakness which went far to give success to the Federal arms. It kept Kentucky from seceding, prevented the region of West Virginia from being of any value to the rebellion, and weakened its control in several other States. In all, somewhere near one hundred thousand recruits came to the Federal army from this part of the South. It is not improbable that to this folk we may attribute the failure of the great revolt.

If the question had been left to an honest vote of the people, perhaps not more than two of the Southern States would have voted for secession. It is interesting to observe that from the States where the Union sentiment was strongest in the South there have come some of the most distinguished men, and undoubtedly the greatest heroes of the South. Virginia and Tennessee are the most notable examples of this fact. The Union sentiment was perhaps stronger in Tennessee than in any one of the eleven States that seceded. Sam Houston was a native of Virginia but Tennessee and Texas were the scenes of his great achievements; David Crockett was a native of Tennessee and he was a fine type of American manhood and patriotism.

Sam Davis, of Tennessee, was one of the heroes of the Nation. In the city of Nashville there is a bronze statue of this young Confederate hero. Every State in the Union contributed to the cost of this monument, through an individual or organization, and a number of the Grand Army posts were most generous in their gifts, and the Grand Army was represented at the unveiling of the statue. Sam Davis was one of Shaw's scouts and was sent by General Bragg with a party into middle Tennessee to secure information regarding the movement of a certain division of Federal troops. When the order was given, the men were told of the extreme danger of the mission and were warned that few were likely to return. Several of the party were killed and Davis was captured. There was found on his person and hidden under the leather of his saddle, maps, descriptions of the fortifications at Nashville, and a full report of the Federal army in Tennessee. Davis knew that death was inevitable. When he was taken before General Dodge no pleadings nor threats could influence him to make any statements concerning the source of his information. In answer to threats and questions, Davis said:

I know that I will have to die, but there is no power on earth that will make me tell you. If I die I will do so with the feeling that I died doing my duty to God and my country.

General Dodge believed to the last that Davis could be prevailed upon to give the name of his informer. As he was mounting the scaffold, Captain Chickasaw, of General Dodge's staff, came with an offer not only of life, but a free pardon, and a good horse and safe conduct into the Confederate lines if he would tell. "It is not too late," the officer pleaded. Young Davis with a quiet dignity said to him: "If I had a thousand lives I would lose them all, here and now, before I would betray my friend or the confidence of my informer." When immunity was offered Nathan Hale his answer was: "I regret that I have but one life to give my country." Sam Davis's answer was: "If I had a thousand lives I would lose them all."

The greatest hero of the World War was Alvin C. York, of Tennessee. Major General George Duncan, who commanded the 82nd Division in which Sergeant York fought, said that he was the most distinguished soldier the world had produced:

York's deeds are of a character that go down in history and make our boys patriots in time of stress. He is not only a very unpretentious soldier but an unassuming, modest man. His achievement was the most outstanding act of gallantry not only that this World War has produced, but that I have ever heard of. He is not only modest, absolutely, but unabashed unafraid, in the presence of any gathering or any enemy.

The world is familiar with the details of Sergeant York's heroic conduct. He killed 25 Germans, captured 132 more, put

35 German machine guns out of commission, and smashed a counter-attack by an entire German battalion. When Sergeant York returned to America he received greater honors than were paid to any other soldier from the United States in the World War. He was not only a hero of the war, but he was no less a hero in peace. He declined numerous attractive offers, to exploit his achievements as a hero of the World War. After his return to the United States, Sergeant York traveled over the country lecturing in the interest of rural schools for his native State. Declining all offers for his services, Sergeant York said:

I did not accept any of the large offers, because I wanted to help the people at my home to get an education which I could not get. I had rather see these children go pattering to and from school than to have a millon dollars and see them without school.

Sergeant William Sandlin, of the 132nd Infantry, is another hero of the World War who was born in the South. He followed the example of Sergeant York in an effort to improve the educational opportunities for the poor people of his native State. Sergeant Samuel Woodfill, to whom General Pershing referred as the outstanding hero of the World War, was born in Indiana. Thus it seems that, in spite of the defaults of the South in the World War, cited in a preceding chapter, which were due, as I have already stated, to the policies of the Oligarchy, the South may justly claim two of the three outstanding heroes of the World War.

In their devotion to their country, Sergeant Jasper, David Crockett, Sam Houston, Sergeants Samuel Davis, Alvin York, Samuel Woodfill and William Sandlin were splendid types of the virile American stock which has saved this Nation in every crisis of its history. It was this British and French race, with the British largely predominating in population and consequently in leadership, that conceived and created the new Republic of the Western Hemisphere. It was substantially the same stock, North and South, differing only in the advantages and opportunities afforded by birth, early environment, education or wealth. The Dutch represented a comparatively small proportion of the original American stock, but they brought with them the spirit of liberty which predominated in the heroic struggle of the Netherlands for political independence and civic progress.

In this virile American stock of British, French and Dutch lineage, there never have been any material points of difference in patriotism and loyalty to democratic institutions, on account of birth, education, wealth or social position. Washington, Franklin, Adams, Lincoln and Roosevelt were in the same class as Americans and patriots. The ancestors of George Washington, John Adams and Benjamin Franklin came from Northamptonshire, England, and they brought with them to America the spirit of Simon de Montfort. Through seven centuries the forefathers of the original American stock slowly evolved the great democratic principles of American institutions. It was a common interest and common purpose of educated and uneducated, rich and poor, an inspiration of Christian civilization, that conceived and wrought out this new federation of democracies. The expansion of this Republic, its growth and development, have been under the guidance and direction of the men and women whose fathers created the Nation and sustained it in its early history. The pioneers and pathfinders who carried the American flag and American institutions to the far West were of the same British and French lineage.

It was the non-slaveholding class of the South who fought the great battles of the Confederacy. There were many of this same American class, including, as we have seen, distinguished leaders, who fought on the Union side. Men of the same stock who fought for the Confederacy were just as conscientious, patriotic and valorous as those who fought for the Union. Those who fought for the Confederacy were influenced by the necessities of their environments.

The poor whites of the South, who live apart and have no voice in the Government which was created through the valor and sacrifices of their fathers, have been not only exploited by an Oligarchy but they have also been grossly misrepresented and traduced by their oppressors. These non-slaveholding whites of the South fought with Lincoln, d'Estang and Pulaski at Savannah; they were with Campbell, Sevier and Shelby at King's Mountain; and these Virginians, Carolinians and Tennesseans were with Morgan, Pickens and McCall at Cowpens, where they defeated Tarleton and his "terrible men," and made possible the capture of Cornwallis at Yorktown. They were with Jackson at New Orleans, where they defeated the British, and with him they defeated the Cherokees, Chickasaws and Seminoles. Their successful campaigns against the Spaniards and Seminoles weakened the power of Spain and made possible the acquisition of Florida. They carried the American flag to the City of Mexico; and of their dauntless courage in Texas it was said that "Thermopylæ had her messenger of defeat; the Alamo had none."

A large majority of the white people of the South, who were opprobriously called "poor whites" because they owned no slaves, were opposed to secession, but when their States called them they answered as their fathers had answered, and they fought with the same spirit and devotion that their fathers had shown in the early history of this country. When the remnant of those brave Americans who had followed Lee, Jackson, Longstreet, Johnston, Bragg and other commanders of the Confederate Army, returned from Appomattox and Durham Station to their ruined homes and impoverished lands, they did not idle, nor did they start a sectional propaganda of hatred against the brave men of the North whom they had so often faced on the battlefield. Nor did the Confederate soldier, who for four years met the Union soldier in the open, begin an inhuman and desultory war against the helpless and defenseless Negroes who had faithfully cared for the families of those who fought for slavery and disunion. With the Confederate soldier the Civil War ended at Appomattox; the racial conflicts were started by the oppressors of the men who fought their battles in the open. The Slave Oligarchy represented less than twenty per cent. of the white population of the South. This privileged class did not fight the battles of the American patriots in the War of the American Revolution, nor did they fight the battles of the Confederacy in the Civil War. With the ascendancy of this Oligarchy of spoilsmen there began a gradual decline in the South; a long period of unrest and provincialism has followed the era of national patriotism and statesmanship.

CHAPTER XXI

The institution of slavery seemed to develop among some of its leading advocates a spirit of law defiance, coarseness, vulgarity and rowdyism. For instance, in 1789, Benjamin Franklin, "then in his eighty-fourth year, the last of his life," signed as President, "an Address to the Public, from the Pennsylvania Society for Promoting Abolition of Slavery, and the Relief of Free Negroes Unlawfully Held in Bondage." This was the first petition for abolition of slavery in America and it was presented during the first session of the first Congress. The signing of this petition was the last public act of Benjamin Franklin, but the name of Franklin did not mollify the champions of slavery.

The address from the Quakers of Pennsylvania, presented to the House on the 11th of February, 1790, was taken up for debate March 17. During the progress of the debate on the address from the Abolitionists, Congressmen Jackson, of Georgia, and Smith, of South Carolina, were very bitter in their attacks on the petitioners. In referring to the debate on this petition, McMaster says:

> The discussion had not gone far before it surpassed in bitterness and vulgarity anything the House had yet listened to. Smith, of South Carolina, and Jackson, of Georgia, could not contain their wrath, and when arguments failed them, fell to abusing the Quakers, their religion, their morals, and their memorial. . . . Language low, indecent, and profane had been used; wit equally wretched and stale had been attempted.

Notwithstanding the opposition to slavery in Georgia and South Carolina, as indicated by laws passed in these colonies, to which I alluded in the preceding chapter, the influence of the minority slave owners and dealers in slaves was so dominant that the article in the original draft of the Declaration of Independence condemning slavery was struck out, as Jefferson explained, "in compliance to South Carolina and Georgia, who had never attempted to restrain the importation of slaves, and who, on the contrary, still wished to continue it."

After the change in their attitude respecting slavery, Georgia and the Carolinas steadily opposed any practicable measures for abolition of the slave trade. And these States particularly demanded that at no future time should slavery be forbidden in territories which they gave up of their own free will, and these territories in time became slave States. It was evident that the dominating Slave Oligarchy intended from the first to preserve and also to extend slavery, although every one of the Southern States had entered into a compact "neither to import or purchase any slave imported from Africa or elsewhere," and this obligation was binding upon each of the Southern States from the date of its adoption. It seems strange that three years after the passage of the Ordinance of 1787, with every vote from the South in its favor, we should find representatives from the South in the House and in the Senate bitterly denouncing petitions from the Society of Friends asking that slavery be abolished.

The history of the South from the time of the inventions which made possible the great economic power of cotton, is the history of a people struggling for existence by means of political subterfuges against the national spirit of Americanism, as well as against the Christian and enlightened spirit of the age. The invention of the Whitney gin was followed by a change of political creed and a new code of ethics in the South. The Southern planters and their close allies and fellow beneficiaries of slavery, the bankers and merchants, united in a demand not only for the perpetuation but also for the extension of slavery. Cotton was king and there was a demand not only for an extension of his domains, but also greater power over his subjects. Calhoun became the leader of the new thought. The Free States were divided; the Slave States were united. The South was solid for slavery and its own peculiar institutions, ready at all times for an alliance with the states rights party and the disgruntled and un-American element of the Northern States.

The change in the South on the slavery question came about gradually, but historians usually state that it was under Jackson's second Administration that this great change was first recognized. As stated in preceding chapters, the administration of Jackson brought many changes in the South, not only in its economic policy but also in the class of political leaders from the Southern States, as well as in the ideals and standards of political morality. It was on March 9, 1836, that Calhoun, in his speech against receiving petitions from Pennsylvania for the abolition of slavery in the District of Columbia, announced the change that had come in the South. He said:

The relation which now exists between the two races in the slaveholding States has existed for two centuries. It has grown with our growth, and strengthened with our strength. It has entered into and modified all our institutions, civil and political. None other can be substituted. We will not, cannot permit it to be destroyed. . . . Come what will, should it cost every drop of blood and every cent of property, we must defend ourselves. I ask neither sympathy nor compassion for the slave-holding States. We can take care of ourselves.

Calhoun was the leader and ablest proponent of the radical pro-slavery element, and he never forgave President Jackson for the toast the President proposed April 13, 1830, on the anniversary of Jefferson's birthday, in these words: "The Federal Union—it must and shall be maintained." It electrified the North and fell like a damper on the followers of Calhoun. Ben Perley Poore writes in his interesting narrative as follows:

It is related that in his last days, Jackson stated to his physician, at the Hermitage, that "posterity will condemn me more because I was persuaded not to hang John C. Calhoun as a traitor, than for any other act of my life."

The Southern "Nullifiers," who had been suppressed by Jackson, began to revive under the more genial rule of Van Buren, and they established an "organ" called *The Washington Chronicle*. After the election of Polk, in 1844, except the interim of the Taylor-Fillmore Administration, the Slave Oligarchy had absolute control of the national Government until the election of Lincoln. The slight changes and nominal surrender of Southern power under Taylor and Fillmore were more than offset immediately after the inauguration of Pierce, who was "proud" and boastful of the fact that he had "never cast a vote, nor given utterance to an opinion antagonistic to the slave interests of the South." He was the faithful Northern ally and subservient tool of the Slave Oligarchy.

From the beginning of the Pierce Administration, the provincial egotism, short-sightedness and rowdyism of the reactionary and extreme pro-slavery leaders in the South knew no bounds. They had forced the Fugitive Slave Law and destroyed the Whig party, and from their narrow vision they had nothing to fear from opposition in America or elsewhere. Senator Hammond, of South Carolina, in a speech in the United States Senate, said:

If no cotton was furnished for three years, England would topple headlong, and carry the whole civilized world with her. . . . The South would never need an army or a navy, beyond a few garrisons on the frontier and a few revenue cutters. Without firing a gun, without drawing a sword, should they make war on us, we could bring the whole world to our feet.

Wigfall, of Texas, not to be outdone in provincial egotism and the gift of prophecy by his colleague in statecraft, predicted short work in destroying all opposition to slavery, the British Empire in particular. He said:

If we stop the supply of cotton for one week, England would be starving. Victoria's crown would not stand on her head one week if the supply of cotton were stopped; nor would her head stand on her shoulders.

It seems unbelievable that intelligent human beings, especially a homogeneous people of the British race, in eleven States of the Union, could have been led or coerced into rebellion by such demagoguery and claptrap of radical leaders of the pro-slavery, secession Oligarchy. But it is a tragic fact in American history that outspoken opposition to slavery in the South declined as the dominion of "king cotton" was extended, and the provincialism and rowdyism of his ministers increased until that ruthless despot demanded not only the bondage of the black man but also the serfdom of the white man. Concerning some of the most active and radical political leaders and protagonists of slavery, the observation of John Stuart Mill, on self-worship, is pertinent:

There is nothing which men so easily learn as this self-worship; all

privileged persons, and all privileged classes have had it. The more we
descend in the scale of humanity, the intenser it is; and most of all in
those who are not, and can never expect to be, raised above any one except
unfortunate wife and children.

The radical leaders of the Slave Oligarchy were exacting in
their sectional policies. They demanded the annexation of
Texas as a slave State. They not only supported but demanded enforcement of the Fugitive Slave Law; they supported the Kansas-Nebraska Bill, and in short, every measure
proposed in Congress and every kind of propaganda, not only
for the protection of slavery in the South but also for the
extension of slavery in every part of the United States, even
to the extent of repealing the Missouri Compromise. Protection for slavery was the dogma of the Slave Oligarchy.

I have already alluded to the fact that South Carolina was
one of the American colonies that protested against slavery
before the War of the American Revolution; and yet, in later
years, this State took the lead in supporting the institution
of slavery to the extent of seceding from the Union. Among
the most radical and virulent leaders of the Slave Oligarchy
were Senators and Representatives in Congress from South
Carolina. With the assumption of greater power and a corresponding disregard for the liberty and best interests of the
mass of the people, there naturally evolved less regard for the
opinions of others. Those who assumed autocratic power could
not tolerate a free discussion of political questions and they
were vulgarly arrogant and overbearing in their social relations. Some of the most partisan leaders of a people who had
justly boasted of their patriotism, personal courage and chivalry soon degenerated into the vulgar practices of mere char-
latans and not infrequently amplified their tirades of racial
and sectional hatreds with the mannerisms and language of
street bullies.

The irascible John Randolph, of Virginia, referred to President Adams as a traitor, Daniel Webster "a vile slanderer,"
and Edward Livingston "the most contemptible and degraded
of beings, whom no man ought to touch, unless with a pair of
tongs." It is related that on one occasion while Randolph in
the Senate was abusing Webster, who was then a member of

the House, a Senator informed him that Mrs. Webster was in the gallery.

He had not the delicacy to desist, however, until he had fully emptied the vials of his wrath. Then he set upon Mr. Speaker Taylor, and after abusing him soundly he turned sarcastically to the gentleman who had informed him of Mrs. Webster's presence, and asked, "Is Mrs. Taylor present also?"

Henry Clay was frequently the object of Randolph's bitter denunciations. Writing about Randolph of Roanoke, Ben Perley Poore says:

He used to enter the Senate Chamber wearing a pair of silver spurs, carrying a heavy riding whip, and followed by a favorite hound, which crouched beneath his desk. He wrote, and occasionally spoke, in riding gloves, and it was his favorite gesture to point the long index finger of his right hand. . . . Every ten or fifteen minutes, while he occupied the floor, he would exclaim in a low tone, "Tims, more porter," and the assistant doorkeeper would hand him a foaming tumbler of potent malt liquor, which he would hurriedly drink.

Senator Cuthbert, of Georgia. also gained notoriety in a very bitter attack on Daniel Webster, because Mr. Webster was opposed to slavery. "The Georgian's declamation was delivered with clenched fist; he pounded his desk, gritted his teeth, and used profane language." Garrett's *Public Men in Alabama* contains the following reference to a speech made in the House by a member from that State, ten years before the outbreak of the war between the States:

The United States Senate passed a resolution of welcome to Louis Kossuth. While this resolution was under consideration in the House, Judge Smith, a Congressman of Alabama, not only attacked the resolution but also engaged in a general onslaught directed against the North and New York in particular.

During Van Buren's Administration, James P. Espey went to Washington to introduce what has grown into the Weather Signal Service. He was born in Pennsylvania and was very poor in his early life; he was seventeen years of age before he learned to read and write.

He subsequently mastered the English language and the classics, and long before he knew why, began to study the mystery of the moving clouds and to form his storm theories. At last he asked of Congress an appropriation of five thousand dollars a year for five years, but he was met with jibes and ridicule.

Senator Preston, of South Carolina, said Espey was a madman, too dangerous to be at large, and the Senator said he would vote for a special appropriation for a prison in which to confine him. When the South Carolina Senator made this speech Espey was in the Senate gallery.

Wounded to the quick, he left the Capitol and went to New York, where he delivered a course of lectures with great success. They were repeated in Boston, and he made money enough to enable him to visit Europe. He was well received in England, and appeared before the British Association of Scientists in London, and later visited Paris where he was well received by the Academy of Sciences.

When it was proposed in Congress to make an appropriation of twenty-five thousand dollars for a series of experiments with "the magnetic telegraph," invented by Morse, Congressman Cave Johnson, a prominent Democrat of Tennessee, "undertook to ridicule the discovery by proposing that one-half of the proposed appropriation be devoted to experiments with mesmerism."

The institution of slavery made the political leaders of the Southern people lawless and provincial, and perhaps unwittingly domineering; the absence of free discussion and full liberty of action necessarily evolved an oligarchic form of government where autocratic power could be assumed with less danger of opposition than it would arouse in any other part of the United States. It was natural and logical, therefore, that those partisan leaders should set at defiance all laws made to check or restrain their power. The cowardly attack on Charles Sumner by Brooks of South Carolina, in the Senate Chamber, was typical of the lawless spirit shown by the radical element of the Slave Oligarchy. As narrated by Rhodes in his *History of the United States:*

At the close of a short session of the Senate, Sumner remained in the chamber occupied in writing letters. Bent over his writing and while in this position he was approached by Brooks, a Representative from South Carolina, and a kinsman of Senator Butler. Brooks, standing before and directly over him, said: ''I have read your speech twice over carefully. It is a libel on South Carolina and Mr. Butler, who is a relative of mine.'' As he pronounced the last word, he hit Sumner on the head with his cane with the force that a dragoon would give to a sabre-blow. Sumner was more than six feet in height and of powerful frame, but penned under the desk he could offer no resistance, and Brooks continued the blows on his defenseless head. The cane broke, but the South Carolinian went on beating his victim with the butt. Brooks took hold of him, and while he was reeling and staggering about, struck him again and again. Sumner fell to the floor, bleeding profusely and covered with his blood.

Several months after this brutal assault, when Brooks returned to his home, there was—

a numerously attended banquet in South Carolina given to Preston S. Brooks by the constituents of his district, where, amid vehement cheering, he was presented with a cane on which was inscribed, ''Use Knock-down arguments.''

Another unfortunate and tragic episode resulting from the lawless radicalism of the extreme secessionists and proponents of slavery, which attracted national attention and caused great indignation among a large majority of the better class of people, was the killing of Senator Broderick in California. Broderick was killed in a duel with Terry in 1859, and the affair was about as infamous as the killing of Hamilton by Burr.

Terry was a Texan, a dead shot. It was arranged that Broderick, whether by intention or accident only Terry and his confederates could know, was assigned a pistol with a very delicate or hair trigger. He had been very ill, and not being accustomed to the use of a pistol, it went off prematurely and the ball entered the ground about four paces in advance of him. Terry then took deliberate aim and shot him through the heart.

Thirty years after killing Broderick, Terry was killed in California by a United States Deputy Marshal, after he had assaulted Justice Field of the United States Supreme Court.

Some of the most radical and unscrupulous leaders of the old Slave Oligarchy were political adventurers from the North. For example, John Slidell, member of Congress from Louisiana, 1834-45, Senator 1853 to 1861, and Confederate Commissioner to France with Mason, was born in New York City. He was generally recognized as the leader of the extreme faction of the Slave Oligarchy in the Senate for several years prior to the Civil War. After he moved to New Orleans, he became the political leader of the most corrupt and lawless element in Louisiana. He was appointed Minister to Mexico in the early months of President Polk's Administration, but the Mexican Government refused to receive him. James Henry Hammond, the ultra radical secession leader of South Carolina, was the son of a New England school teacher but was born in South Carolina.

The political system of the South was an oligarchy. The slaveholders were in a very disproportionate minority in every State. "Two hundred thousand men with pure white skins in South Carolina," said Broderick to the Senators, "are now degraded and despised by thirty thousand aristocratic slave-holders." Referring to the blight of slavery, Rhodes, *History of the United States*, says:

There were 347,525 slaveholders in the South in 1850, who, with their families, may have numbered two million. The total white population of the Slave States was 6,125,000, so that less than one-third of the white people of the South could possibly have derived any benefit from the institution of slavery. In other words, this imperial domain, covering more square miles than there were in the Free States, was given up to two million people, and more than seven millions, bond and free, labored for them or were subservient to their interests. . . . No one seriously maintained that there were any benefits in the system for the poor whites; since it degraded labor, and therefore degraded the white man who had to work with his hands. It is one of the striking facts of our history that these despised people fought bravely and endured much for a cause adverse to their own interests, following Lee and Stonewall Jackson with a devotion that called to mind the deeds of a more heroic age.

Referring to the non-slaveholding whites of the South, Rhodes says:

The poor whites of the South looked on the prosperity of the slave-holding lord with rank and sullen envy; his trappings contrasted painfully with their want of comforts, yet he knew so well how to play upon their contempt for the Negro, and to make it appear that his and their interests were identical, that when election-day came the whites, who were without money and without slaves, did the bidding of the lord of the plantation. When Southern interests were in danger, it was the poor whites who voted for their preservation. The slaveholders, and the members of that society which clustered round them, took the offices. It was extremely rare that a man who had ever labored with his hands was sent to Congress from the South, or chosen to one of the prominent positions in the State.

The political leaders of the South have not only failed to give encouragement and support to men and women of independent thought and high civic ideals, who would not be dominated by the racial and sectional animosities of the Oligarchy, but by a system of narrow provincialism and proscription, the South has persecuted and tried to destroy some of the ablest and most patriotic men and women who were born and brought up in the Southern States. The most distinguished men of the South during the last half century have not attained eminence in the public service of any Southern State. The Hon. Walter Hines Page, born in North Carolina, and one of the most eminent men the South has produced in the past half century, emphasized the plain truth when, in an address before the North Carolina Society of New York, he said:

> Whenever one party by long power breeds intolerance, the other falls into contempt. And what constructive influence have the Southern States in our larger political life? From some of them, where parties have fallen low, we have seen men go to one national convention as a mere unthinking personal following of a candidate. . . . The manhood and the energy and the ambition of Southern men now find effective political expression through neither party.
>
> The South, therefore, neither contributes to the Nation's political thought and influence nor receives stimulation from the Nation's thought and influence. Its real patriotism counts for nothing—is smothered dumb under party systems that have become crimes against the character and the intelligence of the people.

The beginning of the decline of the South, after the Civil War, in the caliber and stamina of its political leaders, was apparent after 1884 when, during the first administration of Cleveland, the present dominant Oligarchy assumed control over the Southern States. For two decades after the war, prominent political leaders of the South were men of ability and high personal character. For example, the late Senator Morgan of Alabama was a pronounced partisan, yet he was a loyal American. He was in the United States Senate for thirty years, and participated at great length in the long and acrimonious discussions following the Reconstruction period when the "bloody shirt was waving," and during his long service he was always a gentleman, showing the highest respect for his

country and its laws. He was an able lawyer and statesman
and never permitted his partisan prejudices or sectional bias
to lead him into rude conduct.

Contemporaneous with Senator Morgan was General Pettus
of Alabama, who served many years in the United States Senate. He was a partisan and a very positive character, fearless
and high-minded; he was a gentleman and never descended to
rowdyism or billingsgate. From other Southern States there
were distinguished Southerners like Gordon, Hill, Lamar and
other Senators and Representatives who observed all the usages
of polite society and parliamentary decorum without surren-
dering their political principles or compromising their partisan
affiliations.

*As to The Leopard's Spots—An Open Letter to Thomas
Dixon, Jr.,* is the title of a pamphlet written by Professor Kelly
Miller, Howard University, Washington, D. C. This writing
is a very clear and forcible protest against the provincialism
and propagandism of race animosity in the South, from which
I take the following:

I am writing you this letter to express the attitude and feeling of ten
million of your fellow-citizens toward the evil of propagandism of race
animosity to which you have lent your great literary powers. Through
the widespread influence of your writings you have become the chief priest
of those who worship at the shrine of race hatred and wrath. This one
spirit runs through all your books and published utterances like the recurrent theme of an opera. . . .

Has it ever occurred to you that the people of New England blood who
have done and are doing most to make the white race great and glorious
in this land, are the most reticent about extravagant claims to everlasting
superiority? You protest too much. Your loud pretensions, backed up by
such exclamatory outbursts of passion, make upon the reflecting mind the
impression that you entertain a sneaking suspicion of their validity.

According to a study of the distribution of ability in the United States,
by Hon. Henry Cabot Lodge, the little State of Massachusetts has produced
more men of distinction and achievement than all the South combined.
. . . But this lack of comparative achievement is not due at all to innate
inferiority of Southern white men to their brethren in higher latitudes.
. . . The white people of the South claim, or rather boast, of a race
prepotency and inheritance as great as that of any breed of men in the
world, but they clearly fail to show its attainments.

The World War brought to the South the greatest opportunity that has come to that section in the past hundred years, and there was scarcely a man in public life from the South that rose equal to the opportunity. In four years of partisan and sectional control in national affairs, during the World War, there was not a political leader from the South who rose to distinction. Instead of dealing with world questions in a broad, humanitarian and statesmanlike manner, the Southern leaders in Congress directed their influence and power to the encouragement of the spoils system and the advancement of provincial politics. The South still has men of marked ability who have sufficient capacity to grasp the great questions of the day, but they are not among the politicians and they were not in Congress.

The decline of the South has been reflected in the character and mental attainments of the men who have been elected to the highest positions of honor and trust during the three decades last past. Some further evidence of the rowdyism and downward course of public affairs in the South is found in the following story from Alabama as published in *The Birmingham Age-Herald:*

The State Legislature will go in a body next Thursday to Demopolis to attend a rooster sale. Four of the roosters to be sold at Demopolis were brought to Montgomery last Thursday and exhibited at the Capitol, where they were admired by the legislators, State officials and visitors. By resolution, both Houses of the Legislature will adjourn next Wednesday afternoon until Friday to enable the members to attend the cock sale.

A few months after witnessing the "rooster sale," the Alabama Legislature, while in session at the Capitol, furnished further entertainment for their constituents as described in *The Birmingham Age-Herald:*

Lawmakers in the House forgot the serious side of their duties Wednesday afternoon and held one of the old-time humorous sessions that make legislatures famous throughout the country. The afternoon session was made up of a score or more first-class acts, each with more humor than the average vaudeville show, but acts which could not be witnessed by the lady gallery attendants who have heretofore been interested spectators at that side of the lawmaking body.

The comedy began in the early afternoon, shortly after several minor local bills had been passed, and when House Bill No. 105, by Mr. Oakley of Wilcox County, was called. The bill is entitled, "To provide for the control of venereal diseases by an ante-nuptial examination of men, which shall be done within 15 days before granting marriage license, fixing penalties for non-compliance.'' . . .

For about an hour the comedy was presented, all women in the gallery having previously been asked to leave, following the adoption of a resolution by one of the members. It was known that this bill would create much discussion and women therefore were asked to leave.

The Senate side of the Legislature had adjourned for the afternoon until 10 o'clock Thursday morning by the time the argument got to its height, and many Senators, the Lieutenant Governor and others came to the House side.

The Chicago Tribune, through Mr. Frazier Hunt, its correspondent in Paris, succeeded in getting the first copy of the Treaty of Versailles that was made public in the United States. It would seem that every respectable citizen of the United States would have felt under some obligation to *The Tribune* for giving information on a matter of vital interest, which the President had withheld not only from the public but also from the United States Senate. However, *The Jackson* (Miss.) *Ledger* took a different view of the matter when it said:

The statement is given out that a newspaper correspondent named **Frazier** Hunt, of *The Chicago Tribune,* managed in some mysterious way to get possession of the Peace Treaty at Paris and brought his copy to America where it fell into the hands of Republican Senators, placed there, doubtless, by this degenerate press reporter . . . who either bought, begged or stole the copy of the Peace Treaty that he brought to Washington, the object being to make sordid dollars by the transaction, and discredit President Wilson. . . . Pity that there is no law by which such men as Hunt could be reached and prosecuted for his dastardly act.

The great wrong of which *The Chicago Tribune* had been guilty was in making it possible not only for the Republican Senators, but also for Democratic Senators, and indeed for the humblest citizen of this country, to learn what obligations the President had undertaken, secretly and without authority, to impose upon this Nation;—practically fulfilling, indeed, the first of the President's own ''Fourteen Commandments'': ''Open covenants, openly arrived at.'' In speaking of the United States Senate, of which he was a member, Senator Williams, of Mississippi was quoted as saying:

The period of great conspiracy started even before one syllable **of** the League of Nations was put on paper. It started in Washington with the announcement that the President would head the Peace Delegation to Paris. It was engineered by a lot of cheap two-by-four politicians. I call them that because that is what they are, I care not how high their station.

A telegram from Hickory, Mississippi, December 14, 1919, stated that—

Senator John Sharp Williams stated in a letter made public to-day: ''I am disgusted with the whole political situation, especially with the treatment of international affairs as if they were questions of party politics.'' The Senator further wrote, ''I would rather be a dog and bay at the moon than to spend one day in the United States Senate after the expiration of my term.''

''By a unanimous vote of the House,'' in the 67th Congress, a Democratic Representative from one of the Southern States was ''censured'' because when he had been allowed by courtesy of the House to print a speech which he did not deliver he inserted ''foul and obscene matter'' which he ''knew he could not have spoken on the floor,'' and—

did insert and cause to be printed in *The Congressional Record* of Saturday, October 22, 1921, a certain letter or communication . . . which said communication contained language that was so indecent, obscene, vulgar, and vile as to render it unmailable had it been contained in any other than an official publication . . . for which he deserves the severe rebuke and censure of the House.

Before a special committee of the United States Senate engaged in an investigation of charges made by Senator Thomas E. Watson of Georgia, against army officers who served in France, Senator Watson insulted and ''denounced, in screaming and excited voice, officers in the United States Army who were in attendance upon the investigation.'' Referring to the presence of the Army officers, the Georgia Senator declared: ''They eyed me with an insolence that aroused my Southern blood.'' . . . He addressed an officer of the United States Army who was present, in these words: ''For two pennies, I would slap your jaws, you lantern-jawed dog.''

The ''Southern blood'' of the Wilson régime did not get very warm and it was not aroused by the atrocious deeds of the German vandals in France and in Belgium and the German pirates on the high seas. It was "too proud to fight" when the *Lusitania* went to the bottom of the sea with men, women and children from America among the innocent victims of that act of piracy. But before a committee of the United States Senate, the "Southern blood" of certain political leaders cannot be kept cool. Its vocal organs become very belligerent. As stated by *The New York Tribune,*—

To conduct unbecoming a Senator of the United States, Tom Watson of Georgia has added conduct unbecoming a gentleman. The spectacle of a Senator of the United States making such an exhibition of himself as he did yesterday is appalling.

In an editorial of greater length, *The New York Times*, by comparison, recalled the splendid career of two distinguished citizens of Georgia, General John B. Gordon and Governor Alfred H. Colquitt. The State was proud of these men, the country esteemed them:

It is not in time a far cry from Gordon and Colquitt to Thomas E. Watson, but what a descent in merit, in manners and character, and, obviously, in usefulness. No one could imagine those Senators of another day grossly insulting a witness waiting to be called at a committee hearing, and threatening him with violence. The exhibition of passion and vulgarity of which Senator Watson was guilty when he heaped abuse and contumely upon Major George W. Cocheu, who, in the uniform of the United States Army, sat quietly and self-containedly in his place, has shocked the country.

During a debate in the Senate, according to newspaper reports, Senator Heflin of Alabama called Senator Glass of Virginia a "liar." Some weeks later, during the same session of the 67th Congress, it was reported that—

with his open palm, Representative Oliver, Democrat, of Alabama, gave Representative Dempsey, Republican, New York, a slap on the cheek in the House, and then as he was attempting to land a second time, members rushed between them.

These outbreaks in Congress which have shocked the whole country have been limited, almost without exception, to radical Democrats from the Solid South. They have also been limited to the territory of their occurrence; they usually happen in the Capitol at Washington during sessions of Congress. Ample opportunity was afforded during the World War, especially after America entered the war, for the free and unlimited exercise of the bellicose predilections of the Senators and Representatives from the South; but it was not improved. The spoils system is the main tenet, while race persecution, bigotry, provincialism and sectionalism are the common practices of this reactionary element in American politics.

CHAPTER XXII

For many years the provincialism and sectional prejudices of the ruling class in the South have been the cause of turmoil and strife in the United States. This condition is an anachronism. It has no place in modern civilization; certainly not in a country that boasts of its democracy and guarantees in its organic law a republican form of government.

There are no longer sectional questions in America; at least there should be none. In our foreign relations, and in every economic, social and political question before the American people, the issues are essentially national. But the plain truth of the matter is that the United States has almost ceased to be a nation; America is only a great aggregation of communities. We are not assimilating a large percentage of the alien element that is being made into citizenship without being able to understand or appreciate American institutions. Added to the menace of this unassimilated and insoluble element we have the more powerful and hardly less dangerous provincial partisans who seem unable, or for selfish reasons are unwilling, to rise above their sectional prejudices and race hatred.

Racial friction in the Southern States is not the result of the economic or moral decline, nor is it due to the vice or lawlessness of the Negro. The Negro in America is not degenerating. He is advancing along all lines that make for a higher and better civilization. Never has there been a race whose leaders, almost without exception, have struggled with more patience and forbearance, or more heroically, than the leaders of the Negroes in America, not only for the uplift of their own race, but also for the maintenance of peace between two races.

Nor is the deplorable situation in the South, in general, and the prevalence of sectionalism in particular, due to attacks from without. No effort has been made to take advantage of unfortunate conditions in the South. No party, faction, or political leader, outside the Southern States, at least since the Spanish-American war, has attempted to arouse sectional animosities. The propaganda of sectionalism in the United States, for more than a quarter of a century, has been limited to the leaders and spoilsmen of the Southern Oligarchy. The constructive thought of America, the great newspapers and periodicals, outside the South, for more than twenty-five years, have steadfastly, earnestly and with great charity, tried to allay sectional prejudice; and they have treated the South, the institutions and the people of the Southern States with every mark of respect, confidence and fraternal consideration.

Every one of the Southern States was under the rule of the Democratic party immediately after the inauguration of President Hayes. In the next Presidential election, 1880, the electoral votes of these States were cast for the Democratic ticket. At that time, leading public officials in the South, as a general rule, especially high State officials, Senators and Representatives in Congress, were men of ability and high character. They were loyal and patriotic. For instance, in his answer to the very bitter attack of James G. Blaine, in the House of Representatives, Benjamin Hill, a talented orator from Georgia, expressed the honest sentiment and loyal feeling of the better class of Southern people when he said:

And now let the voices of patriots from the North, and from the East and from the West, join our voices from the South, and send to heaven one universal according chorus. Wave on, flag of our fathers! Wave forever! But wave over a union of equals, not over a despotism of lords and vassals; over a land of law, liberty and peace, and not of anarchy, oppression and strife.

Another eloquent patriot and statesman from the South, L. Q. C. Lamar, of Mississippi, at the funeral of Charles Sumner, said: "My countrymen, let us know one another, and we will love one another." When partisans of the two great political parties were making their latest desperate effort to keep alive the passions of sectional hatred, there came from the South a true and splendid type of its highest manhood. The illustrious and lamented Henry W. Grady "loved the Nation into peace." His career was short, but his work was an epoch that marked the beginning of a new era. His coming was opportune, and if those who knew and loved him best thought his life too short and his work left unfinished, they found great comfort in the fact that he was appreciated in the North no less than in the South. Grady was admired by all races and in all sections of this country, and the Nation mourned his loss. In the hearts of his people he built a lasting monument. In the words of Colonel Henry Watterson:

He was, indeed, the hope, the expectancy of the young South, the one publicist of the New South, who, inheriting the spirit of the old, yet had realized the present, and looked into the future, with the eyes of a statesman and the heart of a patriot.

Henry Grady was a statesman and his mind took a broad and comprehensive view of national affairs. He was a loyal nationalist, and his speeches in New York and Boston were no less ingenious than patriotic; and those speeches were the foundation of his national fame. But among his own people he spoke with more freedom and greater foresight. In his famous Augusta, Georgia, speech, November, 1887, he said:

I know that the ideal status is that every State should vote without regard to sectional lines. The reconciliation of the people will never be complete until Iowa and Georgia, Texas and Massachusetts, may stand side by side without surprise. I would to God that status could be reached. If any man can define a path on which the whites of the South, though divided, can walk in honor and peace, I shall take that path, though I walk down it alone, for at the end of that path, and nowhere else, lies the full emancipation of my section, and the full restoration of this Union.

It would seem that Grady's Augusta speech was anticipated three years before he made it; and answered in a very broad, patriotic spirit, by one of the most partisan and brilliant, and perhaps the ablest among the leaders of the Republican party at that time, Mr. Blaine, who said:

No man in the North, valuing the freedom for which a great war was waged, desires to control the vote of a single individual in the South. He only desires that every individual in the South, as in the North, shall control his own vote, and when that is done, the result, whatever it may be, will always be cheerfully accepted. Contention between sections, divided by a fixed line, is the most undesirable form of political controversy. . . . But the consolidation on one side tends naturally and always to consolidation on the other side.

A little while before his death, Grady asked in his most famous speech if "bitterness should live in the heart of the conqueror when it had died in the heart of the conquered." It was not more than ten years before Grady made his patriotic speech at Augusta, and only a little more than a quarter of a century after Webster's great speech on *The Constitution and the Union,* that Benjamin Hill said:

There was a South of slavery and secession—that South is dead. There is a South of union and freedom—that South, thank God, is living, breathing, growing every hour.

During President Harrison's Administration the country was agitated by the reopening of the question of Federal supervision of elections. The measure proposed was known as the Lodge bill. It was inopportune, unfortunate for the whole country. Had the bill been enacted it could have been enforced in the South only at the point of the bayonet. But it gave the Southern Oligarchy the opportunity for which they had been watching and praying. "We told you so," they said, and in the dark closets they ransacked for the scarecrow. The bugbear of Negro rule was brought forth, the recalcitrant press was driven back into line, and so brave and prudent a man as General Gordon was aroused to passionate outbursts of sectional feeling.

No man in the South could stand before the storm; the leaders of the New South were panic-stricken and there was a general rush for shelter under the protecting wings of the "grand old rock-ribbed Democracy." Nothing was accomplished in the way of securing honest elections, but the good work of ten years was undone in a day. No progress was made toward the solution of the Negro problem, but the poor Negro got a few extra kicks for staying on the earth while these things happened. At the close of the Harrison Administration the period of reaction had set in, the South was solid again, and there was none who had the temerity to speak of the New South or even suggest the possibility of the South ever being anything but solid for the Oligarchy.

Why the Solid South? is the title of a book published in 1890, containing articles contributed by political leaders and publicists who were prominent in the South at that time. This volume contains a story in detail of corrupt practices in every one of the Southern States during the Reconstruction period and Republican rule, so far as the carpet-baggers were involved. It was published at the time of the agitation for a reduction of representation in Congress from the Southern States. Since publication of this book, the Oligarchy has not deemed it necessary or expedient to offer any further excuses or explanations for the solidarity of the South. The agitation for reduction in representation from the South, continued intermittently until every one of the Southern States had disfranchised the Negro. It received little encouragement in the North and finally died out shortly after the close of the war with Spain. The latest fruitless effort to revive it was in the 59th Congress when Judge Crumpacker of Indiana and General Keifer of Ohio brought forward very illuminating arguments in support of the proposition.

At this place it may be well to recall some of the numerous instances of sympathy, respect and friendly feeling in the North for the Southern people and evidence of a sincere desire on the part of the North to eradicate, so far as possible, all bitterness between the two sections.

It was Senator Sumner who introduced the bill prohibiting the future publication of the names of Union victories in *The Army Register* or their inscription on the regimental colors of the army. This step toward an oblivion of past difficulties was highly acceptable to General Grant. At Camp Chase, Ohio, there is a monument to 2,500 Confederate dead who are buried there, and this monument was erected by subscriptions raised among the veterans of the Union Army. This monument is largely, if not wholly, the result of the earnest patriotic work of Colonel W. H. Knaus of Columbus, Ohio, who was a member of Encampment 78, Union Veteran Legion. He devoted many years of his life to abating the bitterness engendered by the Civil War and it was at his suggestion that the word "Americans" was cut upon the keystone of the arch erected at Camp Chase. There is also a monument in Chicago to the Confederate dead, erected by citizens of that city. When General John B. Gordon delivered an address in Batavia, N. Y., he was escorted to the opera house by the local Grand Army post.

The financial crisis and disastrous industrial depression during the second Administration of Cleveland had impoverished the South, while the corrupt and partisan practices of the Oligarchy during the same period brought distress and unrest to the Southern people. The election of President McKinley was a godsend to the South, a blessing to the whole country. The defeat of Bryan freed the South of the greatest peril to which it has been exposed since the Reconstruction period. From the beginning of his public career Mr. McKinley was a constant friend of the Southern people. No public measure directly affecting the interests of the South escaped his attention.

Before his nomination for President, in 1896, Mr. McKinley made a tour of the South with Mr. Hanna. The purpose of that visit was not to confabulate with venal Negroes and disreputable white Republicans; on the contrary, special effort was made to meet men of character and position, particularly young men, without reference to their political affiliations. He tried to build up the Republican party in the South, to "respectableize" it, as some one well said. Some unfortunate appointments were made, and in some places the venal element was given recognition, but on the whole there was great improvement in the general character and policies of the Republican party in the South during the McKinley Administration.

President McKinley in many ways endeared himself to the South. The prompt recognition given General Fitzhugh Lee at Havana was one of his earliest official acts, and the subsequent advancement of General Wheeler and General Lee, coupled with many other friendly acts, indicated his broad and patriotic policies. While a member of Congress, Mr. McKinley had taken a keen interest in providing for the proper care by the Government of the graves of the Confederate dead, and the establishment of a Confederate section in the Arlington Cemetery was the accomplishment of one of his cherished desires. An article by Colonel Henry Watterson in *The Louisville Courier-Journal* contains the following tribute to McKinley:

He was quick to see the meaning and opportunity of the Spanish War. The last, eternal treaty of peace between the North and the South was written by the pen that signed the commissions as Generals in the Army of the United States of Joseph Wheeler and Fitzhugh Lee and John Breckenridge Castleman, and never did statesman and patriot perform an act greater in reach and more benign in effect than did William McKinley when he restored those Confederate soldiers to the service of a once more united country, literally turning gray into blue, and giving to generations of Southern men yet unborn the sign-manual, along with the deathless assurance, of complete moral emancipation.

At a meeting in honor of the memory of William McKinley, held at Canton, Ohio, General Fitzhugh Lee stated that McKinley once said to him:

Could I write an epitaph upon my tomb, I would say: ''Here lies a President of the United States who has done more to bring all the sections of a common country into more harmonious and closer friendship than any of his predecessors.''

Shortly after Mr. McKinley's death, in the presence of thousands of former Confederate and former Union soldiers, and officers of the United States Army and the G. A. R., at the first formal memorial exercises ever held over the graves in the Confederate section of the Arlington Cemetery, President Roosevelt heartily endorsed the movement to erect a monument to the Confederate dead at Arlington. When a committee, headed by former Secretary of the Navy, Hilary A. Herbert, representing the Arlington Confederate Monument Association, called upon President Roosevelt, in answer to the committee, the President said:

I wish to express my deepest sympathy with and most cordial approval of the purpose and the importance of what you are going to do. The monument to the Confederate dead which you will raise will commemorate, among many scores of thousands that it will thus commemorate, my mother's half brother; and my mother's whole brother went down in the *Alabama,* having fired the last gun from her, but was picked up in the escape and lived for many years afterwards. . . . I feel that among all nations we have been blessed peculiarly beyond all others, because now the memory of the valor shown alike by the men who wore the blue, and the men who wore the gray, is a heritage of honor for the whole country.

Colonel Roosevelt never wavered in his friendship for the South. While President he did not always please the turbulent and vindictive element of the Southern States, and it is perhaps true that some of his appointments were ill-advised and unfortunate, but he never lost an opportunity to speak in terms of the highest respect for the Southern people. He never forgot that his mother was a Southern woman, and he never failed to do all in his power for advancement of the educational interests of the South and all other interests conducive to the uplift and progress of the Southern people. In response to an invitation to address the Southern Commercial Congress at Atlanta, in 1911, he wrote a letter to the Chairman of the Congress in which he said:

I earnestly hope that the young men of the South will never forget the past glories of the South, because I earnestly hope that the young men all over America to-day will keep in mind these glorious memories of every section of our common country, and that the men of the North and of the West will remember the South's past with the same pride that the South itself does for the undying glory, won by the men who so valiantly and who so sincerely fought for their convictions, whether they wore the blue or the gray, is now a common heritage of all of us wherever we dwell.

It was during the Administration of Roosevelt that Congress passed a joint resolution directing the return of the captured Confederate flags, in possession of the War Department at Washington since the close of the Civil War. This joint resolution was adopted without a dissenting vote. The flags were returned to the several States under direction of the Secretary of War. These evidences of a broad, American spirit in the North, and sincere respect and friendship for the Southern people, as shown by the words and in the deeds of the most highly respected and representative men of the North, were fully appreciated by the mass of the Southern people, but they did not appease the political leaders of the South and the propagandists of sectional animosities and race hatred. In 1904, President Roosevelt wrote a letter to Colonel Mosby, noted during the Civil War in the Confederate service, in which he said:

I have always been saddened rather than angered at the attacks upon me in the South. I am half a Southerner myself, and I can say with all possible sincerity that the interests of the South are exactly as dear to me as the interests of the North.

A large number of appointments to the most important Federal offices made by President Roosevelt in the Southern States were among the Confederate veterans. For instance, General Luke E. Wright, one of the most distinguished citizens of Tennessee, was appointed President of the Philippine Commission in 1903, and in 1904 he was appointed by President Roosevelt as Civil Governor of the Philippine Islands, and later was appointed Governor-General to succeed Mr. Taft. Early in 1906, General Wright was appointed Ambassador to Japan and he succeded Mr. Taft as Secretary of War. General Wright was a native of Tennessee, where, at the age of fifteen, he joined the Confederate army.

Not only before the Civil War, but all through the war, Lincoln wrote and spoke in terms of highest regard for the Southern people and, "with malice toward none," his acts were in accord with his words. General Grant was zealous and untiring in his efforts to blot out every trace of sectional prejudice; President McKinley and President Roosevelt, each in his own way, by words and in deeds, earnestly tried to reconcile the South, and to make effective the oft-repeated assertion that the country was re-united. If the South could get rid of its irresponsible leadership of reactionary and provincial partisans and spoilsmen, and accept the friendship of the truly great men and American patriots of the North, and of the Nation, who still feel and express themselves quite as clearly and forcibly as Lincoln, Grant, McKinley and Roosevelt spoke and acted respecting the South, we should soon have little cause to complain about the menace of sectionalism. There would be a new birth of the Nation and this great country would be united in the common cause of democracy and progress of mankind.

The Chicago Tribune has been as bitter as any paper in the North in its attacks on corrupt practices and sectionalism in the South. Concerning white supremacy and sectionalism, *The Tribune,* November 16, 1916, editorially said:

We are for having the South attend to its local political affairs as it sees fit. We concede the South the right to protect white domination. The Negro *en masse* is unfit to rule the South and if the only fashion in which he can be kept from ruling is to keep him from voting, then keep him from voting.

But we do ask the Nation to stop the counting of this unvoted Negro vote. It is counted in the Electoral College. It is not counted in Southern precincts, but it is counted in the vote of the Nation.

After his election, but before his inauguration, President

Harding visited the South, and in all his public utterances he spoke in terms of highest praise of the Southern people. Later, after his inauguration, he endeavored in many ways to be no less sincere in his deeds than in his words. During the first week of January, 1922, it was reported from Washington that President Harding went unannounced to Arlington Cemetery "to participate in the ceremonies attending the decoration of the graves of the Confederate soldiers who are buried there with soldiers who wore the blue." On that occasion the President said:

The spirit which actuated the men in gray to fight for what they believed to be right is the same spirit that now makes them loyally devoted citizens of a re-united country.

In less than three weeks after President Harding attended services and decorated graves in honor of the Confederate dead, and spoke in such esteem of the spirit of the Confederate soldier, the United Confederate Veterans, at their thirty-second annual convention, in Richmond, adopted a report made by the "History Committee charged with the duty of recommending school books to the Board of Education in the South." The report which was adopted "with a rising vote, unanimously and with a rebel yell," said :

The Civil War was deliberately and personally conceived and its inauguration made by Abraham Lincoln, and he was personally responsible for forcing the war upon the South.

As a matter of historical reference, the utterly preposterous assertion and attempted falsification of history would command no attention except as a deplorable and pathetic evidence of the decline of the South and the unfortunate rebirth of rabid and unreasonable sectionalism.

The belated discovery of the alleged authoritative records in the life of Abraham Lincoln, as asserted in the report adopted by the Confederate Veterans at Richmond, came after substantially all the great men of the Confederacy had passed away. More than half a century ago, the greatest intellects and best men and women of the South were engaged in revising histories and other school books, writing and editing new histories, and other text-books for use in the schools of the Southern States. Numerous books were written, numerous articles were contributed to newspapers, periodicals and magazines, in the North and in the South, but one could not find in any of these writings of well-informed, reliable and reputable men and women, scholars, historians, publicists and former officers in the Confederate Army and Navy, anything that would support in the slightest degree the absurd charges contained in the report adopted at a meeting of the Confederate Veterans.

I refer to the resolution adopted by the Confederate Veterans only as cumulative evidence of the rebirth and rapid growth of sectionalism under rule of the present Oligarchy in the South. The veterans of the Confederate Army are passing away; very few are left who are able to attend their meetings. There is not left sufficient physical vitality in the organization to resist the designing and mischievous propaganda of the Southern politicians.

The voice of the great mass of the people in the South is seldom heard through the press and never through the political leaders. The Southern States are only provinces and the people of these States have nothing whatever to do with the affairs of this country; they have no voice and they exercise no influence in the domestic or foreign affairs of this Nation. No other civilized country is so completely isolated as is the South; the people of that section live within a pale.

A striking evidence of the power of sectionalism is observed in the fact that not one of the Southern States elects to the United States Senate or House of Representatives a citizen who was born in one of the Northern States. This custom does not obtain in the North. The fact that a man was born in the South is not in any respect, it matters not with which political party he may be affiliated, a bar to political aspirations in the North. Take for instance, the 65th Congress in which, in addition to twenty-six Senators from thirteen Southern States, including Kentucky and Oklahoma, there were ten Senators from Northern States who were born in the South. Nine of the Senators from Northern States who were born in the South are Democrats and one, Senator Poindexter of Washington, who was born in Tennessee, is a Republican. But the most interesting part of this story is that in the 65th Congress there were six Senators who were born in the State of Mississippi. It is a curious illustration of the political situation in this country when the State that leads in repudiation, lawlessness and illiteracy, and has the lowest per cent. of voters in proportion to its population, also leads the list in the number of United States Senators who are natives of it.

Sectionalism was recognized as a part of our political system from the beginning of our constitutional government. It was made a part of our law when the Constitution provided that representatives in Congress should be apportioned among the States according to their population and not according to the number of citizens who actually participated in the affairs of government, as qualified voters, nor on the population of free persons who were citizens. The population, as basis of representation in Congress, was made to include all the free persons and three-fifths of the slaves. The injustice and peril of this arrangement was apparent to those who framed the Constitution, but it was a compromise measure without which the Constitution would not have been ratified by all of the thirteen States.

The advantage of representation in Congress by the slaveholding States did not satisfy the Slave Oligarchy. Their demand for an extension of slave territory, and the consequent increase of political power, became acute when Missouri applied for admission into the Union. The bill passed by Congress in 1820, known as the Missouri Compromise, marked the second great crisis in our history which was temporarily settled by a compromise on sectional lines. Thirty years later, sectionalism again asserted its power and the Slave Oligarchy finally triumphed when, in 1854, it forced the Kansas-Nebraska Bill through Congress, thereby abrogating the Missouri Compromise and fixing the sectional line of cleavage that terminated in civil war.

Sectionalism and slavery were the disturbing questions in making the Federal Constitution, and these were the vital issues in the Civil War. The men who framed our Constitution accepted a compromise on these two questions because they thought a Constitution with a compromise would be better than an insecure confederation without a Constitution. After seventy years of bitter discussion and strife over these two issues, and after several futile attempts to effect other and further compromises, there came at last that dreadful appeal to arms. When the armies of the Confederate States accepted the liberal terms of General Grant and General Sherman, and surrendered, the citizens of those States also accepted the arbitrament of the sword to which their leaders had appealed.

Volumes have been written to support a plea of justification for the leaders of the political party that coerced eleven States into secession and civil war. This is not the place to discuss the merits of that contention, nor is that phase of the question within the limits of this volume; but it is within the scope of the present work to emphasize the fact that the vital questions of slavery and sectionalism were the two issues that were settled by the war. That settlement was accepted by the States which had attempted to withdraw from the Union and it became a part of our fundamental laws.

In order to make the paramount results of the war effective in our organic law, and to secure, so far as it was possible to secure by law, in perpetuity, the vital principles for which the war had been fought, the Thirteenth and Fourteenth Amendments were adopted. It matters not what construction was placed on the original Constitution, prior to the Civil War; after the results of that war were accepted and ratified, and the war amendments to the Constitution adopted, neither slavery nor sectionalism had any legal or moral standing in the United States.

This brings us face to face with the strange anomaly of the political situation and the distressing conditions that actually prevail in the Southern States, where slavery and sectionalism, and disunion, have been supported and encouraged from the formation of this Government. It was a series of immoral and disloyal steps that led from one point in the downward course to the next, and finally to a cataclysm which, as all thoughtful persons now see, was a dreadful blunder. So clearly was this the case that even the most extreme, honest leaders of the sectional party have admitted that the triumph of the South would have been most disastrous to democratic institutions and civilization.

Now it is a remarkable but distressing fact that precisely the same agencies and the same policies that drove this country into civil war in 1861 are now engaged in a similar line of seditious talk and disloyal practices. To illustrate the present point, it may be well here to recall the familiar truth so clearly emphasized in the last work of Lord Bryce:

> The two safeguards on which democracy must rely are law and opinion. . . . Public opinion is, however, even more important than law, since more flexible and able to reach cases not amenable to legal process. Opinion forms in public life that atmosphere which we call Tone and on whose purity the honour and worth of public life depend.

In the Solid South there is a total absence of the "atmosphere which we call Tone and on whose purity the honor and worth of public life depend." Herein lies a menace to the Nation. It is clear that the present task of America is to maintain order at home and preserve the semblance of democracy. The two safeguards of democracy—law and public opinion—have been set at defiance and contemptuously disregarded.

CHAPTER XXIII

A WARNING TO AMERICA

It was one of the aphorisms of modern history and civic philosophy that was uttered by Abraham Lincoln when he said: "Let the people know the truth and the country is safe." With full knowledge of the truth, will the free and independent citizens of the United States continue to tolerate evil and corrupt practices which impair the economic usefulness and destroy the civic worth of 17,000,000 white people of pure American stock in the Southern States? In the history of civilization, we read the story of the achievements of the progenitors of the white people of the South, and we know that their fathers contributed freely to the progress of democratic institutions in the early history of America.

Are the 8,000,000 Negroes in the South worth saving? In the War of the American Revolution, and in every other war in which America has been engaged, the Negroes of this country fought with valor, heroic patriotism and fortitude, on the side of humanity and liberty. These loyal and long-suffering citizens have been, and they still are, one of the most valuable economic assets of the United States. Yet there is no government in the world that furnishes so little protection to the person and property, civic and political rights, of its citizens or subjects, as the semblance of protection which the State or Federal Government provides for the Negroes who live in the Southern States. In this case, it is clear that "if abuses be not remedied, they will certainly increase."

During the reign of corruption and lawlessness, when America was under rule of the Southern Oligarchy, there began a great movement of Negroes from the South to cities north of the Ohio and Potomac rivers. This migration was the largest and most pronounced manifestation of restlessness among the Negroes that has been observed in the history of this race in the United States. It was the result of economic and social conditions of long growth. The history of the Negro shows that he is not of nomadic habits; in fact, no other race has shown a more persistent attachment for his native locality.

The number of Negroes who moved from the Southern to the Northern States during the second Wilson Administration has been variously estimated at from 400,000 to 750,000. In 1910, the total Negro population of the eleven Southern States (the Solid South) was 80.68 per cent. of the total Negro population of the United States; in 1920, the total Negro population of these States was 76.99 per cent. of the total Negro population of the United States. According to the Fourteenth Census reports, the total increase of the Negro population of the United States (1910-1920) was 635,368. The total increase in the eleven Southern States which composed the Confederacy in 1861, and which now constitute the Solid South, was only 127,651, being 20.09 per cent. of the total increase in the United States. In at least four of the Southern States, the Negro population was less in 1920 than it was in 1910. In Mississippi, for example, where for many years the Negroes have been in the majority, the Negro population was 74,303 less in 1920 than it was in 1910. In eleven Northern States used for comparison, where the total population was practically the same as the total population of the Southern States, the net increase of the Negro population, 1910 to 1920, was 179,686. With these significant facts in view, it is perhaps safe to assume that at least 400,000 Negroes migrated from the eleven Southern States during the Wilson Administration.

This exodus of Negroes from the South has continued since 1916, and at the present time it is steadily increasing. The Negroes are seeking new homes in the North where they can find employment and enjoy some protection of life and liberty. As pointed out in a preceding chapter, the consequent scarcity of labor in the cotton-growing States, added to the increasing ravages of the boll weevil, present the most serious economic problem before the American people.

Not only during slavery, but since his emancipation, the Negro has been, and still is, the main source of labor for the production of cotton. The South has not secured, and under its present system of land tenure and civil administration, it cannot secure white labor to take the place of the Negro migrants. In spite of the progress that has been made in Egypt, and the continued efforts of British spinners for improvement in the production of cotton in Africa and India, the South continues the main source of supply for the cotton mills of the world.

The blockade of the Southern ports was the cause of great distress and suffering in England during the Civil War in America, and the serious questions that arose during the World War in connection with the supply of cotton are among the outstanding evidences of the importance of the cotton crop in the industrial life of civilization. Cotton is usually the largest item of export from the United States, and anything that seriously affects the production of cotton is a matter of first importance in our international commerce. The pernicious results of corrupt practices, the evils of misfeasance and malfeasance in civil administration, and the appalling record of crimes of violence have contributed to the state of unrest in the Southern States, but the principal and immediate cause may be traced to the industrial situation. Increasing tenancy and the wretched condition of the tenants in the South are the outstanding facts in the late history of social and economic unrest.

In the spontaneous migration of so large a population of Negroes, a very large majority of whom were penniless and destitute, necessarily there came with these migrants a large number of the most lawless, vicious and immoral of their race. This fact explains the increase of crimes by Negroes in the Northern States. The movement of so large a population should have been regarded as a warning, indicating a civic and industrial disorder calling for an investigation by the Federal Government.

The influx into the Northern States, in such great numbers, of American citizens who had never enjoyed the civil rights and political privileges of citizens, as these rights and privileges are known and enjoyed outside the Southern States, will develop new and interesting phases of the already complex social and political questions in the United States. These Negro migrants have never had the free use of the ballot; they have enjoyed only a limited exercise of certain civil rights guaranteed under the Federal Constitution, and they have never had the social community privileges which they may freely enjoy in their new homes. While the political and social aspect of the situation is a matter of grave interest, the economic result of this migration of Negroes from the cotton-growing States is a matter of serious concern to the whole civilized world.

It is unreasonable to assume that the white people of the South, among whose progenitors were some of the most heroic patriots and greatest statesmen in the history of civilization, can be held in subjection indefinitely by an Oligarchy of spoilsmen. It is also unreasonable to assume that a race which has proven its loyalty and courage on the battlefield, and which has made the educational and industrial progress that the Negroes have made in America, can be persecuted, robbed and tortured with impunity and indefinitely. If the rule of the Oligarchy continue in the Southern States, the Solid South will soon be the Ireland of America, as Ireland was under the old system of landlordism, with the horrors of a race war added to the bitter strife between the impoverished whites and their oppressors.

The decline of American patriotism, the propaganda of so-called internationalism, the contemptuous disregard of American precedents and traditions, and the coddling of alien and seditious pacifists and non-resistants, during the Wilson Administration, produced radical and deplorable changes in the South. Long years of exploitation by the Oligarchy, consequent industrial depression and loss of civic and political rights, among the mass of the people, have produced results which history teaches us invariably follow a decline of civic virtue, with a corresponding loss of confidence by the people in their government. The misrule of the Oligarchy is the principal cause of the alarming situation; the mischievous agencies at work during the Wilson Administration would have made little impression on the Southern people had they not been reduced to impoverishment and unrest by years of exploitation and maladministration. If it be true, as stated by Macaulay, that "the violence of revolutions is generally proportioned to the degree of maladministration which has produced them," we may safely conjecture that the approaching revolution in the South will be very violent.

The total population of the Southern States in 1920 was 25,106,954, of which 17,029,013 are white and 8,055,760 are Negroes. The whites are the purest British stock in the world, except perhaps the Australians. The white population of the South is also the purest American stock of British and French lineage; the Southern States contain less of the "foreign element" than any other States. The average of the total foreign born population of the South in 1910 was 1.9, less than it was in 1860 when it reached the maximum of 2.56 per cent. In 1920, it was less than one per cent. in seven of these States. In the eleven Northern States which I have used for comparison the average of the foreign born population in 1910 was 19.2 while in the United States the average was 14.7 per cent. The real American stock largely predominates in the rural communities in the United States. In the Southern States the average rural population in 1920 was 75.20 per cent.

The unassimilated foreign stock in the United States has been the cause of apprehension because it affords opportunities for exploitation by demagogues, Bolshevists and other designing enemies of America. But the enemies of democratic institutions in the United States are not limited to the unassimilated foreign stock, nor to the uneducated and ignorant citizens who were born in America, who do not understand the underlying principles of democratic institutions and are frequently misled by designing politicians. In the Congress of the United States, among highly educated authors, magazine and newspaper writers, publicists and lecturers, are some of the boldest and most aggressive enemies of America. Race persecution, religious bigotry, provincialism and materialism are the leading features of an insidious propagandism by radical agitators and certain prominent materialists and political leaders in the United States.

A matter of greater immediate concern than the present attitude of the unassimilated foreign stock in America is the civic and economic situation in the Southern States. Before the beginning of the Wilson Administration, there was no section of the United States where the propaganda of internationalism or Bolshevism would have received so little encouragement, or even toleration, as in the South. The pure American stock in the Southern States, where immigration had been negligibly small compared with immigration to other parts of the United States, in spite of sectional prejudices and racial animosities, has been regarded as impregnable to attacks of radical Socialism or modern Bolshevism. Before the advent of the Wilson régime, the South was properly regarded as ultra conservative on labor questions and modern theories of industrialism; but a radical change has taken place, and from extreme conservatism the Southern States are passing into a menacing attitude of reckless and lawless radicalism.

The proponents of modern radicalism received no support, nor even countenance, from whites nor blacks in the South, before the World War, but a great social and economic revolution has taken place. By rapid transition, the ultra conservative population of the United States, the people of intense sentiments and local attachments are becoming the most radical and dissatisfied. Long years of injustice and oppression have driven them to desperation; they have lost faith in the institutions of their fathers. The ideals and patriotism of their fathers are no longer the tenets of their political faith. The emasculated protagonists of materialism have become the popular leaders of a people whose fathers were among the most virile and heroic patriots and statesmen of modern history. These deplorable facts bring us face to face with the increasing national menace of the situation in the South. It was consideration of the defects in the administration of the American Government, which have made possible this distressing condition, that moved Macaulay to write a memorable letter of prophecy in which he said:

Either some Cæsar or Napoleon will seize the reins of government with a strong hand, or your republic will be as fearfully plundered and laid waste by barbarians in the twentieth century as the Roman Empire was in the fifth—with this difference, that the Huns and Vandals who ravaged the Roman Empire came from without, and that your Huns and Vandals will have been engendered within your own country by your own constitution.

It has been said that history repeats itself by recording the decay and ultimate destruction of any people who, content with past achievement, and a feeling of security from an overweening confidence in their own invincibility, allow the foundations of their government to be undermined by designing enemies. It is as true to-day as it has been in the past that "eternal vigilance is the price of liberty." Not adversity but prosperity brings the greater danger to free institutions, for it is then that the people become so absorbed in money getting and money spending that they are likely to turn aside from the serious affairs of state and leave their government in the hands of men who are always ready to advance their own interests without regard to the security and welfare of the country. Concerning this phase of the subject, the historian, Alison, stated the case very clearly as follows:

It is not, therefore, social evils, but the loss of national virtue, which converts the struggle for liberty into the horrors of revolution. . . . If we would ascertain the causes of the establishment of liberty in any country, we must look for them in the circumstances which have produced in the general mind a predominance of virtue over vice; the secret springs of revolution are to be found in those which have given vice an ascendancy over virtue.

The warning lessons of history should teach Americans some plain truths relative to the social and economic evils which menace the life of this Nation. We are living in a period of revolution; great social and economic changes are taking place. Neither the actual nor the potential wealth of this country will afford protection to America against the political effect of these changes. If we fail to adjust the theories and actual practices of our government to these demands of a new epoch in the progress of civilization, we shall not be prepared to deal peacefully and successfully with the problems of the new era of democracy, liberty and equality, now dawning in the civilized world. When the concentrated power of wealth grows stronger than the power of government by the people and for the people; when property rights are placed above human rights, as they are in the United States, the Nation can not long survive. When proponents of gross materialism and race proscription freely engage in an extensive propaganda against national patriotism and traduce the most sacred traditions of the American people, while a seditious and provincial Oligarchy openly and boastfully violates the fundamental principles of democratic institutions, America cannot long survive the combined attack.

The theory of democracy in a representative form of government like America is that our institutions can be preserved only by respect for law. The United States is theoretically a government of law—not a government of men; and herein lies the wide difference between democratic theories in America and the old absolutism of Europe. The men who made this Nation a federation of democratic states supposed that they had clearly, effectually, and permanently established a government of law. This was the theory in our early history but it is not the present practice in America.

The citizens of the United States need the fostering and the strengthening of a virile national spirit, a rebirth of national pride and a reconsecration to the purposes for which this Government was formed. The greatest need of America is not a readjustment of its economic policies, as much as this may be desired in some respects; America needs a united people, a people who can understand and appreciate democratic principles in practical operation under a republican form of government, constituting one nation with one allegiance and a recognition of the supremacy of law above men. As we read the history of nations, it is plain that the United States is as yet only a nation in the making. Our greatest peril is that sectional prejudices and partisan domination, in connection with gross materialism and the insidious propagandism of race proscription and religious bigotry, will in the end destroy all national pride and respect for law.

Beginning shortly after the foundation of this Government, and for nearly threescore years, we tried by evasions and subterfuges to adjust our civic principles and administration of the Federal Government to the sectional demands of a landed aristocracy and slaveholding oligarchy. The coalition of the Slave Oligarchy with the "dissatisfied element" in the North became so powerful that the Whig party at last surrendered to the provincial demands of a small privileged class and the exactions of its "peculiar institutions." At the Whig National

Convention in 1852, a resolution was adopted declaring that the compromise acts,—

the act known as the Fugitive Slave law included, are received and acquiesced in by the Whig party of the United States as a settlement in principle and substance of the dangerous and exciting questions which they embrace. . . . We insist upon their strict enforcement . . . and we deprecate all further agitation of the question thus settled.

One of the great speeches at the Whig convention, in support of this resolution endorsing the Fugitive Slave law, was made by the talented orator, Rufus Choate, of Massachusetts. In his eloquent defense of the resolution, Mr. Choate said:

Let him who doubts—if such there be—whether it were wise to pass these measures, look back and recall with what instantaneous and mighty charm they calmed the madness and anxiety of the hour. How every countenance, everywhere brightened and elevated itself! How, in a moment, the interrupted and parted currents of fraternal feeling reunited.

While this gifted but not far-seeing Whig compromiser and non-resistant was delivering his fervid oration in which he declared that the "interrupted and parted currents of fraternal feeling" had "reunited," the work of a fearless and patriotic woman was being brought out to show that no compromise of a moral wrong could permanently "reunite the parted currents of fraternal feeling." *Uncle Tom's Cabin* was translated into Danish, Dutch, Flemish, German, Italian, Polish, Magyar and Spanish, before the end of the year 1852. Less than two years after Mr. Choate's speech endorsing surrender to the Slave Oligarchy, the Whig party was dead; within less than five years came the Dred Scott decision; a few years later Sumter was fired upon and eleven States were in open rebellion. The virile American element of the Whig party combined with a remnant of the American spirit in the Democratic party in creating the Republican party.

For nearly half a century, since the Reconstruction period, we have again tried to adjust the principles and policies of our Government in conformity with the sectional demands of a provincial Oligarchy which holds in economic serfdom and political subjection nearly one-fourth of our total population. American institutions cannot survive the increasing propa-

ganda of race persecution and the exacting demands of rapacious landlordism and materialism with the consequent increasing number and greater hardships and suffering of a pro-
letariat. We lagged behind in emancipation of our slaves
until the Slave Oligarchy became so exacting and powerful
that nothing less than civil war would remove the evil. We
still lag behind other advanced countries in dealing with the
pressing social and economic questions of vital interest to the
whole country. The admonitions and prophecies of Harriet
Beecher Stowe, written in 1851, may be as well applied to our
own times as they were applicable to the troublous times in
which this remarkable woman wrote:

This is an age of the world when nations are trembling and convulsed.
A mighty influence is abroad, surging and heaving the world, as with an
earthquake. And is America safe? Every nation that carries in its bosom
great and unredressed injustice has in it the elements of this last convulsion.

Race persecution, injustice, oppression of landlordism, peonage and law defiance have become established practices in the
United States; a condition that exists in no other civilized
country where democratic institutions are the organic principles of a republican form of government. If we continue to
postpone a settlement of these grave matters, by law and the
enforcement of law, we shall at last find, as we found in the
slavery question, that there can be no peaceable settlement.
The admonitions of Harriet Beecher Stowe are as forcible in
America at the present time as they were when written in the
last paragraph of *Uncle Tom's Cabin:*

A day of grace is yet held out to us. Both North and South have been
guilty before God; and the Christian Church has a heavy account to answer.
Not by combining together, to protect injustice and cruelty, and making a
common capital of sin, is this Union to be saved,—but by repentance, justice
and mercy; for not surer is the eternal law by which the millstone sinks
in the ocean, than that stronger law, by which injustice and cruelty shall
bring on nations the wrath of Almighty God.